Legal Issues of Digitalisation, Robotisation and Cyber Security in the Light of EU Law

Legal Issues of Digitalisation, Robotisation and Cyber Security in the Light of EU Law

NADĚŽDA ŠIŠKOVÁ (ed.)

Wolters Kluwer

Citation: Šiškova, N. (ed.) *Legal Issues of Digitalisation, Robotisation and Cyber Security in the Light of EU Law.* 392 pages (Kluwer Law International and Wolters Kluwer CZ 2024)

Published by:
Kluwer Law International B.V.
Zuidpoolsingel 2, 2408ZE
(P.O. Box 316, 2400 AH)
Alphen aan den Rijn
The Netherlands
E-mail: lrs-sales@wolterskluwer.com
Website: www.wolterskluwer.com/en/solutions/kluwerlawinternational

and

Published by:
Wolters Kluwer CZ, U nákladového nádraží 10, 130 00 Praha 3
E-mail: obchod@wolterskluwer.com
Website: www.wolterskluwer.com
1st edition, 2024, 392 pages
Typesetting: Cadis Prag
Printed: Serifa
Printed on acid-free paper

ISBN 9789403502083 (print, Kluwer Law International)
ISBN 9789403502182 (e-book, Kluwer Law International)
ISBN 9789403502281 (ePDF, Kluwer Law International)
ISBN 978-80-7676-791-1 (print, Wolters Kluwer CZ)
ISBN 978-80-7676-792-8 (e-book, Wolters Kluwer CZ)
ISBN 978-80-7676-945-8 (ePDF, Wolters Kluwer CZ)

TABLE OF CONTENT

LIST OF AUTHORS

Editor and author – Assoc. Prof. et Assoc. Prof. JUDr. **Naděžda Šišková**, Ph.D., Jean Monnet Professor, Faculty of Law, Palacký University in Olomouc, Head of Jean Monnet Centre of Excellence in EU Law, President of the Czech Association for European Studies, Coordinator of Jean Monnet Network (Czech Republic)

Assoc. Prof. JUDr. **Jozef Andraško**, PhD., Institute of IT Law and Intellectual Property Law, Faculty of Law, Comenius University in Bratislava (Slovak Republic)

Prof. JUDr. Ing. **Ondrej Blažo**, PhD., Director of the Institute of European Law, Faculty of Law, Comenius University in Bratislava

Prof. Dr. **Volodymyr Denysov**, PhD., Honored Scientist of Ukraine, Department of International and European Union Law, V. M. Koretsky Institute of State and Law of the National Academy of Sciences of Ukraine, Kyiv (Ukraine) ✝[1]

Assoc. Prof. Dr. **Liudmyla Falalieieva**, PhD., Department of International and Comparative Law, V. M. Koretsky Institute of State and Law of the National Academy of Sciences of Ukraine, Kyiv (Ukraine)

Mgr. et. Mgr. **Ondřej Filipec**, Ph.D., Department of Political and Social Sciences, Faculty of Law, Palacký University in Olomouc (Czech Republic)

JUDr. **Ondrej Hamuľák**, Ph.D., Senior Researcher Faculty of Law, Palacký University in Olomouc (Czech Republic) and Adjunct Professor in EU Strategic Legal Affairs, School of Business and Governance, Tallinn University of Technology (Estonia)

Assoc. Prof. **Zsolt Hajnal**, PhD., Department of European and International Law, Faculty of Law, University of Debrecen (Hungary)[2]

Dr. **Ágnes Kasper**, Ph.D., Senior Lecturer, Department of Law, Tallinn University of Technology, Head of Law Branch, NATO Cooperative Cyber Defence Centre of Excellence (Estonia)

---

[1] In memory of Prof. Volodymyr Denysov whose invaluable contribution enriched this book before his passing in September 2023. Professor Denysov's legacy and wisdom will forever remain a vital part of the science in the field of International and European Law.

[2] Holder of the János Bolyai Research Scholarship of Hungarian Academy of Sciences.

Dr. Prof. **Tanel Kerikmäe**, PhD., Prof. of European Legal Policy, Law & Technology, Law School, Tallinn University of Technology (Estonia)

Mgr. **Hovsep Kocharyan**, Ph.D., doctoral candidate, Department of International and European Law, Faculty of Law, Palacký University in Olomouc (Czech Republic)

Mgr. **Martin Mach**, MA, doctoral candidate, Department of International and European Law, Faculty of Law, Palacký University in Olomouc (Czech Republic)

JUDr. **Soňa Matochová**, Ph.D., LL.M., Head of Analytical Department of the Czech Data Protection Office (Prague) and Department of International and European Law, Faculty of Law, Palacký University in Olomouc (Czech Republic)

Prof. Dr. Dr. habil. Dr.h.c.mult. **Peter-Christian Müller-Graff**, Ph. D.h.c., MAE, Honorary Jean-Monnet-Professor

Mgr. **Anett Mádi-Nátor**, doctoral candiate, National University of Public Service Budapest (Hungary)

Assoc. Prof. JUDr. **Mária T. Patakyová**, PhD., Institute of European Law, Faculty of Law, Comenius University in Bratislava (Slovak Republic)

Assoc. Prof. JUDr. **Michal Petr**, Ph.D., Head of the Department of International and European Law, Faculty of Law, Palacký University in Olomouc (Czech Republic)

Mgr. **Pablo Martínez Ramil**, doctoral candidate, Department of International and European Law, Palacký University Olomouc; visiting lecturer of Legal protection of Information Technology products, software, and databases & Technology Law School (Czech Republic, Estonia)

Dr. iur **Rita Simon**, LL.M, B.A., Senior Researcher, Institute of State and Law, Czech Academy of Sciences (Czech Republic)

Prof. Dr. **Kseniia Smyrnova**, Ph.D., Jean Monnet Centre of Excellence and the Institute of International Relations, Taras Shevchenko National University of Kyiv (Ukraine)

Mgr. **Bohdan Strilets**, Ph.D., Department of International and European Union Law, V. M. Koretsky Institute of State and Law of the National Academy of Sciences of Ukraine, Kyiv (Ukraine)

Assoc. Prof. **Yuliia Vashchenko**, Ph.D., Department of Administrative Law and Procedure, Educational and Scientific Institute of Law, Taras Shevchenko National University of Kyiv (Ukraine)

Mgr. **Lusine Vardanyan**, doctoral candidate, Department of International and European Law, Faculty of Law, Palacký University in Olomouc (Czech Republic)

Assoc. Prof. JUDr. **Blanka Vítová**, Ph.D., LL.M., Department of Private Law and Civil Procedure and Jean Monnet Centre of Excellence in EU Law, Faculty of Law, Palacký University in Olomouc, Secretary of Czech Association for European Studies (Czech Republic)

ACKNOWLEDGEMENTS

The book creates a main output of the research project with the title "The EU and the Challenges of Modern Society (legal issues of digitalization, robotisation, cyber security and prevention of hybrid threats)" granted by the EACEA in the category of Jean Monnet Network.

Project id: 611293-EPP-1-2019-1-CZ-EPPJMO-NETWORK.

With the support of the Erasmus+ Programme of the European Union.

Co-funded by the European Union

The European Commission's support for the production of this publication does not constitute an endorsement of the contents, which reflect the views only of the authors, and the Commission cannot be held responsible for any use which may be made of the information contained therein.

PREFACE

JAN PASSER

JUDGE OF THE COURT OF JUSTICE OF THE EUROPEAN UNION

Digitalisation, robotisation and cybersecurity are not entirely new topics; they are areas of human activity and economic activity that have been present in our ecosystem for decades. This has been reflected both in the fact that these are activities and phenomena that have already been regulated to a certain extent, and that this regulation has also been reflected in the case law of the courts.

However, this by no means signifies that these are exhausted topics. On the contrary, they are hot ones, extremely actual and of great importance. The ever-accelerating development of the above-mentioned areas, recently brought about by expectations and fears associated with the advent of Artificial Intelligence, requires a critical evaluation of the effectiveness of the existing regulation and, as a result, proposals for possible changes in the legislation and suggestions for the evolution of case law.

The global nature of the virtual world makes regulation at national level difficult and often literally impossible. The European Union, sometimes referred to as a regulatory power, sets the standard for regulation, which then often serves as a frame of reference in a global context. Therefore, if we are talking about a critical evaluation of existing regulation and related case law, especially in this area naturally falling within the regulatory framework of the European Union, interest must naturally be directed towards EU law.

This has long since gone beyond mainly economic regulation. One example is the area of the protection of fundamental human rights. In this area, there is a great deal of case law communication between the Court of Justice, the European Court of Human Rights and the (mainly constitutional) courts of the Member States. In this dialogue between Europe's top courts, there is no simple equation according to which the European Court of Human Rights is always the inspiration of the Court of Justice. Influence and inspiration are mutual and involve the constitutional courts too. Data protection, the right to be forgotten or the seemingly revolutionary issue of the right of access to the Internet, which are the subject of the first part of this publication, are good examples of the above.

This part is quite naturally followed by a section on consumer protection, which on the one hand is part of "simple", sub-constitutional law, but on the other hand replicates and further develops a number of premises defined in principle in relation to individuals in the protection of fundamental human rights.

Competition law, which is the subject of the next part of the publication, can be an example that the area of digital technologies has long been subject to legal regulation also by the European Union. After all, a historically record fine was once imposed by the Commission in connection with a competition law infringement by the then giant of the digital world. The topicality of the subject is confirmed by the fact that, if the Commission is currently imposing even more record fines, it is imposing them on other – current – giants, again of the digital world. At the same time, the challenges faced by the legislation are constantly evolving and reflect the dynamic and rapid development of the whole sector.

The last section of the book, on cyber security, faithfully reflects not only the digital activities taking place in the shadows and the difficulties faced by individuals, states and supranational entities such as the European Union and NATO, but also the challenges that the advent of certain new technologies will pose precisely in terms of cyber security.

I therefore very much welcome a publication that maps out this dynamically developing area of European Union law, critically and usefully assesses the state of legislation and case law to date, and at the same time reflects on the challenges facing the European Union, its Member States and their citizens.

INTRODUCTION

NADĚŽDA ŠIŠKOVÁ

This book is focused on the key issues of the very specific field of EU law regulation reflecting the fact that currently extremely rapid and dynamic development of modern technologies and the unprecedented degree of their integration into the everyday life of every person are radically changing the previous *modus vivendi* in the society. This is a new born branch of EU law that just now is gaining its basic outlines. Even its name itself is not stable yet that is why we can meet with different names such as: Internet law, Cybernet law, Information technologies law, Digital Law, Modern technologies law, Cyberspace law, etc. This book deals with the different key aspects of this new branch.

Digitalization, robotisation and cyber security should not be a chaotic process, but on the contrary, it must be regulated by the "smart" and appropriate legal rules, which on the one side will reflect the peculiarities of the mentioned phenomena, and on the other side will ensure their compliance with the rule of law principles. The introduction and implementation of new rules, tailored exclusively for these purposes, is extremely crucial right now.

The global spread and usage of modern technologies and their huge interference into each aspect of everyday life is accompanied also by a number of negative trends such as threats to privacy and cyber security or interference into the field of human rights. The monograph focuses on the analysis of the most important and thorny legal issues of the process of digitalisation, robotisation and providing of cyber security and it brings the proposals *de lege ferenda* concerning the optimal ways of legal regulation and the elimination of eventual negative impacts of the mentioned process.

Especially it is dedicated to the main directions of legal regulation in such fields as: e-commerce, usage of Artificial Intelligence, competition law in a digital economy, consumer protection in the on-line world, cyber security and other related issues connected with the integration of modern technologies in the everyday life of every person.

This unique book thus presents the key information and solves the related problems concerning the legal regulation of the usage of modern technologies in everyday life.

The book is conceived in a form of a collective monograph prepared by Jean Monnet Network, which involved an international team of researchers from the leading European Universities (Heidelberg University, Palacký University in

Olomouc, Tallinn University of Technology, Comenius University in Bratislava and Shevchenko University in Kyiv) and the research instituitions (Institute of State and Law of the Czech Academy of Sciences and the V. M. Koretsky Institute of State and Law of the Academy of Sciences of Ukraine) as well as experts from practice, for instance from the National Data Protection office, NATO Cooperative Data Defense Centre of Excellence, etc. This team represents the countries with a high level of integration of modern technologies (Estonia, Germany, Czech Republic, Slovakia) or has unique experience with the provision of cyber security in extreme conditions of war (Ukraine). The contributions of the authors create a coherent text reflecting the different aspects of the general topic and are supplemented by a common introduction and joint conclusions, relating to the whole book. The conclusions summarise the key ideas of the authors and the proposals *de lege ferenda* concerning the whole text.

The authors express their great gratitude for the financial support of this publication and other think-tank activities (conferences, workshops, roundtable debates), which were implemented in the framework of Jean Monnet Network with a title: European Union and the Challenges of Modern Society (Legal Issues of Digitalisation, Robotizatiation, Cyber Security and Prevention of Hybrid Threats).

The book reflects the state of legal regulation until 1. 9. 2023.

PART I.

ISSUES OF DIGITALISATION AND ROBOTISATION IN THE LIGHT OF HUMAN RIGHTS

CHAPTER ONE

GDPR and the Right to Personal Data and Privacy in a Modern Society in the Digital Age

SOŇA MATOCHOVÁ

1. Introduction

It is not going too far to say that the tension between data use and data protection is one of the defining features of the new millennium,[1] also known as the digital age. The protection of personal data and privacy in the context of advanced technological developments and globalisation requires both robust and coherent legal framework that allows individuals to control their own data. In this context, this Chapter addresses questions connected with current European data protection legal framework, e.g. whether the General Data Protection Regulation (GDPR)[2] is successful in practise, what are its problems, specific features and shortcomings and whether there are reasons to reconsider the valid legal framework, either substantially or partially. Although this chapter deals mostly with theoretical issues, it does not neglect practical needs.[3] The red line followed in this contribution are both the special characteristics of the fundamental right to data protection and the assessment of the nature and effectiveness of the current data protection framework. The topic which has been chosen for this collection of contributions focusing on European law issues is highly up to date, containing open questions on the relationship between technology and

1 Paul Craig a Gráinne de Búrca. Series Editors Preface. In LYNSKEY, O. *The foundations of EU data protection law.* First edition. Oxford, United Kingdom: Oxford University Press, 2015. xxiv, 307 pages. Oxford studies in European law. ISBN: 9780198718239.

2 Regulation (EU) 2016/679 of the European Parliament and of the Council of 27 April 2016 on the protection of natural persons with regard to the processing of personal data and on the free movement of such data, and repealing Directive 95/46/EC (General Data Protection Regulation).

3 The author of this article has been analysing personal data protection issues in individual areas of data processing at the Czech data protection supervisory authority for the last seven years, using her previous professional experience in constitutional law and European law.

personal data, which need to be seen from the perspective of legal (including constitutional) and ethical aspects. However, current data processing issues, i.e. questions of personal data in the context of technology development, are often interdisciplinary and complex. Over that, they are closely linked to human rights, democracy and the rule of law, such as the question of surveillance of citizens through technology means.[4]

The framework described above is the reason why the application and interpretation of the fundamental right to data protection could be described as demanding and challenging for the responsible actors (controllers, supervisory authorities, national courts, data subjects, Internet service providers) from a practical point of view, moreover, information and communication technologies are evolving exponentially, while some complex data processing questions are answered by supervisory authorities or by courts gradually and over a long period of time. Data controllers often do not take a comprehensive view of data processing issues from the perspective of the GDPR layered approach, and as a result, they are unable to apply the GDPR principles properly, which leads to formal application of GDPR. Generally, the GDPR requires the qualified application of its general principles in relation to the specific data processing, which presumes not only knowledge of both data protection legal framework and expert fields relating to specific processing (e.g. AML[5] or whistleblowing), but also at least basic understanding of technologies used for data processing. The question for data controllers is how to apply adequately the abstract GDPR principles, if the are to be protected really and effectively, not only formally. It can be noted that only a limited number of data protection authors and commentaries[6] are focusing on specific features of the fundamental right to data protection, most authors limit themselves to state that the right to data protection is a fundamental right. Nevertheless, the understanding to the constitutional dimension of the right to data protection in relation to specific processing[7] poses a challenging and difficult task for data controllers.

---

4 The term technology in the context of this article means any current advanced technological solution in the online environment based on the processing of data, including personal data.

5 AML is used as an abbreviation for anti-money laundering.

6 LYNSKEY, O. *The foundations of EU data protection law.* First edition. Oxford, United Kingdom: Oxford University Press, 2015. xxiv, 307 pp. Oxford studies in European law. ISBN: 9780198718239.
GONZÁLEZ FUSTER, G. *The emergence of personal data protection as a fundamental right of the EU.* Cham: Springer, 2014. xvi, 274 pp. Law governance and technology series, 16. ISBN. 978-3-319-05022-5.
KUNER, Ch. (ed.)., BYGRAVE, L. A. (ed.)., DOCKSEY, Ch. (ed.)., DRECHSLER, L. (ed.). *The EU General Data Protection Regulation (GDPR): a commentary.* First edition. Oxford, New York: Oxford University Press, 2020. ISBN: 9780198826491.

7 Constitutional jurisprudence sometimes uses the term *shining constitutionally protected values into ordinary (simple) law* for explanation of the constitutional law influence in the legal order.

In the area of data protection, there are a number of issues where to reach compliance with the GDPR rules is a difficult task. The risk to the rights and freedoms of natural persons may result from personal data processing which could lead to physical, material or non-material damage, in particular where the processing may give rise to discrimination, identity theft or fraud, financial loss, damage to the reputation, loss of confidentiality of personal data protected by professional secrecy, unauthorised reversal of pseudonymisation, or any other significant economic or social disadvantage.[8] Another example could be when some controllers who process large volumes of data including personal data in connection with services offered by them try to use the collected data, without the consent of data subject, for purposes other than those for which the data was originally collected.[9] In some cases, controllers argue that they have anonymised the data so that they are not processing personal data. However, according to current scientific knowledge it is technically difficult to anonymise personal data in order that they could not be retrospectively de-anonymised, i.e. linked to an original identifiable person. Recently, the so-called Stanford study addressed the issue of de-anonymisation of web browsing data on social networks, concluding that a full 72 % of the data can be linked back to identified or identifiable natural persons, so they are not longer anonymised data.[10] As for another example, there are also different views on the prohibition of data monetisation, although people usually take the view that personal data are not tradable. Also, there are references in European law that the right to data protection as a fundamental right implies that personal data is not a tradable commodity.[11] The task of data protection law and practise is precisely to find answers to such complex questions.

2. The relationship between data protection and privacy in EU law in the digital age

The tension between the free use of data and the protection of personal data has been reflected in Europe since the 1970s, which contributed to evolution

See also judgment of the Constitutional Court of the Czech Republic III. ÚS 139/98.

8 Point 75 GDPR.

9 Point 50 GDPR Preamble.

10 De-anonymising web browsing Data with Social Network. Jessica Su. Sharad Goel. Stanford University. Available at: https://dl.acm.org/doi/pdf/10.1145/3038912.3052714.

11 European Commission. Communication from the Commission to the European Parliament and the Council. Exchanging and Protecting Personal Data in a Globalized World. Brussels, 10 January 2017. *Respecting privacy is a condition for stable, secure and competitive global commercial flows. Privacy is not a commodity to be traded.*

of personal data protection independence.[12] From that time it was clear that for situations of large-scale processing of individual's data, which can in principle be collected, disclosed, copied, processed and replicated without restriction, privacy protection measures are not sufficient. The relationship between the two rights, i. e. privacy and personal data, has gradually evolved and refined against the background of rapid technological development, as reflected by milestones of legal data protection, which are above all the Council of Europe Convention 108 of 1981[13] and later on, Directive 95/46/EC,[14] both of which were based on personal data and privacy protection. While initially the right to data protection was "overshadowed" by the right to privacy, it has become gradually fully emancipated. In EU law, unlike the European Convention on Human Rights,[15] both the right to data protection and the right to privacy are separate fundamental rights regulated by the EU Charter of Fundamental Rights and Freedoms (the EU Charter).[16] Nevertheless, both in practice and in theory these two rights are often not distinguished, they are confused or the right to data protection is considered as part of the right to privacy. There is useful to define their relationship at the outset of described topic clarification.

In general, the right to data protection and to privacy are closely linked and both of them can contribute to protect the values of privacy and integrity of individuals. Nevertheless, these rights are different in terms of their rationale and content. The fact that both rights are independent is also clear from the text of the EU Charter of Fundamental Rights which regulates them separately from 2009. Even during legislative work on the GDPR draft, all references to privacy had been consistently removed from the text. It can be stressed that the EU law has not only enshrined the above two rights by means of different and separate provisions of the EU Charter,[17] but they differ both in terms of their systematic classification, and in terms of data protection exercise and enforcement before relevant authorities and courts. Despite the different procedures,

[12] The concept of personal data first appeared in the 1960s.

[13] Convention 108 for the Protection of Individuals with Regard to Automatic Processing of Personal Data in the wording of its Protocols and Amendments.

[14] Directive 95/46/EC of the European Parliament and of the Council of 24 October 1995 on the protection of individuals with regard to the processing of personal data and on the free movement of such data.

[15] Both the European Convention of Human Rights and the US law are based on the right to privacy.

[16] Charter of Fundamental Rights of the EU. Official Journal of the European Union. 2012/C 326/02.

[17] This is not the case in the Convention for the Protection of Fundamental Rights and Freedoms, which only guarantees the right to privacy. Nor is it the rule that all EU Member States' constitutional orders enshrine both rights.

the enforcement of both rights can contribute to the protection of private space of individual.

For the reasons given above, it is not systematically correct to state that the right to data protection is part of the right to privacy, or *vice versa*, as the relationship between the rights concerned is complex and multi-layered, they can overlap or complement each other in their operation depending on the specific situation, or they may not apply to the concerned situation at all.[18] In some situations, data protection measures may directly or indirectly contribute to the protection of an individual's privacy both as a consequence of general concept and broad interpretation of the right to data protection, which has been repeatedly confirmed by the Court of Justice of the EU (CJEU).[19] This broad concept of data subjects' rights in the GDPR, specifically, for example, the right of access to personal data, the right to be forgotten or the right to rectification, can effectively help to protect privacy.[20] In addition, data protection tools can effectively play a preventive role *pro future* provided the controller remedy the identified deficiency. Often, data protection remedies are in practice more enforceable and effective from the perspective of the individual, whereas privacy remedies pursued through legal actions before the courts could be lengthy and their outcome uncertain. The intertwining of the value of privacy and personal data protection may also partly overcome the division between private and public law, due to the fact that each of these rights may be broader or narrower in relation to the other. On the other hand, the protection of personal data and privacy are often referred to as a single concept, without distinguishing between them, which in principle cannot be objected when speaking generally, but also in view of the broader human rights concept described in the European Court for Human Rights (ECHR) case law, which does not distinguish between the above two rights. On the other hand, precise terminology is necessary when speaking about specific

---

18 GELLERT, R., GUTWIRTH, S. The legal construction of privacy and data protection. *Computer Law & Security Review (CLSR)*. 2013, vol. 29, 522–530 (ISSN 0267-3649). *All in all, data protection and privacy overlap on a mode whereby data protection is both broader and narrower than privacy. It is narrower because it only deals with the processing personal data, whereas the scope of privacy is wider. It is broader, however, because it applies to the processing of personal data, even if the latter does not infringe upon privacy. Privacy is also broader and narrower: it might apply to a processing of data which are not personal but nevertheless affects one's privacy, while it will not apply upon a processing of personal data which is not considered to infringe upon one's privacy. It can be said as well that a processing of personal data can have consequences not only in terms of privacy, but also in terms of other constitutional rights, and most obviously, when the processing of data relating to individuals bears risks in terms of discrimination.*

19 CJEU judgment C-293/12 Digital Rights Ireland of 8 April 2014. Point 48.

20 EDPB Guidelines 1/2022 on data subject rights – right of access of 28 March 2023. Version 2. Point 13. The controller cannot deny the access of data subject to the data which he/she is going to use before court.

legal protection in a particular case. Of course, both rights are execused and enforced quite differently.

The above-mentioned relationship between the right to privacy and the protection of personal data, consisting in their interdependence with ethical values and requirements of the dignity and autonomy of the individual guaranteed in the constitutional order, was precisely expressed by the data protection expert Peter Hustinx[21] when he stated: *"Privacy and data protection – more precisely: the right to respect for private life and the right to the protection of one's personal data –are both fairly recent expressions of a universal idea with quite strong ethical dimensions: the dignity, autonomy and unique value of every human being. This also implies the right of every individual to develop their own personality and to have a fair say on matters that may have a direct impact on them. It explains two features that frequently appear in this context: the need to prevent undue interference in private matters, and the need to ensure adequate control for individuals over matters that may affect them.* "[22] This broader perspective highlights the complexity and interdisciplinarity of the categories of data protection and privacy, which also have ethical and constitutional dimension.

3. The right to the protection of personal data as a fundamental right

The fact that the right to data protection is enshrined as a fundamental right in the EU Charter means that it has a privileged (stronger) position within the legal order than ordinary rights, so it is more difficult to limit it or interfere with it (but this is not excluded as it is not an absolute right). In order to limit the right to data protection, it is necessary to apply the step-by-step assessment (methodology) generally used to assess limitations or conflicts between fundamental rights. This mechanism is provided for in Article 52 (1) of the EU Charter. The fact that the right to data protection is a fundamental right finds its expression in the application and interpretation of this right, both at EU and national law level. The proper application and interpretation of the data protection right by the obliged entities is facilitated by the fact that the various aspects of the data protection law framework are interpreted both by the European Data Protection Board (EDBP) and, above all, by the case law of the CJEU, or the case law of ECHR, where applicable.

[21] Peter Johan Hustinx (born 1945) is a Dutch lawyer who served as European Data Protection Supervisor (EDPS) from January 2004–2014.

[22] Available at: https://edps.europa.eu/sites/edp/files/publication/14-09-08_article_uji_castellon_en.pdf.

The protection of natural persons with regard to the processing of personal data as a fundamental right is enshrined both in Article 8 (1) of the EU Charter of Fundamental Rights of the European Union (hereinafter referred to as the EU Charter) and Article 16 (1) of the Treaty on the Functioning of the European Union (hereinafter referred to as the TFEU), which grant everyone the right to the protection of personal data concerning them. *See Table: Relevant legislation in the field of personal data.* Article 8 of the EU Charter is specific in terms of its wording, structure and content compared to the other rights regulated by the EU Charter. The right to the protection of personal data not only guarantees, but also sets out (specifies) in its Article 8 (2) the conditions for the processing of personal data, which means the correct processing of data, the existence of purpose, the existence of a legal basis for the processing, the guarantee of the right of access to collected personal data and the right to rectification. Article 8 also requires, in paragraph 3, supervision by an independent authority controlling compliance with data protection rules.[23] This way of constructing the right to the protection of personal data in the EU Charter, chosen by the European law-maker in Article 8 of the EU Charter, is specific compared to other rights as in terms of the fact that it describes relatively precisely the content and limits of this right. However, it is clear that the wording pursues a realistic setting of the right to data protection in the form of a data quality requirements of the personal data processing,[24] including the institutional guarantee of supervisory data protection independent authority.

The wording of the right to data protection in the EU Charter is further specified by the GDPR, according to which the right to data protection is not an absolute right; it must be considered in the context of its function in society and, in accordance with the principle of proportionality, it must be balanced with other fundamental rights. The GDPR mentions that it respects all fundamental rights and observes the freedoms and principles recognised by the Charter as enshrined in the Treaties, in particular respect for private and family life, home and communication, protection of personal data, freedom of thought, conscience and religion, freedom of expression and information, freedom of establishment, the right to an effective remedy and to a fair trial, as well as cultural, religious and linguistic diversity.[25] Although the GDPR does not explicitly mention the value of human dignity in the above demonstrative list, it is undoubtedly an essential requirement and an integral part of the right to data protection, which can be significantly affected by the processing of personal data, for example, in the form of

[23] Art. 8(3) EU Charter. Compliance with these rules shall be subject to control by an independent authority.

[24] Art. 8(2) EU Charter contains only some of GDPR principles.

[25] Point 4 GDPR Preamble.

an individual's feeling that he or she is under constant surveillance. The conflict between different rights must always be assessed both according to the nature of rights at stake and the specific circumstances of the processing in question. In practice, this means first to identify the rights and interests that may potentially be affected by the processing. In this respect, personal data processing records are used.[26] In case of some processing, data protection impact assessment (DPA) is obligatory.[27] By the way, the DPA is extremely useful even in situations where the GDPR does not explicitly impose such an obligation on the controller.[28] The balancing of the right to data protection with other (fundamental) rights is realised by applying the proportionality principle based on Article 52 (1) of the EU Charter.[29]

The complex system of assessing the fundamental right to data protection in the EU on multiple levels also reflects the default setting of the GDPR, which envisages both the freedom of data flow and the protection of personal data. This approach emphasising both rights is sometimes referred to as the rights-based approach.[30] The two, in relation to the specific processing contradictory values, pursue quite different goals. While the rationale for enshrining the free movement of data was for the EU states to be able to benefit from the economic and other societal benefits that data processing technologies can potentially bring, including, for example, the exploitation of big data phenomenon, on the other hand side, individuals cannot be deprived of their space of freedom and privacy which has been traditionally recognised in various forms, such as the right to privacy, the right to be left alone, the right to informational self-determination or the right to data protection. These rights are expression of the individual's need to have a certain personal space in which they can develop freely without the supervision of others.[31] From this perspective, collection of personal data by technologies, which in principle can be replicated and disseminated without

---

26 Art. 30 GDPR.

27 Art. 35 GDPR.

28 Art. 35 GDPR. Guidelines on Data Protection Impact Assesment (DPIA) and determining whether processing is likely to result in high risk for the purposes of Regulation 2016/679/EU. WP 248 rev.01.

29 The Constitutional Court of the Czech Republic has expressed its opinion on this issue in its judgment Pl. ÚS 37/17 when it stated: The Constitutional Court in its established case law requires that in the event of a conflict between fundamental rights or freedoms and public interest or other fundamental rights or freedoms, the purpose (objective) of the intervention must be assessed in relation to the means used, with the principle of proportionality being the benchmark of the assessment.

30 LYNSKEY, O. *The foundations of EU data protection law.* First edition. Oxford, United Kingdom: Oxford University Press, 2015, xxiv, 307 pp. Oxford studies in European law. ISBN: 9780198718239.

31 It is claimed that the first mention of privacy in literature can be found in the 1890 article The Right to Privacy by S. D. Warren and L. D. Brandeis. See WARREN, S. D., BRANDEIS, L. D. The Right to Privacy. *Harward Law Review*. 4/1890, no. 5, pp. 193–220.

restrictions, is a massive invasion to personal data and privacy. Therefore, such collection of data should not occur in an arbitrary and purposeless manner. From an ethical perspective, processing of personal data should serve people[32] in the form of some desirable purpose, social good or interest. Accordingly, the EU legal framework for data protection implies that, while the free flow of data must be preserved, there should be no arbitrary, excessive or unnecessary processing of personal data (the principles of the GDPR in Articles 5 and 6 and other provisions serve to prevent such processing). These requirements apply throughout the Union and ensure a consistent and uniform application of the rules on the protection of the fundamental rights and freedoms of natural persons with regard to the processing of personal data.[33]

4. Limitation of the fundamental right to the protection of personal data in the EU

As already mentioned, the data protection legal framework enshrines the right to the protection of personal data as a fundamental right, but at the same time provides that it is not an absolute right and foresees that it can be limited. Such restriction must follow the requirements set out for fundamental rights in Article 52 (1) of the EU Charter. In this spirit, the CJEU also explicitly states that the justification for the interference with the rights guaranteed by Articles 7 and 8 of the EU Charter must be made on the basis of Article 52 (1) of the EU Charter. This Article sets out several cumulative conditions: any restriction on the exercise of the rights and freedoms enshrined in the EU Charter must be provided for by law (1), respect the essence of the rights at stake (2) and, subject to the principle of proportionality (3), restrictions on those rights and freedoms may only be imposed if they are necessary (4) and if they genuinely meet objectives of general interest recognised by the Union or the need for the rights and freedoms of another (5).[34] Each of these abstract requirements set out in Article 52 (1) must be assessed separately and with due care, while the controller does not have absolute certain about the correctness of his/her assessments (based on GDPR requirements and principles). In any case, the assessment of conditions is the responsibility of the controller.[35] These requirements include the principle of necessity, which provides that restrictions may be imposed only if they are necessary, and the principle of proportionality, which is a tool for striking a balance

[32] Point 4 GDPR Preamble.
[33] Point 10 GDPR Preamble.
[34] Art. 52(1) of the EU Charter.
[35] Art. 24 GDPR.

with other rights. The requirement of proportionality can be found in the GDPR not only for balancing competing rights, but also as a general principle applied by the controller in relation to the application of the various measures of the GDPR (e.g. proportionate measures to secure public interest objectives).[36] As a result, the controller must seek an optimal balance between conflicting principles and values. In any case, EU law has set up a very complex multi-level system for assessing the processing of personal data, which places demands on the controller according to the complexity of the personal data it processes.

5. The Principle of Proportionality in the Data Protection Context

With regard to the principle of proportionality, which is an essential component of Article 52(1) of the EU Charter, at the outset it may be briefly mentioned that the search for the measure of things has its origins already in ancient culture. As Pavel Holländer[37] states, the origins of this concept can be found in 19th century German law, but it is only after the Second World War that the principle of proportionality has taken doctrinal form and spread horizontally and vertically to other legal orders and systems. Today, the principle of proportionality is applied as a measure of the limitation of fundamental rights in many, but not all, effective constitutional justice systems. For the sake of completeness, it should be noted that the U.S. constitutional development was and is moving in a different direction, with considerations of the proportionality of values (fundamental rights) stemming from its own historical and constitutional justice trends.[38] In general, the principle of proportionality is a complex abstract tool for measuring fundamental rights, which is not methodologically uniform and is the subject of academic disputes. It is generally true that the essence of the proportionality principle is preserved in case of compliance with the three-step test (appropriateness, necessity and proportionality in the narrower sense) and the principle of compliance of the legal order with the Constitution (constitutional values). However, the application of the proportionality principle does not follow an identical methodology, so there are substantial theoretical differences in this respect. Legal theory has developed complex conceptual constructions of the principle of proportionality, the key ones of which is the model of the prohibition

[36] Point 69 GDPR Preamble.

[37] Pavel Holländer, a former constitutional judge of the Constitutional Court of the Czech and Slovak Federal Republic and of Constitutional Court of the Czech Republic later on, introduced the principle of proportionality into Czech legal discourse.

[38] In the United States so-called balancing test is used as the way competing rights are measured.

of disproportionality (Peter Lerche), the principle of practical concordance (Konrad Hesse) and the interpretation of the principle of proportionality in terms of the command to optimise (Robert Alexy). Thus, it must be stated that there is no uniform methodology of the proportionality principle.[39] It is also important that, in terms of the application of the proportionality test, the decisive problem is often not the proportionality test itself, but the very identification of the rights that (actually) conflict or whose protection is at stake in the case in question.

In terms of content, the principle of proportionality is a designation for the balancing exercise used when two or more protected fundamental rights come into conflict. According to Pavel Ondřejek,[40] the principle of proportionality is based on the concept of the rule of law as an objective order of values in which fundamental rights play a central role. Along with the growing importance of fundamental rights in application practice, there is also a growing need to find an adequate methodology for dealing with conflicts between fundamental rights, or conflicts between a fundamental right and a constitutionally protected public interest. The advantage of this constitutional argumentation method is the maximum consideration of the context of the case, taking into account the facts of the case. The balancing of fundamental rights and public interests is normally conceived as a component of the principle of proportionality and is often described as an alternative method of applying the law alongside subsumption. When measuring, we look at the applied rules as legal principles, in the application of which we can consider the degree of their fulfilment in a particular case, not, as is the case with legal norms, the classification or non-classification of a factual situation under this legal norm.[41] In practice, the doctrine of proportionality is typically used by the highest judicial institutions, and it is also used by the ECHR and the CJEU; however, it is always used with a certain degree of variability, while maintaining the basic set-up as described above.

In data protection practice, the proportionality test is applied with a large degree of flexibility. Controllers, and sometimes also supervisory authorities, are not always able to use use the advanced and complex proportionality test under Article 52 (1) of the EU Charter; instead they use a simplified test, which they refer as the balancing test, although this term is not mentioned both in the GDPR and the CJEU case law. The so-called balancing test is problematic in

[39] HOLLÄNDER, P. *Příběhy právních pojmů*. Vydavatelství a nakladatelství Aleš Čeněk, s. r. o., Plzeň: 2017, pp. 198–231.

[40] Pavel Ondřejek is an associate professor at Charles University. He is the author of the monograph The Principle of Proportionality and its Role in the Interpretation of Fundamental Rights and Freedoms (Prague: Leges, 2012).

[41] ONDŘEJEK, P. Poměřování jako klíčový argument přezkumu ústavnosti v éře proporcionality a některé projevy jeho kritiky. Proportionality as a key argument of constitutional review in the era of proportionality and some of its criticisms. *Právník.* 2016, roč. 155, č. 4, pp. 349–368. Detail článku | Ústav státu a práva Akademie věd České republiky (cas.cz).

some aspects. First of all it is used under the same designation as the test used in the United States, although it is based on different methodology and evaluation. Moreover, the question arises to what extent the implementation of the so-called balancing test, the essence of which is the assessment of the limitation of the fundamental right to the protection of personal data, corresponds to the requirements of Article 52 (1) of the EU Charter or the proportionality test carried out in accordance with the case law of the CJEU. The CJEU has repeatedly provided sufficient guidance on the proportionality test, starting with the Digital Rights Ireland judgment.[42] However, the problematic aspect here, is the difficulty to realise complex constitutional proportionality test for practice, which often leads to the use of a simplified form of the test. However, this can lead to the risk of not finding an optimally balanced solution in data protection processing. It will also always depend on the complexity of the particular processing of personal data. Logically, the more complex is the processing of personal data, the more challenging it is to comply with data protection requirements.

6. The Role of Data Protection Principles

The aim of data protection regulation is the processing of personal data in compliance with the GDPR rules (principles). These general principles (conditions of processing) apply to each individual processing of personal data. In other words, the controller is obliged to assess comprehensively and properly each individual processing of personal data in light of the GDPR principles and, on this basis, to adopt specific measures, solutions and safeguards for the protection of personal data set out in the GDPR. In this context, the GDPR principles under Articles 5 and 6 of the GDPR have their place, but the controller must take also into account other general principles or safeguards, such as the prevention principle and the principles of *privacy by design* and *privacy by default.* Moreover, data protection impact assessments, codes of conduct and other organisational and technical measures have also important role in the search for a balanced protection of personal data. Then, the principle of technological neutrality, based on the application of the general principles of the GDPR to emerging technologies, is also of crucial importance, as the application of these principles can enable to achieve compliance with the GDPR.

With regard to the GDPR, it should be emphasized that the application of the GDPR principles to specific data processing is not realised by way of subsumption in relation to the requirements (provisions) of positive law, but through the

[42] CJEU judgment C-293/12 Digital Rights Ireland of 8 April 2014. Points 32–71. ECLI:EU: C:2014:238.

application of general principles to the specific legal situation of data processing. In this respect, it is the full responsibility of the controller to apply data protection rules in a balanced and reasonable manner in relation to the specific processing and to be fully accountable for the outcome of the application of the principles. The controller is also fully accountable for the outcome of this application of principles. It is therefore the obligation of the controller to demonstrate, for example, that its legitimate interest is not overridden by the interests or fundamental rights and freedoms of the data subject.[43] The title of the GDPR already implies that is based on general rules that need to be applied in specific situation, i.e. case-by-case assessment. This allows the controller to answer the data protection questions in relation to the unique situation of data processing. Specifically, these principles include correctness, fairness, lawfulness, transparency, purpose limitation, data minimization, accuracy, storage limitation, integrity and confidentiality. The most important, however, is the principle of controller's accountability, which means that the controller is responsible for and must demonstrate compliance with data protection requirements.[44]

Before the data protection principles are applied to specific processing, the controller should examine whether the processing of personal data is necessary at all. In fact, there is a lot of personal data processing that is not necessary and in principle, there are no compelling reasons for the processing of personal data. However, if the controller has verified that the processing is indeed necessary, he should answer the following questions:

- What personal data are processed? How is it possible to describe data flow?
- Is there any lawful legal grounds for collecting personal data? Which is it?
- Are the specific personal data of data subjects processed in a transparent manner? Is the information obligation fulfilled?
- Are personal data of data subject collected for an explicit purpose (purpose limitation principle)?
- Are personal data of data subject collected only to the necessary extent (data minimisation principle)?
- Are personal data of data subject processed accurate and up-to-date?
- Are personal data of data subject stored not for longer than necessary for the given purpose (storage limitation principle)?
- Are personal data of data subjects adequately secured by appropriate technical and organisational measures (principle of integrity and confidentiality), such as appropriate IT programmes or equipment and organisational means or internal data protection regulations at the establishment?

---

[43] Art. 6 (2) (f) GDPR.

[44] Art. 63 GDPR.

Answering the above questions will enable the controller responsible for processing data under the GDPR to fulfil its obligations properly.

7. The contribution of EDPB and CJEU to the interpretation of data protection issues

The European Data Protection Board (the EDPB), which was established as a new body under the GDPR, plays an important role in the application and interpretation of the new data protection framework. The way the EDPB is set up and operates, especially its power and independence, corresponds to the considerable value of personal data protected as a fundamental right. The EDPB's primary role is to safeguard the consistent application of the GDPR.[45] The EDPB is an EU body with legal personality, composed of the heads of EU Member States data protection supervisory authorities. Although there is continuity of the EDPB work with the activities of former WP29 Working Party,[46] whose interpretative conclusions (usually opinions and guidelines) were explicitly adopted by the EDPB at its first plenary meeting on 25 May 2018,[47] it represents a qualitatively new body and its powers under GDPR are considerably stronger and extensive. The EDPB is the highest supervisory authority for data protection in Europe, the main task of which is to ensure consistent GDPR interpretation. An effective tool to ensure consistency of interpretation is both the issuance of opinions, guidelines, recommendations, best practices and the mechanism for adjudication of data protection matters by the EDPB. Although the EDPB guidelines, as the most popular EDPB tool, are not legally binding, it is important to underline their considerable importance for practice, which is especially important in relation to complex up to date data protection issues.

It is possible to stress that application of data protection (privacy) is a dynamic concept that evolves through the supervisory authorities' activities and courts decisions. In the area of data protection, the role of the CJEU judgments is significant, as it gradually refines and deepens the existing data processing doctrine based on the EU Charter and the GDPR. The CJEU provides an interpretation on key data protection issues provided it has the opportunity to answer the preliminary question. The CJEU data protection case law is not only "new case law", data protection

---

[45] Art. 63 GDPR.

[46] The Article 29 Working Party (Art. 29 WP) was an independent European Union advisory body on data protection and privacy made up of a representative from the data protection authority of each EU Member State, the European Data Protection Supervisor and the European Commission. The composition and purpose of Art. 29 WP was set out in Article 29 of the Data Protection Directive (Directive 95/46/EC), and it was launched in 1996. It was replaced by the European Data Protection Board (EDPB) on 25 May 2018 in accordance with the GDPR.

[47] Available at:https://edpb.europa.eu/news/news/2018/first-plenary-european-data-protection-board_en.

after the GDPR adoption it has been already developing before the GDPR came into force. The CJEU case law principles have been even incorporated into the new GDPR legal framework, which has thus been developed and strengthened.[48] Currently, the CJEU case law in data protection field is one of the most dynamically developing areas of the CJEU activities in general, fully reflecting the complexity of the relationship between technologies and processing of personal data. The main contribution of the CJEU case law can be seen in relation to the interpretation of the GDPR principles and concepts. So far, the CJEU has spoken out on a number of key issues and continues to do so. For example, it can be mentioned the case law explaining the position of independent supervisory authority as an essential element for the enforcement of the fundamental right to the protection of personal data (CJEU judgments C-518/07, C-614/10 and C-288/12),[49] explaining the broad scope of the concept of personal data (CJEU judgment C-434/16),[50] access to documents containing personal data regardless of whether they relate to professional or private activities (CJEU judgment C-28/08).[51] Recent examples of CJEU case law include the broad interpretation of the right to a copy as the right of the data subject to obtain a faithful and intelligible reproduction of data to exercise effectively the rights under the GDPR (CJEU judgment C-487/21).[52]

8. The support of data protection compliance by activities of controllers and other entities

The compliance with data protection rules should not be achieved solely through enforcement or other activities by supervisory data protection authorities or courts. It envisages activities of controllers and other stakeholders, e.g. civil rights organisations or Internet service providers. The entities dealing with protection of personal data are best placed to deal with often complex issues of data protection in a technology environment that has specificies in particular areas. There are a number of tools foreseen in the GDPR to help meet the data protection obligations. For example, the GDPR foresees the creation of codes of

[48] CJEU judgment C-293/12 Digital Rights Ireland of 8 April 2014 has expressed a number of key principles related to data protection. ECLI:EU:C:2014:238.

[49] Case C-518/07 of 9 March 2010 European Commission v. Federal Republic of Germany, C-614/10 of 16 March 2010 European Commission v. October 2012 European Commission v Republic of Austria and Case C-288/12 European Commission v Hungary of 8 April 2014. ECLI:EU:C:2010:125.

[50] Case C-434/16 of 20 September 2017 Peter Nowak v Data Protection Commissioner, point 34. ECLI:EU:C-2017:994.

[51] Case C-28/08 Bavarian Lager of 6 July 2010. ECLI:EU:C:2010:378.

[52] Case C-487/21, F. F. v Österreichische Datenschutzbehörde of 4 May 2023, point 45. ECLI:EU:C:2023:369.

conduct[53] that should make it easier for data controllers in a given area (banks, insurance, clinical trials of medicines, etc.) to comply with the obligations imposed by the GDPR. However, it is a reality that, contrary to initial expectations, these codes of conduct have been relatively slow to emerge, partly due to the complexy of certain data protection issues. Nevertheless, the codes of conduct will be useful and could make it easier for controllers to fulfil their obligations.

In the context of fulfilling GDPR obligations, a new concept of so-called performance-based rules also emerged, based on a pragmatic reflection of the regulatory architecture of information networks, in which the defining authority plays a central role, setting technical rules that are adequate in the given environment.[54] The more complex is the issue the controller is dealing with, the more complex is to find appropriate solutions from a data protection perspective. In such a situation, the defining authority could perform partly the tasks of the state in given area by setting appropriate rules. However, the shortage of this form consists in the fact that it depends on the discretion this defining authority whether it grants the data subjects the requested right or not. The example of such form could be the implementation of the right to be forgotten by Google in relation to data subject which feels to be affected by publication of data at Google. Data subject can exercise the mentioned right via a pre-set form of a request published on the Internet.[55] In such cases, judicial review cannot be ruled out, but most ligitation can be anicably avoided.

9. The assessment of the GDPR application after 5 years

The GDPR has now been in force for more than five years (since 25 May 2018), which is sufficient time to evaluate the legal regulation and find out what are its successes and failures or what needs to be changed. The GDPR legislation has already undergone several evaluations since its adoption in 2018. Although there are multiple reviews, the evaluation made by the European Data Protection Board, the European Commission and the European Parliament can be emphasized. These evaluations neither lack the necessary insight into the nature of the problems, nor critical comments are useful suggestions for improvement.

According to the European Data Protection Board (EDPB) statement of 18 March 2020,[56] the application of the GDPR has been successful, it has strength-

[53] Art. 40 GDPR.

[54] POLČÁK, R. a kol. *Právo informačních technologií. Information Technology Law*. pp. 13–16.

[55] Available at: https://support.google.com/websearch/troubleshooter/9685456?hl=cs.

[56] Contribution of the EDPB evaluation of the GDPR under Article 97, adopted on 18 February 2020. Available at: https://edpb.europa.eu/sites/default/files/file1/edpb contributiongdprevaluation 20200218.pd.

ened data protection as a fundamental right and harmonized the interpretation of data protection principles. The data subject rights have been reinforced and data subjects are increasingly aware of the modalities to exercise their data protection rights. Moreover, data controllers and processors within the EU benefit from one single set of rules bringing more legal certainty and single interlocutor through a one-stop-shop mechanism. The legal framework provides increased investigative and corrective powers to supervisory authorities, including the significant fines. The GDPR also contributes to the increased visibility of the EU legal framework and is being considered a model outside the EU. Since the entry into force of the GDPR, the EDPB has acted as the new EU body building on the work of Working Party 29 (WP 29). EDPB has adopted various opinions and guidelines to clarify the basic provisions of the GDPR and to ensure consistency in the application of the GDPR by supervisory authorities. Cooperation between supervisory authorities should contribute to the creation of a new data culture and consistent monitoring practices. However, there are currently procedural shortcomings, especially at national level, in the procedures, status of parties, admissibility criteria, duration of proceedings, time limits, etc. At the moment, the EDPB is looking for possible solutions to overcome these shortcomings and to ensure consistent common practices. As regards the GDPR legislation itself, there is no reason to change it.

Two years later, in a letter dated 10 October 2022,[57] EDPB stated that the GDPR is a cornerstone of the digital single market and it is a vital piece of legislation ensuring a human-centric approach to technology. While its enforcement is picking up speed and the efficiency of cross-border cooperation, among supervisory authorities is increasing steadily, the full potential of the GDPR remains to be unlocked. The priority for GDPR cooperation is to develop harmonized provisions at EU level. While it is premature to revise the GDPR, it is necessary to iron out the differences in administrative procedures and practises which may have a detrimental impact on cross-border cooperation. The administrative procedures should be examined and their effectiveness should be improved, specifically as far as parties to the administrative procedure, procedural deadlines, admissibility of complaints, rejection of the complaint and termination of the procedure and investigative powers of supervisory authorities.

The European Commission (EC) issued an evaluation report on the GDPR in 2020,[58] assessing it as having met most of its objectives, i. e. raising people's awareness of their data protection rights, providing citizens with strong

[57] Available at: https://edpb.europa.eu/system/files/2022-10/edpb_letter_out2022-0069_to_the_eu_commission_on_procedural_aspects_en_0.pdf.

[58] Available at: https://commission.europa.eu/publications/communication-commission-european-parliament-and-council-two-years-application-general-data_en.

enforceable rights and creating a new EU-wide system for enforcement and data governance. The GDPR has proved to be flexible enough to offer solutions even in unexpected circumstances such as COVID-19. The report concludes that harmonisation between EU Member States is improving, although there is still a degree of fragmentation and a need to improve the handling of cross-border cases. Didier Reynders, the European Commissioner for Justice, said that the GDPR has successfully achieved its objectives and has become an inspiration worldwide for those countries wishing to provide a high level of protection to their citizens.

In a statement on the 5th anniversary of the GDPR, Věra Jourová, Vice-President for Values and Transparency, and Didier Reynders, Justice Commissioner, stated among others: *Five years ago, in 2018, a groundbreaking act came into force: the General Data Protection Regulation (GDPR). This groundbreaking legislation has given citizens real control over their data and created a level playing field for businesses. The GDPR was a crucial step in shaping the EU's digital transition. Not only have we set global standards for the secure regulation of data flows, but we have also laid the foundation for a human-centred approach to the use of technology. GDPR has strengthened and harmonised the fundamental right to data protection for all citizens in the European Union. Individuals now have the right to know which of their data is being used and for what purpose. They can exercise their rights to access, rectify and delete their data.* [59]

The European Parliament (EP) has also assessed the GDPR in detail. It adopted a resolution of 25 March 2021 on the Commission's evaluation report on the implementation of the GDPR two years after its application, assessing the GDPR in general, in relation to individuals, supervisory authorities and controllers.[60] Firstly, EP welcomed the fact that the GDPR in general has become a global standard for data protection and is an important tool for convergence of data protection standards. He believes that two years after its entry into force, the GDPR has been very successful and agreed with the Commission that it does not need to update it or to revise it. It highlighted that the GDPR provides a robust regulatory framework for emerging technologies by being technology neutral; it considers that any new legislative initiative needs to be carefully considered to ensure consistency and to close legal gaps and it reminded the Commission has obligation to ensure that all legislative proposals must always be fully GDPR compliant. He noted that stronger and more effective enforcement of the GDPR

[59] Communication from the Commission to the European Parliament and the Council – two years of application of the GDPR. Available at:https://ec.europa.eu/commission/presscorner/detail/en/statement_23_2884.

[60] Commission evaluation report on the implementation of the General Data Protection Regulation two years after its application. Official Journal of the European Union C 494/12. Available at: https://eur-lex.europa.eu/legal-content/EN/TXT/PDF/?uri=CELEX:52021IP0111.

is needed on large digital platforms, in integrated businesses and other digital services, especially in the areas of online advertising, micro-targeting, algorithmic processing, classification, distribution and dissemination of content.

With regard to individuals, the EP stated that they are increasingly aware of their rights under the GDPR, but despite this, they continue to face difficulties in exercising them, in particular with regard to the right of access, portability and transparency. It expressed concern that individuals often find themselves under financial pressure to give consent in exchange for discounts or other commercial offers, or they are threatened by the use of "dark patterns", using pervasive surveillance and other unethical practices; it recalled that where a subject has given consent for a particular processing purpose, this original consent cannot legitimise further processing of data and that legitimate interest is often abused as a legal ground for processing; he stressed the need to promote the exercise of the rights set out in the GDPR.

Further on, the EP stated that supervisory authorities have received a massive increase in the number of complaints, while many authorities were unable to deal with the large number of complaints and lack the sufficient number of information technology experts. The EP expressed concern about the uneven and often non-existent enforcement of the GDPR rules by national supervisory authorities and recorded the different levels of fines in different Member States, while some fines imposed on large companies are too low to have a deterrent effect. It warned that prohibiting the processing of personal data obtained in breach of the GDPR, or the obligation to delete it, can have the same deterrent effect as fines, and was concerned about the length of investigation of some cases dealt by supervisory authorities and the negative consequences for effective enforcement and citizens' trust. It was concerned that the Commission has not yet initiated infringement proceedings against Member States that do not comply with their obligations under the GDPR; he noted the discrepancy between some of the Member States' guidelines and the EDPB's guidelines, leading to divergent application of the GDPR.

Finally, the EP reminded controllers of their legal obligation to carry out a data protection impact assessment when the processing of data is likely to result in a high risk to the rights and freedoms of natural persons. It noted that controllers should provide information in a concise, transparent, comprehensible and easily accessible manner and that this obligation must be particularly strictly respected where children are concerned. He also recalled Guideline number 1/2019 on codes of conduct, noting that this tool is currently underused.

10. Conclusion

The above described findings on the legal framework for data protection make it possible to draw the following conclusions:

- It can be summarised that the aim of this chapter has been to address the question of the practical implications of the fact that the right to data protection and privacy are fundamental rights, in other words, principles that are part of an legal order and can be characterised by certain specific features. The normative nature of these rights means that it is difficult to limit them. The fact that the right to data protection and privacy are fundamental rights has a number of implications for its implementation, application and interpretation. In any case, EU law has set up a unique, yet very complex multi-dimensional system pursuing more objectives (basically the right to free movement of data and right to security versus data protection and privacy).
- The doctrine of data protection and privacy in relation to technology development is not new and has been evolving for a long time, while the first data protection laws in Europe have been passed in the 70s. For a long time, the right to data protection was in the shadow of the right to privacy, but gradually the right to personal data protection has become fully independent. This is also clear from the GDPR wording. Nevertheless, the relationship between data protection and privacy continues to exist in various forms, this is complex and multi-layered relationship. A more broadly conceived and readily available data protection framework can in some cases directly or indirectly support the right to privacy.
- Although the right to personal data is a fundamental right, it is not absolute right and it must be balanced both in relation to the free movement of data and in relation to number of other rights, such as the right to information or freedom of expression. The tension between data use and data protection is one of the defining features of the new millennium, which we refer to as the digital age.
- The GDPR has significantly strengthened and refined the legal framework for the protection of personal data, although it is still based on the original principle expressed in in the Directive 95/46/EC and Council of Europe Convention 108 of 1981. The strengthening and refinement of the GDPR rules has also been made possible through the interpretation of the data protection principles contained in the CJEU case law which preceded the adoption of the GDPR. In any case, EU law has set up a unique, yet very complex multi-dimensional system of personal data protection pursuing more objectives.
- Restrictions on the right to data protection are only possible under conditions foreseen in Article 52 (1) of the EU Charter, which include the application of the principles of necessity and proportionality. In practice, however, the

application of the proportionality test could be problem for the controller with regard to its complexity. The practice also often fails to understand the fact that the right to data protection is fundamental right. It is also the reason why controllers often replace the complex evaluation of data flow by formal one, despite the existence of complex and interdisciplinary issues.

- As far as the evaluation of current data protection legal framework, according to the EDPB, EC and EP there are no reason to change GDPR with the passage of time. The assessment of the legislation over time confirms the correctness of the initial setting of the data protection legal framework. Nevertheless, there are number of shortcomings in the enforcement of data protection law in practice and there are inconsistencies in the procedures before supervisory authorities. Different national procedures of supervisory authorities in the course of proceedings before them are considered to be an obstacle to the effective enforcement and consistent interpretation of the GDPR, leading to considerations on the need to harmonise the procedural rules of EU Member States, although these procedual rules are still at least partly within the competence of the Member States. In any case, further reflection on the GDPR in the near future could be conducted in the area of procedural rules reform, at least for cross-border cases.
- Indeed, the requirement to apply and enforce data protection rules stays nowadays essential, given the emerging technologies including Artificial Intelligence and their exponential growth. In this respect, a solid legal framework for the protection of personal data is essentially needed to enable individuals to control their data. The task of promoting data protection and privacy means to defend human beings and the human dimension of society. In this respect, the role of the legal framework for data protection, as a sensitive data protection tool enabling balance, is and will remain crucial criteria also in digital society.

Table 1: Relevant provisions of the Charter ustanovení Listiny základních práv EU a Smlouvy o EU v oblasti ochrany osobních údajů

Art. 7 EU Charter RESPECT FOR PRIVATE AND FAMILY LIFE	Everyone has the right to respect for his or her private and family life, home and communications.
Art. 8 EU Charter PROTECTION OF PERSONAL DATA	1. Everyone has the right to the protection of personal data concerning him or her. 2. Such data must be processed fairly for specified purposes and on the basis of the consent of the person concerned or some other legitimate basis laid down by law. Everyone has the right of access to data which has been collected concerning him or her, and the right to have it rectified. 3. Compliance with these rules shall be subject to control by an independent authority.
Art. 52 para 1 EU Charter SCOPE AND INTERPRETATION OF RIGHTS AND PRINCIPLES	1. Any limitation on the exercice of the rights and freedoms recognised by this Charter must be provided for by law and respect the essence of these roghts and freedoms. Subject to the principle of proportionality, limitations may be made only if they are necessary and genuinely meet objectives of general interest recognised buy the Union ort he need to protect the rights and freedoms of others.
Art. Treaty on EU, ex Article 286 TEC	1. Everyone has the right to the protection of personal data concerning them. 2. The European Parliament and the Council, acting in accordance with the ordinary legislative procedure, shall lay down the rules relating to the protection of individuals with regard to the processing of personal data by Union institutions, bodies, offices and egencies, and by the Member States when carrying out activities which fall within the scope of Inion law, and the rules relating to the free movement of such data. Compliance with these rules shall be subject to the control of independent authorities. 3. The rules adopted on the basis of this Article shall be without prejudice to the specific rules laid fown in Article 39 of the Treaty on European Union.

CHAPTER TWO

The "Right to Be Forgotten" – Some Considerations on a General Concept in the Light of Fundamental Rights

NADĚŽDA ŠIŠKOVÁ

1. Introduction

The right to be forgotten, from the time when the Judgement of the Court of Justice of the EU in the case C-131/12 Google Spain[61] was declared, became the set part of the lexicon of every lawyer.

It is an entitlement with a huge global impact on practically every individual, which is evidenced, among other things, by the very impressive statistical data. According to the Google Transparency Report, from 2014 to the end of 2023 almost 6 million subjects (5,909,323) requested to be delisted, of which more than 1 and a half million (1,530,260) requests were granted and their personal data were delisted.[62] These numbers are not final and are increasing every day.

Despite the fact that this is a concept that came to the attention of the experts (but even the lay public) more than ten years ago, there are still a number of disputable questions associated with this concept, which this chapter will focus on. The analysis below does not aspire to an in-depth approach to all the issues of the mentioned term (in this direction it refers to already numerous scientific works), but selectively focuses on the chosen questions only.

At the beginning of the chapter, I will deal with certain aspects of this concept in relation to the individual in the human rights intentions, i.e. with this entitlement from the point of view of its beneficiary. In particular, I will analyze whether, contrary to the title itself, it is a really autonomous right. Whether it is an absolute right. What is the relationship between this entitlement and other

[61] C-131/12, Google Spain SL and Google Inc. v. Agencia Española de Protección de Datos (AEPD) and Mario Costeja González, ECLI:EU:C:2014:317.

[62] Requests to delist content under European privacy law – Google Transparency Report. Available at: https://transparencyreport.google.com/

fundamental rights, such as the right to privacy and the right to the protection of personal data or the right to information? Also questions of terminology and the definition of this term are not unambiguous and will be explained. Furthermore, I will try to evaluate the effectiveness of this entitlement, especially whether its usage in practice serves for the benefit of the individual in all cases and whether it is not capable to cause the opposite tendencies, known as the "Streisand effect".

2. Evolution of the concept, terminology and definition

For the first time the concept of the right to be forgotten was used in the Communication of the Commission from 4 November 2010 "A Comprehensive Approach on personal data protection in the European Union". [63] Especially, in the light of online social networking, highlighted the European Commission the necessity of "clarifying the so-called 'right to be forgotten', i.e. the right of individuals to have their data no longer processed and deleted when they are no longer needed for legitimate purposes. This in the case, for example, when processing is based on the person's consent and when he or she withdraws consent or when the storage period has expired." [64]

The global publicity and extraordinary interest from the public and the media this term gained only afterwards, based on the hearing of the Google Spain case by the Court of Justice of the EU, which can be considered a groundbreaking judgment.

The concept within this case was mentioned originally already in the Opinion of the Advocate General Niil Jääskinen[65] in Google Spain,[66] (delivered on 25th of June 2013), almost a year before the judgment itself was issued (May 13, 2014), which adopted the mentioned terminology. The Luxembourg Court based its decision on the interpretation of the Directive 95/46/EC[67] and at the same time shaped the idea and clarified the content of this concept.

[63] Communication from the Commission to the European Parliament, the Council, the Economic and Social Commitee and the Commitee of the Regions "A Comprehensive Approach on personal data protection in the European Union", Brussels, 4. 11. 2010, COM (2010) 609 final

[64] Ibid., p. 8.

[65] Opinion of Advocate General in case Google Spain, ECLI:EU:C:2013:424.

[66] C-131-12 "Google Spain and Inc. v. Española de Protección de Datos (AEPD) and Mario Costeja Conzález", ECLI:EU:C:2014:317.

[67] Directive 1995/46/EC – Protection of individuals with regard to the processing of personal data and on the free movement of such data of 24 October 1995, Official Journal L 281, 23/11/1995, pp. 0031–0050.

Subsequently, this concept was further expanded based on the Guidelines of the Working Group WP 29[68], the independent advisory body on data protection and privacy.

And finally, the General Data Protection Regulation (GDPR)[69], which substituted the aforementioned directive, comes with the most advanced version of this concept, including the introduction in its Article 17 (1) of the structural and integral elements of this entitlement. That is why Article 17 (1) of the GDPR is rightfully considered in jurisprudence as the "torso of today's valid right to be forgotten".[70]

It must be emphasized in this context, that the Court of Justice not only provided a clear interpretation and the necessary basis for adequate regulation at the level of the EU secondary law, but also enriched and completed its own judicial doctrine of fundamental rights, which creates an integral part of the general principles of law. This fact will be of particular importance in our further interpretation.

Regarding the terminology itself, it can be stated that while the judgment in the Google Spain case refers to this concept as *the right to be forgotten*, the General Regulation comes even simultaneously with two names, which it uses *promiscue* and in a synonymous sense – especially in Article 17 it operates with the terms *right to erasure* and *right to be forgotten.*

In scientific doctrine it is possible to be met with different definitions of this term, for example as "deletion from all available carriers of such personal data, the retention of which is no longer necessary or the retention of which is not essential and the data subject does not wish for its retention"[71] or minimalistic, and probably the least appropriate approach "the right to silence on past events in life that are no longer occurring",[72] or "the claim of the individual to have certain data deleted so that third persons can no longer trace them".[73]

---

[68] Guidelines on the Implementation of the Court of Justice of the European Union "Google Spain and Inc. v. Española de Protección de Datos (AEPD) and Mario Costeja Conzález" C-131/12 adopted on 26. 11. 2014, 14/EN, WP 225.

[69] Regulation (EU) 2016/679 of the European Parliament and of the Council of 27 April 2016 on the protection of natural persons with regard to the processing of personal data and on the free movement of such data, and repealing Directive 95/46/EC (General Data Protection Regulation).

[70] DENEMARK, J. *Právo být zapomenout v kontextu moderního pojetí ochrany osobních údajů.* Wolters Kluwer, Prague: 2021, p. 13.

[71] Ibid., p. 15.

[72] Pino, Giorgio: "The Right to Personal Identity in Italian Private Law. Constitutional Interpretation and Juge-Made Rights". In VAN HOECKE, M. AND OST, F. (eds.). *The Harmonisation of Private Law in Europe*. Oxford University Press, Oxford: 2000, pp. 225, 237.

[73] MITROU, L., KARYDA, M. EU's Data Protection Reform and the Right to be Forgotten: A Legal Response to a Technological Challenge?, 5th International Conference of Information

Analysis of the wording of the structural elements of this concept, listed in Article 17(1) GDPR, enables us to define the right to be forgotten as *the entitlement of the individual to request from the controller of the search engine the erasure of his/her personal data or information, if they are no longer necessary, or have been unlawfully processed, or the given by individual consent was withdrawn, and there is no legal grounds for processing, or respectfully on other legitimate grounds, as they are stated in Art. 17 (1) of GDPR.*

Despite that the mentioned provision operates with the term *erasure* in the sense of *removal*, the design and the intention of this entitlement doesn't count on complete deletion of the relevant information, but makes it only non-accessible (for details see below).

3. Right to be forgotten and the related fundamental rights – right to the protection of personal data and right to respect for private and family life

The concept of the right to be forgotten cannot be properly understood without clarifying its relationship to certain fundamental rights regulated in the Charter of Fundamental Rights of the EU, in particular the right to the protection of personal data (Article 8 of the Charter), right to respect for private and family life (Article 7 of the Charter) and the right to freedom of expression (Article 11 of the Charter). Similar rights are also protected by the European Convention of Human Rights and Fundamental Freedoms, which creates one of the most important sources of inspiration for the European Union law.

At the level of the Charter of Fundamental Rights of the EU, the right to be forgotten is not *expressis verbis* mentioned. However, as it follows from the case law of the Court of Justice,[74] this entitlement is closely connected with both the right to the protection of personal data and the right to respect for private and family life. Similarly, the European Commission points out on it in its already mentioned Communication.[75]

The analysis of the mentioned judgments allows us to come to the conclusion that the right to be forgotten currently is not yet an autonomous right, but creates one of the structural and integral elements of two other fundamental rights – the

Law and Ethics 2012, Corfu-Greece, June 29–30, 2012. Available at: https://papers.ssrn.com/sol3/papers.cfm?abstract_id=2165245, p. 8.

[74] For instance, the Opinion of Advocate General in the case C-131/12, paragraf 1112-115. ECLI: EU:C:2013:424.

[75] In the Communication from the Commission from 4. 11. 2010 "A Comprehensive Approach on personal data protection in the European Union" / (COM)2010/609 final.

right to respect for private and family life and the right to the protection of personal data, while these rights "also involve a person's entitlement to access, control and sometimes, erase personal data held by others.[76] On the Internet and e-commerce, it can serve as a means to know and control information about one's personal data, and possibly to erase them". [77]

In jurisprudence, the assessment that the right to be forgotten cannot be considered currently as an independent right, is shared by the majority of authors. For example, Jaroslav Denemark states: "... the right to be forgotten cannot be described as a fundamental human right, but rather as a right that enables by its assert the fulfillment and protection of the fundamental human right to the protection of personal data, i.e. protection of privacy".[78]

But the approaches of particular authors differ to the legal identification of this term, especially to what the right to be forgotten currently can be compared to. For example, Denemark perceives that it is "rather a mechanism enabling the exercise of other fundamental human rights, *that means that* it is an integral part of it and cannot stand as an autonomous right without the aforementioned goals". [79]

This formulation in such a wording cannot be considered completely satisfactory (in the sense that the right to be forgotten is a mechanism enabling the exercise of other rights), especially considering that the right to privacy existed and was exercised long before the invention of the Internet and other technical advantages, with which the concept of right to be forgotten is inseparably linked.

At the same time, I consider the right to be forgotten as a directly invokable entitlement of an individual, which currently is implicitly contained in the right to the protection of personal data and the right to respect for private and family life, and which has a real capacity to become an autonomous right or to create in the future an integral part of other digital entitlements of the individual (for details, see below).

From the point of view of the citizen and other beneficiaries of *the right to be forgotten*, this academic discussion regarding the position and place of this concept in the theory of human rights is not as essential as the finding out whether the aforementioned entitlement can be really invoked in practice or not.

The answer to this question is unambiguously "yes", as the enforceability of this entitlement is supported even within several ways and legal instruments.

At the level of primary law, the related entitlement can be found in the Treaty on the Functioning of the EU and in the Charter of Fundamental Rights of the

[76] WERRO, F. (ed). *The Right to Be Forgotten. A Comparative Study of the Emergent Right's Evolution and Application in Europe, the Americas, and Asia*. Cham: Springer, 2020, p. 1.

[77] Ibid., p. 2.

[78] Denemark, p. 15.

[79] Ibid.

EU, since, as was already pointed out above, the right to be forgotten is implicitly contained in two other fundamental rights. In particular, as regards to the right to the protection of personal data, it is a provision of Article 16 TFEU (1), which is a norm with both vertical and horizontal (direct) effect, and therefore individuals can invoke it before national courts against state authorities and institutions as well as towards private entities.

As regards the Charter of Fundamental Rights of the EU, which, from a formal point of view, is not directly a part of primary law, but it was raised to the level of primary law by the reference contained in Article 6(1) EU, the relevant provisions from the point of view of the right to be forgotten are the provisions of Article 8 (Protection of personal data) and Article 7 (Respect for private and family life).

However, the general problem with the Charter of Fundamental Rights of the EU lies in the fact that, although it is a legally binding catalogue of human rights of the European Union's standard, but not all of its provisions are of the same character and can be judicially invokable by individuals. This is because the Explanations Relating to the Charter of Fundamental Rights to the EU[80] divides all the rights mentioned in the Charter into *rights* and *principles*, when "the difference between the two is that *rights* constitute subjective rights which may be directly invoked as such by individuals in Courts, while *principles* defined as objectives to be respected by the EU legislature and which will be invoked once they have been implemented through legislation".[81]

In other words, some provisions of the Charter based on the Explanations can be considered as the real rights on which an individual can rely in asserting his claims, while other, the principles, are considered to be merely the provisions of the character, which define the objectives of the EU. Their enforcement can be done only in cases, if they were implemented by the EU secondary law. [82]

Although the above Explanations do not have the status of a source of the law, the reference to them was incorporated in the text the Treaty of Lisbon itself /Article 6 (1) TEU/, as well as into the Charter of Fundamental Rights of the EU /Article 52 (7)/, and thus the stated limitations in the application of the Charter became binding.

In the light of the above classification of the rights of an individual based on the "Explanations", the *right to be forgotten* undoubtedly belongs to the category

[80] Explanations Relating to the Charter of Fundamental Rights from 14. 12. 2007. 2007/C 303/02.

[81] PIRIS, J-C. *The Lisbon Treaty. A Legal and Political Analysis*. Cambridge: Cambridge University Press, 2010, p. 153.

[82] For details see ŠIŠKOVÁ, N. New Challenges of the EU in the Field of Human Rights. *European Studies. The Review of European Law, Economics and Politics*. 2014, vol. 1, pp. 15–16; see alo ŠIŠKOVÁ, N. *Lidskoprávní mechanismy na úrovni EU a otázky související.* Prague: Wolters Kluwer, 2021, pp. 79–83.

of the real and directly enforceable rights for 2 reasons: on the one hand, considering that this right was already implemented by the act of the secondary law (i.e. GDPR, which as a general regulation has both a vertical and a horizontal effect). Another reason consists in the construction and formulation of the related norms itself in this EU catalogue of fundamental rights/ Article 7 and Article 8 of the Charter/, which operate with formulations "everyone has the right to...", which are inherent just for the directly invokable rights.

This approach for the differentiation between the *rights* and *principles* based on the construction and formulation of norms was proposed by Commissioner Vitorino, who participated in the work of the Convention on behalf of the European Commission. He concluded that "there is a *right* where the holder is clearly designated and that a *principle* where the Union is referred to as having to respect or recognize a specific value such as healthy environment or protection of consumers".[83] This approach and suggestions of Commissioner Vitorino was reflected in the Final Report of Working Group II[84] and were taken over in the final version of the Constitutional Treaty and in the Lisbon Treaty.

Finally, this entitlement uses the protection as a real *right* (not merely as a *principle*) also considering that it was declared as such by the Court of Justice in the framework of the shaping of its doctrine of fundamental rights. This doctrine creates an integral part of general principles of law,[85] when these principles are ranked in the hierarchy of norms of the European law at the same level as the Treaties.

As we can see, the right to be forgotten, as a part of two other personal rights, is protected as a directly applicable and enforceable entitlement in the framework of various mechanisms at the level of European Union law, and has the corresponding analogous also within the European Convention for the Protection of Human Rights, where as it is stated in Explanations, "the meaning and scope of these rights are the same of the corresponding articles of ECHR".[86]

However, this fact does not mean that the right to erasure can be exercised in all the circumstances and that it is an absolute right. On the contrary, the concept of right to be forgotten counts with a number of exceptions and limitations, and therefore this entitlement is not absolute. It was clearly declared by the Court of Justice in a number of its judgments,[87] especially in Google 2 judgment which declared

[83] See CRAIG, P. *The Lisbon Treaty. Law, Politics and Treaty Reform.* Oxford: Oxford University Press, 2010, p. 217.

[84] Conv 354/02, Final Report of Working Group II, 22. 11. 2002, p. 8.

[85] For details see TRIDIMAS, T. *The General Principles of EU Law.* Second Edition. Oxford: Oxford University Press, 2006, pp. 50–56.

[86] Explanation on Art. 7, Official Journal, 2007/C 303/02, from 14. 12. 2007.

[87] See also C-92/09 and C-93/09, EU:C:2010:662, paragraph 48, and Opinion 1/15 (EU-Canada PNR Agreement) of 26 July 2017, EU:C:2017:592, paragraph 136.

that: "The circumstance that Article 17(3)(a) of Regulation 2016/679 now expressly provides that the data subject's right to erasure is excluded where the processing is necessary for the exercise of the right of information, guaranteed by Article 11 of the Charter, is an expression of the fact that the right to protection of personal data is not an absolute right but, as recital 4 of the Regulation states, must be considered in relation to its function in society and be balanced against other fundamental rights, in accordance with the principle of proportionality[88] (for details see below)."

4. Content of the right to be forgotten from the point of its *ratione materiae* and *ratione loci*

The ratione materiae of the right to be forgotten can be identified within Article 17 (1) GDPR, which provides an individual with the right to request the controller to delete his personal data without undue delay. This provision provides a list of 6 reasons on the basis of which the entity is entitled to request the deletion, namely:

- First reason *(Article 17.1.a)* – a. the personal data are no longer necessary in relation to the purposes for which they were collected or otherwise processed;
- Second reason *(Article 17.1.b)* – the data subject withdraws consent on which the processing is based;
- Third reason (*Article 17.1.c)* – the data subject exercised his or her right to object to processing of his or her personal data pursuant to Article 21.1 and 21.2 GDPR;
- Fourth reason *(Article 17.1.d)* – the personal data has been unlawfully processed;
- Fifth reason *(Article 17.1.e)* – the erasure is compliant with a legal obligation;
- Sixth reason (*Article 17.1.f)* – the personal data has been collected in relation to the offer of information society services to a minor *(Article 17.1.f which refers to Article 8.1)*.[89]

Due the limited scope of this chapter, the content and the conditions will not be analysed for applying of all of these reasons, but only one of them will be mentioned. In particular, the third reason stated in GDPR Article 17 paragraph 1.c) deserves a special attention. This is because of the fact, that the wording of this reason is more favourable for individuals in the comparison to the analogous

[88] C-136/17, para 57, ECLI: EU:C:2019:773.

[89] Guidelines 5/2019 on the criteria of the Right to be Forgotten in the search engines cases under the GDPR (part 1), Version 2.0, Adopted on 7 July 2020. Available at: https://www.edpb.europa.eu/our-work-tools/our-documents/guidelines/guidelines-52019-criteria-right-be-forgotten-search-engines_en, p. 6.

provision of Directive 96/46/EC (Article 14), although it was just this directive that the Court of Justice relied on in the case Google Spain when shaping *the right to be forgotten* concept. While the wording of Article 14 of the Directive linked the right to erasure with cases, when an individual raises an objection to processing with "compelling legitimate grounds relating to his (or her) particular situation", on the other hand, the GDPR speaks of a similar reason mentioned in Article 17 paragraph 1c) only "on grounds relating to his (or her) particular situation". Therefore, as is correctly stated in Guidelines 5/2019 on the criteria of the Right to be forgotten in the search engines, the GDPR therefore changes the burden of proof, providing a presumption in favour of the data subject by obliging on the contrary the controller to demonstrate *"compelling legitimate grounds for the processing"* (Article 21.1). As a result, when a search engine provider receives a request to delist based on the data subject's particular situation, it must now erase the personal data, pursuant to Article17.1.c GDPR, unless it can demonstrate *"overriding legitimate grounds"* for the listing of the specific search result, which read in conjunction with Article 21.1 are *"compelling legitimate grounds (...) which override the interests, rights and freedoms of the data subject"*.

Nonetheless, if the search engine provider fails to demonstrate the existence of overriding legitimate grounds, the data subject is entitled to obtain the delisting pursuant to Article 17.1.c GDPR.[90]

As it was already mentioned above, *the right to be forgotten* cannot be considered as an absolute right, as there are a number of exceptions and limitations for the realization of this right. They are listed in Article 17 (3) of the GDPR, which contains 5 exceptions from the application of this entitlement. In particular, the erasure will not be applied, if the retention of personal data is necessary for:

- First exception – for exercising the right of freedom of expression and information;
- Second exception – for compliance with a legal obligation which requires processing by Union or Member State law to which the controller is subject or for the performance of a task carried out in the public interest or in the exercise of official authority vested in the controller;
- Third Exception for reasons of public interest in the area of public health in accordance with points (h) and (i) of Article 9(2) as well as Article 9(3);
- Fourth exception – for archiving purposes in the public interest, scientific or historical research purposes or statistical purposes in accordance with Article 89(1) in so far as the right referred to in paragraph 1 is likely to render impossible or seriously impair the achievement of the objectives of that processing; or

[90] Ibid., pp.8–9.

– Fifth exception – for the establishment, exercise or defence of legal claims.

Other limitations which are not mentioned in the GDPR, stem from the fact that the relevant national legislation is not always adapted for the realization of individual rights arising from the application of RTBF at the national level. The approaches of the particular Member States are very different, they are not yet unified and we can speak of only partial harmonization. For example, in the case of damages, the concept of fault in Germany and the Czech Republic differs considerably. Other differences in the relevant national legislation connected with the application of the right to be forgotten are described in the comparative study.[91]

In respect to the material scope of the RTBF the correct identification of the meaning *erasure*, with which operates GDPR, creates a key question. The Webster's dictionary explains "erasure" as an "act of erasing something" and proposes as synonymous the words "removal", "cancellation", "elimination", "deletion". When we compare the above mentioned meaning with the design of RTBF, we can find out that "this right only affects the results obtained on searchesmade by the name of an individual and never suggests that the complete deletion of the page from the indexes of the search engine is needed".[92]

In other words the personal data of the individual in fact are not erased or deleted, but became only inaccessible (for details see below).

This finding has a direct connection to the territorial scope of this entitlement.

Ratione loci of the right to be forgotten reflects the territorial scope of EU law, which is regulated by Article 52 of the TEU and Article 355 TFEU. The scope of Charter of Fundamental Rights of the EU, which is also relevant in this sense "follows the scope of EU law and not vice versa, as expressively stated in Article 51 (2) of the Charter".[93]

The practical realization of the right to erasure is reached by the technique known as geo-blocking, which covers the entities from the territory of the EU only. Although the fact that this technique has a negative connotation in the EU internal market, but concerning the right to be forgotten is used as a legally approved mechanism, which ensures the non-accessibility of private data. The details of the geo-blocking mechanism were described in Opinion of Advocate General in case C-507/17.[94]

91 WERRO, F.(ed). *The Right to Be Forgotten. A Comparative Study of the Emergent Right's Evolution and Application in Europe, the Americas, and Asia*. Cham: Springer, 2020.

92 Working Party: Guideline on the Implementation of the Court of Justice of the EU Judgement on Google and Inc. v. Agencia Española de Protección de Datos (AEPD) and Mario Costeja González "C-131/12" adopted on 26. 11. 2014, 14/EN, WP 225, p. 9.

93 Viz Opinion of Advocate General in the case C-507/17, ECLI: EU:C:2019:773, para 55.

94 Ibid., para 71.

5. Right to be forgotten versus Freedom of Expression – what is a proper balance?

On the contrary to the harmonious "coexistence" of the right to erasure with the right to protect personal data and the right for privacy in the form of their integral part, the character of correlation between RTBF and freedom of expression is absolutely different. In essence, one can talk about antipoles and opposites, when the exercise of one right interferes into the exercise of another right, thereby restricting or even precluding it, and vice versa. That is why the proper balance between the right to be forgotten and the realization of freedom of expression is always given by the approach of the legislator and his/her preferences in the field of human rights. In this respect two main approaches can be observed – USA approach and EU approach, which are oppositely different.

The EU approach is best summarized by the verdict of the CJEU in the case Google Spain, which states: "As the data subject may, in the light of his fundamental rights under Articles 7 and 8 of the Charter, request that the information in question no longer be made available to the general public on account of its inclusion in such a list of results, those rights override, as a rule, not only the economic interest of the operator of the search engine, but also the interest of the general public in having access to that information upon a search relating to the data subject's name. However, that would not be the case if it appeared, for particular reasons, such as the role played by the data subject in public life, that the interference with his fundamental rights is justified by the preponderant interest of the general public in having, on account of its inclusion in the list of results, access to the information in question."[95]

On the contrary, the American approach clearly prefers freedom of expression, which is based on the First Amendment of the US Constitution, in contrast to the relevant personal rights, which "are derived from individual amendments *ad hoc* by judicial practice, and rather in marginal cases". [96]

With regard to the aforementioned different preferences in the framework of the collisions of the mentioned rights in the EU and the USA, had occurred the designation of these concepts as the access to dignity (Europe) and the access to freedom (USA).[97] Access to freedom then means that the first violin plays the freedom of speech and press incorporated in to the First Amendment of the US Constitution, and is therefore considered the basis of the American legal system.[98]

[95] Judgement of the Court, C-131/12.

[96] Denemark, ibid., p. 9.

[97] WHITMAN, J. The Two Western Cultures of Privacy, Dignity Versus Liberty. 113 *Yale Law journal*. 11 53, pp.1161–1162.

[98] Denemark, ibid., s. 25.

The American approach in this field even had led some authors to the conviction, that "the Americans will never have the right to be forgotten".[99]

Seemingly, the EU citizen or other subject legally residing in the territory of the European Union is in a better situation than their American counterparts in terms of the protection of their personal rights, including the right to be forgotten. However, this comparative advantage is partially lost with a closer inspection, considering the territorial scope of the RTBF. In other words, as it was already mentioned, the right to erasure is currently enforceable only in the Member States of the Union, not beyond its borders. This is clear from the case law of the Court of Justice. In particular, General Advocate Maciej Szpunar in his Opinion in case C-507/17[100] states that "the right to be forgotten must be weighed against other fundamental rights".[101] This reasoning is followed by argumentation that "the EU authorities would not be in a position to define and determine a right to receive information, still less to strike a balance between that right and other fundamental rights to data protection and to private life, a *fortiori* because such a public interest in having access to information will necessarily vary, depending on the geographic location, from one third State to another".[102]

Therefore it can be concluded, that right to be forgotten with regard to its territorial limitations is to some extent an illusory entitlement, because personal data in fact are not deleted, but with the usage of geo-blocking are only hidden or locked in the Member States and are still accessible for the subjects with the domain outside the European Union. As it was stated in the Judgement of CJEU in the case C-507/17: "That operator is not required to carry out that de-referencing on all versions of its search engine, but on the versions of that search engine corresponding to all the Member States, using, where necessary, measures which, while meeting the legal requirements, effectively prevent or, at the very least, seriously discourage an Internet user conducting a search from one of the Member States on the basis of a data subject's name from gaining access, via the list of results displayed following that search, to the links which are the subject of that request."[103]

In the light of the above mentioned paradoxically, just the EU citizens and other entities on the territory of the Union could be at a disadvantage in comparison to the rest of the world, where the right to be forgotten is not applied. This

[99] LUCKERSON, V. Americans Will Never Have the Right to be Forgotten. *TIME*, 14. 5. 2014. Available at: http:// time.com/98554/right-to-be-forgotten/

[100] Opinion in case C-507/17/ Google LLC v. Commission Nationale de l'informatique et des libertes. ECLI:EU:C:2019:15.

[101] Ibid., para 57.

[102] Ibid., para 60.

[103] C-507/17, ECLI:EU:C:2019:772.

opinion is generally shared in jurisprudence, in particular: "Considering the borderless nature and existence of the Internet, any and all decisions made regarding the application of the RTBF in the EU will have global implications through the trickledown effect, in addition to the creation of information asymmetry with regard to accessibility and availability of information in Europe and the rest of the world. As a result, in the long run, on a broader scale, it will be the European countries which will have lesser access to information in comparison to the rest of the world, which would be rather ironic." [104]

In addition to this limitation resulting from the territorial scope of the RTBF which in a specific way affects only EU citizens, there exists another universal negative aspect, which is given by the technological reasons and has global impact on everybody. By this I mean the effect that it's not actually a total erasure and definite removal of undesirable and unwanted (from the point of view of the individual) data, but only making it unavailable. In other words, once the information occurs in cyber space, it will never disappear.

Therefore, the opinion can be shared that: "Wherever data exists, it is vulnerable, and hence the only way to ensure the non-vulnerability of data is for it not to exist."[105]

In other words, while for the users of the Internet the data „were erased", for the controllers it is still an available information which is at their disposal anywhere.

This gives the controllers, especially the Internet giants, enormous power over citizens and even the governments, that can be easily abused in the future. Totalitarian regimes and terrorist organizations can also get hold of this data through guided hacking attacks.

Therefore, the very concept of unlimited data retention in its essence is flawed and must be changed, as it does not serve the entire society, but only to selected individuals and can be misused at any time.

6. Right to be forgotten and the Streisand effect

The impacts of the Google v. Gonzalez Judgement had showed clearly that despite the fact that right to be forgotten creates in principle a very significant instrument for the protection of personal rights but it certain cases in can work in an opposite way, when it is not capable of protecting the applicant for erasure

[104] FARHAAN, U. A. Right to Be Forgotten: a critique of the post-Costeja Gonzalez paradigm. *Computer and Telecommunications Law Review.* 2015, vol. 21, 6, p. 181.

[105] BERNAL, P. A. A Right to Delete? *European Journal of Law and Technology*. 2011, vol. 2, issue 2, p. 8.

but even vice versa, to damage him. It takes place in situations, when the hearing in courts supported by outputs in media concerning the case are resulting in a huge interest from the side of general public to the personal information of the applicant for erasure. In other words it does not lead to the hiding or veiling of the private information but on the contrary to the massive publicity and the capture of the general attention to these matters.

Title of this effect is derived from the name of the famous American singer and actress, who had tried through litigation in Court[106] to have removed the photo of her residence from the open access website but as a result achieved an incomparably larger interest from the side of the general users than before[107] (especially only 4 downloads of the photo before the lawsuit and 420 000 downloads after it).

Also Mario Gonzalez in the same way had become the subject of the enormous interest resulting from the announcement of the Judgement of the Court of Justice of the EU. "Paradoxically on the one hand he achieved what he demanded, on the other hand he brought the same information to the attention of the professional public across continents… After the Judgement the information in the article appeared in several places in different languages making it more accessible to the public…, the case has also become frequently cited in academic publications… Thus in case Google Spain v. Mario Costeja Gonzalez the Streisand effect can be demonstrably confirmed."[108]

The representatives of legal science had analysed the factors which influence whether the Streisand effect will be manifested for a requestor claiming the right to be forgotten, namely:

1) The extent to which the requestor is a public figure;
2) The type of information the requestor wants to hide;
3) The requestor's actual actions;[109]

To the mentioned three factors, on which was pertinently pointed out, two more can be added, which can complete this list, especially:

4) If the dispute is connected with enormous financial sanctions (penalty) or with a great compensation for damage;
5) In the case of a ground-breaking judgement.

In other words, concerning the first factor, the chances for the Streisand effect increase and the prospects for the protection of privacy reduce in case of:

[106] Barbara Streisand v Kenneth Ademan et al, case No 077257 Superior Court of California, County Los Angeles.

[107] CHIPIDZA, W., YAN, J. *Does Flaggin Potus's Tweets Lead to Fewer or More Retweets? Preliminary Evidence From Machine Learning Models*. p. 18. Available at: https://ideas.repec.org/p/osf/socarx/69hkb.html

[108] MACH, M. Streisand effect in the Content of Right to be Forgotten. *European Studies, The Review of European law, Economic and Politics.* 2022, vol. 9, issue 1, pp. 115–16.

[109] Ibid., p. 113.

politicians and other publicly active persons, famous actors, sportsmen, anchor men and commentators (especially if they are working in countrywide media), the participants in various reality shows in the TV and Internet broadcasts, influencers etc.

In some cases taking into account the character of the information they could be even the representatives of teacher's and doctor's professions, on whom the high moral demands are being traditionally placed.

Besides the personality and its status, the key role in the rise of the Streisand effect plays the "explosiveness" of the information itself, which must be blocked. As it was pointed out correctly in the jurisprudence: "the more serious the transgression, the more societal expectations of morality have been violated and the greater chances of the Streisand effect occurring".[110]

The decisive factor creates also the fact whether the applicant themselves doesn't contribute to the spreading of the personal information on different Internet platforms, especially on social media as, "the individual who publicly provides his or her personal information or does not adequately protect it, is less likely to hide his or her information retrospectively".[111]

So, it can be concluded, that under certain circumstances the right to be forgotten doesn't work in a proper way and vice versa could even lead to huge interference in the private sphere of an individual. As such, the right to be forgotten could be compared to a double-edged sword. That is why all the above-mentioned factors must be taken into consideration in advance in order to avoid the negative impacts caused by the Streisand effect.

7. Conclusion

The European Union by regulation of the right to be forgotten (which is embodied in GDPR) had taken a significant step towards the better protection of the personal sphere of the individual, acting as a pioneer in this field.

Nevertheless, in the current form the right to be forgotten couldn't be considered as a really effective instrument, which always serves for the benefits of the citizens and prevents in all the cases the spreading of their personal data via Internet, to some extent it still remains an illusory entitlement, due to the several factors:

1) Due to the design and the concept of this entitlement which despite its title doesn't count on the complete erasure or deletion of relevant information,

[110] Ibid., p. 115.
[111] Ibid.

but only with its being hidden in the territory of the EU by the technique known as geo-blocking, so the data still exists, as geo-blocking counts on their retention.

2) Due to the limits of the territorial scope of this entitlement, which reflects the *ratione loci* of EU law and thus isn't valid over the borders of the European Union. In this sense paradoxically the EU citizens and other entities with the domaine in the Member States are at a disadvantage in comparison with their counterparts in the rest of the world, because their personal data in fact are not deleted and are still available for the entities beyond the Union. This information asymmetry concerning the accessibility of information in the EU and in the rest of the world is obvious and alarming.
3) Third, due to the nature of Internet itself, which never ensures the definite removal of undesirable (from the point of view of the individual) private information. Besides the so-called trickledown effect and the circulation of the uploaded before content there is also a fact that controllers always have at their disposal all the data, which were officially erased. This gives the controllers enormous power over citizens and governments, that can be easily abused in the future. Therefore, the very concept of the unlimited data retention in its essence is flawed and must be changed.
4) Due to the threats and jeopardizing by the eventuality of the Streisand effect, when, despite the intention to erasure, the access to the private information from the side of general public is not reduced, but vice versa it is multiplied greatly. In this respect it can be considered as a double-edged sword.

So the right to be forgotten is a non-absolute entitlement which counts on a number of exceptions and is greatly influenced by some negative factors mentioned above, cannot guarantee the protection of personal data of the individual in all the cases. Nevertheless its regulation creates a step in the right direction, but in the current form is not a sufficient one.

The real effectiveness of it in the optimal way can be reached only, if this entitlement would be applicable in the global scope; if it would count on the complete erasure of data without their retention and if it would be regulated by the international legal instruments of the universal character. This course of action nevertheless strikes with the different approaches of the particular states to the correlation between the right to be forgotten and the freedom of expression.

Therefore in reality the right to be forgotten as a legally binding and invokable entitlement in a global scope cannot be ensured in the near future.

On the other hand, it is worth considering the creation of at least a worldwide digital catalogue of entitlements of the individual, which will be conceived and designed at the beginning as "principles" (not real "rights"). The right to be forgotten will be a part of this catalogue.

This coherent catalogue (in the form of declaration) will reflect the peculiarities of these new entitlements, which stem from the nature of Internet itself and differ greatly from other traditional human rights. To these peculiarities belong for instance the rapidity of the spread of information via Internet, its global impacts, much more devastating character of the eventual damages, etc.

The catalogue of digital rights could consist of both already declared rights, as well as entirely new entitlements of the individual, for instance:

- Right to the access to Internet;
- Right to the communication in cyber space (via email, social media, chats);
- Right to be forgotten (right to erasure);
- Right for information, clear explanation and truthful information in e -commerce;
- Right to communication with a human operator and not to be the subject of the automated decision;
- Prohibition of disriminatory conditions in the transactions made online, especially in e-commerce (personalized pricing, geo-blocking, etc.).

This coherent catalogue (first in the form of declaration) can become in future a proper basis and an eligible platform for formulation of new autonomous rights and their regulation by the universal legal instruments.

At the level of the EU it is worth thinking about incorporation of these entitlements into the Charter of the Fundamental Rights of the EU as the new autonomous right, right to digital integrity. The right to be forgotten will be rightfully a part of it.

CHAPTER THREE

The "Right to Be Forgotten" – by Watchdogs and Open-Source Search Engines

MARTIN MACH

The Judgment of the Grand Chamber of the Court of Justice of the European Union (CJEU) in the case *Google Spain SL and Google Inc. v Agencia Española de Protección de Datos* (AEPD) *and Mario Costeja González* has significantly increased the protection of personal data mainly due to the interpretation of data protection law, while taking into account the facts of the case. The fact that in 2012, when the case started, Directive 95/46/EC was the effective legal regulation was the problematic issue in this case. As soon as then, the concept of a web search engine was well-known, as the first web search engine *Archie* was introduced in 1990 and the search engines *W3Catalog* and *Aliweb* in 1993,[112] however, they were not yet so extensively used, and today's really most commonly used and largest web search engines did not even exist at that time. *Google* was created in 1998, 3 years after the *Directive*, *Bing* in 2009, *Yahoo!* in the year of the *Directive* (1995) and *Yandex* in 2000. There were also approximately 16 million Internet users in 1995, which was 0.4% of the total world population.[113] The aforementioned 16 million users may seem like a large number, but it is a tiny fraction compared to the 3,035 million users (42.3% of the total world population) in 2014, or the 5 473 million (69% of the total world population) in 2022. It may be deduced from this that Directive 95/46/EC was no longer able to fully respond to the situation in 2014 and it was precisely a judicial decision that was needed, together with Directive 95/46/EC, to reflect the current circumstances in relation to the facts of case C-131/12.

[112] HENDY, C. The *History of Search Engine*. [online]. Available at: https://carlhendy.com/history-of-search-engines/?fbclid=IwAR2R4cz3J_f80EsWu0mjQcaeS57StVEBVezp4vfINGWIv-feOWe8CJmvXFw#archie. Accessed 1. 3. 2023.

[113] *Internet Growth Statistics 1995 to 2023 – the Global Village Online*. [online]. Available at: https://www.internetworldstats.com/emarketing.htm?fbclid=IwAR2DVQgzwksJuQ9uBZfhFZcLWw00SJiOVnHrwyYQbQW8McjtwoX76gGq2L0. Accessed 1. 3. 2023.

Two years after the Judgment of the Court in the case *Google Spain v Mario Costeja Gonzales*, a necessary amendment to the data protection legislation was issued, reflecting the conclusions of that judgment. Regulation (EU) 2016/679 of the European Parliament and of the Council of 27 April 2016 on the protection of natural persons with regard to the processing of personal data and on the free movement of such data, and repealing Directive 95/46/EC,[114] also known as GDPR (General Data Protection Regulation), was a welcome strengthening of the protection of personal data also with regard to the position of search engines, which in Article 17 of the GDPR includes the right to be forgotten, i.e. the extended Right to erasure. Both, the *Google Spain v Mario Costeja Gonzales* judgment, and the GDPR Regulation primarily target commercial search engines owned by private companies, such as the aforementioned Google, Bing, Yahoo! The prerequisite here is that the information is removed from the public part of the Internet where it is hosted by a private entity and the conditions of Article 17(1) of the GDPR Regulation are met.[115] However, just as Directive 95/46/EC responded to the situation in 1995 and failed to respond to later developments in search engines and the Internet in general, the GDPR today omits one type of search engine. These are Internet search engines where the source data is not only from the Internet but from public administration.[116] These search engines only started to appear at the time of the introduction of the GDPR and later.[117]

In the context of protecting democracy and transparency and the anti-corruption environment, there are types of search engines called *"watchdogs"*, which

[114] Regulation (EU) 2016/679 of the European Parliament and of the Council of 27 April 2016 on the protection of natural persons with regard to the processing of personal data and on the free movement of such data, and repealing Directive 95/46/EC (General Data Protection Regulation).

[115] (a) the personal data is no longer necessary in relation to the purposes for which they were collected or otherwise processed;
(b) the data subject withdraws consent on which the processing is based according to point (a) of Article 6(1), or point (a) of Article 9(2), and where there is no other legal ground for the processing;
(c) the data subject objects to the processing pursuant to Article 21(1) and there are no overriding legitimate grounds for the processing, or the data subject objects to the processing pursuant to Article 21(2);
(d) the personal data has been unlawfully processed;
(e) the personal data has to be erased for compliance with a legal obligation in Union or Member State law to which the controller is subject;

[116] Data from public administration institutions are also found in commercial search engines, but in a negligible percentage compared to watchdog search engines. Also, commercial search engines have a developed application assessment system, which is lacking in watchdog search engines. Therefore, the chapter focuses primarily on watchdog search engines.

[117] Hlidacstatu.cz, czech watchdog, which contains the most information available on watchdog search engines in EU member states, was created in 2016 as a spin-off from the anti-corruption initiative Rekonstrukcestatu.cz.

are present in every EU Member State. There are big differences between the *watchdogs* search engines of each country: what information they contain, where they draw their information from, and while some are completely free, some require payment to display more information. Another important difference is that while some watchdogs run directly on the official government website,[118] some are set up by non-profit organisations and run on websites separate from the country's government website.[119] This raises the question of whether the right to be forgotten can be applied to these types of search engines as well. If so, how to deal with a request to delete personal information from the results of such search engines by invoking the right to be forgotten in cases where the source of that personal information is public administration? Is there going to be a different approach for watchdog search engines on government websites and watchdog search engines on NGO websites?

As watchdog search engines process personal data, they are also considered data controllers according to Article 4 (7) of the GDPR.[120] Therefore, the right to be forgotten can also be applied to them. However, it should be taken into account that, unlike commercial search engines, the source of information for watchdog search engines is not only freely available content on the Internet, but mostly data from institutions or public administration systems. While freely available information on the Internet[121] may be removed from the search results under the conditions of Article 17(1), the logical question arising here is whether the same may be done in the case of data and information from the state. In the case of such data, while in most cases the data subject cannot withdraw his or her consent to processing, even data provided by the state administration may be inaccurate or the personal data may no longer be necessary for the purposes for which they were collected or otherwise processed and therefore, the data subject should have the right to correct or delete such information in justified cases. However, the application of the right to be forgotten to such personal information could lead to an undesirable situation where a private operator, for example a non-profit organisation operating a *watchdog* search engine, would have to assess the relevance of the information published by the public administration.

[118] For example: *Accueil – data.gouv.fr.* [online]. Available at: https://www.data.gouv.fr/fr/?fbclid=IwAR3KWiC1pOPQqj9RVSUg0zAwVX1izrBJsgdrsObYUwh5p0Z4qGIOBsAVyOc. Accessed 1. 3. 2023.

[119] For example *Hlídač státu.* [online]. Available at: https://www.hlidacstatu.cz/. Accessed 1. 3. 2023. Or *Sieć Obywatelska Watchdog Polska.* [online]. Available at: https://siecobywatelska.pl/?lang=en. Accessed 1. 3. 2023.

[120] Regulation (EU) 2016/679 of the European Parliament and of the Council of 27 April 2016 on the protection of natural persons with regard to the processing of personal data and on the free movement of such data, and repealing Directive 95/46/EC (General Data Protection Regulation).

[121] Art. 17, para 1, ibid.

Nevertheless, this is not legally permissible, since the state, or its institutions, is competent in the exercise of public administration. Alternatively, some of the powers may be delegated, but it is precisely defined in the relevant legislation which powers and to what extent. Search engine watchdog organisations are thus not legally entitled to verify the relevance and accuracy of the information provided by the public administration, or even to modify it subsequently. How to proceed in these cases to guarantee all the rights of the individual, but at the same time not to interfere with the exercise of state administration, since there is no legislative provision to do so in this case?

It is necessary to approach the operation *watchdog* search engines with respect to the fact that their style of operation differs from commercial search engines. The transformation of the information obtained from the government into the form required for the proper functioning of a watchdog search engine is the first significant change. Commercial search engines have a site-specific developed search system. Their work is also facilitated by the keywords that are listed for each page and other search strategies such as the entire SEO (*Search Engine Optimisation*) structure of the website. This is also the focus of website builders, as good SEO will help the page to be better identified by search engines and thus the page will rank higher in search results.[122] Search engines thus get every page ready and tailored to be easily found through commercial search engines. The major commercial search engines are able to ‘click’ through all the links on a website and examine its content in detail, for example, Google uses Googlebot to do this.[123] Watchdog search engines, however, do not have these capabilities. They get large amounts of data that they have to sort and index so that searching them works properly. Some sources are mere scans of documents therefore, conversion to machine-readable text has to take place. Although there are computer programs for converting text into machine-readable form, reliability of these conversions is not 100%, as evidenced by recent research results dealing with automatic conversions of text into machine-readable form. Andrija Cvejić and colleagues even claim that *“... the current results do not indicate that the whole legal corpus can be transformed without any assistance from human experts”.*[124] That is to say, legal acts need to be double-checked by an expert, not

[122] O’NEILL, S., CURRAN, K. The Core Aspects of Search Engine Optimisation Necessary to Move up the Ranking. *International Journal of Ambient computing and Intelligence.* 2011, vol. 3, no. 4, pp. 62–70.

[123] Google Developers. (n.d.). *What Is Googlebot | Google Search Central | Documentation.* [online]. Available at: https://developers.google.com/search/docs/crawling-indexing/googlebot. Accessed 1. 3. 2023.

[124] CVEJIĆ, A. et al. Automatic Transformation of Plain-text Legislation into Machine-readable Format. In ZDRAVKOVIĆ, M., TRAJANOVIĆ, M., KONJOVIĆ, Z. (ed.). *ICIST 2021 Proceedings.* Kopaonik: Information Society of Serbia, 2021, pp. 50–55.

just a layman, when converted into machine-readable form. For the purposes of these conversions, due to the nature of watchdog search engines, the authors do not consider it strictly necessary to have the text checked by a person with a legal background, since in this case, only a check of the verbatim transcription of the text is sufficient. However, mere conversion to machine-readable form is not the final solution. Just as there are *keywords* and *SEO* for commercial search engines, watchdog search engines have to categorize and index all documents so that they are properly searchable. There is also an effort to incorporate programs with algorithms to perform this indexing, however, there is currently no flawless program. The research conducted by Jakub Maroušek investigated text pre-processing through four different classifiers for determining categories, *random forests, word embeddings* (two different solutions) and *wordkeys*, but none of them were error-free.[125] Since there is a need for checking the final text and indexing, for which a checker has to be assigned, this offers the possibility of checking the admissibility of a given document in the results of a watchdog search engine. In establishing internal control mechanisms, one can take inspiration from, for example, the Watchdog State.[126] A good example for Watchdog State is the control mechanism where the received documents[127] undergo a multi-point analysis:

1. Validation of formal data
2. Checking the listed prices with and without VAT to see if they are calculated correctly (thousands of contracts are not)
3. Checking the completeness of contract data, including validation and verification in commercial and other registers
4. Analysis of illegal actions – typically signing a contract before the supplier company was formed
5. Analyzing the relationship of politicians to the contractor in the contract and finding conflicts of interest
6. Statistical calculations (e.g., suppliers with the largest share of orders)
7. Search for suspicious circumstances (contract splitting, contracts with new companies, etc.)[128]

[125] MAROUŠEK, J. *Automated contract classification for portal HlidacSmluv.cz.* Praha: 2020. Thesis. Charles University, Faculty of Mathematics and Physics, Department of Software Engineering.

[126] *Hlídač státu.* [online]. Available at: https://www.hlidacstatu.cz/. Accessed 1. 3. 2023. This watchdog search engine will be mentioned several times in the text as it is an NGO website, but it collects, analyses and offers the largest amount of personal information of all the NGO watchdog search engines in the EU. This is why it is useful to use it as an example of what watchdog search engines can offer in search results and examples of good or bad practice.

[127] For example contracts for public procurement, sponsorship of political parties, relationship between natural and legal persons, etc.

[128] BLÁHA, M. *O Hlídači státu – Hlídač státu.* [online]. Available at: https://texty.hlidacstatu.cz/o-serveru/. Accessed 1. 3. 2023.

In particular, points 1 and 3 could reveal data that are manifestly erroneous or documents with a large amount of missing data that could lead to misidentification of the data subject. However, these errors cannot be explicitly covered by any of the conditions under which the removal of personal data can be requested. If we look at Article 17(1) of the GDPR, which lists the conditions for the application of RTBF, it does not mention the possibility of applying RTBF based on inaccurate or misattributed information. However, there is case law from the CJEU which allows the application of RTBF based on inaccurate or false information.[129] Thus, a multi-point analysis by the watchdog search engine operator is welcome as it checks the accuracy of personal data. Even if this step fails, the right to be forgotten under Article 17 can be applied to inaccurate or misattributed personal data.

However, from the perspective of the right to be forgotten, it is also possible to view the personal data in the search result in the light of Article 17(1)(a), i.e., *“the personal data is no longer necessary in relation to the purposes for which they were collected or otherwise processed”*. How long specific information need to be retained may be decided by national archiving legislation. Only if the legislation in question does not stipulate the necessary retention period, according to the author, it is possible upon the discretion of the operator of the watchdog search engine. Thus, if the state does not stipulate the length of retention and disclosure of information by legal regulation, the watchdog search engine itself may determine the time period for displaying a particular situation, either by setting it within its internal rules or by assessing cases individually. This is the case, for example, with the State Watchdog, which has set time limits for the display of sponsorship donations to political parties, namely 5 years for donations below EUR 210 and 10 years for donations above EUR 210.[130] The removal of search results from a watchdog search engine based on the obsolescence of the information in question, unless otherwise provided for by law, is the only case when it is at the discretion of the operator of the watchdog search engine whether to remove or retain the information in question.

However, for the remaining grounds for the removal of personal data under Article 17(1) of the GDPR Directive, as is the case with commercial search engines, the assessment cannot be left to the discretion of the operator of the watchdog search engine, as the private entity would interfere with the exercise of public administration, which is not possible without a delegation of powers. At the same time, a mere disclaimer cannot be accepted. If personal data was to be included in the search results and there was no one to check and decide

[129] For example C-460/20 Google (Déréférencement d’un contenu prétendument inexact), ECLI: EU:C:2022:962.

[130] From email communication with the author. Author’s archive.

whether to keep or delete it, there would be a significant interference with the data subject's personality rights. The authors do not dispute that it would certainly be possible to go to court to decide on the matter, but a court decision should be a last resort. This is for two reasons. The first one is the speed of the decision. Court proceedings may take months or years, while having personal data on the Internet for that length of time is too significant intervention into an individual's privacy.[131] The second reason is to create a fiction of no liability for information originating from the public administration. If each individual case is decided only by the courts, this could give the impression that verifying the accuracy of the information when it is entered into the systems from which the watchdog search engine draws is not necessary. However, it should be the case that whoever enters personal information into any publicly available system or website on behalf of the government should be held accountable for the accuracy of that information. Since it is the institution that posted the information that is held responsible for it, the right to be forgotten application should be decided by the institution that posted the information. More precisely, the institution on whose behalf the information was published.

There is a big difference between a commercial search engine and a watchdog search engine. Commercial search engines are the arbitrators of requests for the right to be forgotten, while they have to assess these requests, which the European Court of Justice has also pointed out.[132] By contrast, watchdog search engines draw not only on information publicly available on the Internet, but also on public administration sources and therefore have to treat requests differently. Primarily, they need to know where they are drawing the information in connection with which the RTBF takedown request has been submitted from. In the case of a publicly available source, the watchdog search engines should also be the arbitrator of the request. However, in the case of an RTBF takedown request, where the information in question is drawn from a public source, watchdog search engines cannot become arbitrators and assess these requests. In such cases, they should send the request to the institution that published the information for consideration. This is precisely on the basis of responsibility while entering and processing information in question. The authors would recommend that this assessment be made by the Department of Archives if the institution has one. The reason for this is the close monitoring of the right to be forgotten by these very employees, while at the time of the creation of the GDPR, French archivists initiated a petition, *Citoyens contre le projet de réglement européen sur les données*

[131] In the absence of an interim measure.

[132] C-460/20 Google (Déréférencement d'un contenu prétendument inexact), ECLI:EU:C:2022:962.

personnelles,[133] signed by archivists and lay people from all EU countries. The final 50,762 signatures translated into the creation of point d) in Article 17(3) of the GDPR Directive. The topic of the right to be forgotten is very important for archivists in terms of the practical occurrence in their profession, which is why one can also find academic articles and research on this topic.[134]

The assessment of national disclosure requests by state agencies should bring consistency and legal certainty in the form of predictability of the law, as not all non-state watchdogs have legal departments,[135] which could lead to different assessment results. This will therefore also unify the decision-making process, where it will not matter whether the watchdog search engine runs on a government website or a watchdog search engine is run by an NGO. However, the long timeframes are problematic for the government, which is not desirable in the area of data protection. Although paragraph 1 of Article 17 of the GDPR operates with a vague legal concept of *"without undue delay"*, practice and other accompanying documents[136] assign to this concept a time period of approximately 1 month, which is sufficient time even for consideration by state institutions. This will meet the predictability of the law applied within a clearly defined timeframe. The overwhelming of state institutions with requests for RTBF by watchdog search engines could be another problematic point, but current practice does not suggest that the number of requests is large.[137] However, this way of adjudicating applications only complements the first instance decision. In the event that a data subject's request for a right to be forgotten application on his or her personal data is rejected, he or she has the possibility to appeal against the decision. In this case, as is the practice with commercial search engines, the appeal should be lodged with the national office for personal data protection. Since these are state institutions, it will no longer be relevant

---

[133] Text here: The world's platform for change. (n.d.). *Change.org.* [online]. Available at: https://www.change.org/p/citoyens-contre-le-projet-de-r%C3%A9glement-europ%C3%A9en-sur-les-donn%C3%A9es-personnelles-eudatap. Accessed 1. 3. 2023.

[134] For example: ČTVRTNÍK, M. Právo být (ne)zapomenut. Výmazy dějin, inflace historických pramenů, ochrana soukromí, vy(zne)užívání dat a prekérní situace archivů v mladém 21. století – podněty k diskusi. *Archivní časopis 68.* 2018, vol. 3, pp. 266–297. Or: ŠIMŮNKOVÁ, K. GDPR v archivní praxi. *Setkání archivů.* Praha, 18. 1. 2018.

[135] Even the oft-mentioned Hlídač státu doesn't have legal department.

[136] WOLFORD, B. *Everything you need to know about the "Right to be forgotten"* GDPR.eu. [online]. Available at: https://gdpr.eu/right-to-be-forgotten/. Accessed 1. 3. 2023.

[137] For the Google search engine, the number is listed here: Google Transparency Report. (n.d.). [online]. Available at: https://transparencyreport.google.com/eu-privacy/overview. Accessed 1. 3. 2023. In an email communication with the author, Hlídač státu mentions "dozens of applications per year", which is certainly not a large number when sent to multiple institutions for review.

whether the request concerns the removal of personal data from the Internet or personal data from public service sources.

8. Conclusion

The right to be forgotten is known primarily for its possibility to be applied to search results from commercial search engines such as *Google*, *Bing*, *Yahoo!* and others. The legal basis for the obligation of search engines to apply this right to their search results may be found in the GDPR. Search engines meet the definition of *controller*,[138] which imposes this obligation on them. However, so do *watchdog* search engines, which also fall under the definition of *controller* and should therefore have the same obligations as commercial search engines and should be able to apply the right to be forgotten to their search results. However, and this is particularly problematic for watchdog search engines, their source also includes public administration data. However, watchdog search engines, often operated by non-state organisations, cannot arbitrarily judge which data of state organisations they hide or leave visible, as this would be an unlawful interference with the exercise of public administration, which is not possible without an explicit delegation in the law.

In part, information provided may be handled in a preventative manner in an effort to provide correct information and minimize the number of right to be forgotten requests. This is by establishing internal control mechanisms that should be able to detect information that is incomplete or apparently meaningless at first glance. This control mechanism is known from watchdog search engines on non-government websites, but not from watchdogs on government websites. This step is not mandatory as it is not mentioned in any legislation, but it is recommended by the author. Within the given document control and indexing, government documents may also be flagged, which can then provide guidance to the watchdog search engine on how to proceed in the case of a right to be forgotten request. However, these control mechanisms are not 100% reliable and consideration should be given to how to proceed when a right to be forgotten request is applied to watchdog search engine results. In this case the request needs to be considered in terms of the source of information to which the request relates. If the provider is a public administration institution, the request needs to be decided by the public administration institution, specifically, the institution

[138] Art. 4, par. 7, Regulation (EU) 2016/679 of the European Parliament and of the Council of 27 April 2016 on the protection of natural persons with regard to the processing of personal data and on the free movement of such data, and repealing Directive 95/46/EC (General Data Protection Regulation).

that issued the information in question. Since information in question may be covered by the provisions of the national Archives Acts, the author recommends that the archiving departments, if they exist, should be responsible for assessing such requests. The operators of the watchdog search engines themselves will certainly welcome this step, because of the disclaimer, as there are substantial fines for mishandling personal data, which could be devastating, especially for non-profit organisations.[139] It is also beneficial in terms of the predictability of the law. For watchdog search engines, it would be possible to submit a request by simply clicking on the originator of the information in question for consideration. However, it depends on the condition of digitisation of the public administration of the country in question. I t is necessary that RTBF could be applied also to the results of watchdog search engines on government websites. The long timeframe in assessing "right to be forgotten" applications may be a possible concern for public administration involvement. This is not desirable in the case of data protection, but there is a well-established practice of assessment within one month in RTBF, which would also apply to assessment by public administration institutions. In the event of inaction or rejection of a request, there is the possibility of an appeal to the national office for personal data protection, as a public institution, it may assess information from all sources.

[139] Art. 83, Regulation (EU) 2016/679 of the European Parliament and of the Council of 27 April 2016 on the protection of natural persons with regard to the processing of personal data and on the free movement of such data, and repealing Directive 95/46/EC (General Data Protection Regulation).

CHAPTER FOUR

The Right to Internet Acces: A New Fundamental Right or a New "Platform" for Fundamental Rights?

LUSINE VARDANYAN, HOVSEP KOCHARYAN, ONDREJ HAMUĽÁK

1. Introduction

The emergence of the Internet and the continuous development of digital technologies have brought to the fore a number of new legal problems and issues that require timely solution and proper and effective legal regulation from the EU as one of the leading regulators of the digital world. The technological developments have opened a new "window" to the borderless world of Internet, giving a person an opportunity to exercise his/her fundamental rights at a new and unprecedented level. Nowadays digital technologies are so ingrained in human life that it is no longer possible to imagine the existence of a person without the "worldwide digital web". In this paper the authors will focus on the analysis of the main issues and challenges of the right to Internet access, taking into account the existing case-law of the European supranational courts and the legal practice of the EU Member States.

Nowadays the issue of the legal essence and nature of the right to Internet access continues to remain open and insufficiently determined not only in the legal literature, but also in the law-enforcement practice. The relevance of this issue is promoted by the tendency to consider Internet access as a special and extremely significant benefit. Indeed, some EU Member States, such as, for example, France, Greece and Estonia, have even explicitly recognized and enshrined such a right in their national laws. At the same time, the Recommendation CM/Rec (2014)6 of the Committee of Ministers to Member States on a Guide to human rights for Internet users provides that: *"(...) [N]o one should be subjected to unlawful, unnecessary or disproportionate interference with the exercise of their human rights and fundamental freedoms when using the*

Internet. (...) [E]very Internet user should have the greatest possible access to Internet-based content, applications and services of his/her choice, whether or not they are offered free of charge, using suitable devices of his/her choice."[140] Besides, it is even argued that the UN Human Rights Council equates access to the Internet with the basic human rights and thereby prohibits restricting or prohibiting a person from exercising such a right.[141] In this context, the following questions naturally arise:

1. Has the advent of the Internet created a new "platform" for exercising of the classical fundamental rights enshrined in the EU Charter on fundamental rights (hereinafter – the "CFR") or has it granted a person with a new Fundamental Right – the right to Internet access?
2. What role and place should the right of Internet access have in the system of existing fundamental rights?

The objective of the chapter is to identify the essence and nature of the right to Internet access, its role and place in the system of protection of fundamental rights, taking into account the existing case-law of the European supranational courts and the legal practice of the European states that have a rich experience in protecting the right to Internet access. For these purposes the authors will use several approaches to meet the complex issues of the research focus. As a starting point (especially when working with the set of relevant data/documents) we will utilize the analytical approach (the desktop research) in order to identify, systematize and mutually compare the key case-law and doctrinal views, as well as their impact and interpretations. For a more complete disclosure of the content of the research topic, comparative, normative, logical methods, as well as the method of system-structural analysis will be used. In this chapter a special value has the normative approach in the framework of the analysis of the subject of research, the development of scientific and legal concepts, the construction of conclusions based on legal reasoning. The comparative method will be fundamental in the analysis of individual case-law of the CJEU and ECtHR. During our research we use:

1. Deductive approach while testing the hypotheses against the assembled data.
2. Inductive methods while formulating the models of interpretation.

---

[140] Recommendation CM/Rec(2014)6 of the Committee of Ministers to member States on a Guide to human rights for Internet users (Adopted by the Committee of Ministers on 16 April 2014 at the 1197th meeting of the Ministers' Deputies).

[141] See HOWELL, C. & WEST, M. D. *The Internet as a Human Right.* Techtank. Available at: https://www.brookings.edu/blog/techtank/2016/11/07/the-internet-as-a-human-right/. Accessed 25. 6. 2023. See also: *Promotion and protection of all human rights, civil, political, economic, social and cultural rights, including the right to development.* Human Rights Council. Thirty-second session. Agenda item 3. Distr.: Limited 27 June 2016. Available at: https://www.article19.org/data/files/Internet_Statement_Adopted.pdf. Accessed 25. 6. 2023.

3. Comparative methods, while comparing the approach of the case-law and legal practice.
4. Synthesis, while working on the conclusions and defining the nature, contours and scope of the right to Internet access.
5. Prediction in evaluation and extrapolation of the future challenges and developments.

Initial hypotheses of our research are:

1. The right to Internet access shall be recognised as a new fundamental right in the EU law, which has its own material scope, essence and nature, distinguishing it from the other fundamental human rights.
2. There is no need to develop a new legal document at the level of the EU primary law, since ensuring the right to access the Internet will help avoid the need to adopt a new human rights document for the Internet.

Both hypotheses will be tested in parallel via critical analyses of the case-law or case studies and their developments. The originality of this research lies in the fact that the researchers intends to undertake a well-reasoned analysis of the right to Internet access through the prism of judicial approaches of the Court of Justice of the European Union (hereinafter – the "CJEU") and the European Court of Human Rights (hereinafter – the "ECtHR"), in order to clearly show the existing challenges of the legal protection of the right to Internet access in the EU law from the new vision.

In order to find well-reasoned answers to the above-mentioned questions, as well as to test the correctness of the hypothesis, the authors conduct this scientific research.

2. The different doctrinal views on the right to Internet access

The technological developments have opened a new "window" to the borderless world of Internet, giving a person an opportunity to exercise his/her fundamental rights at a new and unprecedented level. Nowadays digital technologies are so ingrained in human life that it is no longer possible to imagine the existence of a person without the "worldwide digital web". In the framework of modern technological realities, a person discloses and receives his/her personal data and other information, uses and provides services, performs various works, exercises his/her right to education primary via Internet technologies, that have already become the main source of human activity in the digital age, especially in the post-Covid world. As Tim Berners-Lee, the inventor of the World Wide Web, noted during the debate "Internet Access: a new Human Right?" organized by the European Parliament at the end of 2020: "In this crisis, for those who have it [internet access], the web is not a luxury. It's a lifeline."[142] Indeed, the Covid-19 pandemic has practically shown how essential the Internet access is for the realization of existing human rights and freedoms, and how dependent we are on technology today. It is precisely this high level of human dependence on digital technologies that brings to the fore questions about the need to recognize the right to Internet access as a new fundamental human right, as well as determine its role and place in the existing EU human rights system, which, in its turn, requires a rethinking of the very legal nature of the EU fundamental human rights. As D. Canetti and R. Shandler point out: "We are faced with a new reality where our reliance on Internet access to fulfil basic civil tasks is threatened by increasing personal and societal cyber vulnerability. This dichotomy of dependence and vulnerability requires a new framework for understanding the legal and human rights status of this evolving technological reality."[143]

Nowadays a number of scholars, such as, for example, M. Estrada,[144] G. Gosztonyi,[145] L. Jasmontaite and P. De Hert,[146] analyzed the essence and nature of the right to Internet access, as well as the problems and issues of its legal protection from the perspective of the European legal reality. In turn, other scholars, such as, for example, F. Scholz, B. Yalcin, M. Priestley[147] and H. Morten Haugen,[148] conducted researches dedicated to the problematic aspects and existing challenges of protection of the right to Internet access for the persons with disabilities. Despite the fact of existence of a large number of research contributions on the

[142] VILLADIEGO, L. Internet access: a new human right? *EqualTimes.org*. Available at: https://www.equaltimes.org/internet-access-a-new-human-right?lang=en#.ZChzo8pBy3A. Accessed 25. 6. 2023.

[143] CANETTI, D., SHANDLER, R. A Reality of Vulnerability and Dependence: Internet Access as a Human Right. *Israel Law Review*. 2019, vol. 52, no. 1, pp. 77–98. DOI: http://dx.doi.org/10.1017/S0021223718000262

[144] ESTRADA, M. Revisiting access to internet as a fundamental right in times of COVID-19. *UNIO – EU Law Journal*. 2020, vol. 6, no. 2, pp. 15–24. URL: https://doi.org/10.21814/unio.6.2.2753

[145] GOSZTONYI, G. European Court of Human Rights: Internet Access as a Means of Receiving and Imparting Information and Ideas. *International Comparative Jurisprudence*. 2020, vol. 6, no. 2, pp. 139. Available at: https://ojs.mruni.eu/ojs/international-comparative-jurisprudence/article/view/6292. Accessed 25. 6. 2023.

[146] JASMONTAITE, L., DE HERT, P. Access to the Internet in the EU: a policy priority, a fundamental, a human right or a concern for eGovernment? *SSRN Working Paper*. 2020, vol. 6, no. 19. Available at: https://www.researchgate.net/publication/339860840. Accessed 25. 6. 2023.

[147] SCHOLZ, Fr., YALCIN, B., PRIESTLEY, M. Internet access for disabled people: Understanding socio-relational factors in Europe. *Cyberpsychology: Journal of Psychosocial Research on Cyberspace*. 2017, vol. 11, no. 1. Available at: https://doi.org/10.5817/CP2017-1-4

[148] MORTEN H. H. Is Internet Access a Human Right – for Everyone, or only for Persons with Disabilities? *Kritisk juss*. 2014, vol. 40, no. 1, pp. 26–51. Available at: https://papers.ssrn.com/sol3/papers.cfm?abstract_id=2553196. Accessed 24. 6. 2023.

right to Internet access and its legal problems, nevertheless, in the conditions of different approaches of legal scholars, such as, for example, O. Pollicino,[149] M. Reglitz,[150] L. Szoszkiewicz,[151] T. Frosini,[152] N. Lucchi,[153] B. Skepys[154] and S. Tully,[155] to the role and place of the right to Internet access in the system of human fundamental rights, this topic still remains relevant and needs further comprehensive and in-depth research. Taking into account the existing scientific contributions about the topic under consideration, it is conditionally possible to generalize the existing positions of researchers, highlighting two opposite positions regarding to the Internet access.

Thus, ***the first group*** of scientists (supporters), such as, for example, M. Reglitz, believe that it is already necessary to recognize the right to Internet access as a fundamental right, arguing their views by the fact that most human rights are already realized through Internet technologies. In particular, the scholar notes that: "Rather than being a mere luxury, Internet access should be considered a universal entitlement because it is necessary for people to be able to lead minimally decent lives. Accepting this claim transforms our conception of the Internet from a technology to that of a basic right."[156] Another supporter of the recognition of this right, S.M. Tabusca, emphasizes in her academic paper that: "The new technologies – such as the Internet, the satellite and the digital broad casting – offer unprecedented opportunities to promote freedom of expression. Therefore,

[149] POLLICINO, O. The Right to Internet Access: Quid Iuris? In VON ARNAULD, A., VON DER DECKEN, K., SUSI, M. (eds.). *The Cambridge Handbook of New Human Rights: Recognition, Novelty, Rhetoric.* Cambridge: Cambridge University Press, 2020, pp. 263–275. Available at: https://papers.ssrn.com/sol3/papers.cfm?abstract_id=3397340. Accessed 22. 6. 2023.

[150] REGLITZ, M. The Human Right to Free Internet Access. *Journal of Applied Philosophy.* 2020, vol. 37, no. 2, pp. 314–331. Available at: https://onlinelibrary.wiley.com/doi/abs/10.1111/japp.12395. Accessed 25. 6. 2023.

[151] SZOSZKIEWICZ, Ł. Internet Access as a New Human Right? State of the Art on the Threshold of 2020. *Przegląd Prawniczy Uniwersytetu im Adama Mickiewicza.* 2018, vol. 8, pp. 49–62. Available at: https://pressto.amu.edu.pl/index.php/ppuam/article/view/21599. Accessed 22. 6. 2023.

[152] FROSINI, T. E. Access To Internet As A Fundamental Right. *Italian Journal of Public Law.* 2013, vol. 5, no. 2, pp. 226–234. Available at: https://www.ijpl.eu/wp-content/uploads/2022/10/7.Frosini.pdf. Accessed 26. 6. 2023.

[153] LUCCHI, N. The Role of Internet Access in Enabling Individual's Rights and Freedoms. *EUI RSCAS Working Paper 2013/47.* Available at: https://cadmus.eui.eu/handle/1814/27435. Accessed 26. 6. 2023.

[154] SKEPYS, B. Is There a Human Right to the Internet? *Journal of Politics and Law.* 2012, vol. 5, no. 4, pp. 15–29. Available at: https://www.ccsenet.org/journal/index.php/jpl/article/view/22541/14534. Accessed 21. 6. 2023.

[155] TULLY, S. A Human Right to Access the Internet? Problems and Prospects. *Human Rights Law Review.* 2014, vol. 14, no. 2, pp. 175–195, Available at: https://doi.org/10.1093/hrlr/ngu011

[156] REGLITZ, M. The Human Right to Free Internet Access. *Journal of Applied Philosophy.* 2020, vol. 37, no. 2, pp. 314–331. Available at: https://onlinelibrary.wiley.com/doi/abs/10.1111/japp.12395. Accessed 25. 6. 2023.

the right to Internet access becomes an indispensable fundamental right needed for the implementation of the freedom of expression, being important not only for individual dignity, but also for the promotion of the democracy."[157]

At the same time, ***the second group*** of scholars (opponents), such as, for example, B. Skepys, argue that access to the Internet " (...) is an enabler of rights, not a right itself", in this connection, there is no need to recognize such a right, since it is already covered by existing rights. In particular, in his research, the author gives five arguments to show the inconsistency of the right to access the Internet, while noting that: "There is not a human right to the Internet, but it would seem that the denial of Internet access is an urgent threat to the human right to assemble, so the Internet demands negative duties not to be denied."[158]

It should be noted that when studying the scientific contributions of various authors, it is possible to notice that often the problem of recognition or non-recognition of the right to Internet access is due to what ideology and/or legal understanding a particular researcher adheres to. For example, if we compare the existing arguments of the EU and US lawyers, it is possible to see their difference in understanding the essence and nature of human rights in general, on the basis of which each of the scholars comes to different results.[159] As one can already understand, the problem of legal protection of Internet access is quite controversial in the legal science, and it is impossible to give an unambiguous answer to this question yet. The reason lies in the fact that both supporters and opponents (critics) of the recognition of the Internet access as a fundamental right give their well-reasoned arguments in defence of their legal positions, which will be discussed in this scientific research in more details. Based on the above, the authors will analyze the main arguments of supporters and critics, which, in turn, will allow to understand the legal nature of Internet access and show the existing risks and current challenges, issues and questions arising in the context of the recognition or non-recognition of the right to Internet access.

---

[157] TABUSCA, S. M. The Internet Access as a Fundamental Right. *Romanian Economic Business Review.* 2010, vol. 4. Available at: https://www.researchgate.net/publication/227487197_THE_INTERNET_ACCESS_AS_A_FUNDAMENTAL_RIGHT. Accessed 25. 6. 2023.

[158] SKEPYS, B. Is There a Human Right to the Internet? *Journal of Politics and Law.* 2012, vol. 5, no. 4, pp. 15–29. Available at: https://www.ccsenet.org/journal/index.php/jpl/article/view/22541/14534. Accessed 21. 6. 2023.

[159] For example, see HEARD, A. Human rights: Chimeras in sheep's clothing. An Introduction to Human Rights Theory, 1997. Available at: https://lawprojects.wordpress.com/2012/03/01/human-rights-chimeras-in-sheeps-clothing/. Accessed 21. 6. 2023.

3. The Internet as a simple means ("platform") for already existing fundamental rights?

One of the most prominent critics of the right to access the Internet as a fundamental right is Vinton G. Cerf. Talking about the nature of Internet, the expert gives an interesting example, comparing the Internet with a horse. In his arguments against the recognition of this right, he argues that "at one time if you didn't have a horse, it was hard to make a living. But the important right in that case was the right to make a living, not the right to a horse".[160] However, in our opinion, it is impossible to agree with such an example: the reason lies precisely in the very unique nature of the Internet as an unprecedented project created by humankind. It should be noted that unlike other means of realization of the existing human rights (i.e., the same Cerf's "horse"), Internet seriously affect both the very nature of the person and his/her rights, in many ways even modifying them. In this context, the Internet is not just a means of exercising already existing human rights, but rather a benefit that requires careful and peculiar legal regulation. In particular, the peculiarity of the Internet is that, unlike other means of communication and/or information exchange (hereinafter referred to as "means of communication"), where a person, as a rule, retains his/her connection with the offline world, for example, in the case of a telephone or radio, newspaper or the same Cerf's "horse", the Internet access brings a person into an information space separate from the offline world, previously unknown to human, where completely different rules and principles of functioning operate.

At the same time, a person, receiving greater autonomy on the Internet, is already the "master" and manager of the information universe ("online world"), which exists in parallel with the offline world created by nature, and the online world is in many ways even ahead of the offline world in its development. In other words, the Internet is a dynamically developing anthropogenic universe of information, distinct and independent from the offline world, where the Internet user is not only the "designer" of his/her digital embodiment, but even the digital embodiment of other Internet users. Simultaneously, such human activity leads to the constant expansion of such an information space. It turns out that through Internet access a person loses his/her connection and "breaks away" from the offline world, getting into a new unlimited information universe, created by humankind. The only thing that connects a person with the offline world is his/her PC or smartphone, i.e., the technical means by which

[160] CERF, V. G. Internet Access is not a Human Right. *The New York Times.* January 4, 2012. Available at: https://cse.sc.edu/~mgv/csce390f20/cerfRight.pdf. Accessed 24. 6. 2023.

a person enters this boundless world of information. This is the main difference between the Internet and other means of communication, which does not allow it to be considered "under the roof" of existing means of communication and extend similar rules to the Internet technologies, not to mention the possibility of obtaining large-scale and easily accessible information on the Internet compared to other means of communication. As one can see, if before the Internet there was no need to consolidate new individual rights, such as, for example, the right to phone, e-mail or TV, since they easily fell under the scope of already existing human rights (for example, freedom of expression and information, private life and/or data protection) through the concept of a living instrument and did not separate a person from the "offline" world, then after the emergence and rapid development of the Internet technologies, the situation is changing significantly. In the era of digitalisation, a person has unlimited access to a new world, where traditionally developed "offline" rules, principles and tools are no longer able to effectively protect him/her and his/her existing rights in the digital world.

The emergence of new social relations requires a new fresh look from lawyers. We shall not forget that digital technologies are developing so rapidly that nowadays they even allow through collection and processing of personal data, as well as the use of hologram-technologies, to reproduce the digital embodiment of any person, and even *post-mortem*,[161] that nothing but a utopian idea could be considered before the development of such digital technologies. If, as a general rule, "offline" human rights ceased after his/her biological death, then after the advent of the digital technologies, such a person can become the subject of digital manipulation by any third party, even after the death of such person. As an illustrative example can be the case of the concert of the American signer *2Pac*, where the concert organizers were able to reproduce the digital embodiment of the singer after his death.[162] Of course, it would be unthinkable to imagine such a situation before the advent of information technology. In other words, if earlier personal data and/or information about a person after a certain period of time was subjected to moral aging and forgotten by society, the Internet allows you to reproduce and use information (personal data) of any person in any corner of the world, by any Internet user and at any time, even without his/her consent and/or

[161] See HAMUĽÁK, O., KOCHARYAN, H., KERIKMÄE, T. The Contemporary Issues of Post-Mortem Personal Data Protection in the EU after GDPR entering into Force. In *Czech Yearbook of Public and Private International Law.* 2020, vol. 11, pp. 225–238. See also MEESE, J., NANSEN, B., KOHN, T., ARNOLD, M., GIBBS, M. Posthumous personhood and the affordances of digital media. *Mortality.* 2015, vol. 20, no. 4, pp. 408–420.

[162] See DODSON, A. (2017). The strange legacy of Tupac's 'hologram' lives on five years after its historic Coachella debut. *Andscape.com*. April 14, 2017. Available at: https://andscape.com/features/the-strange-legacy-of-tupacs-hologram-after-coachella/. Accessed 20. 6. 2023.

his/her knowledge.[163] In such conditions, a person has never been so vulnerable as at present, when Internet-technologies are rapidly developing, and the law continues to lag behind such development. In this context, it is not entirely correct to consider the Internet technologies as just a means (platform) for the realization of already existing human (fundamental) rights, and the comparison of the Internet from the V. Cerf's side with the "right to a horse" is not entirely successful.

In this framework, new and effective mechanisms are needed for the protection of digital existence of a person, and the recognition of the right to Internet access can also serve as one of the legal foundations for the development of such mechanisms. We believe that taking into account the possibilities of dynamically developing information technologies, the principle of simply distributing offline rights to the online environment by analogy with other means of communication cannot become an effective guarantee for human protection in the digital world. If we draw parallels, it is the same as trying to extend the rules of Newton's physics to Einstein's theory of relativity. In particular, the Newton's force of gravity, which acts on the Earth, does not act in the Universe, despite the fact that the Earth is a part of the Universe (i.e., "a world in a world"). Similarly, we are talking about two parallel worlds – offline and online worlds – having different principles and rules of existence.[164] Moreover, we should not forget that the online world is not always a reflection of the offline world: the online world can exist without the offline world. For example, a person can create a bot-user on the Internet that will perform certain functions, but such a bot does not exist in the offline world, but is exclusively a product of the online world. The same can be said about the creation of various social accounts by a person in such social networks as Facebook, Twitter, Instagram, where he/she may not always act under his/her own name. This situation is somewhat reminiscent of the movie "The Matrix", where the main character Thomas A. Anderson is a professional program-writer in a prestigious company, but in the "online world" he lives under the pseudonym "Neo".[165]

---

[163] See KOCHARYAN, H., HAMUĽÁK, O., VARDANYAN, L. "TheRight to be Remembered?": The Contemporary Challenges of the "StreisandEffect" in the European Judicial Reality. *International and Comparative Law Review.* 2022, vol. 22, no. 2, pp. 105–120. DOI: 10.2478/iclr-2022-0017

[164] See JURGENSON, N. Digital dualism versus augmented reality. *The Society Pages: Cyborgology.* February 24, 2011. Available at: https://mxepstein.com/wp-content/uploads/2017./08/Digital-Dualism-versus-Augmented-Reality.pdf. Accessed 19. 6. 2023. See also GOSSE, Ch. "Not the Real World": Exploring Experiences of Online Abuse, Digital Dualism, and Ontological Labor. *The Emerald International Handbook of Technology Facilitated Violence and Abuse.* 2021. Available at: https://www.semanticscholar.org/paper/"Not-the-Real-World"%3A-Exploring-Experiences-of-and-Gosse/4b39d472fb8f95fbc7c48d3ec7322c1f2ae75904. Accessed 20. 6. 2023.

[165] Agent Smith: It seems that you've been living two lives. One life, you're Thomas A. Anderson, program writer for a respectable software company. You have a social security number,

That is, all of the above shows that we are dealing with a dualism of worlds that exist in parallel and do not always intersect. Nowadays, it is not already a utopia – it is a new reality. In these conditions, the lawmakers shall take their timely and effective steps to avoid situation of a big gap between the law and technology. In this light, the recognition of the right to Internet access can become a new legal ground for the existence of *homo digitalis*.[166]

4. Is the Internet access an artificial phenomenon for human nature, and therefore cannot be a human right?

This opinion can be regarded as a continuation of the previous argument of the critics. Some experts often point out that the right to access the Internet is not a right given to human by nature. As an argument, the fact is also given that a person can exist without the Internet, that is, it is not a universal and inalienable human right, as it is enshrined in the Universal Declaration of Human Rights (1948). For example, one of such critics is Neth Daño –the Asia Director of the ETC action group on erosion, technology and concentration. The expert points out that: "Internet or digital connectivity cannot be considered inherent to the human race. The basic rights and services that people should be afforded are more important than the internet."[167] As one can see, such critical views are based on the preamble of the Universal Declaration of Human Rights (1948), which states about *"equal and inalienable rights of all members of the human family"*.[168]

However, we believe that this position is also not without drawbacks. We should not forget that the law is a dynamic phenomenon, and technological progress, of course, could not but affect both a person's life and the development of his/her rights. There is not by chance the CFR specifies in its preamble

pay your taxes, and you... help your landlady carry out her garbage. The other life is lived in computers, where you go by the hacker alias "Neo" and are guilty of virtually every computer crime we have a law for. One of these lives has a future, and one of them does not. (*See:* "The Matrix" (1999). Hugo Weaving: Agent Smith. Available at: https://www.imdb.com/title/tt0133093/characters/nm0915989)

[166] See VARDANYAN, L., STEHLÍK, V., KOCHARYAN, H. Digital Integrity: A Foundation for Digital Rights and the New Manifestation of Human Dignity. *TalTech Journal of European Studies*. 2022, vol. 12, no. 1, pp.159–185. Available at: https://doi.org/10.2478/bjes-2022-0008.

[167] See VILLADIEGO, L. Internet access: a new human right? *EqualTimes.org*. Available at: https://www.equaltimes.org/internet-access-a-new-human-right?lang=en#.ZChzo8pBy3A. Accessed 25. 6. 2023.

[168] UN General Assembly, Universal Declaration of Human Rights, 10 December 1948, 217 A (III). Available at: https://www.un.org/en/about-us/universal-declaration-of-human-rights. Accessed 25. 6. 2023.

that: *"(...) it is necessary to strengthen the protection of fundamental rights in the light of changes in society, social progress and scientific and technological developments by making those rights more visible in a Charter".*[169] Moreover, it is not by chance that human rights instruments are considered by their nature as a "living instrument". Today human rights instruments, such as the ECHR and the CFR, are increasingly adapting to new life situations and previously unknown social relations through the developed standards of the case-law of the European Supranational Courts. This is even indicated in the case of *Loizidou v. Turkey (1995),* which states that: "(...) the Convention is a living instrument which must be interpreted in the light of present-day conditions is firmly rooted in the Court's case-law (see, inter alia, the *Tyrer v. the United Kingdom* judgment of 25 April 1978, Series A, no. 26, pp. 15–16, para. 31). Such an approach, in the Court's view, is not confined to the substantive provisions of the Convention, but also applies to those provisions, such as Articles 25 and 46 (Article 25, Article 46), which govern the operation of the Convention's enforcement machinery. It follows that these provisions cannot be interpreted solely in accordance with the intentions of their authors as expressed more than forty years ago."[170] Moreover, in the process of judicial interpretation of the European supranational courts, new human rights that are not enshrined in the CFR or the ECHR even appear. For example, in the opinion to the case of *Leyla ßahin v. Turkey*, judge Tulkens, referring to the cases of *Keenan v. the United Kingdom* and *Pretty v. the UK*, stressed that the Court has already developed a real right to personal autonomy, based on Article 8 of the ECHR (the right to private life).[171]

The same parallels can be drawn in the case of Internet access. In particular, the case-law of the ECtHR shows that the right to Internet access is most closely related to the freedom of expression and information guaranteed by the Article 11 of the CFR and the Article 10 of the ECHR respectively, which is also confirmed in the judicial practice of the European supranational courts. In particular, when considering the case of *Jankovskis v. Lithuania*, the Court held that there had been a violation of Article 10 of the ECHR (freedom of expression and information) on the part of the Lithuanian authorities, since the national law of Lithuania guaranteed access to information for educational purposes, and the restriction of access to a certain Internet website amounted to "the interference with the applicant's right to receive information cannot be regarded as having

[169] Charter of Fundamental Rights of the European Union, 26 October 2012, 2012/C 326/02.

[170] Case of *Loizidou v. Turkey*, 40/1993/435/514, Council of Europe: European Court of Human Rights, 28 November 1996, para 71. Available at: https://www.refworld.org/cases,ECHR,43de104d4.html. Accessed 25. 6. 2023.

[171] See Judge Tulkens, dissenting opinion to ECtHR [GC] judgment of 10 November 2005, *Leyla ßahin v. Turkey*, appl. no. 44774/98.

been necessary in a democratic society".[172] The Court also follows a similar approach in the case of *Kalda v. Estonia*, where the Court refers to the fact that: "(...) the websites of the Council of Europe Information Office in Tallinn, the Chancellor of Justice, and the *Riigikogu*, to which the applicant wished to have access, predominantly contained legal information and information related to fundamental rights, including the rights of prisoners."[173]

In turn, in the case of *Cengiz and Others v. Turkey*, the ECtHR ruled that: "[T]he Internet has now become one of the principal means by which individuals exercise their right to freedom to receive and impart information and ideas, providing as it does essential tools for participation in activities and discussions concerning political issues and issues of general interest. (…) [A]s to the importance of Internet sites in the exercise of freedom of expression (…), the Internet plays an important role in enhancing the public's access to news and facilitating the dissemination of information in general."[174]

Another judgment devoted to the non-discriminative and open Internet access, is the *Telenor* case, where the CJEU ruled that the "measures blocking or slowing down traffic are applied to the other applications and services available (…) are incompatible with Article 3(2) of Regulation 2015/2120, read in conjunction with Article 3(1) of that regulation, where those packages, agreements, and measures blocking or slowing down traffic *limit the exercise of end users' rights*, and (…) are incompatible with Article 3(3) of that regulation where those measures blocking or slowing down traffic *are based on commercial considerations*".[175]

Taking into account the existing judicial practice of the European supranational courts, S. Tully argues that: "Analysing the views on this issue of the United Nations, the Council of Europe and the European Court of Human Rights, we conclude that the right of access to the Internet is recognized as one of the inalienable human rights, as it is fundamental to ensure dignified existence to all and social development under the conditions of formation and development of the

---

[172] Case of *Jankovskis v. Lithuania* (Application No. 21575/08), Judgment Strasbourg, 17 January 2017, Final 17/04/2017, para 64 // Available at: https://hudoc.echr.coe.int/fre#{%22itemid%22:[%22001-170354%22]}. Accessed 25.06.2023.

[173] Case of *Kalda v. Estonia* (Application No. 17429/10), Judgment, Strasbourg, 19 January 2016, Final 06/06/2016, para 50. Available at: https://hudoc.echr.coe.int/fre#{%22itemid%22:[%22001-160270%22]}. Accessed 20. 6. 2023.

[174] Case of *Cengiz and Others v. Turkey* (nos. 48226/10 and 14027/11,) Judgment, Strasbourg, 1 December 2015, para 49 and para 52. Available at: https://www.echr.coe.int/Documents/FS_Access_Internet_ENG.pdf. Accessed 20. 6. 2023.

[175] Case of Telenor Magyarország Zrt. v Nemzeti Média- és Hírközlési Hatóság Elnöke (Joined Cases C-807/18 and C-39/19) Requests for a preliminary ruling from the Fővárosi Törvényszék, Judgment of the Court (Grand Chamber) of 15 September 2020. Available at: https://curia.europa.eu/juris/document/document.jsf?text=&docid=231042&pageIndex=0&doclang=EN&mode=lst&dir=&occ=first&part=1&cid=477662. Accessed 20. 6. 2023.

information society. The states are then required to refrain from any violation of human rights concerning the Internet. They have a positive obligation to ensure the right to the Internet and to create a safe and favourable online space for all."[176]

Despite the fact that the case-law of the European supranational courts considers the problems of access to the Internet mainly through the prism of freedom of expression and information, nevertheless, the list of human rights realized through Internet-technologies has long been not limited only to freedom of expression and information. This means that it is hardly correct to link the Internet activity exclusively with the realization of the freedom of expression and information. In this case there would be an oversimplification of the phenomenon under consideration. Nowadays the Internet is also a means of realizing of other fundamental and conventional rights, such as the right to education, freedom of entrepreneurial activity, labour rights and even electoral rights through a remote voting system, which, in turn, shows the complex legal essence of the Internet, not limited only to the freedom of expression and information.

At the same time, the phenomenon of dynamism is inherent not only in human rights, but also in law in general, and international and European law, in particular. For example, even when studying the UN Charter itself, it was often noted by the UN Secretary-Generals, such as, for example, K. Waldheim, that this is no longer the document that was originally developed in San Francisco, not to mention human rights instruments themselves. In turn, Kofi Annan also stated in his 1999 Annual Report to the General Assembly that the UN Charter is a "living document, whose high principles still define the aspirations of peoples everywhere for lives of peace, dignity and development".[177] We believe that with the development of human civilization, new human rights will naturally appear in the future. For example, who would talk about international space law, if technologies would not allow us to explore Space, not to mention that if a person can master Space, then it will be possible to talk even about the "cosmic" human rights? Who would talk about the emerging cryptocurrency market and the rapid developments of FinTech law, if there were no advanced digital technologies? It is this dynamic development of social relations that is one of the main reasons for both the emergence of discussion between the scholars and the development of the applicable law (including human rights) in a new direction. Moreover, throughout the history of the formation and development of human rights, one can notice that there have almost always been political, philosophical and/or ideological differences in the recognition of human

[176] TULLY, S. A Human Right to Access the Internet? Problems and Prospects. *Human Rights Law Review*. 2014, vol. 14, no. 2, pp. 175–195. Available at: https://doi.org/10.1093/hrlr/ngu011.

[177] United Nations, The Secretary General's Annual Reports to the General Assembly (20 September 1999), Available at: http://www.un.org/press/en/1999/19990920.sgsm7136.html. Accessed 20. 6. 2023.

rights by the states of international community, starting with the understanding of the nature of human rights in Ancient Greece and Rome (*jus naturale* or *jus civile*) and ending with the French Revolution, the signing of the Declaration of Independence of the USA and even the period from the adoption of the Universal Declaration of Human Rights (1948) to the adoption of two International Human Rights Covenants (1966), in the context of which on the basis of consensus among the countries of the international community, the branch of international human rights law as such began to take shape. It should not be forgotten that when the issue of the adoption of the International Covenant on Human Rights was being resolved, there were political and ideological differences between the governments of the USA and the USSR regarding various human rights (not) enshrined in the Human Rights Covenant, including the rights of the people to self-determination, the right to freedom of movement and others.[178]

As one can see, already in the process of creating universal (international) instruments for the protection of human rights, ideas about human rights differed between the states. That is why it was decided to develop two separate universal (international) human rights covenants in order to enable the development of this branch of law – *the International Covenant on Civil and Political Rights* (1966) and *the International Covenant on Social, Economic and Cultural Rights* (1966). So, it is easy to notice that the history of human rights law itself shows that the law, including human rights, do not stand in one place and are not static in its nature, but are capable of being supplemented with new human rights, one of which may be considered the right to Internet access. In this regard, we adhere to the position that the argument given by critics cannot be considered convincing.

5. Will the recognition of the right to access the Internet lead to inflation and devaluation of human rights?

In addition to the above arguments, the critics also see the risk of human rights inflation when recognizing the right to access the Internet. In particular, they argue that if any new phenomenon is recognized as a right, it can lead to fragmentation of human rights and their permanent infringement. In this context. P. de Hert and D. Kloza[179] in their scientific paper correctly paraphrase

[178] See MÄLKSOO, L. The Controversy over Human Rights, UN Covenants, and the Dissolution of the Soviet Union. *Japanese Yearbook of International Law.* 2018, vol. 61, pp. 260–283. Available at SSRN: https://ssrn.com/abstract=3254490. Accessed 22. 6. 2023.

[179] DE HERT, P., KLOZA, D. Internet (access) as a new fundamental right. Inflating the current rights framework? *European Journal of Law and Technology*. 2012, vol. 3, no. 3. Available at: https://ejlt.org/index.php/ejlt/article/view/123/268. Accessed 18. 6. 2023.

the F. H. Easterbrook's view, arguing that if you go into too much detail, you can get the "right to a horse".[180] Naturally, in the context of any application for recognition of new fundamental rights, including the right to access the Internet, they should always be carefully studied.

With such an argument of critics, of course, one should agree. However, this is only one side of the coin. The other side is that lawyers often adhere to excessive conservatism, which, in turn, can also devalue human rights. In other words, both extremes will have a negative impact on the further development of human rights. Of course, we agree with the critics' argument that it is true that we need to be careful when it comes to recognizing new human rights, but at the same time we believe that there is no need to overdo it. As already noted above, human rights do not exist in statics, but change with the development of human civilization, although they are considered from the point of view of Platonic ideal law. In particular, as the AG Mazak pointed out in his Opinion to the case of *Felix Palacios de la Villa:* "This source of law enabled the Court – often drawing inspiration from legal traditions common to the Member States, and international treaties – to guarantee and add content to legal principles in such important areas as the protection of fundamental rights and administrative law. However, it lies in the nature of general principles of law, which are to be sought rather in the Platonic heaven of law than in the law books, that both their existence and their substantive content are marked by uncertainty."[181] We should not forget that the world is dynamic, and if we adhere to an excessively static (conservative) approach, then such a policy will lead to a gap between the real rights ("living rights") and conventionally fixed rights ("positive law").

Moreover, the endless expansion of the scope of already conventionally enshrined human rights can reduce their original value. Moreover, one should not forget that human rights, although amenable to "live" interpretation, nevertheless, they cannot expand and change all the time. In this regard, human rights can be compared with "rubber" norms, which, with excessive expansion, can simply "break" and lose their true essence. A good example is Article 8 of the ECHR (the right to private life), where, as a result of the judicial interpretation of the Convention, the concept of private life has expanded so much that it has already lost its original purpose and has become an excessively extensive and

[180] EASTERBROOK, F. H. Cyberspace and the Law of the Horse. *University of Chicago Legal Forum.* 1996, vol. 207, pp. 207–2016. Available at: https://chicagounbound.uchicago.edu/uclf/vol1996/iss1/7/. Accessed 23. 6. 2023. See also LESSIG, L. The Law of the Horse: What Cyberlaw Might Teach. *Harvard Law Review.* 1999, vol. 113, no. 2, pp. 501–546. Available at: https://cyber.harvard.edu/works/lessig/finalhls.pdf. Accessed 29. 6. 2023.

[181] Opinion of Mr Advocate General Mazák delivered on 15 February 2007. *Félix Palacios de la Villa v Cortefiel Servicios SA.*, para 86. Available at: https://eur-lex.europa.eu/legal-content/EN/TXT/?uri=CELEX:62005CC0411. Accessed 21. 6. 2023.

incomprehensible legal structure, causing heated discussions in legal science. In this framework, Daniel J. Solove even argues that: "Privacy (…) is a concept in disarray. Nobody can articulate what it means. Currently, privacy is a sweeping concept, encompassing (among other things) freedom of thought, control over one's body, solitude in one's home, control over personal information, freedom from surveillance, protection of one's reputation, and protection from searches and interrogations."[182] Of course, the ECtHR should not be blamed for this: the Court can only interpret existing convention rights and derive new rights from them in accordance with the changing life circumstances. Rather, it is the task of the Council of Europe, which should monitor new trends in the development of human rights, and, if necessary, think about revising the Convention, even though the Council of Europe is used to considering it as a "living instrument".

In this regard, one should adhere to the Aristotle's concept of the "golden mean",[183] where human rights should be recognized and consolidated only when the need for such recognition has clearly matured, and other means of protection will no longer be effective for protecting a person and his/her rights in a changing system of social relations. There is no denying that Internet access has such potential, because with even greater technological development, the gap between law and technology will only worsen. An illustrative example is the practice of international humanitarian law, where military technologies are rapidly developing, and this branch of law does not have time to regulate such development in the spirit of its principles.[184]

Realizing this and understanding the developing potential of digital technologies, it is necessary to take seriously the issue of recognizing the right to access the Internet, and not consider it only as a simple platform for the implementation of existing rights. It is necessary to prevent an excessive split between law and technology, which can lead to negative consequences in the future.

---

[182] SOLOVE, D. J. Understanding Privacy. *Harvard University Press*, 2008. GWU Legal Studies Research Paper No. 420, GWU Law School Public Law Research Paper No. 420, Available at SSRN: https://ssrn.com/abstract=1127888. Accessed 18. 6. 2023.

[183] ARISTOTLE, Nicomachean Ethics II.1

[184] In particular, the ICRC, in its official website notes that: "Technological developments have given rise to new methods and means of warfare, such as cyber-attacks, armed drones and robots, raising novel humanitarian and legal challenges. When developing or acquiring any new weapon, means or method of warfare, it is vitally important that a State assess whether it complies with international humanitarian law. However, applying pre-existing legal rules to a new technology may raise the question of whether the rules are sufficiently clear in light of the technology's specific characteristics and foreseeable humanitarian impact." Available at: https://www.icrc.org/en.

6. If Internet access is a human right, what should it protect?

The international legal practice shows that the consolidation of the right to Internet access exists, although not everywhere. For example, it can be found both at the international and national levels. In this section, we will pay our attention not only to the existing law-enforcement practice of some EU Member States, but also try to give our doctrinal interpretation of the essence and nature of the right to Internet access.

6.1 The law-enforcement practice of some EU Member States

6.1.1 Estonia

For the analysis of the right to Internet access, the legal practice of Estonia is of interest. Its legal experience is one of the leading examples of the systematic application of information (digital) technologies for the realization of human rights. Direct guarantees of the application of right to Internet access can be found in the Law of November 15, 2000 on "Public Information Act".[185] In particular, the paragraph 33 of the specified Law provides for the possibility for everyone to access public information via the Internet. It is often correctly stated in the media news that in the Estonian law, Internet access is actually considered as a human right.[186] At the same time, Estonia, one of the first states that began to build a kind of information system at the state level, as a result of which a whole system of information society, called *e-Estonia*, emerged, providing ample opportunities for the realization of civil rights.[187]

6.1.2 France

Another EU Member State with a remarkable experience with the right to access the Internet is France. It should be noted that, as in Estonia, in French law

[185] Law on Public Information Act, passed 15. 11. 2000, RT I 2000, 92, 597, entry into force: 1. 1. 2001. Available at: https://www.riigiteataja.ee/en/eli/529032019012/consolide. Accessed 27. 6. 2023.

[186] JACKSON, Nicholas. United Nations Declares Internet Access a Basic Human Right. *The Atlantic.* June 3, 2011. Available at: https://www.theatlantic.com/technology/archive/2011/06/united-nations-declares-internet-access-a-basic-human-right/239911/. Accessed 27. 6. 2023.

[187] TROPP, E. M., HOFFMANN, T., CHOCHIA, A. Open Data: A Stepchild in e-Estonia's Data Management Strategy? *TalTech Journal of European Studies*. 2022, vol. 12, no. 1, pp.123–144. Available at: https://doi.org/10.2478/bjes-2022-0006

the right to Internet access is also not enshrined in the Constitution. However, like the Estonian lawmaker, the French legislator nevertheless developed regulation on issues related to such access and Internet opportunities. The motivation for such activity was, in particular, the active discussion of amendments to the Law of December 31, 1979 No. 79-1204 "On the Voluntary Termination of Pregnancy",[188] which would allow blocking websites that contain anti-abortion propaganda. Moreover, the Law of June 12, 2009 No. 2009-669 "On Promoting the Dissemination and Protection of Creative Works on The Internet ", more famous as *HADOPI* law,[189] caused a great resonance in the French society. It was this Law that played the culminating role for the recognition of the right to Internet access in France. In particular, the French Council of State – the judicial body of constitutional control, which was approached by the deputies of the National Assembly with a request to verify compliance with the Constitution of a number of provisions of the law under consideration here –in its Resolution of June 10, 2009 No. 2009-580 DC attributed Internet access to fundamental human rights and freedoms.[190]

6.1.3 Greece

Unlike France and Estonia, Greece has directly enshrined in the Constitution the legal regulation of the right to access the Internet. In particular, part 2 of article 5A of the Greek Constitution of July 11, 1975 (as amended from 2001, 2008) provides for "The right of everyone to participate in the information society".[191] In particular, the Greek Constitution states that: "Facilitation of access to electronically transmitted information, as well as of the production, exchange and diffusion thereof, constitutes an obligation of the State."[192] It is easy to see that this right in its essence and nature is very close to the right to access the Internet.

[188] Law No. 79-1204 of 31 December 1979 and related laws. (Journal Officiel, no. 1, 1 January 1980, p. 3). Available at: https://cyber.harvard.edu/population/abortion/France.abo.htm. Accessed 27. 6. 2023.

[189] Law No. 2009-669 on Promoting the Dissemination and Protection of Creative Works on The Internet (a.k.a. HADOPI law). Available at: https://wilmap.stanford.edu/entries/law-no-2009-669-promoting-dissemination-and-protection-creative-works-internet-aka-hadopi. Accessed 27. 6. 2023.

[190] Decision no. 2009-580 DC of 10 June 2009 Act furthering the diffusion and protection of creation on the Internet. Available at: https://www.conseil-constitutionnel.fr/en/decision/2009/2009580DC.htm. Accessed 27. 6. 2023.

[191] The Constitution of Greece. Available at: https://www.hellenicparliament.gr/UserFiles/f3c70a23-7696-49db-9148-f24dce6a27c8/THE%20CONSTITUTION%20OF%20GREECE.pdf. Accessed 27. 6. 2023.

[192] Ibid.

Moreover, this right also finds its embodiment in the case-law of the Greek courts. For example, in one of the cases, the Greek court ruled to take special technical measures to restrict access to Internet resources on which protected works were posted in violation of the interests of copyright holders, while in another case, the Greek court nevertheless held that the application of such measures contradicts the constitutional principle of proportionality and the constitutional right to participate in information society.[193]

6.2 Doctrinal interpretation: the Swiss experience as a useful guide for the EU?

Despite the fact that some EU Member States recognize the existence of such a right at the legislative level, critics still argue that the Internet access is a complex phenomenon and cannot have a clear scope of regulation, such as other existing human rights. Indeed, it is a problematic question with which right it is necessary to associate it, and in general whether it is necessary to associate it with some existing rights, or is it a separate right in its essence?

However, we adhere to the position that the Internet access is not a separate right by itself, but rather is a part of human integrity. In particular, it is easy to see that the human body is almost always at the centre of all human rights.[194] In particular, the right to life, the right to inviolability, the right to freedom of movement, the right to protection of personal data, the prohibition of torture and slavery and other conventional and/or fundamental rights enshrined in the ECHR and the CFR, as a rule, are embodied through the human body and are inextricably linked with it. For example, it is unthinkable to talk about the right to life, privacy or torture, when a person does not have or once did not have his/her physical embodiment in the offline world. Even when we talk about the right to life of an unborn foetus, we associate this right with its conception and acquisition of a physical embodiment, where the body of the future person is in the process of formation even before his/her "access" to the offline world. In simple words, we are born and live through our body, which is our physical embodiment. This is a kind of "natural title" of our existing fundamental rights. It is not for nothing that international instruments for the protection of human rights mention about

[193] See SYNODINOU, T. A Greek premiere: Greek ISPs ordered to block access to infringing websites. Kluwer Copyright Blog, November 21, 2012. Available at: https://copyrightblog.kluweriplaw.com/2012/11/21/a-greek-premiere-greek-isps-ordered-to-block-access-to-infringing-websites/. Accessed 27. 6. 2023.

[194] See BUBLITZ, Ch. The body of law: boundaries, extensions, and the human right to physical integrity in the biotechnical age. *Journal of law and the biosciences*. 2022, vol. 9, no. 2, pp. 1–26. DOI:10.1093/jlb/lsac032

the rights given to a person for their existence as such. Moreover, it is not for nothing that the CJEU emphasizes that the integrity and dignity of a person is a general principle of EU law.[195] That is, the body (integrity) of a person is a right from which all other rights flow and receive their legal meaning and purpose.

On the Internet ("online world"), the concept of integrity is already changing. This is not a simple transfer of a person's physical body to the digital world.[196] Here we lose our physical body, created by nature for "access" to the offline world. The Internet, created by humankind, is already becoming a window (a kind of "portal") to a new (parallel) world, where, when realizing his/her Internet access, a person is already perceived not through their physical body, but through their digital lifestyle –a set of personal data that can be manipulated much more easily by both its carrier and third parties in the online world, than our physical body in the offline world. On the Internet, the physical body of a person disappears, giving way to data about such a physical body of a person, which together create the digital integrity of a person. For example, we see photos, video files, hobbies and interests of a person, i.e., through his/her digital lifestyle, created as a result of manipulation of personal data (i.e., through his/her digital integrity), we mentally collect the image of such a person in the offline world, even if we have never seen him/her before in the offline world.

However, unlike the offline world, where our integrity has certain boundaries given by nature, where it is connected to our physical body, in the online world, a person's personal data (i.e., the building materials (parts) of digital integrity) is scattered all over the Internet, and a person may not even know about it (for example, a person may not know that some Internet user keeps his/her photos in his/her computer folder). The Internet is not just a window from where we look at another person (neighbour), but a window from where we look at any person (Internet user) anytime and anywhere, about whom we can get even more information than we need to know, and regardless of the will or knowledge of such a person (i.e., the object of observation). This is what makes us vulnerable in the online world much more than in the offline world, given that the Internet not only never forgets such data, but also gives global access to such data from anywhere in the world, at any time and for any Internet user, unlike other means of communication. In this context, a person needs certain effective guarantees that allow us to exist in the digital world without losing control over our digital

[195] Case of *Kingdom of the Netherlands v European Parliament and Council of the European Union*. Judgment of the Court of 9 October 2001. Para 70. Available at: https://eur-lex.europa.eu/legal-content/EN/TXT/?uri=CELEX:61998CJ0377

[196] See VARDANYAN, L., STEHLÍK, V., KOCHARYAN, H. Digital Integrity: A Foundation for Digital Rights and the New Manifestation of Human Dignity. *TalTech Journal of European Studies*. 2022, vol. 12, no. 1, pp. 159–185. Available at: https://doi.org/10.2478/bjes-2022-0008.

integrity. Such a guarantee can be the right to Internet access as the basis of the right to digital birth and existence of *homo digitalis*.[197]

Based on the above, we believe that the right to Internet access should be considered as an integral part of a person's digital life – his/her digital body. For example, if you deprive a person of access to the Internet, a person will no longer be able to protect his/her digital integrity from manipulation by third parties, therefore, this is an important and integral part of a person's digital integrity.[198] In case of deprivation of the right to access the Internet, a person is equated by his/her position to a deceased (sleeping) person, since thereby he/she loses access to his/her digital body as the basis of his/her digital life.

Based on this, we believe that this right is not an independent right, but is an integral part of another fundamental right – the right to digital integrity. Thus, as part of the right to digital integrity, similarly to Article 3 of the CFR (the right to personal integrity), the Internet access should also be considered as a fundamental right.[199] The above concept is similar to the opinion of Swiss data protection experts, who rightly consider the right to Internet access as a part of the right to digital integrity, and are trying so far to consolidate this right not only in the local constitutions (at the cantonal level), and further at the level of Switzerland as a whole.[200] In this framework, as Alexis Roussel, Lusine Vardanyan, Alexander Barclay and Harry Halpin pointed out during the panel discussion devoted to "Right to Digital Integrity – A New Framework For Data Protection" at CPDP2023: "The adoption of the 'right to digital integrity' in the constitutions of Swiss cantons is in full swing, and is already transforming the approach to data protection. For example, the Valais Constituent Assembly has moved away from the classic approach to data protection, which seeks to avoid the 'abusive processing' of data, by proposing a prohibition of 'data processing without consent' as a general rule. In contrast to the GDPR, this means the burden of proof is shifted from those who are the subject of the processing to those who carry out the processing. In the same draft, the 'right to digital integrity' is granted, including through the 'ability to interact freely through digital technologies'. A right to open and non-discriminatory access to the Internet is recognized, as is the right

---

[197] Ibid.

[198] See ROCHEL, J. Connecting the Dots: Digital Integrity as a Human Right. *Human Rights Law Review.* 2021, vol. 21, no. 2, pp. 358–383. Available at: https://doi.org/10.1093/hrlr/ngaa063

[199] For more information on the concept of the right to digital integrity, see the following paper: VARDANYAN, L., STEHLÍK, V., KOCHARYAN, H. Digital Integrity: A Foundation for Digital Rights and the New Manifestation of Human Dignity. *TalTech Journal of European Studies.* 2022, vol. 12, no. 1, pp. 159–185. Available at: https://doi.org/10.2478/bjes-2022-0008

[200] FUMAGALLI, A. Was passiert mit meinen Daten nach dem Tod? Bei der digitalen Integrität gehen erste Kantone in die Offensive. *Neue Zürcher Zeitung.* 5. 10. 2022. Available at: https://www.nzz.ch/schweiz/digitale-integritaet-kantone-gehen-in-die-offensive-ld.1705761?reduced=true. Accessed 24. 6. 2023.

to communicate with the authorities, without being required to exclusively use a specific technology."[201]

7. But is everything so smooth for the right to Internet access to be recognized as a new fundamental right?

In fairness, it should be noted that there are a number of practical and technical issues to be solved in the framework of the recognition of the right to Internet access. In particular, one of such issues is how in practice the EU and its Member States can provide such access to the Internet, and by what technical means can this be achieved? Another issue is whether the recognition of the right to Internet access violate the business interests of Internet service providers (ISP)? When we speak about the fundamental nature of the right to Internet access, is it necessary to recognize as a fundamental right also the right to electricity, as without electricity there will be no Internet access? As one can see, there are a number of practical issues that still require rethinking and which, in its turn, is a subject of another research, which will clarify the contours of this right in more detail.

8. Conclusion

As a result of this research the authors come to the conclusion that the Internet access should not be considered only as a simple "platform" for the realization of existing human fundamental rights, but at the same time it is not an independent human right by itself. The right to Internet access should be considered as an integral part of the right to digital integrity under the Article 3 of the CFR (the right to personal integrity).[202] At the same time, we believe, that securing the right to Internet access, in turn, will avoid the need to adopt a new human rights instrument that "duplicates" the fundamental rights of the existing "offline" rights for the Internet.

Despite the existing grounds for securing the right to Internet access, nevertheless, some practical and technical issues still arise. In particular, how should

[201] ROUSSEL, A. Digital Integrity – disrupting the personal data economy: Five years in, it is clear the GDPR is not enough. The Medium Blog, May 25, 2023. Available at: https://blog.nymtech.net/digital-integrity-disrupting-the-personal-data-economy-509642bc756b. Accessed 20. 6. 2023.

[202] See VARDANYAN, L., STEHLÍK, V., KOCHARYAN, H. Digital Integrity: A Foundation for Digital Rights and the New Manifestation of Human Dignity. *TalTech Journal of European Studies.* 2022, vol. 12, no. 1, pp. 159–185. Available at: https://doi.org/10.2478/bjes-2022-0008

the EU practically and technically ensure the protection of such a right without prejudice to the business interests of Internet providers? This, in turn, is a separate research topic, which need more analysis. Nevertheless, we have reasonable grounds to argue that such issues cannot interfere with the recognition of the right to Internet access at the European level, taking into account the already existing legislative experience of some EU Member States in this matter, such as, for example, France, Estonia, Greece and Switzerland, and the right to Internet access has a big potential to become one of the legal grounds for existing of *homo digitalis* in the digital world.

PART II.

CONSUMER PROTECTION IN THE ON-LINE WORLD

CHAPTER FIVE

Future Challenges and Opportunities in European Consumer Law Protection in the Digital Era

BLANKA VÍTOVÁ

1. Introduction

Consumer protection in the digital world is a complex and evolving area of law that poses unique challenges and opportunities. The digitisation and technology within the innovative digital economy is accelerating. The digital sector is no longer just a specific subdivision of the market, but the basis of all innovative economic systems. Data and information collection and its analyses have become a specific commodity.[203] On the one hand, the consumers may benefit from this fast development – they have access to specific goods and services that make their everyday lives easier[204]. At the same time, the instant development of the digital technologies are raising novel legal issues in the field of consumer protection, such as transparency and fairness of contractual terms[205], access to and the use of data[206], liability, warranties, ethics, etc.

---

[203] MCCHESNEY, R. *Digital Disconnect: How capitalism is turning the internet against democracy*. New York, NY: New Press, 2013; ANGWIN, J. The web's new gold mine: Your secrets: A journal investigation finds that one of the fastest-growing businesses on the internet is the business of spying on consumers. *The Wall Street Journal*. 2010. Available at: http://www.wsj.com/articles/SB10001424052748703940904575395073512989404.

[204] VÍTOVÁ, B. Quo vadis, ochrano spotřebitele aneb personalizovaná tvorba ceny jako férová obchodní praktika? In *Pocta prof. Janu Hurdíkovi k 70. narozeninám*. Brno: Masarykova Univerzita, 2021, pp. 265–285.

[205] VÍTOVÁ, B. Unfair Commercial Practices and Corporate Social Responsibility (CSR) In the Digital World. *European Studies – the Review of European law, Economics and Politics*. 2022, vol. 9, no. 2, pp. 197–212; VÍTOVÁ, B. Limits of fairness and transparency in Internet of Things (IoT) contracts concluded with consumers. *Revue européenne de droit de la consommation (R.E.D.C.)*. Larcier, 2020, pp. 523–541.

[206] RUST, Ronald T., HUANG, Ming-Hui. The service revolution and the transformation of marketing science. *Marketing Science*. vol. 33, no. 2, 2014, pp. 206–221.

As technology continues to advance rapidly, consumers are increasingly engaging in online transactions, using digital services, and interacting with automated systems powered by Artificial Intelligence (AI) and other emerging technologies. While the digital world offers convenience, efficiency, and innovation, it also presents risks to consumers, such as data breaches, fraud, unfair practices, lack of transparency, etc.

The digital world has transformed the way consumers interact with businesses, bringing convenience, accessibility, and innovation. However, this rapid digitization has also raised several challenges for consumer protection, especially in the European context. As consumers increasingly engage in online transactions, data sharing, and digital services, it is crucial to ensure that their rights are safeguarded effectively. European consumer law protection has evolved to adapt to the changing digital landscape, but future challenges are still present.

2. Challenges of Consumer Protection in the Digital World

Consumer protection in the digital world faces several challenges that are connected to European consumer law protection. These challenges arise from the unique characteristics of the digital environment and the rapid pace of technological advancements. Some of the key challenges include:

a) Lack of Transparency, Information Asymmetry and Information Overload

Consumers in the digital world may face challenges related to the lack of transparency and information asymmetry. Businesses may not provide clear and accurate information about their products or services, pricing, or terms and conditions[207]. Consumers may also face challenges in understanding complex technologies, such as AI algorithms or automated decision-making systems. European consumer law protection should ensure that consumers have access to transparent and easily understandable information to make informed choices in the digital marketplace.

One of the key challenges in consumer protection in the digital world is information asymmetry. Information asymmetry refers to the situation where one party has more information than the other, resulting in an imbalance of power.

[207] AKERLOF, G. A. The market for "lemons": Quality uncertainty and the market mechanism. *The Quarterly Journal of Economics*. 1970, vol. 84, no. 3, pp. 488–500.

Some authors point out the difference between earlier thinking about the role of information asymmetries and modern information theory. Whereas the early theories recognised information asymmetries as a brute inequality in the information available to buyers and sellers and wanted to restore the equality through the provision of information to buyers, the modern information theory recognizes the subtle and complex ways in which information affects the dynamics of markets and bargaining settings and also recognizes the cost of becoming informed as an irreducible component of market transactions.[208] In the digital world, consumers often face challenges in obtaining accurate and complete information about the products or services they are purchasing online[209]. This can include misleading product descriptions, fake reviews, hidden fees, and unclear terms and conditions. Information transparency and understanding of contractual conditions are necessary prerequisites also for sustainable consumption but consumers face the complex and often impossible task of assembling and then analysing relevant information.[210]

For example, online marketplaces may have numerous sellers, making it difficult for consumers to ascertain the quality, safety, and authenticity of the products or services they are purchasing. Additionally, online advertisements can be misleading or deceptive, leading consumers to make uninformed decisions[211]. This information asymmetry can result in consumers being duped into purchasing counterfeit or substandard products, falling victim to fraudulent activities, or being exposed to unfair contractual terms. Asymmetric consumer information also enables those who own the means of production to more effectively extract surplus, which further entrenches class divisions.[212]

Furthermore, with the increasing use of automated decision-making systems, such as recommendation algorithms and personalized pricing algorithms, consumers may not fully understand how their data is being used, and how decisions are being made.[213] This lack of transparency and understanding can lead to consumer confusion, loss of privacy, and potential discrimination.

---

208 HADFIELD, G. K., HOWSE, R., TREBILCOCK, M. Information-Based Principles for Rethinking Consumer Protection Policy. *Journal of Consumer Policy*. 1998, no. 21, pp. 131–169.

209 NEGROPONTE, N. *Being Digital.* New York, NY: Vintage Book, 1996.

210 WELLS, P. E. *Business Models for Sustainability*. Edward Elgar Publishing, Northampton, MA, 2013.

211 KERBER, W. Digital markets, data, and privacy: competition law, consumer law and data protection. *Journal of Intellectual Property Law & Practice.* Vol. 11, no. 11, 2016, pp. 856–866.

212 PARK, D. Individualization, information asymmetry, and exploitation in the advertiser-driven digital era. *The Political Economy of Communication*. Vol. 5, no. 2, pp. 22–44. Available at: http://www.polecom.org/index.php/polecom/article/view/83.

213 SOLOVE, D. J. Introduction: Privacy self-management and the consent dilemma. *Harvard Law Review*. 2013, 1880. Available at: https://papers.ssrn.com/sol3/papers.cfm?abstract_id=2171018#.

Addressing information asymmetry requires robust consumer protection regulations that ensure transparency, accuracy, and completeness of information provided by businesses in the digital marketplace. European consumer law protection should mandate clear and easily accessible disclosures of product information, pricing, terms and conditions, and data usage practices[214]. Additionally, businesses should be held accountable for the accuracy and integrity of user-generated content, such as reviews and ratings, on their platforms. Consumers should also be educated and empowered to critically evaluate online information, understand the implications of automated decision-making, and protect their privacy rights.

The challenge for consumer protection in the online space is not only information asymmetry, information overload (or information anxiety and technostress[215]) also plays an important role, as consumers can be so overwhelmed by the amount of information about products, businesses and consumer rights that they are unable to navigate it and assess their options in a relevant way. Some of the earlier studies show that more information tends to decrease the quality of consumer decision performance.[216] This has been confirmed by more recent studies which showed that the "combination of number of attributes and distribution of attribute levels is a better predictor of information overload than the number of alternatives or attributes alone. Increasing the number of attributes from 9 to 18 significantly imposed information overload on subjects and led to negative effect on choice quality. When combined with equal distribution of attribute levels across alternatives, the negative effect of information overload was increased".[217] In the online environment, consumers often do not rely on the information provided by the business, but take advantage of the sharing of experiences of other consumers who share their knowledge through online reviews. However, this too requires cognitive processing, which places additional demands on consumers. As Han-fen Hu and Anjala S. Krishen state, even when a consumer reaches a decision and purchases online after reading reviews, they can experience decision difficulty and reduced decision satisfaction.[218] The issue

[214] FAINMESSER, I. P., GALEOTTI, A., MOMOT, R. Digital Privacy. *Management Science*. 2022, vol. 69, no. 6, pp. 3157–3173.

[215] See AL-YOUZBAKY, B. A., HANNA, R. D. The Effect of Information Overload, and Social Media Fatigue on Online Consumers Purchasing Decisions: The Mediating Role of Technostress and Information Anxiety. *Journal of System and Management Sciences*. 2022, vol. 12, no. 2, pp. 195–220.

[216] JACOBY, J., SPELLER, D. E., KOHN, C. A. Brand choice behavior as a function of information load. *Journal of Marketing Research*. 1974, no. 11, pp. 63–69.

[217] LEE, B. K., LEE, W. N. The effect of information overload on consumer choice quality in an on-line environment. *Psychology & Marketing*. 2004, vol. 21, no. 3, pp. 159–183.

[218] HU, H., KRISHEN, A. S. When is enough, enough? Investigating product reviews and information overload from a consumer empowerment perspective. *Journal of Business Research*.

of communicating sufficient information to consumers also has an impact on ecological issues, because if consumers do not have enough appropriate information or are overwhelmed by information, they return goods, which has an impact on the carbon footprint[219] and responsibility for sustainable consumption.[220]

b) Data Privacy and Security

With the increasing reliance on digital technologies, cybersecurity has become a critical concern for consumer protection. According to Kerber, the voluntary and involuntary disclosure of consumers' private data allows enterprises to capture substantially more information about the preferences and behaviour of their customers. Whereas this enables enterprises to offer new and better-matching products and services, there are also serious concerns that this new distribution of information can enable companies to pursue strategies possibly detrimental to consumers.[221] Data breaches, where consumers' personal and financial information is compromised, have become a prevalent threat in the digital world. Such breaches can result in financial losses, identity theft, and reputational harm for consumers. Moreover, the ever-evolving nature of cyber threats makes it challenging for consumer protection mechanisms to keep pace with the rapid changes in technology. Ensuring robust cybersecurity measures, such as encryption, multi-factor authentication, and data breach notification requirements, is crucial to protect consumers' personal data in the digital world.

European Union sees privacy as a fundamental right through which every person should have control of their personal data[222]. In order to ensure consistent protection of individuals' rights and facilitate data flows within the European

2019, vol. 100, pp. 27–37.

[219] LV, J., LIU, X. The Impact of Information Overload of E-Commerce Platform on Consumer Return Intention: Considering the Moderating Role of Perceived Environmental Effectiveness. *International Journal of Environmental Research and Public Health*. 2022, vol. 19, issue 13, 8060.

[220] MAK, V., TERRYN, E. Circular Economy and Consumer Protection: The Consumer as a Citizen and the Limits of Empowerment Through Consumer Law. *Journal of Consumer Policy.* 2020, vol. 43, no. 1, pp. 227–248.

[221] KERBER, W. Digital markets, data, and privacy: competition law, consumer law and data protection. *Journal of Intellectual Property Law & Practice.* vol. 11, no. 11, 2016, pp. 856–866.

[222] See e.g. Art. 7 and 8 of the Charter of Fundamental Rights of the European Union; Directive 95/46/EC of the European Parliament and of the Council of 24 October 1995 on the protection of individuals with regard to the processing of personal data and on the free movement of such data; Regulation (EU) 2016/679 of the European Parliament and of the Council of 27 April 2016 on the protection of natural persons with regard to the processing of personal data and on the free movement of such data, and repealing Directive 95/46/EC (General Data Protection Regulation).

Union, it is necessary for all Member States to have equivalent safeguards for processing personal data. The GDPR, which sets out rules for the protection of personal data in the EU, has been a significant step towards addressing these challenges (such as right to compensation[223], right to know the value of your personal data[224], right to reset the user profile[225] etc.). However, the complexities of data privacy and security in the digital world require ongoing efforts to ensure that consumer data is adequately protected. General Data Protection Regulation on one hand states that processing of personal data should be designed to serve mankind, however the right to the protection of personal data is not an absolute right because it must be considered in relation to its function in society and be balanced against other fundamental rights (using the principle of proportionality). The GDPR encompasses the handling of personal data across various sectors and contexts, with certain exceptions such as activities directly related to crime prevention, investigation, detection, or prosecution (as specified in Article 2 of the GDPR). It has two primary goals outlined in Article 1 of the GDPR. Firstly, it seeks to safeguard the personal data of individuals (as stated in Article 1, Section 2, GDPR), secondly, it aims to govern the unrestricted flow of personal data (as stated in Article 1, Section 3, GDPR). According to Article 4 GDPR personal data means any information relating to an identified or identifiable natural person (a person who can be identified, directly or indirectly[226], in particular by reference to an identifier such as a name, an identification number, location data, an online identifier or to one or more factors specific to the physical, physiological, genetic, mental, economic, cultural or social identity of that natural person). The information may be open to public or kept private.[227] The GDPR sticks to strict principles[228], namely that personal data must be processed lawfully, fairly, and transparently in relation to the individual concerned, collected only for specific, explicit, and legitimate purposes. Personal data must be always adequate,

[223] WALREE, T. F., WOLTERS Pieter T. J. The Right to Compensation of a Competitor for a Violation of the GDPR. *International Data Privacy Law*. 2020, vol. 10, no. 4, pp. 346–355.

[224] MALGIERI, G., CUSTERS, B. Pricing privacy – the right to know the value of your personal data. *Computer Law & Security Review*. 2018, vol. 34, no. 2, pp. 289–303.

[225] ESKENS, S. A right to reset your user profile and more: GDPR-rights for personalized news consumers. *International Data Privacy Law*. 2019, vol. 9, no. 3, pp. 153–17.

[226] E.g. by the name. See LAMBERT, P. *Understanding the New European Data Protection Rules*. New York: Auerbach Publications, 2017.

[227] CUSTERS, B., SEARS, A. M., DECHESNE, F., GEORGIEVA, I., TANI, T., VAN DER HOF, S. Introduction – The Netherlands. *EU Personal Data Protection Policy and Practice*. Information Technology and Law Series; Asser Press. The Hague, The Netherlands, 2019, vol. 29.

[228] TRZASKOWSKI, J. GDPR compliant processing of big data in small business. In PEDERSEN, C. L., LINDGREEN, A., RITTER, T., RINGBERG, T. (eds.). *Big Data in Small Business: Data-driven Growth in Small and Medium-sized Enterprises*. Edward Elgar Publishing, 2021, pp. 27–29.

relevant, and limited to what is necessary for the purposes for which they are processed, they must be accurate and, where necessary, kept up to date (reasonable measures must be taken to promptly rectify or erase inaccurate personal data in relation to the purposes for which they are processed). Personal data must be retained in a form that allows identification of data subjects for no longer than necessary for the purposes for which the personal data are processed[229], and also processed in a manner that ensures appropriate security of personal data, including protection against unauthorized or unlawful processing, accidental loss, destruction, or damage.

c) E-commerce and Online Marketplaces: Place for Fraud and Unfair Practices

E-commerce has revolutionized the way consumers shop, offering convenience, choice, and competitive prices. However, it also presents challenges related to consumer protection. Online marketplaces, where consumers purchase products and services from third-party sellers, raise concerns about product safety, counterfeit goods, and consumer remedies. Apart from the economic interests of consumers, some aspects of predatory business models may cause a risk for human dignity, human well-being, social welfare and democracy[230]. Some authors claim that fake news are not only used in politics but also in online marketing.[231]

Consumers may also face challenges in resolving disputes, as online marketplaces are often intermediaries that may not be held liable for the actions of third-party sellers. On the other hand, as consumers gain knowledge about digital technologies, they may be more likely to adopt a proactive strategy and take preemptive, protective measures when interacting with firms.[232] However, the increasing dominance of certain e-commerce platforms may raise competition

[229] See GONZÁLEZ, E. G., DE HERT, P. Understanding the legal provisions that allow processing and profiling of personal data. An analysis of the GDPR provisions and principles. *ERA Forum*. 2019, vol. 19, pp. 597–621.

[230] TRZASKOWSKI, J. Data-driven value extraction and human well-being under EU law. *Electron Markets*. 2022, vol. 32, pp. 447–458; TRZASKOWSKI, J. Lawful distortion of consumers' economic behaviour – collateral damage under the Unfair Commercial Practices Directive. *European Business Law Review*. 2016, vol. 27, no. 1, pp. 25–49.

[231] DI DOMENICO, G., VISENTIN, M. Fake news or true lies? Reflections about problematic contents in marketing. *International Journal of Market Research*. 2020, vol. 62, no. 4, pp. 409–417; DI DOMENICO, G., SIT, J., ISHIZAKA, A., NUNAN, D. Fake news, social media and marketing: A systematic review. *Journal of Business Research*. 2021, vol. 124, pp. 329–341.

[232] QUACH, S., THAICHON, P., MARTIN, K. D., WEAVEN, S. Digital technologies: tensions in privacy and data. *Journal of the Academy of Marketing Science*. 2022, vol. 50, no. 1, pp. 1299–1323.

concerns, limiting consumer choice and bargaining power. Croxson, Frost, Gambacorta and Valletti state that "platforms are highly scalable, making use of network effects and economies of scale and scope in multi-sided markets. In some cases, this has allowed them to lower costs and achieve impressive gains in financial inclusion. In other cases, it has allowed them to serve existing customers with new, more personalised offers. Yet often, these gains have been accompanied by pressing risks, particularly from market dominance, data privacy and financial stability given the potential for systemic importance of platform providers".[233]

The digital world presents opportunities for fraudsters to engage in various deceptive practices, such as phishing, fake online stores, and false advertising. Consumers may fall victim to such practices and suffer financial losses. European consumer law protection addresses these challenges by imposing strict rules and penalties on businesses that engage in fraudulent activities, and by providing effective mechanisms for consumers to seek redress, not only through the GDPR mentioned above, but also by the means of the Unfair Commercial Practices Directive (2005/29/EC). The UCPD regulates the unfair commercial practices, including unfair advertising, which directly or indirectly harm consumers' economic interests and protects consumers from the consequences of such unfair commercial practices. If any of the commercial practice targeting privacy does not also concern the economic interests of consumers, it is from a marketing perspective a matter of taste and decency, which is controlled under national law.[234]

d) Digital Services and Subscription Models

Digital services, such as streaming platforms, cloud storage and subscription-based models, have become increasingly popular in the digital world. While these services offer convenience and accessibility, they also raise challenges related to consumer protection. Subscription-based models, for instance, may involve automatic renewal of subscriptions, hidden fees, and unclear cancellation policies, leaving consumers vulnerable to unfair practices. Digital services may also raise concerns about data privacy, as these platforms collect and analyse vast amounts of consumer data to deliver personalized content and advertisements. Not many users are aware of the magnitude of the collection of data and the

[233] CROXSON, K., FROST, J., GAMBACORTA, L., VALLETTI, T. Platform-based business models and financial inclusion. *Journal of Competition Law and Economics.* 2022, vol. 19, no. 6, pp. 75–102.

[234] TRZASKOWSKI, J. Data-driven value extraction and human well-being under EU law. *Electron Markets*. 2022, vol. 32, pp. 447–458.

extent to which they are addressed and targeted based on that data[235]. Moreover, issues related to contract terms, transparency, and dispute resolution may arise, as digital services are often provided through complex terms of service agreements that consumers may not fully understand.

e) Accountability for AI and Automated Systems

Automated decision-making, powered by Artificial Intelligence (AI) and machine learning algorithms, is increasingly being used in various aspects of the digital world, such as personalized pricing, product recommendations, credit scoring, and content filtering. While these technologies offer benefits such as efficiency, convenience, and personalization, they also raise concerns in terms of consumer protection. For example, there is reason to believe that profiling, automated decision-making, and credit-scoring are not declared as often as they are used.[236]

One of the challenges associated with automated decision-making is the lack of transparency and explainability. Consumers may not fully understand how decisions are made by algorithms and may not be able to challenge or appeal against unfair or discriminatory decisions. For example, personalized pricing algorithms may result in discriminatory pricing based on factors such as location, browsing history, or demographic information, leading to price discrimination. Some authors even claim that the consumer has a right to impersonal prices under the GDPR legal provisions[237].

Price discrimination can be defined as charging of different prices to end consumers based on a discriminatory variable[238] or ability to charge different prices to different consumers[239]. Another challenge is the potential for bias in automated decision-making. AI and machine learning algorithms are trained on large datasets, which may contain biased data that can result in biased outcomes. For instance, credit scoring algorithms may perpetuate existing biases in lending

[235] MCDONALD, A., CRANOR, L. Beliefs and behaviors: Internet users' understanding of behavioral advertising. Proceedings of the 2010 Research Conference on Communication, Information and Internet Policy, 2010.

[236] WULF, A. J., SEIZOV, O. "Please understand we cannot provide further information": evaluating content and transparency of GDPR-mandated AI disclosures. *AI & Society*. 2022. Available from: https://link.springer.com/article/10.1007/s00146-022-01424-z#citeas

[237] ESPOSITO, F. The GDPR enshrines the right to the impersonal price. *Computer Law & Security Review*. 2022, vol. 45, 105660.

[238] REINARTZ, W. Customizing prices in online markets. *Emerging Issues in Management*. 2002, vol. 1, pp. 55–65.

[239] GHOSE, A., HUANG, K. Personalized pricing and quality customization. *Journal of Economics & Management Strategy*. 2009, vol. 18, no. 4, pp. 1095–1135.

practices, resulting in discrimination against certain groups of consumers, such as minorities or individuals with low incomes. This belongs to so called price discrimination which results in offering of different prices to different customers based on their pervious purchase history or factors such as place of purchase, time of the day, type of smart devices used and other variables[240].

Moreover, there may be issues related to accountability and liability in cases where automated decision-making results in harm to consumers. It may be challenging to determine who is responsible when decisions are made by algorithms, and consumers may face difficulties in seeking compensation or redress.

European consumer law protection should address these challenges by ensuring transparency, explainability, and fairness in automated decision-making, since the requirements of the GDPR are too vague and leave substantial room for interpretation. Although the GDPR is the most advanced legislation on data protection we have, the guidance that it provides on how companies should inform data subjects about AI and automated decision-making appears to be too superficial and too vague to interpretation [241]. Regulations should mandate businesses to disclose when decisions are made by algorithms and provide explanations to consumers. There should also be mechanisms for consumers to challenge or appeal against decisions made by algorithms. Additionally, consumer protection laws should require that algorithms are trained on unbiased and representative data, and that businesses are held accountable for the outcomes of automated decision-making processes. This may include establishing liability frameworks that clarify the responsibilities of businesses, manufacturers, and developers in cases of harm caused by automated decision-making.

f) Changing Business Models

The digital world has disrupted traditional business models, and new models such as platform-based and subscription-based models have emerged. While these models offer convenience and accessibility to consumers, they also present challenges for consumer protection.

For instance, in platform-based models, businesses act as intermediaries connecting buyers and sellers, but they may not have control over the quality, safety, and legality of the products or services being offered. Consumers may face challenges in resolving disputes, obtaining refunds, or holding businesses

---

[240] CAILLAUD, B., DE NIJS, R. Strategic loyalty reward in dynamic price discrimination. *Marketing Science*. 2014, vol. 33, no. 5, pp. 725–742.

[241] WULF, A. J., SEIZOV, O. "Please understand we cannot provide further information": evaluating content and transparency of GDPR-mandated AI disclosures. *AI & Society*. 2022. Available from: https://link.springer.com/article/10.1007/s00146-022-01424-z#citeas.

accountable for their obligations. Moreover, in subscription-based models[242], consumers may face difficulties in understanding the terms and conditions, canceling subscriptions, or getting refunds.

Another example is the "freemium" model[243], where businesses offer free basic services but charge for additional features. In such cases, consumers may face challenges in understanding the true cost of the services[244], hidden charges[245], and the impact on their privacy rights when using free services.

In many cases, consumers are not paying for the services with subscription fees or any kind of monetary payment, but with their personal data. Consumers' personal data represents value which is exchanged for certain services, often implicitly, without users knowing which data they actually provide and what the value of their personal data is to these data controllers[246].

To address these challenges, European consumer law protection started to adapt to changing business models and ensure that consumers are adequately protected[247]. This includes regulations that mandate clear disclosures of terms and conditions, pricing, refund policies, and cancellation procedures. It may also require businesses to have robust dispute resolution mechanisms in place, and to be transparent about the quality, safety, and legality of products or services offered on their platforms. Consumer education and awareness about different business models, their implications, and available consumer protection mechanisms can also play a crucial role in mitigating these challenges.

---

242 PUNJ, G. The relationship between consumer characteristics and willingness to pay for general online content: Implications for content providers considering subscription-based business models. *Marketing Letters*. 2013, vol. 26, no. 2, pp. 175–186.

243 HAN, C., REYES, I., BAR ON, A. E., REARDON, J., FEAL, Á., BAMBERGER, K. A., EGELMAN, S., VALLINA-RODRIGUEZ, N. Do You Get What You Pay For? Comparing The Privacy Behaviors of Free vs. Paid Apps. Available from: https://dspace.networks.imdea.org/bitstream/handle/20.500.12761/691/Do_You_Get_What_You_Pay_For_2019_EN.pdf?sequence=1&isAllowed=y

244 Information asymmetry in the context of in-game purchasing refers to a relationship between the game and the player whereby the game system has significantly more information about the player than the player has (or is able to acquire) about the game. KING, D. L., DELFABBRO, P. H., GAINSBURY, S. M., DREIER, M., GREER, N., BILLIEUX, J. Unfair play? Video games as exploitative monetized services: An examination of game patents from a consumer protection perspective. *Computers in Human Behavior*. 2019, vol. 101, pp. 131–143.

245 KING, D. L., DELFABBRO, P. H. Video game monetization (e.g., 'loot boxes'): A blueprint for practical social responsibility measures. *International Journal of Mental Health and Addiction*. 2019, vol. 17, pp. 166–179; GRIFFITHS, M. D. Is the buying of loot boxes in video games a form of gambling or gaming? *Gaming Law Review*. 2018, vol. 22, no. 1, pp. 52–54.

246 CUSTERS, B., MALGIERI, G. Priceless data: why the EU fundamental right to data protection is at odds with trade in personal data. *Computer Law & Security Review*. 2022, vol. 45, 2022, 105683; MALGIERI, G., CUSTERS, B. Pricing privacy: the right to know the value of your personal data. *Computer Law & Security Review*. 2018, vol. 34, no. 2, pp. 289–303.

247 See e.g. Digital Content and Digital Service Directive (EU) 2019 /770, Article 3(1).

g) Enforcement Challenges in the Digital World: Technological Illiteracy, Dispute Resolution and Cross-Border Challenges

Not all consumers are technologically proficient, and many may lack the necessary skills and knowledge to navigate the complexities of the digital world. Technological illiteracy can make consumers vulnerable to various risks, such as falling for scams, making uninformed choices, or failing to protect their personal data. European consumer law protection tries to take into account the needs of technologically illiterate consumers and provide adequate measures, such as educational campaigns and accessible information, to empower consumers to make informed choices and protect their rights in the digital world.

Although recent cases demonstrate the serious struggles of the courts when it comes to the enforcement of the EU consumer protection law[248], enforcement of consumer protection laws in the digital world presents even more unique challenges. Traditional enforcement mechanisms may not be fully effective in addressing violations that occur in the digital realm.[249] For instance, online businesses may be based in multiple jurisdictions, making it difficult to determine the applicable laws and enforcement agencies. Additionally, digital platforms may be intermediaries that may not be held directly liable for the actions of third-party sellers or service providers, resulting in accountability gaps. The anonymous nature of online transactions and the speed at which digital transactions occur may also make it challenging to track and prosecute wrongdoers. Moreover, the lack of consumer awareness and education about their rights in the digital world may further hinder effective enforcement.

The digital world has facilitated cross-border transactions, allowing consumers to access products and services from different countries. However, this has also resulted in challenges related to consumer protection. Consumers may face difficulties in asserting their rights when dealing with businesses from different jurisdictions. Disputes may arise regarding issues such as contract enforcement, product quality, and liability. Additionally, the complexity of cross-border transactions may create information asymmetry, leaving consumers vulnerable to scams, fraud, and unfair practices.

Online dispute resolution constitutes an implementation of existing forms of general alternative dispute resolution with the use of the Internet; the main

[248] MIŠĆENIĆ, E. The Effectiveness of Judicial Enforcement of the EU Consumer Protection Law. In MEŠKIĆ, Z., KUNDA, I., POPOVIĆ, D., OMEROVIĆ, E. (eds.). *Balkan Yearbook of European and International Law*. Cham: Springer, 2019.

[249] PONTE, L. M. Throwing Bad Money After Bad: Can Online Dispute Resolution (ODR) Really Deliver the Goods for the Unhappy Internet Shopper? *Tulane Journal of Technology and Intellectual Property*. 2001, vol. 3, pp. 55–92.

assumption of alternative methods of dispute resolution –the presence of a third party during the process of reaching an agreement – remains unchanged.[250] The ODR platform serves as a resource for general information on resolving contractual disputes between traders and consumers arising from online sales and service contracts. It facilitates the independent, impartial, transparent, effective, fast and fair out-of-court resolution of disputes between consumers and traders online.[251] The platform's purpose is to transmit the consumers' complaints to a competent ADR entity that can handle the specific dispute. Additionally, the ODR platform provides a free electronic case management tool, enabling ADR entities to carry out the dispute resolution process with the involved parties through the platform. Loutocký states that "negotiation is generally considered as the initial stage of the alternative proceedings where the parties have the possibility of resolving the dispute by active communication to reach mutual agreement. While it may seem at first glance that this kind of solution of the dispute does not motivate parties to end their dispute much, the opposite is true especially in the online environment. Modern technologies in this stage show their greatest potential and allow the parties to settle the dispute quickly and efficiently just by using convenient environment to negotiate between each other".[252]

3. Opportunities for Consumer Protection in the Digital World

While the digital world poses significant challenges to consumer protection, it also presents opportunities to enhance consumer rights and interests. These opportunities arise from the potential of technology to provide innovative solutions and empower consumers. For instance, data analytics and AI could be used to detect and prevent fraud, identify potential consumer risks, and personalize consumer protection measures. AI-powered chatbots can provide instant and personalized assistance to consumers, helping them navigate complex terms and conditions, and resolve disputes efficiently. Data analytics can also be used to

[250] MANIA, K. Online dispute resolution: The future of justice. *International Comparative Jurisprudence*. 2015, vol. 1, no. 1, pp. 76–86.

[251] Regulation (EU) No 524/2013 of the European Parliament and of the Council of 21 May 2013 on online dispute resolution for consumer disputes and amending Regulation (EC) No 2006/2004 and Directive 2009/22/EC (Regulation on consumer ODR) which builds upon the Alternate Dispute Resolution (ADR) Directive (Dir. 2013/11/EU). See also BOGDAN, M. The New EU Regulation on Online Resolution for Consumer Disputes. *Masaryk University Journal of Law and Technology*. 2015, vol. 9, no. 1, pp. 155.

[252] LOUTOCKÝ, P. Online Dispute Resolution to Resolve Consumer Disputes from the perspective of European Union Law: Is the Potential of ODR Fully Used? *Masaryk University Journal of Law and Technology*. 2016, vol. 10, no. 1, pp. 113–127.

identify patterns of consumer complaints or issues, which can inform regulatory efforts to address emerging consumer protection challenges.

In addition, technology could enable consumer empowerment by providing consumers with tools and information to make informed choices. If used properly, price comparison websites, consumer reviews, and product ratings can help consumers make informed decisions about the quality, safety, and price of products or services. Digital platforms can also provide mechanisms for consumers to leave feedback, report issues, and seek redress, creating a feedback loop that can drive improvements in consumer protection.

3.1 Enhanced Transparency

Technology can also enable greater transparency in the digital marketplace, allowing consumers to access accurate and comprehensive information about products, services, prices, and terms and conditions. For example, online reviews, comparison websites, and rating systems can empower consumers to make informed choices and hold businesses accountable for their products or services. However, information does not equal transparency because information must be read, decoded and understood and consumers must make a vast number of decisions every day based on goals, preferences, experience and available information. In general, efficient decisions rely on consumers' ability to overcome the searching costs, switching costs (the cost of changing providers and testing new brands or products) and bounded rationality (biases and heuristics in human decision making)[253]. Thus, the European consumer law protection could leverage technological tools to promote transparency in the digital world and empower consumers to make informed decisions.

3.2 Enhanced Personalization and Customization

Technology can enable businesses to offer personalized and customized products or services to consumers. For example, AI-powered recommendation systems can analyse consumer preferences and behaviours to offer tailored recommendations. However, such personalization should be carried out in a transparent and ethical manner, respecting consumers' privacy and consent. European consumer law protection should ensure that businesses comply with the principles

[253] TRZASKOWSKI, J. Behavioural innovations in marketing law. In MICKLITZ, H., SIBONY, A. L., ESPOSITO, F. (eds.). *Handbook of Research Methods in Consumer Law*. Edward Elgar Publishing, 2018.

of transparency, fairness, and consumer consent in their personalized offerings, and that consumers have control over their personal data and the use of AI in their transactions. The consent mechanism regulation would however benefit more from the introduction of an opt-in system instead of an opt-out system, so that every consumer is not bothered with constant urge to confirm his or her consent and only an informed and persistent consumer is able to protect his or her rights and privacy.

3.3 Strengthening Data Protection and Cybersecurity Measures

Although consumers have become increasingly concerned about data privacy, fueled by negative publicity about data breaches, they are also disclosing more information than ever before.[254] Robust cybersecurity measures should be in place to protect consumers' personal data from data breaches and other cyber threats. This may involve imposing strict cybersecurity standards on digital businesses, including encryption, multi-factor authentication, and data breach notification requirements. Digital platforms should also be held accountable for protecting consumer data and taking appropriate measures to prevent data breaches. It may not be worthwhile for companies to circumvent data protection rules because it can affect the value of the company.[255] In this regard, European consumer law protection can play a crucial role in setting cybersecurity standards for digital businesses.

3.4 Strengthening Enforcement Mechanisms and Improved Access to Justice

Effective enforcement mechanisms are crucial for ensuring that consumer protection laws are upheld in the digital world. Despite the existence of consumer protection laws, violations can still occur, and consumers may face challenges in seeking redress. Therefore, enforcement mechanisms should be strengthened to effectively investigate and prosecute wrongdoers and provide effective remedies for consumers.

Technology can enable innovative dispute resolution mechanisms, such as online mediation, online arbitration, and blockchain-based dispute resolution.

[254] BEKE, F. T., EGGERS, F., VERHOEF, P. C., WIERINGA, J. E. Consumers' privacy calculus: The PRICAL index development and validation. *International Journal of Research in Marketing*. 2022, vol. 39, no. 1, pp. 20–41.

[255] MARTIN, K. D., BORAH, A., PALMATIER, R. W. Data privacy: Effects on customer and firm performance. *Journal of Marketing*. 2017, vol. 81, no. 1, pp. 36–58.

These mechanisms can provide efficient, cost-effective, and accessible ways for consumers to resolve disputes with businesses in the digital world. European consumer law protection should keep pace with technological innovations in dispute resolution and explore the potential of such mechanisms to enhance consumer protection in the digital world. It should also promote the use of technology to improve access to justice for consumers, particularly in cross-border disputes and complex digital transactions.

Enforcement mechanisms should be strengthened to effectively address violations of consumer protection laws in the digital world. This may involve empowering consumer protection agencies with adequate resources and authority to investigate and prosecute wrongdoers. Digital platforms should also be held accountable for the actions of third-party sellers or service providers operating on their platforms. Cooperation among EU Member States and international cooperation in cross-border cases should be enhanced to tackle jurisdictional challenges.

3.5 Enhancing Consumer Awareness and Education and Empowered Consumer Voice

Consumer awareness and education play a crucial role in empowering consumers and protecting their rights in the digital world. Many consumers lack awareness about their rights and responsibilities when using digital services[256], including issues related to data privacy, online transactions, and dispute resolution mechanisms. Therefore, efforts should be made to educate consumers about their rights and responsibilities in the digital world and equip them with the necessary knowledge and skills to make informed decisions.

In this regard, European consumer law protection tries to implement consumer education programs that provide resources and information on digital platforms, data privacy, and online transactions. This involves collaborations between consumer protection agencies, educational institutions, and other stakeholders to develop and disseminate educational materials, conduct workshops and seminars, and promote digital literacy among consumers.

Technology can also amplify the consumer voice, allowing consumers to share their experiences, feedback, and opinions about products or services in

[256] LOBSCHAT, L., MUELLER, B., EGGERS, F., BRANDIMARTE, L., DIEFENBACH, S., KROSCHKE, M., WIRTZ, J. Corporate digital responsibility. *Journal of Business Research*. 2021, vol. 122, pp. 875–888.

the digital world[257]. Social media, online forums, and review platforms provide consumers with a platform to voice their concerns, share feedback, and hold businesses accountable for their practices. European consumer law protection can leverage the power of technology to empower consumers to exercise their consumer rights, voice their opinions, and engage in consumer activism in the digital world.

3.6 Enhanced Product Safety

Technology can play a crucial role in enhancing product safety in the digital world. For example, connected devices, also known as the Internet of Things (IoT), can enable real-time monitoring of product performance and provide early warnings of potential safety risks[258]. Additionally, advanced data analytics and machine learning algorithms can analyse large datasets to detect patterns and trends that may indicate safety concerns, such as identifying potential defects in products or identifying patterns of product misuse that may lead to safety hazards. European consumer law protection should promote the use of technology in ensuring product safety in the digital world, such as setting standards for IoT devices, regulating data analytics in product safety monitoring, and encouraging businesses to use advanced technologies for proactive product safety measures.

3.7 Enhanced Market Surveillance

Technology can enable more effective market surveillance to detect and address unfair practices, scams, and counterfeit products in the digital world. For example, automated systems can monitor online marketplaces for fraudulent activities, analyse customer reviews for patterns of deceit, and use machine learning algorithms to detect fake products. European consumer law protection should leverage technology to enhance market surveillance efforts, collaborate with relevant stakeholders, such as consumer organizations and technology companies, and establish robust mechanisms to detect and combat unfair practices in the digital world.

[257] LABRECQUE, L. I., VOR DEM ESCHE, J., MATHWICK, Ch., NOVAK, T. P., HOFACKER, Ch. F. Consumer Power: Evolution in the Digital Age. *Journal of Interactive Marketing*. 2013, vol. 27, no. 4, pp. 257–269. Available at: https://journals.sagepub.com/doi/pdf/10.1016/j.intmar.2013.09.002

[258] VÍTOVÁ, B. Limits of fairness and transparency in Internet of Things (IoT) contracts concluded with consumers. *Revue européenne de droit de la consommation (R.E.D.C.)*. Larcier, 2020, pp. 523–541.

4. Conclusion

Consumer protection in the digital world is a complex and evolving field that requires robust and adaptive regulatory frameworks, innovative technological solutions, collaboration among stakeholders, and widespread education and awareness. While there are challenges associated with the digital world, such as privacy risks, security concerns, automated decision-making, and cross-border transactions, there are also opportunities for leveraging technology, collaboration, and education to enhance consumer protection and improve the overall consumer experience.

European consumer law protection continues to evolve to address the emerging challenges and opportunities of the digital world, ensuring that consumers are protected in their interactions with businesses and that their rights are safeguarded in the online environment. By adopting a multi-stakeholder approach, promoting transparency, fairness, and accountability, and leveraging technology and education, consumer protection in the digital world can be strengthened, enabling consumers to confidently participate in the digital economy and enjoy the benefits of technological advancements while being protected from potential harms.

CHAPTER SIX

Key Challenges to the Implementation of the Digital Content Directive in Hungary and Czech Republic

ZSOLT HAJNAL, RITA SIMON

1. Introduction – national contractual law before the implementation

The Directive on Digital Content and Services (hereafter DCD) was expected to be implemented by the European Member States by the end of 2021, in order to better tackle the challenges of our Digital Age and to fill the gaps in the national Sales Laws concerning contractual relations regarding digital products or products with digital elements. The Directive served also for harmonization of European private law to enable firms to trade cross-border in a less diverse legal framework. However, the integration of harmonized contractual requirements into the national private codes is a very challenging discipline, due to the fact that contract law is one of the most significant pillars of national law, bringing together the essence of the national legal culture and tradition. This chapter compares the main difficulties of the Hungarian and Czech legislator in the implementation of the DCD with the main focus being the chosen integration model (2) and shaping data as counter-performance (3), as one of the most problematic, legally unconventional elements of the implementation, after a short introduction on these national laws before the implementation (1).

1.1 From the Austrian heritage to the recodification

Both Hungarian and the Czech national contract law underwent a similar historical development. Besides the common Austrian legal heritage, a similar destiny and timing of the legislation processes should be highlighted. The Austrian ABGB was not only an official legal source for a good hundred years in both countries, in the Czech Republic between 1811–1964[259] and in Hungary between 1852–1959[260]; but it also heavily influenced the first national drafts of their own Civil Codes in both countries. A further similarity is that despite the enthusiastic codification in the first 2 decades of the XX. century, neither the Czech[261] nor the Hungarian draft[262] on the Private Law Code could enter into force, due to the quick communistic penetration in the civil law. Unluckily, both countries enacted a communistic Civil Code in the 1950-s, which was their first modern and independent Private Law Act. The last parallel between the Hungarian and Czech civil law development is, that both national legislators completed the recodification of their Civil Codes with one year difference. The Czech Republic published its reshaped Civil Code in 2012[263] and Hungary in 2013[264]. Both codes eliminated the remaining communistic elements and transposed as much European consumer law into their new code as possible. However, the Hungarian legislator was influenced by the modernization of the German BGB[265], the Burgerliche Wetbok[266] of the Netherlands and Quebecian Civil Code[267]; the Czech legislator resorted to the old Czech draft from 1937, following again the Austrian tradition.

1.2 Lack of regulation of digital content before the DCD

Besides the similar historical development some further similarities and differences concerning the regulation of digital content should be noted. In both countries – similarly to most European countries, with exception of Ireland, the Netherlands and the UK – before the transposition of the DCD, a concrete

[259] BERGER, E. Österreichs Allgemeines Bürgerliches Gesetzbuch (ABGB): Eine europäische Privatrechtskodifikation. *Band III: Das ABGB außerhalb Österreichs*. Schriften zur Europäischen Rechts- und Verfassungsgeschichte, vol. 57, Wien: Duncker & Humblot GmbH, 2010, pp. 227–290.

[260] Ibid., pp. 33–134.

[261] Vládní návrh československého občanského zákoníku v r. 1937, see KOBER, J. (ed.). Osnova československého občanského zákoníku. Praha: Ústav státu a práva AV ČR, 2021, pp. 1–473.

[262] 1928. évi magánjogi törvényjavaslat. Available at: https://net.jogtar.hu/ezer-ev-torveny?docid=92800000.TVJ&searchUrl=/ezer-ev-torvenyei%3Fpagenum%3D52. Assessed 8. 7. 2023.

[263] Zákon č. 89/2012 Sb., občanský zákoník (Act No. 89/2012 Coll., Civil Code).

[264] 2013. évi V. Törvény a Polgári Törvénykönyvről (2013, Act. No. V Civil Code).

[265] Bürgerliches Gesetzbuch (BGB). Available at: https://www.gesetze-im-internet.de/bgb/. Assessed: 8. 7. 2023.

[266] Burgerlijk Wetboek. Available at: https://wetten.overheid.nl/BWBR0002656/2023-07-01. Assessed: 8. 7. 2023.

[267] Civil Code of Québec, Available at: <https://www.legisquebec.gouv.qc.ca/en/document/cs/ccq-1991. Assessed 8. 7. 2023.

definition of digital content was missing.[268] Although digital content fulfilled the definition of goods in both countries – according to Section 489 CzCC – the responsible ministries assumed that the existing intellectual property rights[269] were not sufficient to use them by analogy for digital content and digital services, because the two target different situations[270]. The digital content by its nature would not fit into the Hungarian concept of *things,* which refers to physical objects that can be taken into possession being able to be objects of ownership and the same rules shall be applied to money and securities as well as to natural forces usable as things under HunCC Section 5:14 1-2. Despite the lack of digital content definition and the narrow approach regarding things, digital contents and services are compatible with the service focused concept of Hungarian contract law (HunCC Section 6:1.). However, the Hungarian Code included some important requirements concerning electronic contracting acc. Section 6:82 HunCC and electronic contract declaration and confirmation acc. Section 6:84. HunCC.

Furthermore, both codese acknowledged the protection of personal data, a fact which will be important for the next chapter.

Both countries transposed the rules of contractual conformity and the remedies in case of lack of conformity in their actual Civil Codes, during the implementation of the last European Sales Law Directive, the Directive on Sale of Consumer Goods 1999/44, and due to the minimal harmonisation approach of this older directive, these remedies could been little different in these countries, delivering a common bases for the contractual disputes concerning sales of digital content. Interestingly, the Hungarian legislator extended the rules of the Sale of Consumer Goods Directive to legal relations other than consumer contracts (B2B), to avoid a two-track regulation approach[271], at the same time, it prohibited derogations in consumer contracts, while it laid down dispositive provisions in other legal relationships. As opposed to this solution, the Czech legislator did not provide "gold plating", but rather created different conformity rules and remedies for B2B and B2C relations in the Code.

---

[268] RAFEL, R. M. The Directive Proposals on Online Sales and Supply of Digital Content (Part I): will the new rules attain their objective of reducing legal complexity? *IDP: Revista d'Internet, Dret i Política*, 2016, no. 23, and DE FRANCESCHI, A., SCHULZE, R. (eds.). *Harmonizing Digital Contract Law. The Impact of EU Directives 2019/770 and 2019/771 and the Regulation of Online Platforms A Handbook.* Baden-Baden: Hart/Nomos, 2023, pp. 1–332.

[269] Zákon č. 121/2000 Sb., o právu autorském (Act No. 121/2000 Coll. on Copyright).

[270] Explanatory Notes to Sněmovní tisk 947/21 (Parliamentary Press 947/21), p. 79.

[271] VÉKÁS, L. Az uniós fogyasztói szerződési jog megújítása és az új irányelvek átültetése. Magyar Jog. 2021, vol. 68, no. 2, pp. 65–75.

2. Different transposition approach in the implementation of the Digital Content Directive

The twin directives on Digital Content and Services (hereafter DCD) and on the Sale of Goods (SGD) were expected to be implemented by the European Member States to reshape their national Sales Law regulations by the end of 2021, so they could better tackle the challenges of our digital age. However, as an important change to the older directive from 1999, the European legislator changed its harmonisation approach at drafting these twin directives to achieve a higher level in harmonisation and moved from minimal to the maximum harmonisation approach, thus limiting the room for discretion of the Member States. A relatively narrow margin of manoeuvre has been left to the national legislators in transposing the European directives; and the danger arose, that legal concepts or institutions that are alien to national private law should been transposed in the national legal system.

Due to the implementation period acc. Article 24 of the DCD the Member States had to transpose the DCD by 1 July 2021 and apply them to contracts concluded on or after 1 January 2022. However, Hungary fulfilled its transposition obligation by promulgating Government Decree No. 373/2021 (VI.30.) on the Detailed Rules of Contracts between Consumers and Undertakings on the Sale of Goods and on the Performance of Digital Content and Digital Services (hereinafter Implementing Decree, short HunID) on 30 June 2021 and its entry into force on 1 January 2022; the Czech legislator was unable to comply with the implementation period. Although the Czech amending drafts[272] were delivered in due time – in September 2020 – to the Parliament, the Czech implementation entered into force only on 9 January 2023 with Act no 374/2022 Coll.[273] This delay will presumably disadvantage Czech consumers, leaving them without concrete norms on digital content. Furthermore, the consumer-friendly innovations in the twin directives, e.g. the one year long reversed burden of proof in contractual disputes will be available for the Czech consumer only with a year delay, than for consumers' living in other Member States.

Concerning the transposition approach, both legislators have chosen a different integration model, which both bringing different benefits and disadvantages for consumers in these two countries. The elementary question, whether to involve

[272] Sněmovní tisk 994/0, Novela zákona č. 89/2012 Sb., občanský zákoník (Parliamentary Press 994/0, Amendment to the Civil Code). Available at: https://www.psp.cz/sqw/historie.sqw?o=8&t=994. Assessed: 8. 7. 2023.

[273] Zákon č. 374/2022 Sb., zákon, kterým se mění zákon č. 634/1992 Sb., o ochraně spotřebitele, ve znění pozdějších předpisů, a zákon č. 89/2012 Sb., občanský zákoník (Act No. 374/2022 Coll. Act amending Act No. 634/1992 Coll., on Consumer Protection, and Act No. 89/2012 Coll., Civil Code).

more legislative effort and upgrade the Civil Code suitable for future digital issues, or rather place the partially technical norms outside of the Code, was raised by all legislators[274]. Because both legislators used a different transposition method, the Czech using the integration model, the Hungarian the separation approach, the next chapter will deal with the advantages and disadvantages of both Model.

2.1 Benefits of the integration model – the Czech example

The Czech legislator transposed the majority of the DCD – with exception of the enforcement rules of Article 21 DCD – into the Czech Civil Code[275] (hereafter: CzCC). From the perspective of the legislator's technique, the Czech Republic followed the path of those countries (e.g. Germany and the Netherlands), which included their substantive consumer legislation in their Civil Code; however, part of the Czech recodification committee originally planned not to include consumer law into the new Civil Code[276], due to the risk of making it a constant construction[277] caused by the ever-changing EU consumer law. The integration model is to be praised because on one hand it undoubtedly raises the gravity of the codification, expecting a smooth creation of further building blocks; and on the other hand, it enables the Code to solve future challenges, and provides easier usability for practitioners.

This transposition approach was also kept during the implementation of the DCD, however the legislator needed to intervene in the structure of the existing code, to create a new contract type, *"providing digital content"*. The chapter was placed at *Book IV. Relative Property Rights, II. Obligation arising from judicial Acts, – Chapter 2 Relinquishing a thing to be used by another*, in a new *Division 6.* This new contract type follows the *licence contracts,* where provisions on licence contracts, on items protected by the Copyright Act, on publishing and on the rights of database authors are collected. This structural decision closed a long debate on the affiliation of digital contracts; and although the similarities to licence contracts were often mentioned to keep the rules under one division,

[274] See DE FRANCESCHI, A., SCHULZE, R. (eds.). *Harmonizing Digital Contract Law. The Impact of EU Directives 2019/770 and 2019/771 and the Regulation of Online Platforms.* A Handbook. Baden-Baden: Hart/Nomos, 2023, p. 15.

[275] Zákon č. 89/2012 Sb., občanský zákoník (Act No. 89/2012 Coll. Civil Code).

[276] The plans of the Czech recodification committee are available 1.2.3.1 of the Substantive intent of the Civil Code, Available at: http://obcanskyzakonik.justice.cz/images/pdf/vecny_zamer_OZ_2000.pdf. Assessed: 8. 7. 2023.

[277] DAUBNER-LIEB, B., LANGEN, W. (eds.). *Schuldrecht.* Nomos, 2021, p. 5. However, the Czech recodification committee originally planned not to include consumer law into the new Civil Code see 1.2.3.1 of the Substantive intent of the Civil Code, Available at: http://obcanskyzakonik.justice.cz/images/pdf/vecny_zamer_OZ_2000.pdf. Assessed 8. 7. 2023 and

the unique characteristics of providing digital content and services deserved separate norms. This separate placement is to be praised also for suitability for practitioners.[278]

The main added value of the amendments is in establishing a new, advanced framework for the terminology of the digital environment. Defining the essence of digital content, and even more of digital services[279], was an urgent necessity in the Czech Republic, because neither the understanding of digital content, nor the classification of digital services was consistent. Therefore, clear definitions and concrete requirements for the supply of digital content were welcomed both by the consumer and the businesses.

It is very important to underline that the Czech legislator widened the applicability of the DCD rules also to B2B relationships, however with a two-track solution, creating more user- friendly rules for consumers. Concerning these new divisions the general requirements on digital content and services, such as the undue performance of supply, the necessity for updates and the reversed burden of proof on conformity of items, are valid in both B2B and B2C relations; while the remedies for lack of conformity are different for the two kinds of buyers, enabling only consumers to enjoy more strict remedies. Presumably also businesses, especially SMEs, will welcome these new general rules, enabling them to enforce remedies against bigger platforms.

Otherwise the transposition of the DCD did not impact the structure of other fields of law, such as the law on intellectual property or data protection.

2.2 Separate norm for technical rules – the Hungarian approach

As opposed to the Czech implementation approach, the Hungarian legislator did not vote for an integrative solution. None of the Twin Directives, not even the requirements of the SGD were implemented into the HunCC. This solution was disputed in the literature, because the former chairman of the Committee for the Codification of the Civil Code proposed the transposition of the SGD into the HunCC, while the transposition of the DCD into Government Decree 45/2014 (II.26.) on the detailed rules of contracts between consumers and businesses, which is the implementing decree of the Consumer Rights' Directive.[280] Such a solution would

[278] WENDEHORST, Ch. Die neuen Regelungen im BGB zu Verträgen über digitale Produkte. *NJW.* 2021, pp. 2913–2914.

[279] RICHTER, S. Směrnice EU 2019/770 o některých aspektech poskytování digitálního obsahu a digitálních služeb jako nástroj ochrany spotřebitele. *Jurisprudence*. 2020, no. 4., p. 16.

[280] VÉKÁS, L. Az uniós fogyasztói szerződési jog megújítása és az új irányelvek átültetése. *Magyar Jog*. 2021, vol. 68, no. 2, pp. 65–75.

undoubtedly have involved greater risks and more legislative effort, but it would have eliminated regulatory stratification and created a more consumer-friendly regulatory environment. Nevertheless, due to casuistic rules of the two directives and to the diverging levels of abstraction (especially of the DCD) the legislator chose the safer route and transposed the rules of both directives into a separate Implementing Decree. This separative approach, on the one hand opened the way for a separate private consumer law code,[281] but on the other hand it led to cumulatively applicable, parallel legal regimes. As a result of this solution essentially provisions eg. among others defective performance, warranty and guaranty redresses, cancellation of the contract, presumption of non-conformity, requirements for conformity can be found parallel in the HunCC and in the HunID, [282] although they apply cumulatively. The establishment of coherence will be left within the euroconform interpretation of the Hungarian jurisdiction. Furthermore, essential parts of civil law, e.g. subjective and objective requirements on conformity of contract, were delivered to the HunID, although these could also be derived from the HunCC but at the same time the rules for the conformity of the contract were maintained in unchanged form in the HunCC applicable for all contractual relations.

The derogation options offered by the directives to Member States have mostly been used by the Hungarian legislator. Among these, it is worth highlighting the provision[283] that does not consider deviation from the objective reasons for conformity with the contract as non- conformity if the consumer was specifically informed about this at the time of conclusion of the contract and accepted this deviation separately and explicitly. Based on the previous rule, under the Section 6:157 HunCC, the obligee's performance shall not be defective if the consumer was aware of the defect at the time of conclusion of the contract or should have been aware of the defect at the time of conclusion of the contract. The twin directives' proposed solution is a better option for the consumer.

The Hungarian legislator did not used the opportunity to extend the scope of the DCD rules to B2B relations, which is criticised in the literature.[284]As a further negative development it should be added that on the altar of maximum harmonisation, the Hungarian legislator sacrificed the consumer's self-help remedies in B2C relations, by which the consumer would be entitled to repair the defect him

[281] SZILÁGYI, F. The Implementation of Directives 2019/770 and 2019/771 in Hungary. *Journal of European Consumer and Market Law.* 2021, vol. 10, no. 6, pp. 267–272.

[282] FUGLINSZKY, Á. In DE FRANCESCHI, A., SCHULZE, R. (eds.). *Harmonizing Digital Contract Law. The Impact of EU Directives 2019/770 and 2019/771 and the Regulation of Online Platforms*. Baden-Baden: Hart/Nomos, 2023, p. 365.

[283] HunID 8 § (4), 18 § (2).

[284] FUGLINSZKY, Á. In DE FRANCESCHI, A., SCHULZE, R. (eds.). *Harmonizing Digital Contract Law. The Impact of EU Directives 2019/770 and 2019/771 and the Regulation of Online Platforms*. Baden-Baden: Hart/Nomos, 2023, p. 337.

or herself or by someone else at the expense of the obligor. The survival of these remedies would have better served the circular economy, sustainability and right to repair movements in the EU.[285]

Similarly, the DCD did not deal with the qualification and typification of digital contracts, the Hungarian legislator did not define it either. Theoretically, this solution, does not create a problem concerning the scope of the Implementing Decree, but if issues outside the scope of this Decree will be dealt, it will be a challenging issue. Since the Hungarian jurisdiction must classify contracts not based on their form, but on their content, it is incumbent on the jurisdiction to judge whether a contract for work, a leasing contract, a licence contract or a mixed or atypical contract was agreed[286].

Other discrepancies were maintained, or with other words weren't dissolved by this technique of transposition. The source of the problematic goes back to the nature of the maximum harmonisation clause of the directives, which do not leave the room for discretion to the Member States. However, from the point of view of the functioning of European law, it is impossible for the European legislator to use terminology that fits the different private law of all Member States.

This approach is mirrored the most by creating uncertain and unambiguous definitions and regulatory situations, as the problematic nature of data provided on durable medium.

2.3 Data provided on durable medium

In both countries it was contested whether data belongs to digital content, if provided on a durable medium (e.g. DVD or pen drive). This issue gained attention in both countries. In the Czech Republic the national market surveillance – carried out by the Czech Trade Inspectorate- interpreted that if the digital content was delivered on a durable medium then it should be taken as a classic purchase of goods.[287] The problem was that this practice did not take into consideration whether or not it served exclusively as a carrier of digital content. Moreover,

[285] ULRICH, Á. A digitális tartalom szolgáltatására és digitális szolgáltatások nyújtására irányuló szerződések egyes vonatkozásairól szóló (EU) 2019/770 irányelv legfontosabb rendelkezései, valamint az irányelv hazai átültetése. *Európai Jog.* 2022, vol. 23, no. 3, pp. 1–10.8; FUGLINSZKY, Á. In DE FRANCESCHI, A., SCHULZE, R. (ed) *Harmonizing Digital Contract Law. The Impact of EU Directives 2019/770 and 2019/771 and the Regulation of Online Platforms.* Baden-Baden: Hart/Nomos, 2023, p. 332.

[286] VÉKÁS, L. Az uniós fogyasztói szerződési jog megújítása és az új irányelvek átültetése. *Magyar Jog.* 2021, vol. 68, no. 2, pp. 65–68.

[287] See Czech Trade Inspection, Available at: https://www.coi.cz/faq/a-co-je-vlastne-digitalni-obsah/. Assessed 8. 7. 2023.

goods with digital elements which required digital content or a digital service in order to perform their functions were also not defined; not to mention how digital services were classified. These uncertainties should be abolished by the new rules with the implementation of the DCD. In Hungary, several authors[288] considered the rules of the Twin Directives to be inconsistent in excluding digital content and services supplied on tangible media from the scope of the SGD and placing them within the scope of the DSD. The easiest regulatory way could be to handle these as consumer goods with digital elements under the scope of the SGD.

3. Data as Counter-Performance

The acknowledgement of personal data as counter-performance is what Alex Metzger considers "one of the innovative elements" of the DCD, but "empirically, it is nothing more than the approval of a social practice"[289]. Changing the synallagmatic performance of users in this way was not only a doctrinal change, but it clearly intensifies the duties and rights of both the consumer and the supplier. On one hand, consumers are entitled to have the digital content or service brought into conformity (e.g. through updates), but, on the other hand, the consumer's duty to provide data is emphasised.

3.1 A broad interpretation in Czech Republic

The new Czech wording, (Section 2389a CzCC), that "the *user* undertakes to pay a reward" is very broad. It can be immediate performance or a future one, and the rule is applicable to both B2B and B2C relations. The new rule does not further regulate whether the supplier and the user should clarify the submission of personal data as a separate contract. Neither the conclusion, nor the nullity nor the contractual obligation on data submission is specified; therefore, general contract law shall also apply to this type of counter-performance. Taking into consideration that the data are the main reward for a digital content or service, (no further fees should be paid for the digital content), the supplier will have a justifiable interest in the contractual performance of the consumer. However,

[288] FUGLINSZKY, Á. In DE FRANCESCHI, A., SCHULZE, R. (eds.). *Harmonizing Digital Contract Law. The Impact of EU Directives 2019/770 and 2019/771 and the Regulation of Online Platforms*. Baden-Baden: Hart/Nomos, 2023, p. 342; VÉKÁS, L. Az uniós fogyasztói szerződési jog megújítása és az új irányelvek átültetése. *Magyar Jog*. 2021, vol. 68, no. 2, p. 68.

[289] METZGER, A. Data as Counter-Performance: What Rights and Duties do Parties Have? *JIPITEC*. 2017, vol. 8, p. 1.

the Czech rules, similarly to the DCD, unfortunately misses the opportunity to go into more detail on which types of data could be counter-performance (e.g. only personal data in a narrow sense or data that are also sensitive[290]) or when the submission of data in the future is fulfilled. Those clarifying rules would protect consumers from contested "over-performance". The only clarification that is made in the new rules concerning contracts on digital content that are rewarded with data is that the remedies for the lack of conformity or failure to supply are only valid in B2C relations. This means that, for B2B contract relations, general contract law is applicable. Processing personal data only for the purpose of providing digital content or only to fulfil traders' legal obligations are both out of the scope of the reward.

How far the introduction of data as counter-performance will change the existing doctrine on synalagmatic performance has attracted little comment in the Czech literature; however, the Czech Authority for the Protection of Personal Data emphasized the immaterial values of personal data, which prevent them from being seen as counter-performance, which shows presumable practical problems in the future. Some of scholars criticize the legislator for not dealing conceptually with the contractual problem of data as counter-performance.[291] Štepán Richter warns further that the broad definition of data under Article 4 No 1 of the GDPR, which is also applicable to the DCD[292], can be inappropriately broad in terms of contract law. The treatment of those data that are not in *stricto sensu* personal data, but are used as such by traders because they have significant commercial value could also be problematic, because their position is not clarified by the DCD.[293] If they were to be taken as part of the reward, a disparity between the performances of the parties could occur.

3.2 Data as counter performance in Hungary

The presentation of personal-data as counter performance is undoubtedly (practically but not dogmatically) the most controversial provision of the twin directives. On the one hand, regulation can be seen as the European

[290] See clarification of Art. 4 and Art. 9 of Regulation (EU) 2016/679 of the European Parliament and of the Council of 27 April 2016 on the protection of natural persons with regard to the processing of personal data and on the free movement of such data, and repealing Directive 95/46/EC (General Data Protection Regulation).

[291] RICHTER, S. Ochrana osobních údajů v kontextu poskytování digitálních dat spotřebitelům. *Právnik*. 2021, no. 9, pp. 745–750.

[292] See Art. 2 subpara 8 of DCD.

[293] RICHTER, S. Směrnice EU 2019/770 o některých aspektech poskytování digitálního obsahu a digitálních služeb jako nástroj ochrany spotřebitele. *Jurisprudence*. 2020, vol. 4, p. 11.

legislator's response to the digital revolution and the phenomenon of big data. Regardless of whether the provision of personal data as counter performance could be integrated into the intersection of traditional private law and data protection law, it had to be adapted to the real economic circumstances: Consumers should be protected in the same way when paying with their data as if they were paying a price.

Nearby the protection of the personal data at fundamental law level, professional concerns have also been expressed about regulations encouraging payments with personal data. "The European Data Protection Supervisor warned against any new provision introducing the idea that people can pay with their data the same way as they do with money. Fundamental rights cannot be reduced to simple consumer interests, and personal data cannot be considered as a mere commodity."[294]

The Hungarian legislature did not specify whether the transfer of personal data should be regarded as a gratuitous or non-gratuitous contract. The situation can be seen a *Gordian knot*, which the European legislator did not dare to cut. The DCD accepts the real business models, that personal data are required in exchange for digital services and content, while recognising the fundamental rights protection of personal data.

The creation and transposition of the directive paved the way for personal data to be referred to in national private laws as a *special concept of consideration* or as *an extension of the scope of traditional consideration to personal data*. Although Hungarian law, with the exception of the ID, does not regulate and permits the transfer of personal data as counter performance, the question arises the same way: How to qualify these contracts, especially the tranfer of personal data? Section 6:61 of the HunCC on *the presumption of reciprocity* can help to find a way: "A consideration shall be due for a service stipulated in a contract, unless it follows otherwise from the contract or the circumstances." Since neither the parties' contract nor its circumstances imply otherwise, since they provide digital content or services in exchange for personal data, there should be presumed the reciprocal character of the contract. [295]

The question arises whether consideration must have an identifiable and measurable value? Today, business models and monopoly market players owe their success to the collection of personal data. Personal data assets become truly valuable when they are analysed, evaluated, sampled, profiled and sold for

[294] Summary of the Opinion on the Proposal for a Directive on certain aspects concerning contracts for the supply of digital content OJ C 200, 2017.6.23, pp. 10–13.

[295] Following the same logic, see FUGLINSZKY, Á. In DE FRANCESCHI, A., SCHULZE, R. (eds.). *Harmonizing Digital Contract Law. The Impact of EU Directives 2019/770 and 2019/771 and the Regulation of Online Platforms.* Baden-Baden: Hart/Nomos, 2023, p. 334.

targeted advertising. Google Services generated $69.4 billion from 2021 profits from parent company Alphabet Google, so from the market perspective, the value of personal data assets is clear, but questions remain about its quantifiability in the legal relationship between consumers and businesses.

At the same time, there are countless types of contracts in Hungary where the value of the consideration is uncertain and cannot be determined precisely; for example, in the case of maintenance and annuity contracts, but its reciprocal nature is out of question.[296] Until a special data specific measurement standard is established in order to handle the value proportionality issues, like *laesio enormis,* there will be many unresolved questions, but in fact consumers are already exchanging their personal data for digital contents and services, and they have to be protected.

3.3 Collision between DCD rules and data protection

More contested in the Czech literature is how the application of the new DCD rules will collide with the principles of data protection.[297] The protection of persons and personal data are, according to Article 8 of the Czech Constitution,[298] human rights, further specified by Article 10 Sec. 3 of the Charter of Fundamental Right and Freedoms[299], which is part of the constitutional order, where everyone is protected against unauthorized collection, disclosure or other misuse of personal data. These principles are also mirrored in the re-codified Civil Code, where the CzCC dedicates a *Division 6 Personality rights* for individuals in *Chapter II Persons.* The Czech jurisdiction gives very broad protection to personality rights. According to Section 87 CzCC, a person can anytime withdraw his or her consent for usage of personal data, also if it was given for a fixed period of time. However, the unlimited withdrawal right is also a principal idea of the GDPR, to which the DCD is without prejudice;[300] but the GDPR does not care about civil law. It can create practical problems when the consumer withdraws their consent, and how far the supplier's performance is disputed; not to mention that the consumer will hardly be able to check whether the trader has stopped using their personal data or not. The Explanatory Notes of the Act itself comments that the personal data

---

[296] FUGLINSZKY, Á. In DE FRANCESCHI, A., SCHULZE, R. (eds.). *Harmonizing Digital Contract Law. The Impact of EU Directives 2019/770 and 2019/771 and the Regulation of Online Platforms*. Baden-Baden: Hart/Nomos, 2023, p. 345.

[297] RICHTER, S. Ochrana osobních údajů v kontextu poskytování digitálních dat spotřebitelům. *Právnik*. 2021, no. 9, pp. 745–749.

[298] Ústavní zákon č. 1/1993 Sb. (Act. No. 1/1993 Coll. Constitution).

[299] Listina základních práv a svobod zákon č. 2/1993 Sb. (Act. No. 2/193 Coll. Charter of Fundamental Right and Freedoms).

[300] See Reference 37 of DCD.

provided by the consumer may be misused for purposes other than those specified in the contract.[301] Nevertheless, this risk should be minimized, primarily using the GDPR with its mechanisms and sanctions provided for by national law, but the *Division 6 Personality rights* mentioned can also be beneficial as judicial protection in civil proceedings.

Similar to the Czech law, the Hungarian Fundamental Law Article VI. Para (3)–(4) defines the right for the protection of the personal data, which is supervised by an independent authority. The HunCC nominates the personal datas' protection under the XI. Title General rules and certain personality rights 2:43 § e), that "violation of personality rights means, in particular, the violation of the right to privacy and the protection of personal data".

The final wording of the DCD and its verbatim transposition into the HunID do not provide a crystal clear doctrine of the classification of personal data as counter performance. On the one hand, the legislator ensured the enforcement of the GDPR and the protection of personal data under fundamental rights, and on the other hand, it had to ensure the acceptance of personal data as consideration in order to enable the consumer to became entitled against defective performance of contracts and to exercise warranty rights.[302] However, it considers only the supply of personal data as consideration, which risks that the "payment" with non-personal data will no longer be subject to the provisions of the DCD and the HunID.

Under DCD and HunID, we may divide the data into two main groups (personal and non-personal data of the consumer) and further sub-groups, which will be relevant for the determination of onerous nature of the contract and the consequences of termination.

In the DCD and the HunID 1 § (3) a) the personal data is referred to in three contexts: first, to personal data as counter-performance; second to personal data, provided by the consumer, which are exclusively processed by the trader for the purpose of supplying the digital content or digital service the trader does not process those data for any other purpose; and third to personal data for allowing the trader to comply with legal requirements to which the trader is subject, and the trader does not process those data for any other purpose. The distinction between personal and the differenct types of other thanpersonal data will be relevant in the context of termination of the contract. Difficulties of interpretation and application may arise from the fact that the DCD refers to several categories of

[301] Explanatory Notes to Sněmovní tisk 947/21 (Parliamentary Press 947/21), p. 98.

[302] FUGLINSZKY, Á. In DE FRANCESCHI, A., SCHULZE, R. (eds.). *Harmonizing Digital Contract Law. The Impact of EU Directives 2019/770 and 2019/771 and the Regulation of Online Platforms*. Baden-Baden: Hart/Nomos, 2023, pp. 343, and DCD Preambel 24.

data without precise definition, all of which may fall within the broad definition of personal data under the GDPR.

Non-personal data are categorised into two main groups based on the trade's postcontractuals usage rights and the duty for making these available upon the request of the consumers after termination of the contract. In generell the trader should refrain tu use the non personal datas after termination of the contract with a few exemptions under (HunID 25 § (2) a-c). Concerning non-personal data, which has been generated jointly by the consumer, and other consumers are able to continue to make use of the content, the trader should make it available at the request of the consumer after terminating the contract by the HunID 25 § (2) d).

4. Conclusion

The European legislator has long undermined national contract laws with its efforts to unify the law, which Member States have so far successfully resisted. However, digital challenges have made it necessary to harmonize consumer sales law in the European Union at a maximum level. While the primary objective of regulation was in addition to a high level of consumer protection, to remove barriers from the internal market, created by the differences in national legal systems,

Despite the maximum harmonisation approach of the Digital Content Directive, Member States' specificities did not disappeared. Based on the comparison of the Hungarian and Czech implementation of the DCD it can be summarized, that notwithstanding the similarities in the historical development of both civil law, and the common aims of national legislators to eliminate conceptual and dogmatically inconsistencies and incompatibilities between civil law and data protection; our report detects several differences in the new regulation. Companies offering digital content and services cross border will be challanged also in the future with differeces between national laws. However, the most challanging common issue in both countries will be presumably consumers' data performance as reward for digital services. The application of the new DCD rules in case of collision with the principles of data protection will definitelly create practical problems. Therefore, it will stay interesting to compare how different national courts will tackle this issue.

PART III.

COMPETITION LAW IN A DIGITAL ECONOMY

CHAPTER SEVEN

EU Regulation of On-Line Platforms: between Competition Law and Digital Markets Act

MICHAL PETR

I. Introduction

In the last decade, competition authorities have been focusing their attention on digital markets, and in particular, digital platform services. As these markets exhibit some characteristics believed to make application of "classical" competition law especially difficult, a consensus began to form in the EU that a new regulatory approach to these markets might be necessary.[303] The EU decided to adopt a specific regulatory framework concerning the digital markets, specifically, the "gatekeeper" platforms.

The new "Digital Markets Act"[304] (hereinafter referred to as "DMA") was finally adopted in 2022 and entered into force in mid-2023; thus, as of now, there is no experience with its application. In this Chapter, we would like to address several issues connected with the regulatory characteristics of the DMA. First, we will briefly introduce the specific properties of digital markets and providers of platform services from the point of view of competition law. Second, we will outline the DMA and compare its regulatory approach to the one of competition law on the one hand and sector-specific regulation on the other. Third, we will discuss whether there really was a gap in enforcement of competition law vis-à-vis

[303] For a summary of the debate, see e.g. OECD (2021). *Ex ante regulation of digital markets. OECD Competition Committee Discussion Paper*. [online]. Available at: https://www.oecd.org/daf/competition/ex-ante-regulation-and-competition-in-digital-markets-2021.pdf. Accessed 10. 5. 2023. For an overview of relevant literature, see e.g. BOTTA, M. Sector Regulation of Digital Platforms in Europe: Uno, Nessuno e Centomila. *Journal of European Competition Law & Practice*. 2021, vol. 12, no. 7, p. 501.

[304] Regulation (EU) 2022/1925 of the European Parliament and of the Council of 14 September 2022 on contestable and fair markets in the digital sector and amending Directives (EU) 2019/1937 and (EU) 2020/1828 (Digital Markets Act).

digital markets, and whether the DMA is suitable to fill this gap. And finally, we will discuss the potential conflicts between the DMA and competition law and sector-specific regulation, in particular the issue of the *ne bis in idem* principle.

II. Characteristics of Digital Markets

The economic significance of digital markets is enormous, and it continues to grow. Even before the pandemic of COVID-19, which enabled an unprecedented expansion of some digital services, it was estimated that the digital economy stands for 15.5 % of the world GDP.[305] Necessarily, competition authorities throughout the world have shifted their attention to digital services. Already in 2012 had the OECD organised its first roundtable, an informal discussion among leading competition authorities, on digital economy;[306] more than 20 roundtables have since been organised on topics closely related to digital economy.[307] Similar discussion took place in competition authorities in crucial jurisdictions; the Commission published a study *Competition Policy for Digital Era* (hereinafter referred to as the "Study")[308] in 2019.

Competition-related issues in digital markets are typically associated with core platform services.[309] Platforms may be characterised as undertakings providing services to different groups of interconnected consumers;[310] frequently, the platforms are multi-sided, meaning that the platform is active in a market where it sells different products to different groups of consumers, while the demand from one group of consumers depends on the demand from other groups of them.[311] For example, a digital content platform may feature content creators on one side, viewers of content on the other and advertisers on another.[312] As summarised by the OECD: "*Digital platforms, like any other multi-sided market, feature cross-platform network*

[305] OECD (2021), op. cit., p. 6.

[306] OECD (2102) *The Digital Economy. OECD Hearings.* [online]. Available at: https://www.oecd.org/daf/competition/The-Digital-Economy-2012.pdf. Accessed 10. 5. 2023.

[307] The documents concerning the OECD best practice roundtables on competition policy are available at: https://www.oecd.org/daf/competition/roundtables.htm. Accessed 10. 5. 2023.

[308] CREMER, J., MONJOYE, Y. A., SCHWEITZER, H. *Competition Policy for the Digital Era.* [online]. Available at: https://ec.europa.eu/competition/publications/reports/kd0419345enn.pdf. Accessed 10. 5. 2023.

[309] EVANS, D. S. The Antitrust Economics of Multisided Platform Markets. *Yale Journal on Regulation.* 2023, vol. 20, no. 2, pp. 325–381.

[310] OECD (2022) *OECD Handbook on Competition Policy in the Digital Age*. [online]. Available at: https://www.oecd.org/daf/competition/oecd-handbook-on-competition-policy-in-the-digital-age.pdf. Accessed 10. 5. 2023, p. 10.

[311] Ibid.

[312] Ibid, op. cit., p. 13.

effects, which mean that a firm's decisions in one side of the market for example on pricing, affect demand on another. These network effects can lead to market power and amplify the impacts of anti-competitive conduct, but they may also [...] generate significant consumer benefits, for example by enabling cross-subsidisation."[313]

Innovation is often disruptive. The characteristic feature of platforms is that they typically do not enter into existing markets or expand them: they create new markets and replace the traditional ones with them.[314]

New market definitions therefore need to be found for digital platforms. This is however complicated by the multi-sided nature of these markets, uncommon to traditional competition law, and by the fact that the services of the platforms are frequently not paid for by final consumers;[315] conversely, in traditional competition law, market definitions are based on price-related tests.[316] Without the price, platforms generally compete on quality and innovation,[317] and compete rather for attention of the consumers than directly for their money.[318] The consumers' choice is however limited by network effects – the quality of a platform is frequently defined by the number of people using it. Thus, consumers may be dissuaded from switching to a more innovative, higher-quality platform simply because it is not (yet) used by a sufficient number of other users.

Digital economy and platforms in particular are characterised by extreme return to scale, network externalities and the role of data.[319] This generally gives them significant market power. Because of these characteristics, digital platform services are of interest to competition authorities.

Indeed, the number of investigations in digital markets has grown significantly in the past years. The proceedings are however characterised by extraordinary length;

---

[313] Ibid, p. 17. It adds that: *"Advertising plays a particularly important role in many of these multi-sided digital markets, especially when services are provided to consumers free of charge, as is often the case for search-engines and social networks.* "

[314] Cohen, J. E. Law for the Platform Economy. *Georgetown Law Technology Review*. 2018, vol. 2, no. 2, p. 191.

[315] Even though this may be offset by charging other sides of the market. OECD (2022), op. cit., p. 17: *"Advertising plays a particularly important role in [...] multi-sided digital markets, especially when services are provided to consumers free of charge, as is often the case for search-engines and social networks.* "

[316] Solek, L. Need to Revise or Apply the Concept of Market Definition with a View to 'Zero-Price' and Overarching Markets. *Journal of European Competition Law & Practice*. 2021, vol. 12, no. 8, p. 595.

[317] JENNY, F. Changing the way we think: competition, platforms and ecosystems. *Journal of Antitrust Enforcement.* 2021, vol. 9, 3.

[318] EVANS, D. S. *The Economics of Attention Markets.* [online]. Available at: https://ssrn.com/abstract=3044858. Accessed 10. 5. 2023; NEWMAN, J. M. *Antitrust in Attention Markets: Defintion, Power, Harm. University of Miami Legal studies Research Paper No 3744839.* [online]. Available at: https://ssrn.com/abstract=3745839. Accessed 10. 5. 2023

[319] The Study, p. 2.

also, the threat of a sanction must not be a sufficient deterrent for tech business and the *ad hoc* remedies, imposed in individual cases, may not be sufficient to address the systemic problems in the relevant markets.[320] The question therefore emerged, whether competition law alone is able to effectively regulate these markets.

In the EU, the Study concluded it is not. It described the characteristics of digital economy, the role of competition policy in its effective functioning and possible regulatory changes that might be necessary in order to unlock its full potential. It stressed that it is necessary to promote both the competition for the market (i.e., enable other platforms to acquire critical mass of users) and in the market (i.e. prevent abusive behaviour of the dominant platform).[321] It however concluded that a vigorous enforcement of competition law in digital markets may not be enough, as *"[i]n some areas, we propose that a regulatory regime may be needed in the longer run"*.[322]

This thinking was translated into the DMA. It focuses on three broadly understood activities of providers of platform services:[323] entrenching and strengthening the position of a gatekeeper on a specific platform; leveraging the market power from the platform to adjacent activities; and exploitation of the position of the gatekeeper within the platform. With regard to these activities, the DMA introduces a new regulatory regime of obligations, as will be described below.

III. Regulatory Characteristics of DMA

On the first sight, DMA is not a part of competition law. It expressly tells so in its preamble.[324] Many scholars support this view, while others oppose it, as will be discusses below. It nonetheless needs to be observed that there are significant differences between "classic" competition law and the DMA. Whereas the competition law decides in principle *ex post* whether competition rules had been broken, DMA imposes *ex ante* obligations. Arguably, DMA also pursues different objectives than the competition law. The DMA is therefore often described as more akin to sector-specific regulation, in particular the regulation of electronic communications, than to competition law;[325] even in this regard, however, the differences prevail.

---

[320] BOTTA, M., op. cit., p. 501.
[321] The Study, p. 6.
[322] Ibid., p. 126.
[323] IBÁŇEZ COLOMO, P. The Draft Digital Markets Act: A Legal and Institutional Analysis. *Journal of European Competition Law & Practice*. 2021, vol. 12, no. 7, p. 563.
[324] DMA, par. 10: the DMA *"aims to complement the enforcement of competition law"*.
[325] IBÁŇEZ COLOMO, P., op. cit., p. 562.

In order to understand the regulatory character of the DMA, we will first discuss the objectives of the DMA, followed by analysis of the way it pursues them, compared with the regulatory regime of electronic communications, and on the basis of this, attempt to describe its position vis-à-vis competition law.

1. DMA's Objectives

The DMA's purpose *"is to contribute to the proper functioning of the internal market by laying down harmonised rules ensuring for all businesses, contestable and fair markets in the digital sector across the Union where gatekeepers are present, to the benefit of business users and end users"*.[326] The DMA thus seems to be pursuing two objectives: first, that the markets become and remain contestable, and second, that the functioning of these markets is fair.[327]

These on the first sight diverge from the objectives of the competition law; as the DMA itself puts it: competition rules *"have as their objective the* ***protection of undistorted competition*** *on the market. This Regulation pursues an objective that is* ***complementary to, but different*** *from that of protecting undistorted competition on any given market, as defined in competition-law terms, which is to ensure that* ***markets where gatekeepers are present are and remain contestable and fair****,* ***independently*** *from the actual, potential or presumed* ***effects of the conduct of a given gatekeeper*** *covered by this Regulation* ***on competition on a given market****. This Regulation therefore aims to protect a different legal interest from that protected by those rules and it should apply without prejudice to their application"*.[328]

On a closer look, however, these sets of goals are not as far removed from each other as the proposal would like to suggest.[329] Indeed, both competition law and the DMA seek to promote contestability and fairness in markets.[330] As summarised by Professor Komninos, *"the 'DNA' of the DMA is competition law and* ***both of the two proclaimed objectives of the DMA, fairness and contestability, are inextricably linked with competition law****"*.[331]

---

[326] DMA, Art. 1 (1)

[327] DMA, paras 4–8; IBÁÑEZ COLOMO, P., op. cit., p. 563.

[328] DMA, para 10; emphasis added.

[329] LAROUCHE, P., DE STREEL, A. The European Digital Markets Act: A Revolution Grounded on Traditions. *Journal of European Competition Law & Practice*. 2021, vol. 12, no. 7, p. 544.

[330] MONTI, G. The Digital Markets Act: Improving the Institutional Design. *Journal of European Competition Law & Practice*. 2021, vol. 12, no. 2, p. 98.

[331] KOMNINOS, A. *The Digital Markets Act: How Does it Compare with Competition Law*. [online]. Available at: https://papers.ssrn.com/sol3/papers.cfm?abstract_id=4136146. Accessed 10. 5. 2023, p. 6; emphasis added.

However, even though competition law and the DMA aim at – at the least – similar goals,[332] their regulatory approach is clearly different: for the competition law to be enforced, it must in principle be established that the conduct in question has as its object or effect distortion of competition in the market; the undertakings concerned may claim efficiencies and objective justification for their conduct.[333] Conversely, nothing similar needs to be established under the DMA regime, only the fact that its rules have been broken; for the DMA to be breached, it is not necessary to establish that the conduct in question actually affected fairness or contestability of the market.[334]

The logic of intervention is thus completely different: whereas the key obligation of undertakings under competition law is not to engage in behaviour capable of distorting competition and the competition authority assesses *ex post* whether there had been an infringement, in case of DMA, it is for the undertakings to define *ex ante* how they intend to comply with the obligations set by the DMA, and for the enforcement authority to check whether they adhere to these rules.[335]

As summarised by Professor Petit: *"the DMA, unlike the system of control of abuse, is not a system of discretionary supervision of bad behaviour by firms with gatekeeping positions. A specified list of prescriptive and proscriptive rules applies as soon as a firm is designated as a gatekeeper. There is no requirement of 'improper' use of gatekeeping power that triggers application of the rules. And there is no process of evaluation of 'improper' purpose or effect, negligence or deliberateness. The DMA is both a 'no fault' regime and a per se prescription and proscription system."*[336]

Coming back to the question of objectives, even though the DMA pursues similar objectives as the competition law – a functioning competition – they aim to protect the competition from different dangers: whereas the competition law aims at preventing the distortion of competition by market power of the undertakings concerned, the DMA is not limited in this way. Thus, the scope of the DMA is broader, and, arguably, the objectives of the two sets of regulation differ.

---

[332] PETIT, N. The Proposed Digital Markets Act: A Legal and Policy Review. *Journal of European Competition Law & Practice*. 2021, vol. 12, no. 7, p. 530.

[333] DMA, recital 10, characterises competition law as rules *"that are based on an individualised assessment of market positions and behaviour, including its actual or potential effects and the precise scope of the prohibited behaviour, and which provide for the possibility of undertakings to make efficiency and objective justification arguments for the behaviour in question"*.

[334] KOMNINOS, A., op. cit., p. 2.

[335] IBÁŇEZ COLOMO, P., op. cit., p. 562.

[336] PETIT, N., op. cit., p. 532.

Finally, is also necessary to compare the objectives of the DMA with the objectives of sector-specific regulation; in the latter, case, it is the liberalization of the market.[337] It is widely accepted that the objectives of sector-specific regulation and of the competition law differ. As summarised by AG Bobek in the recent case *bpost*: *"[S]ectoral and competition proceedings seem to be linked to the protection of a different legal interest and to a legislation pursuing a different objective. First, in terms of the protected legal interest, achieving liberalization of certain, previously monopolistic, markets follows a different logic than the ongoing and horizontal protection of competition. Second, that is also evident with regard to the undesirable consequences that punishment of each of the offences is intended to prevent. If the aim is to liberalise a sector, than potential harm caused to competition upstream or downstream is not necessarily an issue that the sectoral regulatory framework must tackle. By contrast, an abuse of a dominant position that results in a distortion of competition upstream or downstream from the dominant undertaking is very much a concern of competition rules."*[338]

In our opinion, the same logic applies to the relationship between the DMA and sector-specific regulation. Thus, to summarise, we take the view that the DMA indeed pursues a specific objective, complementary, but not identical with that of competition law and sector-specific regulation. That will be particularly relevant for the discussion of the *ne bis in idem* principle in the Section below. Before that, we will first discuss the regulatory characteristics of the DMA itself.

2. Obligations imposed by the DMA

After outlining the objectives of the DMA, it is necessary to discuss the means by which it aims at fulfilling them. On the basis of this, we shall outline the regulatory character of the.

The DMA regime applies to gatekeepers, i.e. to undertakings providing core platform services.[339] Without going into details on this issue, an undertaking shall be designed as a gatekeeper if it (i) has a significant impact on the internal market; (ii) provides a core platform service which is an important gateway for business

[337] C-117/20 bpost SA v. Autorité belge de la concurrence, ECLI:EU:C:2022:202, para 45.

[338] Opinion of AG Bobek in case C-117/20 bpost SA v Autorité belge de la concurrence, ECLI:EU:C:2021:680, para 162.

[339] DMA, Art. 1 (2). By core platform services, the DMA, Art. 2 (2), understands online intermediation services, online search engines, online social networking services, video-sharing platform services, number-independent interpersonal communication services, operating systems, web browsers, virtual assistants, cloud computing services and online advertising services. For the definitions of these terms, see DMA, Art. 2 (3)–(13).

users to reach end users; and (iii) enjoys an entrenched and durable position, in its operations, or it is foreseeable that it will enjoy such a position in the near future.[340] Unlike in case of dominant position under competition law, where the actual market power of the undertaking in question needs to be measure in every case, the characteristics of the gatekeeper may be presumed if the undertaking in question exceeds the turnover thresholds, prescribed by the DMA.[341]

This presumption may only be rebutted if the undertaking provides sufficiently substantiated arguments demonstrating that due to the circumstances in which the relevant core platform service operates, it does not satisfy the requirements listed above.[342] Similarly, an undertaking providing core platform services may be designated a gatekeeper even if it does not exceed the prescribed turnovers.[343] Notwithstanding this, the position of a gatekeeper will generally rely on its turnover, not actual determination of its market power. Thus, the concept of gatekeeping appears broader than the concept of dominance, in the sense that several platforms might be gatekeepers of a similar core platform service, like for example, application stores.[344]

Similarly, the obligations imposed by the DMA, in particular in its Articles 5, 6 and 7, contain prohibitions, applicable without measuring their actual effects on the market; these are in essence *per se* rules, independent from any assessment of their specific impact on competition.[345] Unlike the competition law, which contains prohibitions of competition-distorting conduct, the DMA is proscriptive and prescriptive.[346]

The individual obligations fall within four distinctive categories: (i) preventing opaque and asymmetric access to data and information, (ii) limiting obstacles to interoperability, (iii) setting conditions for obtaining access to end-users and (iv) empowering consumers.[347] It is not our intention to discuss the content of these obligations in detail.[348] It is however remarkable that many of these prohibitions reflect activities, enforceable under competition rules,[349] including for example the most-favoured nation clauses,[350] self-preferencing[351] or other

[340] DMA, Art. 3 (1).
[341] DMA, para 23 and Art. 3 (2).
[342] DMA, Art. 3 (5).
[343] DMA, Art. 3 (8).
[344] PETIT, N., op. cit., p. 532.
[345] PETIT, N., op. cit., p. 530.
[346] PETIT, N., op. cit., p. 535.
[347] CHIRICO, F. Digital Markets Act. A Regulatory Perspective. *Journal of European Competition Law & Practice*. 2021, vol. 12, no. 7, p. 495.
[348] For a detailed description, see e.g. IBÁÑEZ COLOMO, P., op. cit., pp. 564–566
[349] KOMNINOS, A., op. cit., p. 4; PETIT, N., op. cit., p. 535.
[350] DMA, Art. 5 (3). This was investigated for example in the *Booking.com* case.
[351] DMA, Art. 6 (2) and 5, resembling the investigation of *Google Search (Shopping)* and *Amazon*.

practices currently under investigation, e.g. the possibility to install third-party software applications and software application stores.[352]

It has been observed that the list to some extent resembles a guidance paper, running ahead of competition law developments and trying to pre-emptively lay down the rules.[353] Still, the DMA remains an *ex ante* tool laying down future obligations, not a set of *ex post* prohibitions. Thus, many obligations contained in the DMA go beyond the current focus of competition law, including e.g. the end users' right to un-install unwanted software applications[354] or a broadly-framed obligation to enable interoperability for software and hardware.[355]

In accordance with the *ex ante* approach, the gatekeeper shall ensure and demonstrate compliance with these obligations, while the implementing measures need to ensure effectivity in achieving the objectives of the DMA.[356] This leads us back to the question, to what extend does the regime of the DMA resemble competition law or sectoral regulation.

Even though on the first sight, the DMA is similar to sectoral regimes, in particular the Electronic Communications Code,[357] the differences are significant. Crucially, the objective of sectoral regulation is to *promote competition* in the provision of electronic communications networks and associated facilities;[358] the Electronic Communications Code *"aims to progressively reduce ex ante sector-specific rules as competition in the markets develops and,* ***ultimately, to ensure that electronic communications are governed only by competition law****"*.[359] The DMA does not have any such ambition, its scope is not time-limited.

Similarly, any *ex ante* intervention on the basis of the Electronic Communications Code is conditional on finding that market is not effectively competitive and competition law alone is insufficient to adequately address the market failure;[360] obligations are imposed on "undertakings with significant market power", defined as a "position equivalent to dominance", as understood in the competition law.[361] Unlike the DMA, the framework of the Electronic Communications Code is thus *"expressly biased against intervention"*,[362] which is subsidiary to the tools of competition law; conversely, the DMA foresees a permanent overlap

[352] DMA, Art 6 (4), resembling the investigation of *Apple Store*.
[353] LAROUCHE, P., DE STREEL, A., op. cit., p. 547.
[354] DMA, Art. 6 (3).
[355] DMA, Art. 7.
[356] DMA, Art. 8 (1).
[357] Directive (EU) 2018/1972 of the European Parliament and of the Council of 11 December 2018 establishing the European Electronic Communications Code (Recast).
[358] Electronic Communications Code, Art. 3 (2) (b).
[359] Electronic Communications Code, recital 29; emphasis added.
[360] Electronic Communications Code, Art. 67 (1).
[361] Electronic Communications Code, Art. 63 (2).
[362] IBÁŇEZ COLOMO, P., op. cit., p. 569.

with competition law.[363] The intervention under the DMA is dependant solely on the question whether an undertaking is designated as a gatekeeper, not the actual effects of its conduct.

Thus, in most cases, the analysis under the Electronic Communications Code is much more similar to the competition law than to the DMA.[364] In case of electronic communications, the regulatory authority needs to define the relevant market, find an undertaking with significant market power and devise appropriate remedies; conversely, in case of the DMA, irrespective of the quality of competition in the market, the gatekeepers are themselves to implement measures securing compliance with the DMA-imposed obligations.

The similarities and differences among the DMA, the competition law and sector-specific regulation are summarised in a simple table below. As is evident from the above, no simple pattern may be discerned.

	Competition	**Sector-specific**	**DMA**
Scope			
Sector-specific		X	X
Time-limited		X	
Intervention			
General rules	X	X	
Effects-based	X	X	
Ex ante obligations		X	X

The regulatory approach of the DMA is clearly not a sector-specific regulation, akin to Electronic Communications Code; only the *ex ante* approach is similar, as well as the limited scope. At the same time, it is questionable whether the DMA is part of competition law. Even though heavily inspired by it, the legislator insists it is not;[365] many scholars agree. Conversely, others argue that the DMA is in fact a sector-specific competition law[366] or *ex ante* competition law.[367]

The question whether the DMA is a specific competition law or not is however mostly an academic one, without specific practical consequences. It is however clear that the DMA brings more obligations than the "traditional" competition law would. The next question, addressed in the following Sections, therefore is, whether these new obligations are justified.

---

[363] Ibid., p. 570.

[364] Ibid., p. 571.

[365] KOMNINOS, A., op. cit., p. 1.

[366] PETIT, N., op. cit., p. 529.

[367] KOMNINOS, A., op. cit., p. 7.

3. More than competition law

Given the fact that a significant number of prohibitions contained in the DMA correspond with the cases actually investigated by the competition authorities under the competition rules currently in place, it can legitimately be asked whether there really was a need for the adoption of the DMA.

As has already been observed, the DMA significantly diverges from the competition law. First, by not requiring the proof of significant market power and its abuse amounting to the distortion of competition, the enforcement is significantly easier. As observed by Professor Monti: *"not that there is an absence of law in relation to regulating platforms, but [...] procedural and substantive requirements in competition law are seen as a barrier to effective enforcement."*[368]

Are practical difficulties with establishing an infringement in itself a sufficient reason to introduce new regulation? Arguably not; it may be argued that when the traditional antitrust is sufficiently effective in other markets, the enforcers may – even with an extra effort and with the help of interim measures and other less commonly used instruments – succeed in digital ones as well.[369]

A more convincing argument might be that the scope of the DMA is broader, covering practices of undertakings not necessarily wielding significant market power and unfair practices which do not necessarily produce anticompetitive effects.[370] Thus, instead of broad prohibitions of practices linked with the abuse of market power, the DMA introduces a long list of *per se* rules.[371] Such a system may be effectively enforced, it is however not flexible, which may be a problem in dynamic markets.[372]

Most persuasive may therefore be the argument that the DMA strives not only to prohibit specific kinds of conduct, but to set general rules for the market; thus, activities distorting the market only in connection with other measures may effectively by regulated.[373] Instead of prohibitions, it contains prescriptive obligations. Thus, as argued by Professor Monti: *"the DMA is more than an enhanced and simplified application of Article 102 TFEU: while the* obligations *may be criticised as being based on existing competition concerns, they are*

[368] MONTI, G., op. cit., p. 90.

[369] GÖNENÇ, G., KAĞAN, A. U., YILDIZ, G. Is there a Need for a Visible Hand in Digital Markets? *European Competition and Regulatory Law Journal*. 2022, vol. 6, no. 4, p. 316.

[370] LAROUCHE, P., DE STREEL, A., op. cit., p. 545.

[371] KOMNINOS, A., op. cit., p. 3.

[372] Ibid., p. 4.

[373] MONTI, G., op. cit., p. 91: *"Arguably, this framework is more effective in achieving contestability than the use of competition law: not only is this conduct prohibited automatically without the need to show likely anticompetitive effects, but the comprehensive list of prohibitions targets various forms of conduct which cumulatively restrict market access."*

forward-looking in trying to create a regulatory environment where gatekeeper power is contained and perhaps even reduced."[374]

It may be questioned whether the digital economy indeed requires a specific regulation;[375] however, as we have discussed in Section 2, the specifics of platforms are such that it cannot be simply ruled out. In any event, the shortcomings of the markets dominated by gatekeeper platforms seems to be adequately addressed by the DMA. This leads us to the final question: may the DMA be applied in parallel with the competition law and/or the sector-specific regulation, and would such a parallel application be in line with the *ne bis in idem* principle?

IV. Conflicts with Competition Law and Sector-specific Regulation

As has been discussed above, both competition law and sector-specific regulation address similar issues in the market, focussing on the competitiveness of the markets in question. These regulations are applied by distinct enforcers – competition authorities, both the Commission and National Competition Authorities (hereinafter referred to as "NCAs"), on the one side, and National Regulatory Authorities (hereinafter referred to as "NRAs"), on the other; these regulators conduct different proceedings according to different rules. It may therefore happen that the same conduct of the same undertaking breaches at the same time both sets of rules, and may therefore be subject to parallel proceedings of the competition authorities and the NRAs. Below, we will discuss the case-law of the Court of Justice of the European Union (hereinafter referred to as "CJEU") addressing the question, under what conditions are such parallel proceedings in line with the *ne bis in idem* principle, guaranteed by Article 50 of the Charter of the Fundamental Rights of the European Union (hereinafter referred to as the "Charter").

May similar issue of parallel proceedings appear with respect to the DMA? Arguably, it may. The DMA may be applied only by the Commission. Even though most probably, the Commission would opt to avoid two sets of proceedings concerning the same conduct of the same undertaking, the parallel proceedings are in principle imaginable. In addition to that, the EU competition

---

374 Ibid., p. 92.

375 GÖNENÇ, G., KAĞAN, A. U., YILDIZ, G., op. cit., p. 312: *"The recent extensive legislative efforts in a market which corrects itself are simply the results of ongoing lobbying activities against tech giants or hindsight bias. Even if introduced, these regulative efforts would only serve to punish market leaders, undermining the level playing field in digital markets under the guise of public interest."*

law may be applied not only by the Commission, but by the NCAs as well; in that case, the NCAs would have no obstacles intervening on the basis of Article 102 TFEU. The same applies to the possibility of parallel application of the DMA by the Commission and sector-specific regulation by the NRAs.

May such parallel proceedings be in breach of the *ne bis in idem principle*? To answer this question, we will first discuss the recent *bpost* judgment of the CJEU, concerning the parallel enforcement of competition law and sector-specific regulation. We will then move to the DMA.

1. *Ne bis in idem in the bpost case*

The issue of the *ne bis in idem* principle, as applied in the area of competition law and compared to the "general" interpretation of this principle by the CJEU and the European Court of Human Rights, has been subject to discussion for many years.[376] The latest addition to this debate have been two recent judgments of the CJEU, one concerning the competition law itself[377] and the other – the *bpost* judgment – concerning the relationship between the competition law and sector-specific regulation.

The case itself was concerned with the conduct of the incumbent postal services provider in Belgium, specifically its tariffs for the distribution of addressed advertising material and administrative mail items. This system was found to be in breach of postal regulation by the Belgian Institute for Postal Services and Telecommunications, the Belgian NRA, in particular because of alleged discrimination. A year later, the same tariff was scrutinised by the Belgian NCA, that found an exclusionary abuse of dominance. This latter decision was found in breach of the *ne bis in idem* principle by a court. On appeal, a question concerning the interpretation of this principle was addressed to the CJEU.[378]

The CJEU, recalling its *Menci* judgment,[379] repeated that the *ne bis in idem* principle is based on *idem factum*, not idem *crimen*,[380] i.e. only the facts of the case are decisive, not their legal qualification: *"the relevant criterion for the purposes of assessing the existence of the same offence* ***identity of the material acts****, understood as the existence of a set of concrete circumstances which are*

[376] See e.g. PETR, M. Twice about ne bis in idem: Conflicting Approach of European Courts to the Same Principle. *Czech Yearbook of Public & Private International Law*. 2017, vol. 8, p. 210.

[377] C-151/20 Bundeswettbewerbsbehörde v Nordzucker AG and Others, ECLI:EU:C:2022:203.

[378] For details on this case DEWISPELAERE, J., GHYSELS, T. The Duplication of Proceedings and Penalties under Sectoral Rules and Competition Law Recast: Toshiba Is Dead, Long Live Bpost? *European Competition and Regulatory Law Journal*. 2022, vol. 6, no. 3, pp. 278–283

[379] C-524/15 Criminal proceedings against Luca Menci, ECLI:EU:C:2018:197.

[380] AG opinion in C-117/20 bpost, op. cit., paras 40 and 41.

inextricably linked together [...]. ***[T]he legal classification*** *[...] of the facts* ***and the legal interest protected are not relevant*** *for the purposes of establishing the existence of the same offence."*[381]

That would clearly prevent the parallel application of competition law and sector-specific regulation; parallel investigations concerning the same facts, despite on the basis of different sets of regulation, *"would constitute a limitation of the fundamental right guaranteed by Article 50 of the Charter"*.[382] The CJEU however added that a limitation of a fundamental right may be justified on the basis of Article 52 (1) of the Charter,[383] according to which: *"Any limitation on the exercise of the rights and freedoms recognised by this Charter must be provided for by law and respect the essence of those rights and freedoms. Subject to the principle of proportionality, limitations may be made only if they are necessary and genuinely meet objectives of general interest recognised by the Union or the need to protect the rights and freedoms of others."*

The CJEU requires that not only is the possibility of parallel proceedings provided for by law, but also that the different sets of legislation "*pursue distinct legitimate objectives*".[384] As discussed above, this is generally the case with competition law and sector-specific regulation.

Further, for the principle of proportionality to be met, the additional burden on the infringer, caused by the duplication of proceedings, must be justified by the two objectives pursued and not be excessive: *"public authorities can legitimately choose complementary legal responses to certain conduct that is harmful to society through* ***different procedures forming a coherent whole*** *so as to address different aspects of the social problem involved, provided that the accumulated legal responses do not represent an excessive burden for the individual concerned."*[385] Again, this requirement is generally met with respect to competition law and sector-specific regulation.

And finally, in order to meet the criterion of strict necessity of the duplication of proceedings, the parallel proceedings must be predictable, coordinated and conducted within a proximate timeframe, with the second penalty taking into account the first one.[386] These conditions were also satisfied in the *bpost* case.

[381] C-117/20 bpost, op. cit., paras 33 and 34.

[382] Ibid., para 39.

[383] Ibid., para 40.

[384] Ibid., para 44. The CJEU concluded in para 47: *"It is therefore legitimate, for the purposes of guaranteeing the ongoing liberalisation of the internal market (...), while ensuring the proper functioning of the market, for a Member State to punish infringements, on the one hand, of sectoral rules (...), and, on the other, of the rules applicable to competition law."*

[385] Ibid., para 49.

[386] Ibid., para 51: *It is necessary to assess whether there are clear and precise rules making it possible to predict which acts or omissions are liable to be subject to a duplication of proceedings and penalties, and also to predict that there will be coordination between the different*

May these conditions be met with respect to the parallel proceedings on the basis of the DMA on the one hand, and competition law or sector-specific regulation on the other?

2. *Ne bis in idem and the application of the DMA*

Having in mind the conclusions of the CJEU in the *bpost* case, enforcement of the DMA in parallel with competition law or sector-specific regulation would infringe Article 50 of the Charter, it might however be justified according to Article 52 (1) of the Charter.

Concerning the competition law, we have suggested above that the objectives of the DMA and competition law are not identical. The DMA envisages parallel proceedings and sets specific rules for the cooperation and coordination with NCAs.[387] We put forward that in this regard, the *bpost*-test may be met.

The situation is less clear concerning the sector-specific regulation. The objectives of the DMA and the sector-specific regulation differ, as has been discussed above. The possibility of parallel proceedings and their coordination is outlined only very lightly in the DMA,[388] it however broadly corresponds with the *bpost* requirements. The predictability of parallel proceedings is also less certain; but admittedly, it is significantly less probable than parallel proceedings with competition law. We thus put forward that the *bpost* test would be met in case of parallel proceedings with sector-specific regulation as well.

V. Conclusion

The DMA is a brand-new piece of legislation, designed to remedy specific problems in digital markets dominated by the providers of core platform services. Its regulatory characteristics differ significantly from both the competition law and sector-specific regulation. Crucially, these three sets of regulation seem to have different objectives and employ different tools to achieve them.

---

authorities, whether the two sets of proceedings have been conducted in a manner that is sufficiently coordinated and within a proximate timeframe and whether any penalty that may have been imposed in the proceedings that were first in time was taken into account in the assessment of the second penalty, meaning that the resulting burden, for the persons concerned, of such duplication is limited to what is strictly necessary and the overall penalties imposed correspond to the seriousness of the offences committed".

387 DMA, Art. 38.

388 DMA, para 86 and Art. 37.

On the first sight, the tools introduced by the DMA seem to be adequate to address the specific problems associated with the regulation of digital markets; only the future practice of the Commission may however confirm this presumption.

The application of the DMA is not exclusive, the same conduct of the same undertakings might be investigated also by competition authorities or, more exceptionally, by national regulatory authorities. Even though specific circumstances of individual cases would be decisive to assess it, we believe that in principle, such a parallel application would be in line with the *ne bis in idem* principle, as interpreted by the CJEU.

CHAPTER EIGHT

Private Enforcement of the Digital Markets Act: Filling Holes and Creating New Ones in Harmonized Enforcement

ONDREJ BLAŽO

1. Introduction

The recent decade has witnessed several new elements or innovations in the European Union: partial regulation of damages claims related to harm caused by violation of competition rules,[389] strengthening powers of national competition authorities (NCAs)[390] and a new pro-competition instrument on ex-ante regulation of designated gatekeepers – the Digital Markets Act (DMA).[391] Along these legislative acts, update of block exemptions and the soft law of the European Commission reflect current challenges of the digital economy and functioning of digital markets, as well as sustainability and green transition aspects. The adoption of the DMA was followed by vigorous discussion in academia, on the position of the DMA, its legal basis, its provisions and its relationship with competition law and to ex-ante regulation.[392] These discussions are not surprising

[389] Directive 2014/104/EU of the European Parliament and of the Council of 26 November 2014 on certain rules governing actions for damages under national law for infringements of the competition law provisions of the Member States and of the European Union Text (OJ L 349, 5. 12. 2014, pp. 1–19) (hereinafter "Damages Directive").

[390] Directive (EU) 2019/1 of the European Parliament and of the Council of 11 December 2018 to empower the competition authorities of the Member States to be more effective enforcers and to ensure the proper functioning of the internal market (OJ L 11, 14. 1. 2019, pp. 3–33) (hereinafter "ECN+ Directive").

[391] Regulation (EU) 2022/1925 of the European Parliament and of the Council of 14 September 2022 on contestable and fair markets in the digital sector and amending Directives (EU) 2019/1937 and (EU) 2020/1828 (Digital Markets Act) (OJ L 265, 12. 10. 2022, pp. 1–66).

[392] E.g., PETIT, N. The Proposed Digital Markets Act (DMA): A Legal and Policy Review. *Journal of European Competition Law and Practice.* [online]. 2021, vol. 12, no. 7. DOI: 10.1093/jeclap/lpab062; IBÁÑEZ COLOMO, P. The Draft Digital Markets Act: A Legal and Institutional Analysis. *Journal of European Competition Law & Practice.* [online]. 2021, vol. 12, no. 7. DOI: 10.1093/jeclap/lpab065; LAMADRID DE PABLO, A., BAYÓN

because the DMA did not come out of the blue but it is an apparent reaction to previous and pending cases against the BigTech launched under EU or national competition law.[393] The regulation of BigTech became the EU's existential due to the economic power of the BigTech and the limits of traditional ex-post control by competition law in the dynamic digital markets.[394]

The enforcement regime is 'Commission-centric' – Article 16 to 36 DMA provide a comprehensive system of investigation and sanction powers of the

FERNÁNDEZ, N. Why the Proposed DMA Might Be Illegal under Article 114 TFEU, and How to Fix It. *Journal of European Competition Law and Practice.* [online]. 2021, vol. 12, no. 7. DOI: 10.1093/jeclap/lpab059; ŠMEJKAL, V. Abuse of Dominance and the DMA – Differing Objectives or Prevailing Continuity? *Auc Iuridica.* [online]. 2023, vol. 69, no. 2. DOI: 10.14712/23366478.2023.13; PODSZUN, R. From Competition Law to Platform Regulation – Regulatory Choices for the Digital Markets Act. *Economics.* [online]. 2023, vol. 17, no. 1. DOI: 10.1515/econ-2022-0037.

393 PARKER, G., PETROPOULOS, G., VAN ALSTYNE, M. Platform mergers and antitrust. *Industrial and Corporate Change.* [online]. 2021, vol. 30, no. 5. DOI: 10.1093/icc/dtab048; BOTTA, M., WIEDEMANN, K. The interaction of EU competition, consumer, and data protection law in the digital economy: The regulatory dilemma in the facebook odyssey. *Antitrust Bulletin* [online]. 2019, vol. 64, no. 3. DOI: 10.1177/0003603X19863590; PATAKYOVÁ, M. T., MAZÚR, J. Facebook – Global Issue without (Existing) Solution? In KLIEŠTIK, T. (ed.). *18th International Scientific Conference Globalization and Its Socio-Economic Consequences.* Žilina: 2018; MAZÚR, J., PATAKYOVÁ, M. T. Regulatory Approaches to Facebook and Other Social Media Platforms: Towards Platforms Design Accountability. *Masaryk University Journal of Law and Technology* [online]. 2019, vol. 13, no. 2. DOI: 10.5817/MUJLT2019-2-4; BOTTA, M., WIEDEMANN, K. Exploitative conducts in digital markets: Time for a discussion after the facebook decision. *Journal of European Competition Law and Practice* [online]. 2019, vol. 10, no. 8. DOI: 10.1093/jeclap/lpz064; CARUGATI, Ch. The 2017 facebook saga: A competition, consumer and data protection story. *European Competition and Regulatory Law Review* [online]. 2018, vol. 2, no. 1. DOI: 10.21552/core/2018/1/4; VAN DEN BERGH, R., WEBER, F. The german facebook saga: Abuse of dominance or abuse of competition law? *World Competition.* 2021, vol. 44, no. 1; CHIRITA, A. Google's Anti-Competitive and Unfair Practices in Digital Leisure Markets. *The Competition law review.* 2015, vol. 11, no. 1; JAKAB, M. Google Android: Behavioural Theories of Harm in the Light of New Judgments and Regulatory Tools. *Auc Iuridica* [online]. 2023, vol. 69, no. 2. DOI: 10.14712/23366478.2023.17; GAUDIN, G., MANTZARI, D. Google Shopping and the As-Efficient-Competitor Test: Taking Stock and Looking Ahead. *Journal of European Competition Law and Practice* [online]. 2022, vol. 13, no. 2. DOI: 10.1093/jeclap/lpac006; NICOLI, N., IOSIFIDIS, P. EU digital economy competition policy: From ex-post to ex-ante. The case of Alphabet, Amazon, Apple, and Meta. *Global Media and China* [online]. 2023, vol. 8,, no. 1. DOI: 10.1177/20594364231152673.

394 E.g., GERBRANDY, A., PHOA, P. The Power of Big Tech Corporations as Modern Bigness and a Vocabulary for Shaping Competition Law as Counter-Power. *Wealth and Power* [online]. New York: Routledge, 2022. DOI: 10.4324/9781003173632-11; ROBERTSON, V. Delineating Digital Markets under EU Competition Law: Challenging or Futile? *The Competition Law Review.* 2017, vol. 12, no. 2; ROBERTSON, Victoria H.S.E. Antitrust, Big Tech, and Democracy: A Research Agenda. *Antitrust Bulletin* [online]. 2022, vol. 67, no. 2. DOI: 10.1177/0003603X221082749; EZRACHI, A. *The Goals of Eu Competition Law and the Digital Economy* [online]. Available at: https://www.beuc.eu/publications/beuc-x-2018-071_goals_of_eu_competition_law_and_digital_economy.pdf

European Commission and only "residual" powers to enforce national laws [Article 38(1) to (3) DMA] and to support the European Commission's investigation [Article 38(6) and (7) DMA] are left to NCAs. Moreover, the DMA stresses multiple times that the European Commission is the sole enforcer of the DMA.[395]

Thus, the DMA explicitly restricted the manoeuvring space of other measures of public enforcement of the DMA than the European Commission. The research questions for this chapter are focused on the extent of possible private enforcement of the DMA, its limits and challenges, and comparison of the private enforcement of the DMA with private enforcement of the EU competition rules and their possible interplay. For the purposes of this chapter, private enforcement of the DMA will be understood as employment of any measures by private parties against designated gatekeepers in the case of violation on non-compliance of the DMA, enforcement of the DMA by private actors vis-à-vis other private entities, private law consequences of application or violation of the DMA, including claims for damages.

2. Explicit private-enforcement provisions in the DMA

The DMA contains two explicit binding provisions on the possibility of private enforcement of the DMA at national courts:

(1) Article 39(1) DMA explicitly awaits the possibility of proceedings at national court for the application of the DMA. This provision does not refer to the type of action. However, since the NCAs cannot apply the DMA (corresponding national rules only), it is obvious that parties other than public bodies are expected to be parties to the proceeding mentioned in Article 39(1) DMA, i.e., private parties.

(2) Article 42 DMA expects "the representative actions brought against infringements by gatekeepers of provisions [the DMA] that harm or may harm the collective interests of consumers…".

Despite these explicit references to the possibility of private enforcement of the DMA, the DMA in its binding provisions remained silent on precise substantive rights of individuals that can be enforced via a court proceeding. Some hints of possible rights of individuals are mentioned in the preamble of the DMA: "… to raise concerns about unfair practices by gatekeepers raising any issue of non-compliance with the relevant Union or national law with any relevant administrative or other public authorities, including national courts." (Rec. 42), "… to complain about different types of unfair practices, such as discriminatory access conditions, unjustified closing of business user accounts or unclear grounds for product de-listings." (Rec. 42). The DMA does not contain any explicit direct

[395] DMA, Rec. 91, Art. 38(7).

substantive rights of individuals in relation to the market behaviour of gatekeepers and from the wording of Rec. 42, Article 39(1) and Article 42 DMA It is obvious that the DMA understands these rights as mirror counterparts to the obligations of gatekeepers under the DMA.

Hence the DMA contains two limbs of reference to private enforcement – procedural aspects and substantive aspects – these elements will be analysed in the further text separately.

2.1 Procedural aspects of private enforcement in the DMA

Compared to the Damages Directive, the DMA sets no further procedural rules on private enforcement at national courts, except the framework for collective redress and cooperation between national courts and the European Commission.

In the context of possible representative actions by consumers it refers merely to Directive (EU) 2020/1828.[396] On the basis of this reference (Article 42 DMA), consumers can employ instruments of collective redress not only when consumers are actually harmed by non-compliance with the DMA but also when there is such a threat. In comparison, consumers cannot use these mechanisms in cases of violation of Article 101 and 102 TFEU.

Cooperation between the European Commission seems to be the most precise provision on private enforcement of the DMA. The purpose of Article 39 is to avoid non-harmonious application of the DMA by the European Commission and national courts of the Member States (NCAs are excluded from enforcement of the DMA itself). It must be recalled that uniform application of the rules for gatekeepers is the rationale of adoption of the DMA relying on harmonization clause of Article 114 TFEU as its sole legal basis.[397]

It is apparent that the DMA follows the provision of Regulation No 1/2003[398] on cooperation with national courts and on uniform application of EU competition law:

[396] Directive (EU) 2020/1828 of the European Parliament and of the Council of 25 November 2020 on representative actions for the protection of the collective interests of consumers and repealing Directive 2009/22/EC (OJ L 409, 4. 12. 2020, p. 1).

[397] LAMADRID DE PABLO, A., BAYÓN FERNÁNDEZ, N. Why the Proposed DMA Might Be Illegal under Article 114 TFEU, and How to Fix It. *Journal of European Competition Law and Practice.* [online]. 2021, vol. 12, no. 7. DOI: 10.1093/jeclap/lpab059; COLANGELO, G. The European Digital Markets Act and Antitrust Enforcement: A Liaison Dangereuse. *European Law Review*. 2022, vol. 47, no. 5; BLAŽO, O. The Digital Markets acts: Between market regulation, competition rules and unfair trade practices rules. *Strani pravni zivot* [online]. 2022, vol. 66, no. 1. DOI: 10.5937/spz66-34993

[398] Council Regulation (EC) No 1/2003 of 16 December 2002 on the implementation of the rules on competition laid down in Articles 81 and 82 of the Treaty (OJ L 1, 4. 1. 2003, pp. 1–25)

1) right of the national courts to request the European Commission to transmit "... information in its possession or its opinion on questions concerning..." the application of the DMA [Article 39 (1) DMA corresponds to Article 15(1) Regulation No 1/2003];
2) duty to forward judgment involving the application of the DMA [Article 39(2) DMA corresponds to Article 15(2) Regulation No 1/2003];
3) right of the European Commission to act as *amicus curiae* in court proceedings [Article 39(3) and 39(4) DMA correspond to Article 15(3) Regulation No 1/2003];
4) avoiding judgments that can frustrate the effects of the decisions of the European Commission [Article 39(5) DMA corresponds to Article 16(1) Regulation No 1/2003].

While the first three rules handle the European Commission and the national courts of the Member States almost as enforcement partners, the fourth is a confirmation of supremacy of EU law and specific provision on application of the principle of loyalty[399] enshrined in Article 4(3) TEU. The equivalent provision was inserted into Article 82(3) of the Digital Services Act (DSA).[400]

The obligation of national courts (1) not give a decision that is contrary to a decision adopted by the European Commission under the DMA but also to (2) avoid giving decisions that would conflict with a decision contemplated by the European Commission in proceedings it has initiated under the DMA is a "codification"[401] the of case law of *Delimitis*[402] and *Masterfoods.*[403] The CJ EU found that the application of supremacy of the decisions of the European Commission in the cases handled by a national court does not violate principle of legal certainty of in any direction: (1) the European Commission can adopt a decision even in the situation when the contemplated decision is in conflict with any judgment of a national court and (2) the national court shall avoid giving decisions which would conflict with a decision contemplated by the European Commission.[404]

[399] KOMNINOS, A. P. The Digital Markets Act and Private Enforcement: Proposals for an Optimal System of Enforcement. In CHARBIT, N., GACHOT, S. (eds.). *Eleanor M. Fox | Antitrust Ambassador to the World – Liber Amicorum* [online]. 2021, p. 443. DOI: 10.4324/978 1315696195-186

[400] Regulation (EU) 2022/2065 of the European Parliament and of the Council of 19 October 2022 on a Single Market For Digital Services and amending Directive 2000/31/EC (Digital Services Act) (OJ L 277, 27. 10. 2022, pp. 1–102).

[401] Judgment of 9 December 2020, Groupe Canal + v European Commission, C-132/19 P, ECLI:EU:C:2020:1007, para 112.

[402] Judgment of 28 February 1991, Stergios Delimitis v Henninger Bräu AG, C-234/89, ECLI:EU:C:1991:91.

[403] Judgment of 14 December 2000, Masterfoods and HB, C-344/98, ECLI:EU:C:2000:689

[404] Delimitis, para 47, Masterfoods, para 51.

In order to avoid abovementioned conflicts, under the Article 39(5) DMA "... national courts may assess whether it is necessary to stay its proceedings". Moreover, the DMA stresses, that provision of Article 39 is without prejudice to the right of submit preliminary reference under Article 267 TFEU. Both these "rules" have, in fact, limited "legal added value", that is, they do not create new rights or duties.

First, the "right" of a national court to stay its proceeding appears to be a mere suggestion to a national judge what to do in order to avoid possible conflict with the decision of the Commission rather than normative permission. The DMA does not regulate the course of court proceedings within the Member States. The only situation that may contravene this rule under the DMA is the explicit prohibition for the court to stay its proceeding in general or in the case of application of the DMA. However, this hypothetical situation is quite extreme and not very probable. Therefore, the DMA, in general, leaves the decision to stay its proceeding to the national court itself.

Second, the right of a national court for preliminary reference to the CJ EU under Article 267 TFEU cannot be subject to secondary legislation. Secondary legislation may neither broaden the rights under Article 267 TFEU nor limit them.

However, although Article 16 Regulation No1/2023, Article 82(3) DSA, Article 39 DMA are deemed codifications of *Delimitis* and *Masterfood* case law; their content is limited by the possible scope of secondary legislation. The CJ EU went in its interpretation of [current] Article 4(3) TEU further that it was reflected in the above-mentioned regulations (and rules stemming from interpretation of Article 267 TFEU) stressing. "An obligation of sincere cooperation between the national courts, on the one hand, and the Commission and the Community Courts, on the other, in the context of which each acts according to the role assigned to it by the Treaty"[405]:

(1) If the European Commission already issued a decision that is under the pending review by the CJ EU "... it is for the national court to decide whether to stay proceedings until a definitive decision has been given in the action for annulment or in order to refer a question to the Court for a preliminary ruling".[406]
(2) "When the outcome of the dispute before the national court depends on the validity of the Commission decision, it follows from the obligation of sincere cooperation that the national court should, in order to avoid reaching a decision that runs counter to that of the Commission, stay its proceedings pending final judgment in the action for annulment by the Community Courts, unless it considers that, in the circumstances of the case, a reference to the Court of

[405] Masterfoods, para 56.
[406] Masterfoods, para 55.

Justice for a preliminary ruling on the validity of the Commission decision is warranted."[407] Although the DMA seemingly lefts the decision whether to stay its proceeding or not to the national court, the CJ EU limits the manoeuvring space for a national court by the principle of sincere cooperation as explained in *Masterfoods.*

(3) "If a national court stays proceedings, it is incumbent on it to examine whether it is necessary to order interim measures in order to safeguard the interests of the parties pending final judgment."[408] Similarly, the principle of sincere cooperation requires a national court to examine the necessity of interim measure. In this context, different separation of powers under the DMA and pursuant to Regulation No 1/2033 analysed in the further text of this chapter shall be noted.

The substantial difference between the DMA and Regulation No 1/2003 lies in the powers of the European Commission and administrative bodies and courts of the Member States. Rec. 7 Regulation No 1/2003 stresses that "[n]ational courts have an essential part to play in applying the Community competition rules. When deciding disputes between private individuals, they protect the subjective rights under Community law, for example, by awarding damages to the victims of infringements. The role of the national courts here complements that of the competition authorities of the Member States. They should therefore be allowed to "apply Articles 81 and 82 of the Treaty in full". This aim was embedded in Article 6 Regulation No 1/2003 under which "[n]ational courts shall have the power to apply Articles [101] and [102] of the [TEFU]". Compared to cooperative co-enforcement of competition rules [with precedence of the European Commission under Article 11(6) Regulation No 1/2003], the DMA stresses that the European Commission is a "sole enforcer".[409] The enforcement monopoly of the European Commission is even stronger compared to the competition rules: enforcement action of the European Commission relieves NCAs from application of Article 101 and 102 TFEU[410] while DMA the enforcement action of the European Commission all rules mentioned under Article 1(6) DMA[411] if they

[407] Masterfoods, para 57.

[408] Masterfoods, para 58.

[409] DMA, Rec. 91, Art. 38(7).

[410] Regulation No 1/2003, 11(6).

[411] "... the application of Articles 101 and 102 TFEU. [...] ... the application of:
(a) national competition rules prohibiting anti-competitive agreements, decisions by associations of undertakings, concerted practices and abuses of dominant positions;
(b) national competition rules prohibiting other forms of unilateral conduct insofar as they are applied to undertakings other than gatekeepers or amount to the imposition of further obligations on gatekeepers; and
(c) Council Regulation (EC) No 139/2004 (23) and national rules concerning merger control."

cover measures against non-compliance with obligations corresponding to those under Art. 5, 6 and 7 DMA, including national rules.

Furthermore, the NCAs and national courts are empowered to apply competition rules under Art. 101 and 102 TFEU in full (respecting enforcement precedence of the European Commission) while some considerations under the DMA are reserved solely to the European Commission. In particular, the European Commission can decide on designation of gatekeepers only, under Art. 3 and 4 DMA and therefore the national court cannot decide on the status of the undertaking as a gatekeeper. Moreover, it cannot refer this question to the CJ EU without the existence of a decision of the European Commission. On the other hand, a national court can challenge the validity of the decision of the European Commission on the designation of a gatekeeper via preliminary reference.

Regarding the scrutiny of the compliance with the obligations of gatekeepers, the DMA does not induce enforcement monopoly of the European Commission and therefore interplay between ex offo investigation by the European Commission (as well as NCAs), complaints lodged by private parties at the European Commission, and private court actions at national courts can take place. Of course, considering the enforcement precedence of the European Commission.

Regarding the obligation of gatekeepers, the European Commission has additional powers to "adjust" them:

(1) under Article 8(2) DMA, the European Commission may, on its own initiative or on request of a designated gatekeeper, adopt an implementing act, specifying the measures that the gatekeeper concerned is to implement in order to effectively comply with the obligations laid down in Article 6 and 7 DMA ("specification decision");

(2) under Art. 9 the European Commission may exceptionally suspend, in whole or in part, the specific obligation if the gatekeeper demonstrates that compliance with a specific obligation laid down in Article 5, 6 or 7 DMA would endanger, due to exceptional circumstances beyond the gatekeeper's control, the economic viability of its operation in the EU ("suspension decision");

(3) under Article 10 DMA the European Commission may adopt an implementing act exempting gatekeeper, in whole or in part, from a specific obligation laid down in Article 5, 6 or 7 DMA due to interests of public health or public security ("exemption decision").

All three, "specification decisions", "suspension decisions" and "exemption decisions" are, again, in the full competence of the European Commission and a national court cannot assess the fulfilment of the conditions for specification, suspension or exemption. Similarly to designation decisions, it can challenge their validity via preliminary reference to the CJ EU. It should be noted that the grounds for judicial review of these "decisions" are limited due to discretionary powers of the European Commission and separation powers between executive and judicial bodies (in this context, the "decisions" of the European Commission do not fall into the scope of "criminal charge" and therefore the full jurisdiction of the CJ EU is not applicable).

While "suspension decision" and "exemption decisions" relieve the gatekeeper in issue from the obligations under Article 5, 6 or 7 DMA *ex nunc*, the effects of "specification decisions" have been discussed: Podszun et al. suggest that "Private enforcement can only work with clear-cut obligations, however, which means that the regulatory dialogue according to Article [8] would shield gatekeepers from private enforcement as long as there are no clear decisions on the exact obligations,"[412] while Komninos suggests that obligations of gatekeepers "are complete and apply, irrespective of a possible 'regulatory dialogue' between the Commission and the gatekeeper and a possible specification decision. Thus, in conclusion, the possible 'specification' process would not make the Article 6 rules less unconditional or less susceptible of direct effect."[413]

First of all, "specification" procedure under Article 8(2) et seq. DMA is not mandatory and gatekeepers are obliged to follow their obligations stemming from Article 5, 6 and 7 DMA notwithstanding the "specification" procedure, as it is stressed in Article 8(1) DMA. Furthermore, the European Commission has a full discretion to launch a "specification" procedure[414] and therefore a gatekeeper cannot shield itself by lodging a request for a "specification decision". On the other hand, principles of sincere cooperation between national courts and the European Commission based on Article 39 DMA and principles derived *mutatis* mutandis from *Delimitis* and *Masterfoods* are relevant not only with respect to non-compliance decisions[415] but also with respect to "specification decisions".[416]

Apart from preliminary references that allow national courts to challenge decisions of the European Commission, they can provide incentives to review them under the mechanisms provided by the DMA. Within the request for the opinion under Article 39(1) to the European Commission a national court can

[412] PODSZUN, R., BONGARTZ, P., LANGENSTEIN, S. Proposals on how to improve the Digital Markets Act. *SSRN Electronic Journal.* [online]. 2021, p. 9. DOI: 10.2139/ssrn.3788571

[413] KOMNINOS, A. P. The Digital Markets Act and Private Enforcement: Proposals for an Optimal System of Enforcement. In CHARBIT, N., GACHOT, S. (eds.). *Eleanor M. Fox | Antitrust Ambassador to the World – Liber Amicorum.* [online]. 2021, p. 430. DOI: 10.4324/9781315696195-186

[414] DMA, Art. 8(3).

[415] Pursuant to Art. 29 DMA.

[416] KOMNINOS, A. P. The Digital Markets Act and Private Enforcement: Proposals for an Optimal System of Enforcement. In CHARBIT, N., GACHOT, S. (eds.). *Eleanor M. Fox | Antitrust Ambassador to the World – Liber Amicorum.* [online]. 2021, pp. 430–431. DOI: 10.4324/9781315696195-186

suggest reviewing decision on designation[417] or reopening proceeding on specification.[418] Suspension decisions and exemption decisions do not provide such an option because they shall be reviewed only periodically.[419]

On some occasions, not only the European Commission can have a 'blocking' effect on the national court proceeding but the 'cooperation' can run also in opposite directions: if a case is handled by the national court prior to adopting a decision of the European Commission, the national judge can refer a preliminary question under Article 267 TFEU, and thus the European Commission will be facing a dilemma whether to proceed in own decision-making or to wait for the CJ EU judgment if the interpretation can be relevant for the decision of the European Commission itself.

2.2 Substantive aspects of private enforcement in the DMA

It is easy to say that the DMA as a regulation has direct effect, including vertical and horizontal, under Art. 288 TFEU, and obligations levied on designated gatekeepers correspond to the right of individuals that are enforceable vis-à-vis gatekeepers. Indeed, even provisions of a regulation can be deprived their direct horizontal effect if they are subject to further implementation based on discretion of Member States.[420] Equally, a provision loses its direct horizontal effect if it shall be subject to discretion of an institution of the EU. None of the obligations set in Art. 5, 6 and 7 DMA has such a "conditional" character. The rest of the provisions are not relevant for possible private enforcement because they have either purely procedural character or impose obligations of gatekeepers explicitly towards the European Commission or NCAs.

Even though it is undoubtedly possible to identify precise obligations of gatekeepers, it does automatically mean that all of them are obligations *erga omnes*. The DMA mentions in the preamble to the two groups of possible plaintiffs: "business users and end users" (Rec. 42) while the right to establish alternative dispute resolution rules or agree on competent court sees only within the relationship between business users and gatekeepers.

The DMA explicitly mentions right of consumers for representative actions within the ambits of Directive (EU) 2020/1828 and thus implies that consumers can have "collective" substantive rights stemming from the DMA. The notion

[417] DMA, Art. 4.
[418] DMA, Art. 8(9).
[419] DMA, Art. 9(2) and 10(2).
[420] Judgment of 11 January 2001, Azienda Agricola Monte Arcosu Srl v Regione Autonoma della Sardegna, Organismo Comprensoriale n° 24 della Sardegna and Ente Regionale per l'Assistenza Tecnica in Agricoltura (ERSAT), C-403/98, ECLI:EU:C:2001:6, para 28.

"consumer" is not mentioned as a beneficiary from of obligations of gatekeepers under the DMA nonetheless consumers can be identified as "end users"[421] in the terminology of the DMA.[422]

From the point of view of entitled from obligations of gatekeepers, the set of obligations under the DMA is not homogenous and the following beneficiaries can be identified:

(1) end users: Article 5(2) and 5(5) to 5(8), Article 6(3), 6(6) and 6(9), Article 7(2) and 7(3) DMA;
(2) business users: Article 5(3) and 5(4), Article 5(6) to 5(8), Article 6(2), 6(7), 6(10), and 6(12) DMA
(3) advertisers: Article 5(9) and Article 6(8) DMA;
(4) publishers: Article 5(10) and Article 6(8) DMA;
(5) any third parties: Article 6(4), 6(5) and 6(8) to 6(11) DMA;
(6) providers of services and providers of hardware: Article 6(7) DMA;
(7) without specific beneficiary: Article 6(4) and 6(13), Article 7(1), 7(4) and 7(5) DMA.

Along with these "explicit" addressees of obligations of gatekeepers, there are "derived" benefits stemming from the functioning of the system of protection as a whole or opportunities created by the DMA regulation.[423] E.g., ensuring, free of charge, effective interoperability [Art. 6(7)] clearly aim to increase competitiveness of the digital market and obligations seem to be addressed to providers of services and providers of hardware as well as to business users, but also consumers (as end users) can clearly benefit from such competitive environment.[424]

Although the DMA itself is silent on subjective rights of individuals that are counterparts to the obligations of gatekeepers stipulated by the DMA, by the reference Directive (EU) 2020/1828[425] collective rights of consumers under the EU law are identifiable. In the event of infringement of the DMA by a gatekeeper (as a trader in law on consumers protection), qualified entities are entitled to seek at least

[421] MOSKAL, A. Highlight Digital Markets Act (DMA): A Consumer Protection Perspective. *European Papers* [online]. 2022, vol. 7, no. 3, p. 1117. DOI: 10.15166/2499-8249/615

[422] Under Art. 2 (20) DMA " 'end user' means any natural or legal person using core platform services other than as a business user"; and under Art. 2 (21) DMA " 'business user' means any natural or legal person acting in a commercial or professional capacity using core platform services for the purpose of or in the course of providing goods or services to end users".

[423] ANDRIYCHUK, O. Do DMA obligations for gatekeepers create entitlements for business users? *Journal of Antitrust Enforcement.* [online]. 2023, vol. 11, no. 1, p. 131. DOI: 10.1093/jaenfo/jnac034

[424] MOSKAL, A. Highlight Digital Markets Act (DMA): A Consumer Protection Perspective. *European Papers.* [online]. 2022, vol. 7, no. 3, p. 1117. DOI: 10.15166/2499-8249/615

[425] Directive (EU) 2020/1828, Art. 2(1).

injunctive measures[426] and redress measures.[427] [428] Thus, the DMA is not completely "silent" on private claims.[429] On the other hand, the European Commission was quite optimistic about private enforcement of the DMA in its Q&A: "The DMA is a Regulation, containing precise obligations and prohibitions for the gatekeepers in scope, which can be enforced directly in national courts. This will facilitate direct actions for damages by those harmed by the conduct of non-complying gatekeepers."[430] The "facilitating" element of the DMA regarding damages claims lies merely in existence of list of duties of gatekeepers and except collective rights of consumers it does not actually facilitate damages claims. The DMA does not even contain a clause similar to Art. 54 DSA[431] stipulating the right to compensation caused by violation of the DSA.[432] Moreover, other types of civil claims – "injunction measures" and "redress measures" other than damages – are somehow neglected (as it is also the case in private enforcement of the core competition law[433]).

Without explicit rules stipulating possible individual rights, the private law claims under the DMA shall be construed on a basis of combination of several sets of rules: (1) EU law – the TEU and the TFEU, the CJ EU's case law, and the DMA; and (2) national law in application of the principle of procedural autonomy, subject

[426] Under Art. 8(1) Directive (EU) 2020/1828 an injunctive measure is:
"(a) a provisional measure to cease a practice or, where appropriate, to prohibit a practice, where that practice has been deemed to constitute an infringement as referred to in Article 2(1);
(b) a definitive measure to cease a practice or, where appropriate, to prohibit a practice, where that practice has been found to constitute an infringement as referred to in Article 2(1)."

[427] Under Art. 9(1) Directive (EU) 2020/1828 a redress measure "shall require a trader to provide consumers concerned with remedies such as compensation, repair, replacement, price reduction, contract termination or reimbursement of the price paid, as appropriate and as available under Union or national law".

[428] Directive (EU) 2020/1828, Art. 7(4).

[429] Cf., KOMNINOS, A. P. The Digital Markets Act and Private Enforcement: Proposals for an Optimal System of Enforcement. In CHARBIT, N., GACHOT, S. (eds.). *Eleanor M. Fox | Antitrust Ambassador to the World – Liber Amicorum.* [online]. 2021. DOI: 10.4324/9781315696195-186; PODSZUN, R. Private Enforcement and Gatekeeper Regulation: Strengthening the Rights of Private Parties in the Digital Markets Act. *Journal of European Competition Law & Practice* [online]. 2022, vol. 13, no. 4. DOI: 10.1093/jeclap/lpab076

[430] EUROPEAN COMMISSION. *Questions and Answers: Digital Markets Act: Ensuring fair and open digital markets.* [online]. Available at: https://ec.europa.eu/commission/presscorner/api/files/document/print/en/qanda_20_2349/QANDA_20_2349_EN.pdf

[431] "Recipients of the service shall have the right to seek, in accordance with Union and national law, compensation from providers of intermediary services, in respect of any damage or loss suffered due to an infringement by those providers of their obligations under this Regulation."

[432] For critical view on consumer protection in DSA see, e.g., CAUFFMAN, C., GOANTA, C. A new order: The digital services act and consumer protection. *European Journal of Risk Regulation.* [online]. 2021, vol. 12, no. 4. DOI: 10.1017/err.2021.8

[433] PODSZUN, R. Private Enforcement and Gatekeeper Regulation: Strengthening the Rights of Private Parties in the Digital Markets Act. *Journal of European Competition Law & Practice.* [online]. 2022, vol. 13, no. 4, p. 254. DOI: 10.1093/jeclap/lpab076

to the usual limits established by the principles of effectiveness and equivalence.[434] Therefore, claims are based rather on national law than EU law (the DMA) and apparent violation of an obligation stipulated in the DMA is "merely" a vehicle for proving wrongful act as an element of liability for damage under national law.

3. Implied elements of private enforcement of the DMA

The pure existence of the duties of gatekeepers does not automatically generate a standing in civil proceedings for individual claims. Since these individual claims were not regulated by the EU law, it remained completely within the competence of the Member States under the principle of procedural autonomy shaped by requirements of effectiveness and equivalence.[435]

The national law of the Member States can provide a catalogue of possible remedies: injunctions, i.e. order to fulfil an obligation or not to continue in violation of an obligation, damages, nullity of contracts, etc. The following text will focus on three possible civil remedies: injunctions, nullity and damages.

The national legal orders of the respective Member States can attach to these civil claims different conditions, procedural rules, essential elements of an action or a burden of proof and a burden of evidence. In other words, due to the enforcement of the DMA, the Member States are not obliged to develop new rules of civil substantive and procedural law. There is a question whether and to what extent the Member States are obliged to provide remedies for the non-compliance with the DMA obligations, whether it is obliged to provide framework also for stand-alone actions or for follow-on actions only. The German law is an example of providing legal framework for claims of private parties to stop the infringement of competition law[436] and this framework will be expanded to the DMA infringements by the 11th Amendment to the German Act against Restriction of Economic Competition (GWB)[437] (expanding the scope of §33b GWB also to the violations of the DMA and decisions of the European Commission under the DMA).

The settled case law of the CJ EU confirmed that a possibility for private persons to bring a direct action due to claim rights under the EU law "it was not

---

[434] AMARO, R. Weaving Penelope's Shroud ... Some Comments on the Private Enforcement of the DMA. *Competition Forum.* [online]. 2022, no. 0042, p. 4. Available at: https://competition-forum.com

[435] Judgment of 16 December 1976, Rewe-Zentralfinanz eG and Rewe-Zentral AG v Landwirtschaftskammer für das Saarland, 33–76, EU:C:1976:188, para 5.

[436] PODSZUN, R. Private Enforcement and Gatekeeper Regulation: Strengthening the Rights of Private Parties in the Digital Markets Act. *Journal of European Competition Law & Practice.* [online]. 2022, vol. 13, no. 4, pp. 255–257. DOI: 10.1093/jeclap/lpab076

[437] Avaible at: https://dserver.bundestag.de/btd/20/068/2006824.pdf

intended to create new remedies in the national courts to ensure the observance of [EU] law other than those already laid down by national law"[438] as well as it is for "national law to determine an individual's standing and legal interest in bringing proceedings".[439] For the private enforcement of the DMA is crucial also the other "limit" of the procedural autonomy of the Member States set by the CJ EU: "It would be otherwise only if it were apparent from the overall scheme of the national legal system in question that no legal remedy existed which made it possible to ensure, even indirectly, respect for an individual's rights under [EU] law."[440]

The content and the rationale of the DMA put the procedural autonomy of the Member States to different light than, e.g., competition law. The DMA stresses that the European Commission is the "sole enforcer" of the DMA and, in the same time, the rationale of adoption of the DMA was to centralize enforcement. The DMA allows business users and end users, competitors or any other third parties to inform an NCA or directly the European Commission about possible non-compliance of the obligations under the DMA.[441] If the European Commission finds an infringement of the obligations of a gatekeeper, it shall issue "non-compliance decision" in which it "shall order the gatekeeper to cease and desist with the non-compliance within an appropriate deadline and to provide explanations on how it plans to comply with that decision".[442] Within the proceeding, third parties can submit their observations. Finally, the "non-compliance decision" can be enforced by periodic penalty.[443] It is apparent that the DMA provides comprehensive "injunction" mechanism in order to compel gatekeepers to observe their obligations under the DMA and thus provide a "protection shield" for any third parties, including business users, competitors and end users, in order not to be harmed by the anti-DMA behaviour of gatekeepers. In this situation, the Member States can hardly be compelled to develop their national system of stand-alone injunction remedies if such a remedy does not exist in national law at all or access to such a remedy is somehow limited. Any Member State can claim that is not obliged to develop any new injunction remedies for enforcement of the DMA because, even in a case of their complete non-existence, there is an effective mechanism run by the European Commission.

[438] Judgment of 13 March 2007, Unibet (London) Ltd and Unibet (International) Ltd v Justitiekansler, C-432/05, ECLI:EU:C:2007:163, para 40.

[439] Judgment of 13 March 2007, Unibet (London) Ltd and Unibet (International) Ltd v Justitiekansler, C-432/05, ECLI:EU:C:2007:163, para 42.

[440] Judgment of 13 March 2007, Unibet (London) Ltd and Unibet (International) Ltd v Justitiekansler, C-432/05, ECLI:EU:C:2007:163, para 41.

[441] DMA, Art. 27.

[442] DMA, Art. 29(5).

[443] DAM, Art. 31.

The situation is completely different in the case of damages claims because the DMA does not establish any enforcement system for damages claims. In fact, these claims cannot be relying on the Damages Directive due to its limited scope. However, competition law provides examples of shaping private claims in this area out of the scope of explicit EU rules, e.g., *Courage/Crehan,*[444] *Manfredi*[445] confirming right to claim damages or *Cogeco Communications*[446] on limitation periods. The *ratione temporis* scope of the Damages Directive (as well as national transpositions) had been limited and therefore its rules cannot be "transferred" to the previous cases. However, *Cogeco Communications* the CJ EU used some of the principles of the Damages Directive (limitation period) even to the pre-Damages Directive case employing the principle of effectiveness. Although the Damages Directive does not apply directly to damages claims under the DMA, it still can serve as an inspiration. And, in practise, not only as inspiration, but also as a benchmark of the EU's understanding of effective enforcement of damages claims in the economic law sphere aimed at achieving contestability in the internal market, *Cogeco Communications* can be used as an example of this transfer. On the other hand, some rules of the Damages Directive can hardly be transferred to the DMA enforcement, e.g., order to access to file, presumption of harm caused by cartel infringement, because they are closely linked to particularities of competition rules. Indeed, compared to stand-alone claims in abuse of dominant cases, national courts can benefit from *per se* prohibitions stipulated by the DMA.[447] And in the same time, the enforcement of the DMA can face the same challenges as enforcement of competition rules, e.g. "prices" on zero-markets, non-pecuniary harm.[448]

The nullity of contracts or unilateral acts of individuals is the third limb of possible private enforcement of the DMA. Explicit nullity under EU law is quite rare, and in competition law can be found only in the context of agreement restricting competition, and, moreover, it must be distinguished between the voidness of an "agreement" within the meaning of Art. 101 TFEU and civil law

[444] Judgment of the Court of 20 September 2001, Courage Ltd v Bernard Crehan and Bernard Crehan v Courage Ltd and Others, C-453/99, ECLI:EU:C:2001:465.

[445] Judgment of 13 July 2006, Vincenzo Manfredi v Lloyd Adriatico Assicurazioni SpA (C-295/04), Antonio Cannito v Fondiaria Sai SpA (C-296/04) and Nicolò Tricarico (C-297/04) and Pasqualina Murgolo (C-298/04) v Assitalia SpA, Joined cases C-295/04 to C-298/04, ECLI:EU:C:2006:461.

[446] Judgment of 28 March 2019, Cogeco Communications Inc v Sport TV Portugal SA and Others, C-637/17, ECLI:EU:C:2019:263.

[447] AMARO, R. Weaving Penelope's Shroud ... Some Comments on the Private Enforcement of the DMA. *Competition Forum.* [online]. 2022, no. 0042, p. 3. Available at: https://competition-forum.com

[448] E.g., SOUSA FERRO, M. De Gratis Non Curat Lex : Abuse of Dominance in Online Free Services. *The Competition Law Review*. 2017, vol. 12, no. 2.

contract under national law.[449] In abuse of dominance cases, which resembles the DMA possible infringements, the EU remained silent. It is obvious that national court cannot provide any legal protection to acts contrary to obligations stemming from the DMA or decision based on the DMA. Again, the Member States enjoy procedural autonomy in how to deprive infringements of the DMA legal protection: nullity or voidness, pure non enforceability, absolute or relative, of entire act or contract or of partial, only. Hence, the solutions can vary EU-wide in their responses to the question whether the invalidity of parts of an agreement that violates public policy.[450] Nevertheless, this divergence in approaches to nullity or ineffectiveness contracts and acts contrary to the DMA obligation does not seem to cause major disruptions in the harmonized DMA enforcement.

4. Conclusion

The DMA created a set of obligations of gatekeepers that appear to be self-executing. Although the European Commission in its press release declared that the DMA is precise enough to be enforced via private claims, the language of the DMA does not follow this "wishful thinking". The DMA does contain any provisions on harmonization of private enforcement rules, although the harmonization of possible rules on prohibition of certain practices of the BigTech was the main objective of the DMA. Furthermore, the DMA does not even contain a general clause on the right to compensation as does the "sibling" regulation – the DSA. At the same time, it directly refers to the collective rights of consumers who can rely on the catalogue of claims stipulated in Directive (EU) 2020/1828.

Henceforth, the whole system on private enforcement, apart from the regime of representative actions, will be govern by the principles of effectiveness and equivalence of enforcement if the EU within the ambits of procedural autonomy of the Member States. The approaches to three analysed limbs of private claims showed three different situations. In the sphere of injunction measures, the activity of national authorities is suppressed by the powers of the European Commission as a "sole enforcer". The national courts of the Member States are not deprived their competence to decide on possible injunctions, but they cannot contravene actual or contemplated decisions of the European Commission. This factor of "sincere cooperation" can hinder speed of injunction proceedings in the national court or

[449] CAUFFMAN, C. The impact of Article 101(2) TFEU Nullity on Private Law. In MICKLITZ, H., SIEBURGH, C. (eds.). *Primary EU law and Private Law Concepts*. Cambridge: Intersentia, 2017.

[450] ULLRICH, H. Private Enforcement of the EU Rules on Competition – Nullity Neglected. *IIC International Review of Intellectual Property and Competition Law.* [online]. 2021, vol. 52, no. 5, p. 621. DOI: 10.1007/s40319-021-01054-w

the willingness of judges to be "overly active" in them. The Member States are not obliged to create any brand new system of injunctions to enforce obligations under the DMA (on the other hand, they can create them, as Germany did). Even in a case of their absolute non-existence, the Member State cannot be blamed by the European Commission for underenforcement because there shall exist an enforcement system created by the DMA. Compared to competition rules, there is no explicit provision on the duty of the bodies of the Member States to engage any precise form of enforcement of the DMA (i.e., general implementation duty under Art. 291(1) TFEU[451]). The situation differs in regards of damages claims. The EU law does not provide any measure to claim damages stemming from non-compliance with the DMA obligations. Therefore, the Member State shall provide this type of remedy due to the direct effect of the DMA, i.e. creating horizontal obligations and rights between individuals. In a situation of non-existence of harmonizing directive similar to the Damages Directive, risk of divergence of standards of damages claims can emerge regarding the DMA. This legal regime can work for a certain time (depending also on the level of public enforcement) based on analogy with the Damages Directive and competition case law regarding private enforcement as well as based on case-by-case development of the CJ EU case law, in the long-term horizon is not sustainable and a "DMA Damages Directive" or a "DMA Private Claims Directive" will be desirable in the future.

The aim of the DMA was to remove obstacles caused by possibly different national regulation and the EU lawmaker saw "preventive harmonization" under Article 114 TFEU as a sufficient legal basis (although it has been criticized, or at least discussed[452]). In these aspects, the DMA failed to achieve this objective in the terms of private enforcement and created new sets of possible tensions between regulations of the Member States that can lead to underenforcement or overenforcement.

---

[451] Member States shall adopt all measures of national law necessary to implement legally binding Union acts.

[452] E.g., LAMADRID DE PABLO, A., BAYÓN FERNÁNDEZ, N. Why the Proposed DMA Might Be Illegal under Article 114 TFEU, and How to Fix It. *Journal of European Competition Law and Practice.* [online]. 2021, vol. 12, no. 7. DOI: 10.1093/jeclap/lpab059; FRANCK, J. U., MONTI, G., STREEL, A. Legal Opinion commissioned by the Federal Ministry for Economic Affairs and Energy concerning Article 114 TFEU as a Legal Basis for Strengthened Control of Acquisitions by Digital Gatekeepers. In [accessed 15.11.2021]. Available at: https://www.bmwi.de/Redaktion/EN/Publikationen/Wirtschaft/article-114-tfeu-as-a-legal-basis-for-strengthened-control-of-acquisitions-by-digital-gatekeepers.pdf?__blob=publicationFile&v=5; VAN DEN BOOM, J. What does the Digital Markets Act harmonize? – exploring interactions between the DMA and national competition laws. *European Competition Journal.* [online]. 2022. DOI: 10.1080/17441056.2022.2156728; BLAŽO, O. Bypassing Competition Law, Bypassing through Competition Law. *EU ANTITRUST: HOT TOPICS & NEXT STEPS, Proceedings of the International Conference*. Prague: 2022; BLAŽO, O. The Digital Markets acts: Between market regulation, competition rules and unfair trade practices rules. *Strani pravni zivot.* [online]. 2022, vol. 66, no. 1. DOI: 10.5937/spz66-34993

CHAPTER NINE

Pricing Algorithms and Anticompetitive Agreements

MÁRIA T. PATAKYOVÁ

Introduction

This chapter is dedicated to one of the pillars of EU competition law, namely prohibition of anti-competition agreements. The notion of anti-competitive agreements was challenged by the introduction of the digital age. Cartels, traditionally committed in smoke-filled rooms, have moved to digital environments. In order to execute and control a cartel, algorithms may be of great use. What is even more, there are voices claiming that algorithms may facilitate tacit collusion, thus moving the borderline between legal and illegal behaviour to the benefit of cartelists.

This chapter will dive into the problems of anticompetitive agreements in the digital age. From various problems arising in this field, it will focus on pricing algorithms. It analyses how pricing algorithms may facilitate collusions and what are the proposals which should address the issue of pricing algorithms. For this purpose, the chapter analyses a model situation from substantive and procedural (enforcement) point of view. The model situation also tests three proposals de lege ferenda, showing their strong sides and weaknesses. The chapter will primarily focus on EU law, however, it will be supplemented by discussions from OECD and ICN, as this issue is well-known on these platforms. The aim of the chapter is to present the problem of pricing algorithms in relation to anti-competitive agreements and to present and analyse certain solutions of the problem.

Cartels are one of the most harmful conducts for the competition. Undertakings on the market exchange competition for cooperation. Therefore, competition is not functional and it may not provide its efficiencies, such as productive efficiency, allocative efficiency and innovation.[453] Therefore, anticompetitive agreements shall be prohibited.

[453] WHISH, R., BAILEY, D. *Competition Law. Eight Edition*. Oxford: Oxford University Press, 2015, pp. 5–6; LIANOS, I., KORAH, V., SICILIANI, P. *Competition Law. Analysis, Cases, & Materials*. Oxford: Oxford University Press, 2019, p. 90 et seq.

However, the borderline between legal and illegal conduct from competition law perspective proved to be very thin. A shining example is the difference between explicit and tacit collusion. The same economic outcome, prices on a supra-competitive level, is illegal if gained through explicit collusion; and is legal if gained through natural behaviour of competitors on the market.[454]

How is this long lasting competition law riddle influenced by employment of algorithms? There are voices insisting on the fact that the riddle is getting more complex, or more spread, by algorithms.[455] Others are more sceptical and point out rather minimal effect of algorithms on the tacit collusion.[456] It is not the aim of this chapter to cut this Gordian knot.

The aim of this chapter is to look at the problem of pricing algorithms from a bottom-up perspective. We will conduct a little "theoretical experiment", or rather, a case study. We will assess the challenges brought by pricing algorithms. In particular, we will discuss them from the substantive point of view of (whether a hypothetical situation on the market is against Article 101 TFEU) as well as the procedural point of view (whether the hypothetical behaviour, if illegal, is likely to be enforced). Subsequently, we will look into three possible solutions in order to establish whether they could improve the enforcement possibilities of a competition authority.

Thus, the chapter is organised as follows: the first part briefly presents the notions of agreements and concerted practices, in order to establish what is actually forbidden by Article 101 TFEU. The second part presents the model situation which serves as our petri dish and it analyses it from substantive and procedural (enforcement) perspective. The third part outlines three possible solutions which might improve the enforcement of competition law with respect to pricing algorithms. The findings are summed up in the conclusion.

Section 1 – Article 101 in a nutshell

Article 101(1) TFEU prohibits "[…] *all agreements between undertakings, decisions by associations of undertakings and concerted practices which may*

[454] WHISH, R., BAILEY, D. *Competition Law. Ninth Edition*. Oxford: Oxford University Press, 2018, p. 573.

[455] See, for instance, OECD: *Algorithms and Collusion, Background Note by the Secretariat*. [online]. Available at: https://one.oecd.org/document/DAF/COMP(2017)4/en/pdf. Accessed 25. 1. 2021, p. 38; EZRACHI, A., STUCKE, M. E. Sustainable and Unchallenged Algorithmic Tacit Collusion. *Northwestern Journal of Technology and Intellectual Property*. vol. 17, no. 2, 2020, p. 221.

[456] See, for instance, literature mentioned by VAN UYTSEL, S. *Artificial intelligence and collusion: a literature overview*. [online]. Available at: https://papers.ssrn.com/sol3/papers.cfm?abstract_id=3656822_. Accessed 25. 1. 2021, p. 8.

affect trade between Member States and which have as their object or effect the prevention, restriction or distortion of competition within the internal market [...]".

As we pointed out elsewhere[457], several important elements must be fulfilled before a dealing is considered to be against Article 101 TFEU. First, it shall have an effect on trade between Member States; second, it shall have as its object or effect the restriction of competition within the internal market; third, it shall be conducted by undertakings or association of undertakings; fourth, it shall take a form of agreement, concerted practice or decision by association of undertakings.

Neither of these requirements is defined in the primary law. The interpretation has been formed by case law. Bearing in mind the aim of this chapter, we shall further focus on second and forth point. Let us start with the latter, whereas we will deliberately omit the discussion on decisions by association of undertakings.

1.1 Understanding of agreements

The notion of agreement requires several elements to be met[458]. First, an agreement presupposes the presence of at least two parties. These two parties may not fall within one undertaking.[459] A unilateral conduct escapes the prohibition in Article 101 para 1 TFEU.[460] It may, however, be prohibited based on Article 102 TFEU[461]. To distinguish between what is and what is not a unilateral conduct proved to be onerous.

The existence of agreement was questioned in the case *Bayer*[462]. The Court acknowledged in *Bayer* that *"the existence of an agreement* [...] *can be deduced*

[457] PATAKYOVÁ, Mária, T. Notion of Anticompetitive Agreement Challenged in Digital Environment. *European Studies. The Review of European Law, Economics and Politics.* 2020, vol. 7, pp. 237–252.

[458] For the definition of agreement, see, for instance: OECD: *Algorithms and Collusion, Background Note by the Secretariat.* [online]. Available at: https://one.oecd.org/document/DAF/COMP(2017)4/en/pdf. Accessed 25. 1. 2021, p. 36.

[459] To the notion of undertaking, see, for instance, KALESNÁ, K., PATAKYOVÁ, M. T. Subjects of Legal Regulation – Different Approaches of Competition, Public Procurement and Corporate Law. In MILKOVIC, M., KECEK, D., HAMMES, K. (eds.). *Economic and social development.* Varazdin: Varazdin Development and Entrepreneurship Agency, 2019, pp. 210–219.

[460] Case 107/82 AEG v Commission [1983] ECLI:EU:C:1983:293, para 38; joined cases 25/84 and 26/84 Ford and Ford Europe v Commission [1985] ECLI:EU:C:1985:340, para 21; case T-43/92 Dunlop Slazenger v Commission [1994] ECLI:EU:T:1994:79, para 56, case T-41/96 Bayer AG v Commission of the European Communities [2000], ECLI:EU:T:2000:242, para 66.

[461] 102(1) TFEU: *Any abuse by one or more undertakings of a dominant position within the internal market or in a substantial part of it shall be prohibited as incompatible with the internal market in so far as it may affect trade between Member States.*

[462] Case C-2/01 P Bundesverband der Arzneimittel-Importeure eV and Commission of the European Communities v Bayer AG [2004] ECLI:EU:C:2004:2.

from the conduct of the parties concerned"[463]. At the same time, it ruled that "*such an agreement cannot be based on what is only the expression of a unilateral policy of one of the contracting parties, which can be put into effect without the assistance of others*".[464]

The outcome of *Bayer* is that the existence of an agreement cannot be taken for granted. Special attention should be given to situations where the anticompetitive goal may be achieved by acting of one undertaking.

Second element as to the formal requirements, "[...] *it is sufficient that the undertakings in question should have expressed their joint intention to conduct themselves on the market in a specific way* [...]"[465]. Once there is a concurrence of wills of the undertakings concerned, the form in which it is presented is of no particular importance.[466] Naturally, the form may be important from the enforcement perspective, as it is far easier to assess an agreement which is actually written or recorded.

Third, as to the time perspective, the moment when the agreement origins is the moment when the concurrence of wills occurs. Thus, no implementation is necessary for existence of the anti-competitive agreement.[467]

1.2 Understanding of concerted practices

If the definition of agreement is broad, the understanding of concerted practices is even broader. However, it is not without boundaries, as parallel behaviour on the market, without an explicit collusion, is not forbidden.[468]

Taking a case-based approach, we may identify the following definition elements of the concerted practices:

[463] Ibid., para 100.

[464] Ibid., para 101.

[465] Case T-41/96 Bayer AG v Commission of the European Communities [2000] ECLI:EU:T:2000:242, para 67. See also case 41/69 ACF Chemiefarma v Commission [1970] ECLI:EU:C:1970:71, para 112; joined cases 209/78 to 215/78 and 218/78 Heintz van Landewyck SARL and Others v Commission of the European Communities [1980] ECLI:EU:C:1980:248, para 86; case T-7/89 SA Hercules Chemicals NV v Commission of the European Communities [1991] ECLI:EU:T:1991:75, para 256.

[466] Case T-41/96 Bayer AG v Commission of the European Communities [2000], ECLI:EU:T:2000:242, para 69.

[467] WHISH, R., BAILEY, D. *Competition Law. Ninth Edition.* Oxford: Oxford University Press, 2018, p. 104.

[468] The same economic result is either prohibited (concerted practice) or not (tacit collusion). This has been criticised by e.g. THOMAS, S. *Harmful Signals. Cartel Prohibition and Oligopoly Theory in the Age of Machine Learning.* [online]. Available at: https://ssrn.com/abstract=3392860. Accessed 22. 1. 2023, p. 4.

- coordination between undertakings may become apparent from the behaviour of undertakings on the market;[469]
- concerted practice may be based on a parallel behaviour if it leads to abnormal conditions on the market;[470]
  - above-competition level of prices may be explained by a concerted practice;[471]
  - possible evidence of concerted practice may consist in price developments in particular Member States;[472] instructions to raise prices[473] and contacts between undertakings[474];
  - concerted practice is a form of coordination without a proper agreement being concluded, however, where undertakings knowingly substitute risk of competition for practical cooperation, this establishing abnormal conditions on the market.[475] In other words, independent behaviour[476] on the market is not covered by 101 TFEU;
  - concerted practice implies "besides undertakings' concerting with each other, subsequent conduct on the market, and a relationship of cause and effect between the two"[477];
  - however, an undertaking may clear itself if it can produce sufficient evidence which would question the causal nexus[478];
- the existence of a concerted practice must be inferred from a number of coincidences and indicia which, taken together, may constitute evidence of an infringement of the competition rules; this is, however, presumed by the fact that there is no other plausible explanation[479];
- undertakings may be presumed to participate in a concerted practice, if they were aware of it and if they did not publicly distance themselves or if they did not

[469] Case 48/69 Imperial Chemical Industries Ltd. v Commission of the European Communities [1972] ECLI:EU:C:1972:70, paras 65–68.

[470] Ibid.

[471] Ibid.

[472] Ibid., paras 69 et seq.

[473] Ibid., p. 642, para 88.

[474] Ibid., para 96.

[475] Joined cases 40 to 48, 50, 54 to 56, 111, 113 and 114–73 Coöperatieve Vereniging "Suiker Unie" UA and others v Commission of the European Communities [1975] ECLI:EU:C:197 5:174, para 26.

[476] WOLF, M. *Algorithm-based pricing in online retailing as concerted practice. Covering the "predictable agent" with Article 101 (1) TFEU.* [online]. Available at: https://ssrn.com/abstra ct=3536959. Accessed 16. 6. 2020, p. 13.

[477] Case C-199/92 P Hüls AG v Commission of the European Communities [1999] ECLI:EU:C:1 999:358, para 161. See also case T587/08 Fresh Del Monte Produce, Inc. v European Commission [2013] ECLI:EU:T:2013:129, para 298.

[478] WHISH, R., BAILEY, D. *Competition Law. Ninth Edition.* Oxford: Oxford University Press, 2018, p. 118.

[479] Case C-634/13 P Total Marketing Services v Commission [2015] EU:C:2015:614, para 26.

rebutted the presumption otherwise[480]. Therefore, illegal concerted practice occurs when the undertakings (humans within them) have the knowledge about it[481].

In relation to concerted practices, one must discuss the concept of exchange of information. It is often questioned to what extent may undertakings reveal information between each other. The basic rule states that if the exchange of information *"reduces or removes the degree of uncertainty as to the operation of the market in question, with the result that competition between undertakings is restricted"*[482] such exchange of information may be incompatible with Article 101 TFEU. It is presumed that the undertakings take into consideration the exchanged information if they take part in a concerted action, unless they prove otherwise.[483]

1.3 Restriction of competition

The existence of an agreement or a concerted practice is not, in itself, prohibited. If it was so, there could never be any contract between two companies not belonging to one undertaking.

Pursuant to Article 101 para 1 TFEU, we may distinguish between by object restrictions and by effect restrictions. If the very object of an agreement/concerted practice is to prevent, restrict or distort competition[484] and if the agreement/concerted practice, by their very nature, can be viewed as injurious to the proper functioning of normal competition;[485] such agreement/concerted practice restricts the competition by object. In other words, if an agreement/concerted practice *"reveal[s] a sufficient degree of harm to competition that it may be found that there is no need to examine their effects"* it restricts competition by object.[486]

[480] Case C-74/14 "Eturas" UAB and Others v Lietuvos Respublikos konkurencijos taryba [2016] ECLI:EU:C:2016:42.

[481] PICHT, P., G., FREUND, B. Competition (law) in the era of algorithms. *Max Planck Institute for Innovation & Competition Research Paper*. 2018, no. 18–10. [online]. Available at: https://doi.org/10.2139/ssrn.3180550. Accessed 23. 2. 2023, p. 17.

[482] Case T587/08 Fresh Del Monte Produce, Inc. v European Commission [2013] ECLI:EU:T:2013:129, para 303; case C194/99 P Thyssen Stahl v Commission [2003] ECLI:EU:C:2003:527, para 81.

[483] Case T587/08 Fresh Del Monte Produce, Inc. v European Commission [2013] ECLI:EU:T:2013:129, para 298.

[484] Case C105/04 P Nederlandse Federatieve Vereniging voor de Groothandel op Elektrotechnisch Gebied v Commission [2006] ECLI:EU:C:2006:592, para 125.

[485] Case C209/07 Beef Industry Development Society and Barry Brothers [2008] ECLI:EU:C:2008:643, para 17; case C8/08 TMobile Netherlands and Others [2009] ECLI:EU:C:2009:343, para 29.

[486] Case T587/08 Fresh Del Monte Produce, Inc. v European Commission [2013] ECLI:EU:T:2013:129, para 304, case C209/07 Beef Industry Development Society and Barry

As presented by Jones and Sufrin in a lucid manner, if there is by object restriction, there is a presumption of illegality of the conduct. The presumption is a rebuttable one, as the undertakings concerned may prove that their agreement is exempted by Article 101 para 3 TFEU. Although, the exception from by object agreement is a very unlikely to occur. On the other hand, if there is no by object restriction, there still may be by effect one.[487] This, however, puts a higher requirements on a competition authority, since it requires a deep economic analysis of the market. [488] It is necessary to establish adverse impact on the parameters of competition.[489]

This definition of by object and by effect restriction presented above is very simplified. Yet, we believe that it is sufficient for the purposes of this paper. One may not omit, however, that there has been an important development during the past decade as to the borderline between the by object and by effect restriction, as well as to the depth of the analysis required in the case of by object restrictions.[490]

Section 2 – Assessment of the model situation

In this section, we will show how the employment of an algorithm may facilitate collusion and how difficult it may be to distinguish between anti-competitive and legitimate behaviour once pricing algorithms are employed. We will use a model situation for this purpose.

Brothers [2008] ECLI:EU:C:2008:643, para 15, case C8/08 TMobile Netherlands and Others [2009] ECLI:EU:C:2009:343, para 28.

[487] JONES, A., SUFRIN, B. *EU Competition Law. Text, Cases and Materials. Sixth Edition.* Oxford: Oxford University Press, 2016, p. 191.

[488] With by object restrictions, adverse impact on the market is to great extent taken for granted. See WHISH, R., BAILEY, D. *Competition Law. Ninth Edition*. Oxford: Oxford University Press, 2018, p. 127.

[489] Case C-382/12 P MasterCard Inc. and Others v European Commission [2014] ECLI:EU:C:20 14:2201, para 93.

[490] Case C-67/13 P Groupement des cartes bancaires (CB) v European Commission ECLI:EU:C: 2014:2204; C-32/11 Allianz Hungária Biztosító Zrt. and Others v Gazdasági Versenyhivatal ECLI:EU:C:2013:160; case C-373/14 P Toshiba Corporation v European Commission ECLI: EU:C:2016:26; case C-469/15 P FSL Holdings and Others v European Commission [2017] ECLI:EU:C:2017:308; case C-228/18 Gazdasági Versenyhivatal v Budapest Bank Nyrt. and Others ECLI:EU:C:2020:265.

2.1 The model situation

Our model situation is as follows.[491] Suppose there is a pricing algorithm on the market which is used by undertakings to calculate the price for their product or services. This pricing algorithm is developed by a third party, a software company. Undertakings have purchased the pricing algorithm from the third party and they have not concluded a written agreement among themselves, especially not such which would contain an obligation to purchase the particular price algorithm from the third party. The market is characterised by a relatively small number of undertakings and high barriers to entry. This parallel use of the same algorithm will lead to supra-competition prices.

In the well-known terminology used by Ezrachi and Stucke[492], the model situation falls within the second category of collusion – *"Hub and Spoke"*, i.e. *"the use of a single algorithm to determine the market price charged by numerous users"*.[493] For instance, Uber (hub) sets the prices for taxi drivers (spokes).[494]

Yet, there is a difference between our model situation and the situation in Uber. In the latter, there are other relations between Uber and the taxi drivers.[495] We believe that this category covers our model situation none the less.[496]

Alternatively, the algorithm can be viewed as falling within the Predictable Agent category. This would be supplemented by the fact that the algorithm is implemented by undertakings independently, or at least so it seems. However, as opposed to a pure Predictable Agent, the undertakings do not develop the pricing algorithms on their own[497]; they purchase the same pre-existing algorithm from a third party.

In the terminology of OECD's Background Note, Algorithms and Collusion, the hypothetical algorithm is viewed as a *Parallel algorithm*. Actually, the situation of several undertakings having their pricing algorithms made by the same

[491] We have analysed a similar situation in our previous work. PATAKYOVÁ, M., T. Notion of Anticompetitive Agreement Challenged in Digital Environment. *European Studies. The Review of European Law, Economics and Politics.* 2020, vol. 7, no. 1, pp. 237–252.

[492] EZRACHI, A., STUCKE, M. E. *Artificial intelligence & collusion: when computers inhibit competition.* [online]. Available at: https://papers.ssrn.com/sol3/papers.cfm?abstract_id=259 1874. Accessed 23. 2. 2023.

[493] Ibid., p. 1782.

[494] Ibid., p. 1788.

[495] For further discussions regarding Hub and Spoke conspiracies, see EZRACHI, A., STUCKE, M. E. *Virtual Competition. First Edition.* Cambridge, Massachusetts: Harvard University Press, 2016, pp. 46 et seq.

[496] Ibid., p. 49.

[497] Ibid., p. 56.

programmers is explicitly recognised and it is understood as a Hub and Spoke scenario; the programmers being the same Hub.[498]

In this regard, OECD opines that *"concerns for competition might arise if companies start sharing the same dynamic pricing algorithm, which may be programmed not to compete against other firms, but to set anti-competitive prices".*[499] Thus, such algorithm allows undertakings first, to collude; and second, to automatically react to changes on the market.

Concerns were also expressed by ICN in the paper *Big Data & Cartels*. It recognises that, in most jurisdictions mere parallelism is not prohibited.[500] This is the case also for EU competition law, under 101 TFEU, there is a necessity for the concerted practice to be proved, i.e. a proof of concertation is required. However, as stated by ICN: "[...] *evidence on common understanding may be difficult to obtain on digital markets, it could be useful to establish under which circumstances using algorithms based on the same or similar formula aligning competitors' prices will constitute a concerted practice."*

2.2 Analysis of the model situation from the substantive point of view

Would the model situation be prohibited by Article 101 TFEU? Several aspects must be considered. Kindly note that, in this part of the chapter, we will discuss if the conduct of the undertakings is prohibited, not whether it could be successfully enforced. We will also limit ourselves to the horizontal agreement/concerted practice among the undertakings.

Scenario 1 – the undertakings agreed that they would purchase the same pricing algorithm. In such case, there was a horizontal agreement in place. Such agreement might have the same characteristics as agreement on setting the prices and it could be by object agreement, if the aim of the undertakings was to set the prices. Exception under 101 para 3 TFEU is improbable.

Scenario 2 – undertakings agreed on purchasing of the same algorithm, however, there was a benign reason behind this. This scenario seems rather difficult to imagine, as one can hardly think of a reason why undertakings *agree* to purchase the same algorithm, if we are not in an Uber-like scenario, which we excluded above.

[498] OECD: *Algorithms and Collusion, Background Note by the Secretariat.* [online]. Available at: https://one.oecd.org/document/DAF/COMP(2017)4/en/pdf. Accessed 25. 1. 2021, p. 26 (para 68).

[499] Ibid., p. 26 (para 67).

[500] ICN: *Big Data & Cartels*. [online]. Available at: https://www.internationalcompetitionnetwork.org/portfolio/big-data-cartels-scoping-paper/. Accessed 29. 10. 2021, p. 7.

Let us be open-minded and suppose that the undertakings wanted to have a discount from the supplier; or that they wanted to support the supplier, e.g. a start-up.

Would such horizontal agreement be prohibited? The answer is rather in the affirmative. One may still claim that it is by object restriction, as undertakings are supposed to develop their pricing policies on their own. On the other hand, there is a need to assess the content of the agreement as well as its goals.[501] Even if the object of such agreement was not anti-competitive, its effects were.

Scenario 3 – there was no agreement between the undertakings. In such case, we are experiencing the same behaviour on the market, however, the mere parallel behaviour is not a prohibited practice. What makes it illegal is an orchestration of such parallel behaviour, i.e. an unnatural practice on the market. In the supposed scenario, this would mean that the undertakings wanted to collude, they knew that all of them would use the same pricing algorithm and they took advantage of it, without an explicit agreement. The risks seem to be similar to those described in relation to exchange of information.

Therefore, if there were contacts among the undertakings, if an exchange of information took place, if the concertation is the only plausible explanation of the parallel behaviour, then there is a concerted practice. If none of these took place, the parallel purchase of the same software is not prohibited.

Scenario 4 – there was no agreement between the undertakings and there were no contacts between the undertakings. In this scenario, we are facing the oligopoly problem, i.e. that kind of situation on the market where prices are set on a supra-competitive level even without exchange of information or communication between the undertakings.[502] However, the tacit collusion in itself is out of scope of EU competition law. *"In the absence of communication and explicit co-ordination, the applicability of provisions on agreements is not straightforward. Mere parallel conduct, such as simultaneous price increases by competitors, is insufficient to indicate co-ordination since it can result from independent and rational behaviour."*[503] It is a highly discussed topic nowadays whether to

[501] Joined cases C-501/06 P, C-513/06 P, C-515/06 P a C-519/06 P GlaxoSmithKline Services Unlimited v Commission of the European Communities (C-501/06 P) and Commission of the European Communities v GlaxoSmithKline Services Unlimited (C-513/06 P) and European Association of Euro Pharmaceutical Companies (EAEPC) v Commission of the European Communities (C-515/06 P) and Asociación de exportadores españoles de productos farmacéuticos (Aseprofar) v Commission of the European Communities (C-519/06 P) [2009] ECLI:EU:C:2009:610, para 58; case C-306/20 SIA "Visma Enterprise" v Konkurences padome, ECLI:EU:C:2021:935, para 62.

[502] OECD: *Algorithms and Collusion, Background Note by the Secretariat.* [online]. Available at: https://one.oecd.org/document/DAF/COMP(2017)4/en/pdf. Accessed 25. 1. 2021, p. 34.

[503] Ibid., p. 35.

broaden the realm of competition law as a reaction to algorithms spreading the tacit collusion (if this proves to be the case).[504]

2.3 Analysis of the model situation from the enforcement point of view

Suppose there is one of the abovementioned infringements of Article 101 TFEU. Would such infringement of Article 101 TFEU be enforceable by a national competition authority?

Scenario 1 – the undertakings agreed that they would purchase the same pricing algorithm. As stated above, this is by object agreement. The position of the competition authority is relatively easy, as the amount of information necessary for proving the infringement is lower compared to by effect restriction. However, the existence of the agreement needs to be proven. Although the competition authorities have at their disposal strong investigatory powers, including inspections[505], one cannot exclude a possibility that there is no evidence on agreement between undertakings. In such a case, the authority is in the same situation as in the Scenario 3 or Scenario 4.

Scenario 2 – undertakings agreed on purchasing of the same algorithm, however, there was a benign reason behind this. This scenario is very similar to the Scenario 1. Once the agreement is proven, the competition authority will have relatively easy job to do, though, as we stated above, it is possible that the undertakings will claim that there is no by object restriction in this case. In such a case, the enforcement authority would need to prove the anti-competitive effects of the agreement. As we assume in the model situation that the parallel use of the same algorithm leads to the supra-competition prices, the by effect restriction is present. Of course, in theory the undertakings may attempt to fulfil the conditions under 101 para 3 TFEU, but their fulfilment seems improbable.

Alternatively, if the agreement cannot be proven, the authority is once again in the same situation as in the Scenario 3 or Scenario 4. Yet, as opposed to Scenario 1, in Scenario 2, the undertakings had a benign reason to conclude the agreement, therefore, the undertakings have possibly less incentive to hide the existence of the agreement.

---

[504] Ibid., p. 35. The broadening of the 101 para 1 TFEU is also advocated by THOMAS, S. *Harmful Signals. Cartel Prohibition and Oligopoly Theory in the Age of Machine Learning.* [online]. Available at: https://ssrn.com/abstract=3392860. Accessed 22. 1. 2023.

[505] Strong investigatory powers are also provided by DIRECTIVE (EU) 2019/1 OF THE EUROPEAN PARLIAMENT AND OF THE COUNCIL of 11 December 2018 to empower the competition authorities of the Member States to be more effective enforcers and to ensure the proper functioning of the internal market.

Scenario 3 – there was no agreement between the undertakings. Even if the existence of agreement cannot be proven based on any evidence, there is a possibility to prove at least the existence of a concerted practice. The fact that all undertakings on the market use the same algorithm may be clear. However, is this the result of abnormal conditions on the market, possibly due to concerted practice? Or, is this the result of a perfectly normal behaviour on the market? Naturally, one would need to establish whether the purchase of the pricing algorithm was rational or not. If it was irrational, then there was probably a concerted practice in relation to purchase the algorithm. If the purchase was rational, the competition authority is in a particularly difficult situation.

The (supra-competition) prices are the result of the pricing algorithm. Therefore, they appear to be out of reach for the undertakings. However, any output (price) produced by the pricing algorithm depends on the input (data inserted into the algorithm), based on which the algorithm calculates the output (price). If the input was given by each undertaking manually, it would be suspicious that the output was the same in each case and it was even a supra-competition price. However, if the algorithm was collecting its input on its own (e.g. by using Internet), the competition authority will find this way of proving the existence of the concerted practice fruitless.

How difficult it would be for the competition authority to prove the concerted practice may be illustrated by looking at the case *ICI v Commission* mentioned in the section 1.2. above. In non-digital settings, competition authorities might possibly base the illegal practice on the following pieces of evidence:

- parallel behaviour leading to abnormal conditions on the market;
- parallel behaviour stabilises price on an above-competition level;
- price developments of undertakings;
- instructions on price developments;
- contacts between undertakings.

However, without a piece of evidence on collusion, such as instructions on price developments or contacts between undertakings, it may be difficult to establish that the undertakings colluded. The pieces of evidence such as current prices and price developments of particular undertakings may not prove the concerted practice itself, as all undertakings use the same pricing algorithm which may explain their similar or even identical pricing behaviour.

Therefore, in our view, the competition authority would need to focus on two sets of evidence. First, evidence on the reasonability of the purchase of the same pricing algorithm. If there was more than one pricing algorithm which had been appropriate, the use of the very same algorithm throughout the sector might seem unnatural. Second, evidence on the input and the use of the pricing algorithm. The pricing algorithm might not lead to the same price if, for instance, each undertaking demands different profit. If the costs are more or less similar for all the undertakings and if they use the same system (pricing algorithm) which calculates the final price, what might be (and should be) different is the margin. Therefore, if the undertakings work with the same margin, this once again might seem as a concerted practice. However, an economic analysis is needed in order to see the specificities of the market.

Scenario 4 – there was no agreement between the undertakings and there were no contacts between the undertakings. Under 101 TFEU in its current use, the mere parallel use of algorithms is not forbidden by EU competition law. Therefore, there is nothing for competition authorities to enforce. If there was no concertation among the undertakings, there is no concerted practice.

2.4 The outcome of the analysis

The purpose of the analysis above was to show that there seems to be a difficulty with substantive assessment and, in particular, with enforcement of collusion which is done through a pricing algorithm. Unsurprisingly, the core stone of the issue lies in the differentiation of the illegal concerted practice and legal parallel behaviour. Even though the result on the market is the same (supra-competition prices), Article 101 TFEU captures only the former. This is nothing new. However, what is new (or, relatively new, given the fact that algorithms are used on the market for some decades already) in an algorithmic setting as opposed to a non-algorithmic setting is how to prove that there is a concerted practice.

As we suggested elsewhere,[506] the use of algorithms is making the liability becoming more subjective. The intention of the undertakings may prove to be crucial from the enforcement perspective.[507] The importance of intention was also highlighted by Ezrachi and Stucke[508].

In our view, the competition authority in the model situation might focus on evidence on the reasonability of the purchase of the same pricing algorithm and

[506] PATAKYOVÁ, M. T. *Employment of Algorithms in Cartels. Drifting Away from Objective Liability in Competiton Law?* Presented during 15th Annual ASCOLA (Virtual) Conference, 27 June 2020.
See also BLOCKX, J. *Antitrust in Digital Markets in the EU: Policing Price Bots.* [online]. Available at: https://papers.ssrn.com/sol3/papers.cfm?abstract_id=2987705. Accessed 20. 1. 2021, pp. 6–7.

[507] The importance of the subjective criteria was presented also by THOMAS, S. *Harmful Signals. Cartel Prohibition and Oligopoly Theory in the Age of Machine Learning.* [online]. Available at: https://ssrn.com/abstract=3392860. Accessed 22. 1. 2023, p. 16.

[508] EZRACHI, A., STUCKE, M. E. *Artificial intelligence & collusion: when computers inhibit competition.* [online]. Available at: https://papers.ssrn.com/sol3/papers.cfm?abstract_id=2591874. Accessed 23. 2. 2023, p. 1784.

evidence on the input and use of the pricing algorithm. However, if the purchase of the algorithm was rational and if the possibility to influence the input and use of the algorithm is very limited, the competition authority will arguably not be able to prove that there was a concerted practice, especially if there is no evidence of prior contact among undertakings.

Section 3 – Proposals de lege ferenda

This section presents proposals which could improve the enforcement of concerted practices in algorithmic settings by competition authorities. For the purposes of this chapter, we have selected three solutions which we apply to the model situation in order to establish whether such proposal would improve the situation of the competition authority. The proposals are inspired by work of other scholars. In this manner, we test the suitability of their proposals.

3.1 Rule of reason analysis

Gal presented a concept of algorithm being a plus factor.[509] She acknowledged that algorithms have many positive effects and it would be wrong to see them in a bad light only; and that it should be clear what is prohibited and what is not. She developed the following rule of reason analysis[510]:

- *"Does the algorithm facilitate or strengthen in a non-negligible way the ability to reach or maintain a jointly profitable market equilibrium?"* If no, the algorithm is legal. If yes, the test continues:
- *"Is the use of the algorithm justified by neutral or procompetitive considerations?"* If no, the algorithm is illegal. If yes, the test continues:
- *"Do these considerations outweigh the algorithm's coordination-facilitating effects, and are the latter needed in order to enjoy the former?"* If yes, the algorithm is legal. If no, the algorithm is illegal.

The use of this rule of reason seems to be clear and understandable. It incorporates elements which suggest the problematic character of pricing algorithms and therefore formulates a meaningful test for assessment the legality of the assessed pricing algorithm.

[509] GAL, M. *Algorithms as illegal agreements*. [online]. Available at: https://papers.ssrn.com/sol3/papers.cfm?abstract_id=3171977. Accessed 23. 1. 2021, p. 37.

[510] Ibid., p. 39. Quotations which follow are from this page.

The problem arising from the test is the necessity to assess the source code of the algorithm. This is not an easy task to do.[511] If we applied this test to the pricing algorithm in our model situation, the answer to the first question is already unclear. The coordination-facilitating effect arises from the fact that more than one undertaking uses this pricing algorithm. The algorithm in itself, used separately, does not have to lead to coordination of prices.

The necessity to analyse the pricing algorithm as such may lead to the unwillingness of (especially smaller) competition authorities to enforce the possible concerted practice. Moreover, if the pricing algorithm contains elements of Artificial Intelligence ("AI"), it will develop over time. Therefore, the algorithm as it departs from the software company, will have different results, compared to the same algorithm after certain time of using.

3.2 Red flags

Gal presented other interesting approach to the pricing algorithms. She listed *"five cases which raise red flags and therefore are good candidates for a repository of cases characterized by prima facie justification for further examining their legality".*[512] The cases are, namely:

1. *"Suppliers consciously use similar algorithms even when better algorithms are available to them."*[513]
2. *"Firms make conscious use of similar data on relevant market conditions even when better data sources exist."*[514]
3. *"Programmers or users of learning algorithms give them similar case studies from which to learn despite those not being the best case studies readily available."*[515]
4. *"Users take actions that make it easier for their competitors to observe their algorithms and/or their databases, and their competitors take actions to observe them."*[516]

---

[511] Evaluation of the source code may be difficult task for competition authorities. This was recognised also by e.g. CAFORIO, V. *Algorithmic tacit collusion: a regulatory approach.* [online]. Available at: https://ssrn.com/abstract=4164905. Accessed 22. 1. 2022, p. 18.

[512] GAL, M. *Algorithms as illegal agreements.* [online]. Available at: https://papers.ssrn.com/sol3/papers.cfm?abstract_id=3171977. Accessed 23. 1. 2021, p. 40.

[513] Ibid., p. 41.

[514] Ibid., p. 41.

[515] Ibid., p. 41.

[516] Ibid., p. 41.

5. *"The user technologically 'locks' the algorithm so that it is difficult to change it."*[517]

The red-flag approach might be beneficial for competition authorities, as it will help them priorities the problematic algorithms. Moreover, the assessment of red-flags does not necessary requires a detailed dive into the source code. For instance, in order to find out whether there is a better algorithm, a better data source, a better case study, competition authority may request this information from relevant parties.

Gal observes that existence of some of the red flags should trigger a deeper investigation.[518] This, however brings the case back to the competition authorities. Essentially, the red-flags should serve for better enforcement prioritisation, however, it does not ease the work for the competition authority.

How many red flags would there be present in the model situation?

The first red flag was already mentioned in part 2.3. above under Scenario 3. We went even further and claimed that presence of this red flag was a piece of evidence in relation to the existence of a concerted practice. The same applies to the second red flag and we refer to our discussion on input to the pricing algorithm.

The third red flag is partially inapplicable, as the undertakings use the very same pricing algorithm. However, if the algorithm contains elements of AI and undertakings teach the algorithm on their own, the use of the same case studies is suspicious. On the other hand, if the teaching is provided by the software company only, the use of the same case studies is not suspicious, as it is used by the one developing software company in relation to their own singular product.

Information related to the forth red flag were not explicitly provided in the model situation. The supra-competition prices are the result of the parallel use of the same algorithm. They are independent from the fact whether one undertaking lets the algorithm "on display" and the other undertaking observes it. However, if the supra-competition prices were reached precisely due to the fact that a database used by each undertaking were "on display" and the algorithm worked also with the databases of the other undertakings, such red flag might be present. One can even say that this appears to be an exchange of information between undertakings, which is a prohibited practice in itself.

As to the fifth red flag, it seems irrelevant in the model situation. The supra-competition prices are reached by the parallel use of the same algorithm. However, if the "locking" of the algorithm helps to reach or maintain the supra-competition prices, and if this was done by the undertakings, this red flag

[517] Ibid., p. 42.

[518] Ibid., p. 42.

would be present. Again, we could even claim that this would be a piece of evidence that a concerted practice exits.

3.3 Broadening the notion of agreement

Another suggested and discussed solution consists in broadening of the notion of agreement.[519] OECD has considered an option to understand "meeting of algorithms" as "meeting of minds".[520] This, however, might catch all situations of parallel pricing algorithms, though not all of them must be harmful. Pricing algorithms may be beneficial for competition.[521] Although, as presented in the beginning of this paper, the notion of agreement is only one element which must be fulfilled for a breach of Article 101 para 1 TFEU to occur. Thus, even if we broaden the notion of agreement to cover tacit collusion between pricing algorithms, this does not lead to the automatic outcome of their illegality. It would still be necessary to prove by object or by effect restriction; and the undertaking could still exempt itself using Article 101 para 3 TFEU. Pricing algorithms may have pro-competitive effects, such as optimisation, innovation and consumer welfare efficiencies.[522]

Applying this solution to the model situation, the undertakings would be caught by Article 101 para 1 TFEU. This would be the case in Scenario 3 as well as in Scenario 4. All parallel pricing algorithms would be caught, although no concertation between undertakings took place. Since, in the model situation, we assume that there are supra-competition prices on the market, the effect of the "meeting of algorithms" will be restriction of competition, therefore, it is prohibited by Article 101 para 1 TFEU. Article 101 para 3 TFEU will most probably not be fulfilled. There is no suggestion of improving the production or distribution of goods or to promoting technical or economic progress; neither any presence of allowing consumers a fair share of the resulting benefit.

From the competition authority's perspective, the model situation is easily solved by this solution. However, how should this be approached from the perspective of undertakings? Although the liability under Article 101 is an objective

[519] OECD: *Algorithms and Collusion, Background Note by the Secretariat*. [online]. Available at: https://one.oecd.org/document/DAF/COMP(2017)4/en/pdf. Accessed 25. 1. 2021, pp. 35–37.
[520] Ibid., p. 37.
[521] GAL, M. *Algorithms as illegal agreements*. [online]. Available at: https://papers.ssrn.com/sol3/papers.cfm?abstract_id=3171977. Accessed 23. 1. 2021, p. 39.
[522] CAFORIO, V. *Algorithmic tacit collusion: a regulatory approach*. [online]. Available at: https://ssrn.com/abstract=4164905. Accessed 22. 1. 2022, pp. 5–7.

one and we are not too concerned for the knowledge of the undertakings;[523] we should not be blind to the point of view of undertakings. How are they to know that there is a tacit collusion in place? How should the undertakings prevent the infringement of Article 101? Should they check what type of pricing algorithm is used by their competitors? This would seem as an exchange of information, which is prohibited by Article 101, as mentioned above. Should they get an assurance from the software company, that the software is not prone to tacit collusion? Yet, the algorithm itself does not have to be prone to tacit collusion, it might be the parallel use of the same algorithm which leads to the supra-competition prices. Should it be the task of the software company to prevent the sale of the same pricing algorithm to several undertakings on the same market? It might be a difficult task for the software company, especially given the fact that the definition of the relevant market may not be straightforward; therefore, the software company does not have to be aware of the fact that its customers are competitors.

Prohibiting the tacit collusion was criticised by Thomas, pointing out a similar point as we have just done above. Thomas claims that undertakings would not know what they should do in order to escape a sanction.[524]

Broadening of the notion of agreement was also advocated by Louis Kaplow[525] and criticized by Calforio. In her view, first, capturing of tacit collusion by Article 101 would essentially lead to price regulation, since tacit collusion, i.e. rational market behaviour leading to supra-competition prices would be prohibited.[526] Second, this broadening might be at odds with the principle of proportionality, given pro-competitive effects of algorithms mentioned above.[527] At this point it should be counterclaimed that pro-competitive effects could still be taken into account within Article 101 para 3 TFEU. Third, Calforio points out to the problem

[523] BLOCKX, J. *Antitrust in Digital Markets in the EU: Policing Price Bots*. [online]. Available at: https://papers.ssrn.com/sol3/papers.cfm?abstract_id=2987705. Accessed 20. 1. 2021, pp. 6–7.

[524] THOMAS, S. *Harmful Signals. Cartel Prohibition and Oligopoly Theory in the Age of Machine Learning.* [online]. Available at: https://ssrn.com/abstract=3392860. Accessed 22. 1. 2023, p. 20.

[525] KAPLOW, L. *Competition Policy and Price Fixing.* Princeton: Princeton University Press, 2013.
More precisely, as interpreted by Posner, Kaplow advocates that, while assessing whether antitrust law was infringed or not, the central focus should be given to the economic outcome, not to the existence of communication. See POSNER, R. A. REVIEW OF KAPLOW, 'COMPETITION POLICY AND PRICE FIXING.' *Antitrust Law Journal.* vol. 79, no. 2, 2014, pp. 761–68, p. 761.

[526] CAFORIO, V. *Algorithmic tacit collusion: a regulatory approach.* [online]. Available at: https://ssrn.com/abstract=4164905. Accessed 22. 1. 2022, p. 13.

[527] Ibid., p. 14

of who should be responsible for the conduct, since algorithmic tacit collusion may be achieved without independently and unilaterally by pricing algorithm.[528]

Conclusion

Pricing algorithms as a challenge for competition law has been discussed for several years. Article 101 TFEU is capable of capturing pricing algorithms with certain limits. In order to analyse this, we presented a model situation, which is close to Hub and Spoke situation in the nomenclature of Ezrachi and Stucke, or parallel algorithms in the OECD's nomenclature. We analysed how the model situation would be assessed from the substantive perspective, and whether and how it could be enforced by a competition authority.

Unsurprisingly, the core stone of the problem lies in distinguishing the mere parallel use of algorithms on the one hand, and concerted practice on the other. As we demonstrated, certain traditional pieces of evidence, such as price development, are fruitless in these situations. None the less, there are other types of evidence which might be used, such as evidence on the rationality of the purchase of the algorithm and evidence on the use of the algorithm, including data used as input for the algorithm.

Furthermore, we have presented three solutions proposed by other authors and we applied them to the model situation. The rule of reason analysis is fruitful, yet it requires analysing the source code of the pricing algorithm, which may be onerous. The red flags are very tempting solution, though it might be beneficial to shift the consequence of a red flag presence from the mere prioritisation to a higher level. In other words, the fact that a red flag is present should lead not only to the fact that a competition authority will look deeper into the case, but it should mean that a concerted practice did probably occur. The last presented solution is, in our opinion, unwelcome.

[528] Ibid., p. 14.

CHAPTER TEN

Does E-commerce Change the ordinary Competitive Conditions? Current Investigations of Geo-blocking and Geofiltering in EU Practice

KSENIIA SMYRNOVA

1. Introduction

Today, it hardly comes into question that competition in the field of e-commerce is specific as compared to 'ordinary' competition. Both various competition authorities and the weight of scholarly publications recognise that the spread of electronic commerce has influenced the way in which competition law had normally operated. With respect in particular to access restriction practices, which have collectively become known as geo-blocking, such measures may be required by the retailer's suppliers, distributors or other relevant contractors, thus constituting an agreement for the purposes of Article 101 of the TFEU. Alternatively, a geo-blocking action can be launched by the retailer himself thus being a unilateral measure. Such measure may be abusive, but in general there is an apparently sound economic justification for limiting access to online stores to foreign customers. The idea of such justification is that increased territorial coverage will entail increased logistics and delivery costs, and these costs should be covered by charging higher prices from foreign customers, failing which an overall increase in retail price would be introduced. This may sound reasonable, however at no point does the effective EU competition law and practice offers guidance as to whether such rationale outweighs the restrictive effects of geo-blocking. This chapter covers the analysis of recent Commission case Guess as a first case where geo-blocking and geo-filtering measures were investigated. And thus, the new legal instruments that prevent restrictive conduct should be discovered by the European Commission, as well as in the updated VBER.

Already in 2002 Balekjian commenting on certain initial developments of e-commerce in the EU observed that 'the mutual relevance of European

Community competition law and e-commerce is being increasingly recognized'[529]. His question at this point ('will the existing rules of competition law be analogously applicable to e-commerce too, or will the specific technicalities of competition in e-commerce generate rules specific to competition in the domain of e-commerce'[530]), however, still remains largely unanswered.

E-commerce opens unprecedented width of client reach and flexibility in options to interact with the client.[531] In itself, the spread of e-commerce is generally a positive development. In wake thereof, market entry and expansion is greatly facilitated, consumers benefit from more choices available, lower prices attainable and overall better quality of services.[532] However, along with positive aspects, several issues of concern have also arisen in connection with the development of e-commerce. In the EU, perhaps the major of such issues is the applicability of the EU rules on competition to anticompetitive conduct of e-undertakings.

Simply put, Article 101.1 of the TFEU prohibits 'all agreements between undertakings, decisions by associations of undertakings and concerted practices' affecting trade between Member States. Conversely, Article 102 of the TFEU outlaws 'any abuse by one or more undertakings of a dominant position within the internal market or in a substantial part of it'. It is a fairly basic exercise to distinguish 'agreement between undertakings' from 'abuse of dominant position' as applied to 'ordinary' business entities. In e-commerce, however, it is not always plain, whether an action affecting competitive conditions is an agreement or a unilateral measure. Moreover, if the measure at issue appears to be in fact unilateral, additional unclarity arises as to whether such measure does qualify for the abuse of dominant position or not.[533]

Turning to practical situations, suppose a large clothing retailer runs an online shop distributing merchandise under the retailer's own brand. In principle,

[529] *E-Commerce and European Competition Law.* In *E-Commerce: Law and Jurisdiction. The Comparative Law Yearbook of International Business.* Special Issue. Ed. by Dennis Campbell, Susan Woodley. Kluwer Law International, 2002, p. 79.

[530] Supra note 1, p. 80.

[531] E-commerce and its impact on competition policy and law in Singapore. A DotEcon study for the Competition Commission of Singapore. Final Report – October 2015, p. 38. Available at: http://www.dotecon.com/assets/images/DotEcon-Ecommerce-Final-Report.pdf (last accessed 14. 6. 2016, 22:19).

[532] Lim Wei Lu, Jaime Pang et al. *E-Commerce in Singapore – How it affects the nature of competition and what it means for competition policy.* 2 December 2015, paras 1–2, p. 1. Available at: https://www.gov.sg/~/sgpcmedia/media_releases/CCS/press_release/P-20151201-1/attachment/Annex%20C_CCS%20Paper%20on%20ECommerce%20in%20Singapore.pdf (last acces sed 14. 6. 2016, 22:26).

[533] Lars Kjølbye, Alessio Aresu, Sophia Stephanou. *The Commission's E-Commerce Sector Inquiry – Analysis of Legal Issues and Suggested Practical Approach.* p. 3. Available at: SSRN: http://papers.ssrn.com/sol3/papers.cfm?abstract_id=2620569 (last accessed 14. 6. 2016, 22:09).

the retailer is fully in a position to determine prices at which it offers its goods in different Member States. Furthermore, the retailer can limit access to its online store for nationals of certain Member States or generally for persons residing abroad. However, whether such conduct would be voidable under either Article 101 of the TFEU or Article 102 of the TFEU is an issue of elaborate fact analysis.

With respect in particular to access restriction practices, which have collectively become known as geo-blocking, such measures may be required by the retailer's suppliers, distributors or other relevant contractors, thus constituting an agreement for the purposes of Article 101 of the TFEU. Alternatively, a geo-blocking action can be launched by the retailer himself thus being a unilateral measure. Such measure may be abusive, but in general there is an apparently sound economic justification for limiting access to online stores to foreign customers. The idea of such justification is that increased territorial coverage will entail increased logistics and delivery costs, and these costs should be covered by charging higher prices from foreign customers, failing which an overall increase in retail price would be introduced.[534] This may sound reasonable, however at no point does the effective EU competition law and practice offers guidance as to whether such rationale outweighs the restrictive effects of geo-blocking.

The same is applicable also to another popular model of e-commerce – an online marketplace or a site selling products of other manufacturers. In this case, a critical issue of applicability of the Competition Law is whether the marketplace operates without being appointed as distributor to manufacturers or, vice versa, acts in the basis of a distribution or agency agreement with the manufacturers.

Thus, it is apparent that a number of critical issues of competition law have either to be established in a slightly different way (as in the second situation outlined above) or balanced out against non-traditional considerations (as in the first situation outlined above). Therefore, ordinary competitive conditions do function differently as applied to e-commerce. Ideally, the conclusion should also cover the competition law rules, which should reflect and accommodate that difference. As of the present standpoint, it remains largely only to be seen, whether they will eventually do.

The Digital Single Market constitutes one of the key political priorities of the European Commission (EC) through which it seeks to improve access to

[534] European Commission's initial findings on geo-blocking practices in EU e-commerce, Antitrust Update. Available at: https://www.dlapiper.com/en/uk/insights/publications/2016/03/european-commission-findings-on-geo-blocking/ (last accessed 15. 6. 2016, 03:03).

cross-border e-commerce for consumers and businesses throughout the European Union[535]. To achieve its ambitions, the EC:

– has intensified the enforcement of competition law with regard to restrictive practices related to online sales; and
– has been updating and modernising the applicable legislative framework as well as creating new legislative instruments[536] with a view to lessen and ultimately remove barriers impeding the increased use of online trade.

2. Anticompetitive restrictions in e-commerce

At the point when the European Commission introduced A Digital Single Market Strategy for Europe one of the key apparatuses intended to guarantee the working of the computerized single market (by relationship with the working of the European market) is antitrust law. Simultaneously, the Commission started concentrating on the internet-based trade market, and in May 2017 introduced a report on the aftereffects of its work[537].

The Commission's report takes note of that makers are attempting to deal with the appropriation chain of their items utilizing three key techniques:

– sales directly to customers through their own online stores, thus competing with traditional distributors;
– application of selective distribution systems, in which the goods are delivered only to authorized retailers;
– the inclusion in the distribution agreement of a number of restrictions on pricing, the use of price comparison sites or online tools in general.

There are several issues concerned restrictive measures taken into account by European Commission: geoblocking; regulatory pricing, price parity or "Most-Favorite nation clause"; internet search discriminatory practices; vertical restraints in the sphere of e-commerce.

[535] EU Digital Single Market. Available at: https://eufordigital.eu/discover-eu/eu-digital-single-market

[536] Such practices include, for example, fixing a distributor's or buyer's resale margin, fixing the maximum level of discount that a distributor can grant from a prescribed price level, making the granting of rebates or the reimbursement of promotional costs subject to the observance of a given price level, imposing minimum advertised prices (MAPs) that prohibit distributors from advertising prices below a level set by the suppliers and linking sales prices to those of competitors.

[537] European Commission, Final report on the E-commerce Sector Inquiry. 10. 5. 2017. Available at: https://ec.europa.eu/competition/antitrust/sector_inquiry_final_report_en.pdf

2.1 Geoblocking

The concept of "Geo-blocking" could be described in several ways. According to European Commission staff working document[538], "geo-blocking refers to commercial practices whereby online providers prevent users from accessing and purchasing consumer goods/digital content services offered on their website based on the location of the user in a Member State different from that of the provider". Basically, the same meaning was referred by European Parliament in it`s briefing papers "Geo-blocking usually refers to discriminatory practices that prevent online customers from accessing and purchasing a product or a service from a website based in another Member State, automatically re-route them to a local site, and refuse delivery or payment based on the location or place of residence of the user. As a result, consumers face different selling conditions for products or services purchased online on the basis, for instance, of their IP address, their postal address or the country of issue of their credit card. These practices which limit cross-border trade in the internal market and result in geographical market segmentation have long been a concern for consumer protection, competition and copyright laws".[539]

Furthermore, legislation of the European Union has got specialized legislation based on the prohibition of the geo-blocking, represented by Regulation (EU) 2018/302 of 28 February 2018. Even, the regulation has got direct definition of the "geo-blocking" in it's term, the preamble which describes the aim of the act has got described, that geo-blocking occurs where traders operating in one Member State block or limit access to their online interfaces, such as websites and apps, by customers from other Member States wishing to engage in cross-border transactions. It is not sufficient to abolish state barriers between Member States in order to realize the full potential of the internal market, which is defined as an area without internal borders in which the free movement of, among other things, goods and services is ensured, in order to realize the full potential of the internal market. It is possible for private parties to hinder such abolition by putting in place restrictions that are incompatible with internal market freedoms. It can also arise when particular businesses impose different general terms of access to their goods and services to consumers from other Member States than they do to their own customers, whether they do so online or in person. Some traders' practices deny or limit access to goods or services by customers who wish to engage in cross-border

538 Available at: https://ec.europa.eu/competition/antitrust/ecommerce_swd_en.pdf#page=17

539 Available at: https://www.europarl.europa.eu/RegData/etudes/BRIE/2016/586620/EPRS_BRI%282016%29586620_EN.pdf#:~:text=Geo-blocking%20usually%20refers%20to%20discriminatory%20practices%20that%20prevent,location%20or%20place%20of%20residence%20of%20the%20user

transactions, and some traders apply different general conditions of access in this regard, which are not objectively justified. Although different treatment may be justified in some cases, in other cases, some traders' practices deny or limit access to goods or services by customers who wish to engage in cross-border transactions, or some traders apply different general conditions of access in this regard, which are not objectively justified. The mentioned regulation consists of the description of both geo-blocking and geo-filtering. From the mentioned above definitions, in the narrow sense, we may presume, that geo-blocking practice, is a practice when the online customer automatically relocation of customer from the chosen platform, to the platform, based on his geolocation.

However, the mentioned regulation includes quite a more subject of regulations, that describes nature of geo-blocking: "1. A trader shall not, within the range of means of payment accepted by the trader, apply, for reasons related to a customer's nationality, place of residence or place of establishment, the location of the payment account, the place of establishment of the payment service provider or the place of issue of the payment instrument within the Union, different conditions for a payment transaction..." Generally, this makes the context of geo-blocking wider, than just rerouting. It includes the concept of declining of payments, from those whose payment provided registered in the area, chosen for geo-blocking by provider of goods or services. In this meaning, we shall conclude, that geo-blocking, consists of all actions, directly or indirectly aimed at restricting access of customer from the specific geographical place to the goods, services or content proceeded through the Internet.

In it`s wiling to boost the European digital market, and make it as place "without borders" to avoid discrimination and ensure the united market, commission set out several examples, when geo-blocking couldn't be justified:

- Sale of products without delivery: in case when a customer buys a product, such as electronics, clothes, sportswear or a book, which the trader does not deliver cross-border to the customer's Member State. Foreign customers should be entitled to delivery in the country of the trader in the same way as local customers.
- Sale of electronically supplied services: in case when a customer buys an electronically delivered service, such as cloud services, data warehousing, website hosting.
- Sale of services provided in a specific physical location: in case when a customer buys a service which is supplied in the premises of the trader or in a physical location where the trader operates. This category covers services such as concert tickets, rental of summer accommodation and car hire.

Some of these rules are also compliant with the Directive 2006/123/EC of the European Parliament and of the Council of 12 December 2006 on services in the internal market where stated, that: "The principle of non-discrimination within the internal market means that access by a recipient, and especially by a consumer, to a service on offer to the public may not be denied or restricted by application of a criterion, included in general conditions made available to the public, relating to the recipient's nationality or place of residence. It does not follow that it will be unlawful discrimination if provision were made in such general conditions for different tariffs and conditions to apply to the provision of a service, where those tariffs, prices and conditions are justified for objective reasons that can vary from country to country, such as additional costs incurred because of the distance involved or the technical characteristics of the provision of the service, or different market conditions, such as higher or lower demand influenced by seasonality, different vacation periods in the Member States and pricing by different competitors, or extra risks linked to rules differing from those of the Member State of establishment. Neither does it follow that the non- provision of a service to a consumer for lack of the required intellectual property rights in a particular territory would constitute unlawful discrimination." Such regulations are also specifically described in the Regulation, where stated, that

1. A trader shall not apply different general conditions of access to goods or services, for reasons related to a customer's nationality, place of residence or place of establishment, where the customer seeks to:

(a) buy goods from a trader and either those goods are delivered to a location in a Member State to which the trader offers delivery in the general conditions of access or those goods are collected at a location agreed upon between the trader and the customer in a Member State in which the trader offers such an option in the general conditions of access;

(b) receive electronically supplied services from the trader, other than services the main feature of which is the provision of access to and use of copyright protected works or other protected subject matter, including the selling of copyright protected works or protected subject matter in an intangible form;

(c) receive services from a trader, other than electronically supplied services, in a physical location within the territory of a Member State where the trader operates.

The mentioned above practices, in all cases considered as discriminative practices in the meaning of Directive 2006/123/EC of 12 December 2006 on services in the internal market, and those which not comply with Regulation (EU) 2018/302 of 28 February 2018. Basically, in the sphere of trade of goods this is the main vision related to the geo-blocking, applied by the European Commission, however, due to the emerging web-technologies, it brings us novelty, but European Commission has got also responds to it, by analyzing novelty practices.

As practice shows the following examples could be considered as restrictive, such as:

- Access to websites: to ban the blocking of access to websites and to use of automatic re-routing without the customer's prior consent. This will increase price transparency by allowing customers to access different national websites. This provision also applies to non-audio-visual electronically supplied services, such as e-books, music, games and software.
- Non-discrimination in payments: while brokers stay allowed to acknowledge whatever installment implies they need, the proposition remembers a particular arrangement for non-segregation inside those installment implies. It covers circumstances when diverse treatment is a consequence of the area of the installment account, the spot of foundation of the installment administrations supplier or the spot of issuance of the installment instrument.

Diverse treatment is precluded assuming these three conditions are met: installments are made through electronic exchanges by credit move, direct charge, or card-based installment instrument; the broker can demand solid client confirmation by the payer, and; the installments are in a money that the dealer acknowledges.

Through this we might see that EC methodology is focused on formation of brought together single market, and geo-obstructing is considered as an instrument, which didn't permit to make a solitary, bound together internal market.

Nonetheless, there are a few special cases from the boycott of geo-blocking:

First and foremost, geo-blocking could be applied, provided that there are severe measures in the neighborhood enactment concerning indicated circles of the economy (for instance, in case the buying of cigarettes permitted uniquely to residents);

Secondly, European Commission described some spheres, where ban of geo-blocking is not related. These spheres include:

- Transport services: These services are avoided from the proposition as existing EU transport enactment as of now expressly denies separation dependent on ethnicity and spot of home for three kinds of transport: air flight tickets, transport and mentor transport and waterborne vehicle. As a feature of the continuous survey of the guidelines for rail traveler freedoms, the Commission intends also to incorporate a comparable restriction into the forthcoming change for rail transports.
- Retail financial services: Access to these administrations is excluded from the proposition as the forthcoming subsequent archive to the Green Paper on retail monetary administrations will address segregation when getting to administrations like taking out a home loan, opening a ledger, or purchasing

cross-line protection. In any case, the proposition covers all distinctions in treatment worked by specific installment implies.

- Audiovisual services: Working with the admittance to varying media administrations across borders is essential for different drives under the Digital Single Market technique. The Commission today introduced refreshed EU decides for varying media that strikingly reinforce the advancement of European works (official statement). Under its continuous modernisation of the EU copyright system, the Commission introduced in December 2015 a proposition permitting Europeans to go with the advanced substance – films, sports communicates, music, digital books and games – that they have bought or preferred at home (official statement). Following stages identified with the modernisation of EU copyright rules in 2019[540].

As a component of its Digital Single Market Strategy, the Commission was attempting to permit Europeans to have better admittance to advanced items and administrations just as to a more extensive substance across Europe. To accomplish this objective, the Commission is chipping away at various drives in corresponding to address the specificities of various kinds of items, administrations and content. For instance, under the computerized contracts drive the Commission has proposed to completely orchestrate the vitally required buyer freedoms appropriate to the stock of advanced substance and distance deals of items. When embraced, these recommendations will lessen the expenses coming about because of contrasts in agreement law, make lawful sureness for organizations, and assist buyers with benefiting as much as possible from shopping on the web across the EU.

These standards are unmistakably identified with the relations with clients. Be that as it may, for this situation the issues with contest guideline is additionally in vital significance.

What are the ties between geo-blocking and anticompetitive practices? Starting around 2010, the European Commission's Regulation on Vertical Agreements in the EU has denied the limitation of merchants' more right than wrong to online deals – such activities are alleged no-nonsense limitations, which are disallowed paying little heed to the piece of the pie of members in such arrangements, except if the gatherings can demonstrate that the adequacy of such limitations might offset their enemy of serious impacts.

The European Commission's Guide to Vertical Restraints, which clarifies the arrangements of the guideline, forbids confining a merchant's right than to online deals. Additionally, both dynamic –when the merchant intentionally draws

[540] Directive (EU) 2019/790 of the European Parliament and of the Council of 17 April 2019 on copyright and related rights in the Digital Single Market and amending Directives 96/9/EC and 2001/29/EC (Text with EEA relevance.) OJ L 130, 17. 5. 2019, pp. 92–125.

in purchasers from "unfamiliar" regions, for instance, through publicizing, email mailings to clients from regions allocated to another wholesaler, and latent – when the merchant "comes" purchasers from different domains without reason the wholesaler's activities to draw in them. Specifically, it is denied to oblige the wholesaler: to deny admittance to his webpage or naturally divert clients from "unfamiliar" domain (counting selective) to the destinations of those merchants to whom the pertinent region is allocated; decline to sell the merchandise/pay if, as indicated by the charge card, the purchaser has a place with the region appointed to another merchant (counting elite); put down certain boundaries on the portion of online deals in the all out deals of the wholesaler (for instance, to sell close to half of merchandise by means of the Internet); pay more for an item for online deals than for a comparable item available to be purchased in a supposed "block" store. The severity of the prohibition on limiting web-based deals is affirmed by EU case law. In 2011, on account of the beauty care products organization Pierre Fabre (brand names Klorane, Avène), which sells beauty care products and cleanliness items essentially through drug stores, the European Court thought that it is hostile to cutthroat to sell just in a "customary" store with a drug specialist.

2.2 Regulatory pricing. Price parity or "Most-Favorite nation clause"

In general, the condition of price parity obliges the supplier to provide a product or service at a price not lower and / or on terms no less favorable than those already provided to other consumers. The essence of this approach stems from the vertical relationships established between online platforms and providers of goods and services sold on them. By setting price parity conditions, online platforms eliminate the risk of free use of their infrastructure by suppliers who can use the "name" of the platform to advertise their product but sell it through other channels.

In addition, by closing" suppliers and their products and services on their platform, digital companies receive significant sets of large data on products, prices, demand dynamics, the analysis of which, in turn, can further strengthen the market power of online platforms.

With the development of e-commerce, the establishment of conditions on price parity has been repeatedly criticized by antitrust authorities in Sweden, Germany, France, Italy, Japan, the United States.

At the same time, despite the decisions taken by some antitrust authorities of these countries to recognize the conditions of price parity as anti-competitive practice, such actions were recognized as legal in the courts.

For example, since 2015, Booking has been facing accusations from antitrust authorities (mostly European) about its pricing policy. The main claim against the company is the use of the condition of price parity in contractual relations with hoteliers.

In the context of hotel reservations, there are two options for establishing price parity. In a broad interpretation, the condition of price parity requires the accommodation facility to provide rooms on the booking portal on terms no less favorable than those that already exist for any online or offline distribution channels, including the official website of the accommodation facility. In a narrow sense, the condition of price parity gives the hotel the opportunity to offer to read the terms through any other sales channels other than its official website.

Widespread application of the price parity problem is a problem for the development of competition, while opinions on the narrow application of this condition differ widely: in some jurisdictions this interpretation is considered anti-competitive (for example, France has legally prohibited the use of any form of price parity conditions for hotel reservations), and in others – a necessary measure to prevent situations where the hotel will actually use the Booking site for free.

It should be noted that after the announcement by several European competition authorities, in particular Germany, France, Italy and Sweden, of their concerns about the development of competition in the online hotel booking market due to Booking, in 2015 the company excluded from its contracts with hotels application of the condition of price parity, leaving only a narrow interpretation. As a result of these actions, the antitrust authorities of France and Italy terminated the relevant investigations.

In turn, the Federal Office for Cartels of Germany (case No. B 9-121/13 of 22 December 2015) initiated an investigation into the Expedia and Booking platforms on the grounds of using price parity conditions in their relations with accommodation facilities. According to the German Federal Cartel Office, the narrow application of the price parity condition is no less anti-competitive than the broad one. Thus, the agency explains that by setting price parity conditions, Booking distorts competition, both between booking platforms and between hotels. The narrow application of the price parity condition limits the incentives for hotels to offer different prices on different platforms. Technically, price parity conditions in the narrow sense allow hotels to set different prices, but on its official website room rates must be no lower than on the Booking website (in case of a reduced price on its own website, the hotel must also lower the price on the Booking platform). This provision also applies to price offers to participants in hotel loyalty programs. This circumstance limits the independence of hotels in setting prices and reduces their incentives to offer a better price than on their own website or Booking platform.

To get on the Booking platform, hotels enter into an agreement with the company, which stipulates that part of the proceeds from the sale of each number reserved through the Booking platform is transferred to the account of the online platform. Overall, Booking receives 10-15% from each booking. In some cases (for example, in high season) Booking income can be 30–50% of each booking. The Booking business model is like the business models of its competitors in Germany – the HRS61 and Expedia platforms.

The decision of the German antitrust authorities, according to which Booking's actions were found to be in breach of German antitrust law, was subsequently overturned by the Düsseldorf Regional Regional Court. The court's decision is based on the results of a survey of consumers and hoteliers. The Court ruled that, unlike the widespread application of the price parity condition, the narrow application of this principle does not restrict competition but, on the contrary, is necessary to establish a fair and balanced relationship between platform companies such as Booking and hotels. The narrow application of the price parity condition prevents the hotel from using unfair publicity when it is listed on one well-known platform, and all transactions are made through another or through its official website, where lower prices are offered. The court called such behavior "inappropriate redirection of customer bookings."

In 2018, the Swedish Patent Court (Case No. RMT. 7779-18 of 9. 5. 2019) considered the lawsuit of the Visita travel business association and found Booking guilty of violating EU competition law by abusing its dominant position in the markets of online travel agencies and hotel reservation systems. The complainant argued that the provisions on price parity adversely affect competition in these markets, as hotels are less likely to offer better conditions and prices to other booking systems, which will lead to weakening price competition, as well as increasing barriers to market entry.

In turn, Booking explained that these provisions are necessary to avoid the irreversible use of invested funds and to ensure that its service functions as a reliable tool for comparing prices for hotel rooms. Deciding that these provisions imply potential anti-competitive effects as they do not allow hotels to apply lower prices on their own sites than on Booking.

At the same time, the decision of the Patent Court was appealed to the Court of Appeal, which overturned the original decision because Visita had failed to sufficiently prove that the price parity conditions could have an anti-competitive effect. In particular, the Court of Appeal points to the lack of coverage of the survey conducted by Visita, which covered only large hotels in Sweden, and also found that decisions on prices through Booking are made by hotels themselves, and therefore the latter are relatively free to choose pricing policy. In 2015, the European Commission opened a case (No. AT.40153 dated

4. 5. 2017) against the digital company Amazon on the grounds of abuse of a dominant position in the market of online e-book sales, which in agreements with suppliers of e-books intended for circulation in the territory The EU set the conditions for price parity.

As part of the investigation, the EC concluded that the agreements between Amazon and e-book providers contain provisions on the conditions for price parity. Amazon required e-book providers to notify the establishment of more attractive terms and prices for the sale of e-books on other sites, and to offer the same or similar conditions to Amazon.

In addition, some agreements contain provisions on parity of choice, which means that e-book providers, when placing alternative versions of books with better functionality (e.g supplemented versions; versions with more interactive elements, etc.), are required to offer Amazon these ebook versions. If such versions are not supported by the Amazon Kindle reader, e-book providers must adjust the format of their books to the specifications of the device.

According to the EC, the inclusion of price parity conditions in contracts reduces the incentives for e-book suppliers to offer more favorable terms prices to other sites and distribution channels, as well as to create fundamentally new business models. The stipulation of price parity agreements reduces the potential for competing platforms where suppliers could potentially sell e-books and strengthens Amazon's market position. Amazon disagreed with the EC's findings, but proposed a number of conditions that would address the Commission's concerns about the restriction of competition in the English and German e-book retail markets by making the following commitments for a period of 5 years from the EC decision:

1) to eliminate from agreements with suppliers of e-books intended for realization in the territory of the EU conditions on price parity (and other parity conditions which caused concerns of the EC). Amazon undertakes to notify each e-book provider within 7 days that these contract terms will expire;
2) not to include conditions on price parity (and other parity conditions that have caused concerns of the EC) in new agreements with suppliers of e-books intended for sale in the EU, regardless of the language of their writing.

2.3 Internet search discriminatory practices

Anti-competitive practices in the Internet search market are very diverse. Antitrust investigations in this market, which ended in record fines, have already been completed in several jurisdictions, such as European Union. In a dynamically changing Internet search market, search algorithms and search engine user interface tools, once developed, can be used without significant variations in different countries. Accordingly, the unscrupulous practices of multinational corporations, such as Google, in the Internet search market of different countries are often similar, as these countries may use a similar version of the search algorithm.

Summarizing the existing practice of suppressing anti-competitive behavior in the Internet search market, it can be stated that entities with greater market power in these markets may abuse such power by discriminating against certain services, for example by:

- providing preferential terms for own services by placing information about them on the top lines of search results;
- application of algorithms aimed at lowering the rating of competing services;
- ignoring the relevance of search results.

In turn, in a number of antitrust proceedings, the practice of providing preferential terms for own search engine services, as contrary to antitrust law was not recognized due to the fact that the use of prioritization of own services aimed at improving search quality and usability.

In the case before the European Commission (case No. 39740 of 27 June 2017), actions by Google were found to be an abuse of a dominant position in the general search market on the Internet, by giving its shopping comparison service an advantage that limited competition in the comparative shopping market.

In particular, the EC notes that since 2008, Google has begun to implement fundamental changes in European markets in a strategy aimed at promoting its shopping comparison service, which was based on Google's dominance in the general Internet search market by:

- systematically giving priority to their own the shopping comparison service (when a consumer enters a query into the Google search engine for which the Google shopping comparison service wants to show results, they appear at the top of or next to the search results);
- downgrading competing purchase comparison services in search results (Competing purchase comparison services appear in Google search results based on Google's general search algorithms. Google has included several criteria in these algorithms, resulting in lower competitive price comparison services. The facts show that even the most A reputable competing service appears on average only on the fourth page of Google search results, and others even lower. Google's own shopping comparison service does not follow Google's general search algorithms, including such reductions. Google, while competing shopping comparison services are much less noticeable).

This means that by giving priority only to its own shopping comparison service and lowering the level of competitors, Google has gained a significant advantage over competitors.

Google has introduced this practice in all 13 countries of the European zone, where its shopping comparison service has been introduced[541].

Since the beginning of each abuse, Google's shopping comparison service has increased its traffic 45 times in the UK, 35 times in Germany, 19 times in France, 29 times in the Netherlands, 17 times in Spain and 14 times in Italy. At the same time, the attendance of competing price comparison services has dropped significantly. For example, the EC found concrete evidence of a sudden drop in traffic to certain competing websites by 85% in the UK, to 92% in Germany and 80% in France. These sharp differences also could not be explained by other factors. Some competitors have adapted and managed to recover some of the traffic, but not completely. In its decision, the EC concludes that Google dominates the common Internet search markets throughout the EEA (in all 31 countries) in most cases by more than 90%.

There are high barriers to entry into these markets, in part because of network effects: the more consumers use a search engine, the more attractive it becomes to advertisers. The profits can be used to attract even more consumers, and the data that the search engine collects about consumers can also be used to improve their business.

In this way, Google abused its dominant position in the general search on the Internet, giving its price comparison service an illegal advantage and restricting competition in the markets of comparative purchases.

Following the hearing, the EC found a violation by Google. The European Commission has fined Google 2.424 billion euros. In accordance with the 2006 Guidelines on the methods of setting fines imposed under Article 23 (2) (a) of Regulation No. 1/2003, the fine was calculated on the basis of the amount of Google's revenue from its purchasing comparison service in 13 EEA countries.

The European Commission's Decision also requires Google to cease its illegal activities within 90 days of the Decision and to refrain from any measures having the same or equivalent object or effect. If Google does not comply with the decision of the European Commission, it will be liable for non-compliance with the requirements of up to 5% of the average daily world turnover of Alphabet, the parent company of Google.

2.4 Vertical restraints in the sphere of e-commerce

Vertical restraints became a crucially important tool, in the sphere of e-commerce. While online sales became more and more popular in the modern world,

541 European Commission, E-Commerce Sector Inquiry, paras 181.

vertical restraints are usually provided in distributive agreements and contains aspects of behavior, which distributor shall adhere. Thus, not all vertical agreements are anti-competitive practice in the framework of the EU legislation. In some cases, the vertical agreements could be beneficial for the market, it`s important to differentiate the practice of infringement from the normal practice of vertical restraints.

Accordingly, to the OECD report, the most common practices of the infringement of competition law through the vertical restraints are:

Selective and exclusive distribution models. According to the OECD, exclusive model are defined as: "Exclusive distribution refers to vertical arrangements by which a supplier contracts to sell their goods to one single distributer within a specific territory <...>" and selective distribution model defined as: <…> vertical arrangements by which a supplier defines minimum standards for admission to its distribution network, agreeing to supply all distributors which meet these requirements[542]." It`s important to notice, that selective and exclusive distribution notices are also used in offline commerce, however, according to the European Commission Inquiry on e-commerce and OECD background documents[543] on the infringements of competition in e-commerce, there is a special "internet addendums" which limit the possibilities of online sale.

In fact, selective and exclusive distribution models are not itself direct infringement of EU competition rules. It`s. important to access, what was the purpose of this vertical measures. In this issues, the distributive models applied for the e-commerce are not too different from the standard distribution models, used for the standard "offline" distribution practices. Furthermore, all distributions explications are standard subject to the related article of TFEU, and all consequent acts.

Furthermore, it`s important to notice, that many suppliers use the "mixed" types of exclusive and selective models of distribution.

Online sales bans. By and large restrictions on web deals establish the clearest vertical impediment to Internet business: such conditions force a direct legally binding denial on resale of the important item in the web-based climate. Regarding EU law, the Pierre Fabre case obviously settled such preclusions as "by object" infringement of Article 101(1) TFEU. Indeed, Pierre Fabre didn't include an express internet-based deals boycott, however rather a prerequisite inside a specific circulation framework that a certified drug specialist should be available at the actual retail deals point of the items concerned (beauty care products

[542] MARSDEN, P., WHELAN, P. (2010) Selective Distribution in the Age of Online Retail. 31 p. *European Competition Law Review.* 26 p.; BUCCIROSSI, P. (2015) Vertical Restraints on E-Commerce and Selective Distribution. *Journal of Competition Law and Economics.* vol. 11, 747 p.

[543] Available at: https://one.oecd.org/document/DAF/COMP(2018)3/en/pdf

and other cleanliness items)[544]. This the Court interpreted as a true prohibition on web deals, and, as needs be, an item limitation, holding that:

The "by object" treatment of online deals boycotts seemingly appears to be legit with regards to the creating Digital Single Market inside the EU, by which the disallowance of online deals divergently affects possible clients from other Member States, who are denied maybe the main practicable means to source labor and products cross-border. This is predictable with the methodology of the European Commission towards different limitations to Internet business, for example, the alleged geo-impeding, which is the subject of ongoing EU optional enactment to a great extent restricting such practices[545]. A somewhat unique methodology has been pushed in Australia to what in particular is named "worldwide value segregation": the public Competition Policy Review contended that such worries are better addressed through buyer schooling instead of any authoritative arrangement[546].

Outside the market mix setting, a profound suspicion of online deals boycotts can in any case be safeguarded, regardless, to the extent that such forbiddances address an unbalanced constraint of intra-brand contest to accomplish real efficiencies, like securing retailer venture, guaranteeing arrangement of valuable administrations and taking care of the issue of free-riding. As per Marsden and Whelan[547], these efficiencies can ordinarily be gotten through less prohibitive means. Specifically, a prerequisite that internet-based retailers should likewise keep up with no less than one physical outlet, to guarantee satisfactory arrangement of in-person client administrations, is by and large viable with Article 101(1) TFEU. Altogether online deals boycotts have likewise been held unlawful by different public contest specialists, remembering for the United Kingdom[548] and France[549].

Online marketplace bans. Online commercial center boycotts address a less widely inclusive assortment of online deals boycott: rather than a sweeping preclusion of web based business channels, retailers are authoritatively kept

[544] C-439/09 Pierre Fabre Dermo-Cosmétique SAS v Président de l'Autorité de la concurrence and Ministre de l'Économie, de l'Industrie et de l'Emploi. ECLI:EU:C:2011:649.

[545] See Council of the European Union Press Release. "Geo-blocking: Council adopts regulation to remove barriers to e-commerce." Published 27 February 2018. Available at: online at http://www.consilium.europa.eu/en/press/press-releases/2018/02/27/geo-blocking-council-adoptsregulation-to-remove-barriers-to-e-commerce/

[546] Commonwealth of Australia (2015), Competition Policy Review. Final Report, published March 2015.

[547] Footnote 10.

[548] Competition and Markets Authority Press release. "CMA fines Ping £1.45m for online sales ban on golf clubs," published 24 August 2017. Available at: https://www.gov.uk/government/news/cma-fines-ping-145m-for-online-sales-ban-on-golf-clubs

[549] Décision n° 12-D-23 du 12 décembre 2012relative à des pratiques mises en œuvre par la société Bang & Olufsen dans le secteur de la distribution sélective de matériels hi-fi et home cinema. Available at: http://www.autoritedelaconcurrence.fr/pdf/avis/12d23.pdf.

from exchanging merchandise through web-based commercial centers worked by outsider go-betweens. On the other hand, retailers are by and large allowed to sell through their own Internet based outlets. The chief justification for why makers wish to confine deals through outsider web-based stages identifies with brand picture and situating: makers might be worried that relationship with an internet based commercial center might decrease customers' view of the quality or worth of its items. Other recognized worries incorporate a craving to battle the offer of fake items, the need to guarantee satisfactory arrangement of explicit pre-and after-deals benefits, the counteraction of free-riding on existing dispersion channels and an absence of client assistance communication at stage level. The topic of how such limitations ought to be drawn closer under contest law is quite discussed[550]. Contending for a "by object" judgment and identical characterization of such conditions as no-nonsense limitations under the VBER, accentuated the crucial job of online commercial centers in supporting the lively aggressive elements which mark the Internet business area today. Such stages lower hindrances to passage for online retailers, while at the same time expanding value straightforwardness and diminishing quest costs for clients. This distrust is noticeable in a few choices taken at public level inside the European Union, especially inside Germany. The Bundeskartellamt's examination of Adidas gives a valuable representation. Adidas had precluded retail resale by means of "open" commercial centers, including those which worked with distributed exchanges, the offer of recycled merchandise, or which acknowledged postings of similar item by a few venders. The German rivalry authority, taking the view that the disallowance couldn't comprise a subjective basis for the motivations behind the Metro standards administering particular dissemination under EU law, arrived at a primer resolution that it penetrated Article 101 TFEU and the same homegrown arrangement. The case was at last settled by the respondent, which changed its states of dispersion. he more extensive view, notwithstanding, is that internet based commercial center boycotts are for the most part faultless under contest law to the degree that these don't block online deals all the more comprehensively[551]. This is predictable with the discoveries of the European Commission's E-Commerce Sector Inquiry, which contended against any as such judgment of provisos on the premise that commercial center boycotts don't confine either dynamic or aloof deals, nor do they focus on division of the computerized single market[552].

[550] Oxera (2017), "No Free Rides? Platform Bans in Light of the Coty Case" Oxera Agenda, December 2017.

[551] Witt, A. C. (2016). "Restrictions on the Use of Third-Party Platforms in Selective Distribution Agreements for Luxury Goods. *European Competition Journal.* vol. 12, 435 p.

[552] European Commission, E-Commerce Sector Inquiry, paras 506-9.

This perspective is further clear in the new judgment of the Court of Justice in Coty[553].

Price comparison tool bans. Examination devices help purchasers in finding the best Internet based arrangements, expanding market straightforwardness and driving value contest inside the online business area. The evaluating data that is collected and positioned by value examination instruments is, ordinarily, given by the web-based retail outlets themselves, which also generally pay a for every snap expense to the correlation webpage for every client that hence gets to their site. Numerous makers view value correlation locales as for the most part useful to their organizations, upgrading brand perceivability and customer data in regards to their products. In certain events, notwithstanding, providers try to restrict retailer commitment with value examination apparatuses, essentially on the premise that such destinations over-accentuate the significance of value contest, in this way lessening other significant elements of the retail offering, which might have thump on adverse consequences for the provider's image picture. Whether or not limiting admittance to value examination instruments is viable with rivalry law remains generally unanswered. In contra-qualification to its somewhat harmless way to deal with commercial center boycotts, the European Commission declined to embrace a position either possibly in support of such limitations in its E-Commerce Sector Inquiry. It noticed that value examination devices don't address an unmistakable Internet based retail channel, yet rather intend to improve shoppers' collaborations with existing channels. Denying access doesn't hence confine a retailer's capacity to shape an immediate relationship with explicit clients yet may make it more hard for retailers to draw in clients at first, or for clients to find fitting retailers. Then again, to the degree that restriction on plan of action to value correlation devices is expected principally to smother value contest, a similarity might be attracted to value solidifying impacts of circuitous types of RPM, which result at last in more exorbitant costs to shoppers. This worry is perceptible in the Bundeskartellamt's requirement activity against ASICS for keeping a preclusion on seller utilization of value correlation motors, hence maintained by the most noteworthy public court. The encroachment choice underscored the damage to buyers particularly that follows from disavowal of admittance to such destinations: buyers lose the capacity to sift through the most reasonable proposition that is accessible on the web.

[553] Case C-230/16 Coty Germany GmbH v Parfümerie Akzente GmbH EU:C:2017:94

3. Shifting of EU legal regulation

On 10 May 2022, the EC published its new Vertical Block Exemption Regulation (VBER) and new Vertical Guidelines, which entered into force on 1 June 2022. The new legislation will be valid for 12 years with an evaluation report after eight years. The new VBER provides for a transitional period for existing agreements until 31 May 2023, by which time those agreements must be aligned with the new regime.

The EC's revisions to the previous regime reflect changes in market dynamics and the platform economy since the VBER was adopted in 2010 and come after an extensive public consultation process that began in 2019. The final version of the new VBER and Guidelines follows an earlier draft published by the EC in July 2021. One of the main objectives of the revisions was to provide up-to-date guidance on online restrictions and ensure a harmonised approach across the EU, as the previous set of rules did not offer sufficient clarity. As a result, national authorities and courts had interpreted the prior legal framework with wide discretion, which led to contradictory and often inconsistent enforcement practices.

Although the new VBER and Guidelines clarify the applicable legal framework concerning exclusive and selective distribution and online sales restrictions, uncertainty still arises, especially with regard to the new online sales hardcore restriction[554]. As the Guidelines constitute soft law, national authorities and courts are still susceptible to interpret the views expressed by the EC differently Outright bans on Internet sales constitute by-object restrictions of competition within the meaning of Article 101(1) of the Treaty on the Functioning of the European Union (TFEU) and correspond to hardcore constraints under the new VBER. Such practices survive antitrust scrutiny only where the four criteria under Article 101(3) TFEU are cumulatively met.

Discussing specifically the context of platform competition, Ezrachi[555] has cautioned that a distinction should be drawn between competition law analysis and state intervention through legislation or regulation, which frequently reflect an alternative, though legitimate, political or social agenda. The latter may be required if competition analysis reveals an absence of cognisable harm in the technical antitrust sense, yet where the state is concerned with wider distributional or other consequences. Three such alternative regulatory avenues will be surveyed here: issue-specific legislation; consumer protection and data protection laws; and quasi-utilities regulation of online platforms.

---

[554] Decision of the EC in Asus, AT. 40465; Denon & Marantz, AT. 40469; Philips, AT. 40181; and Pioneer, AT. 40182.

[555] EZRACHI, A. (2015). The Competitive Effects of Parity Clauses on Online Commerce. *Oxford Legal Studies Research Paper*. N. 55/2015.

4. Geo-blocking and geo-filtering regulation

Geo-blocking encompasses various practices through which online sellers restrict cross-border sales based on consumers' nationality, residence or place of establishment. Frequently, online sellers allow consumers to access and purchase goods or services cross-border, but nonetheless extend different terms and conditions if the customer is in a different Member State (geo-filtering).

Geo-blocking may take many forms, including but not limited to:

- blocking users access to websites if they are located in another Member State;
- automatically rerouting users to another website of the same or a different service provider (possibly with a different price);
- refusing the delivery of goods or services based on the user's location or place of residence; and
- refusing certain payment methods based on geographic criteria related to the location of the user, their bank or credit account, or their banking institution.

It clearly follows from the above that such practices essentially constitute a form of discrimination based on unjustified geographic criteria: online sellers treat EU consumers differently for reasons related to the users' nationality, place of residence or establishment.

By blocking or, at the very least, restricting EU consumers' access to cross-border trade, those practices de facto amount to geographical market segmentation and, therefore, contravene the EU's core free movement principles as well as the digital single market objective.

The EC's Final e-Commerce Sector Inquiry Report published in May 2017 documented the extensive use of geo-blocking: 38 per cent of the responding retailers selling consumer goods online and 68 per cent of the responding digital content providers affirmed that have made recourse to geo-blocking mea sures[556].

On 28 February 2018, the EU adopted Regulation (EU) 2018/302 (the Geo-blocking Regulation), which entered into force on 22 March 2018 and became applicable as of 3 December 2018.

The Geo-blocking Regulation seeks to remove unwarranted, discriminatory restrictions to users' access to cross-border trade and services and obliges online sellers to treat similarly situated EU consumers in the same manner, irrespective of their nationality, place of residence or establishment.

---

[556] Report from the Commission to the council and the European Parliament Final report on the E-commerce Sector Inquiry. Available at: https://ec.europa.eu/competition/antitrust/sector_inquiry_final_report_en.pdf

5. Evolution of jurisprudence of European Court of Justice in geo-filtering cases

5.1 Pierre Fabre case

The Court of Justice of the EU (CJEU) first addressed restrictions on online sales through its judgment in Pierre Fabre. Members of Pierre Fabre's selective distribution system were required to sell cosmetics and personal care products only at brick-and-mortar stores and in the presence of a trained pharmacist [557]:

The CJEU held that a general and absolute ban on Internet sales in the context of a selective distribution network constitutes a restriction of competition by object within the meaning of Article 101(1) TFEU. It reasoned that such a ban 'considerably reduces the ability of an authorised distributor to sell the contractual products to customers outside its contractual territory or area of activity. It is therefore liable to restrict competition in that sector.'

The CJEU further held that the restriction in question could not be justified on the basis of any safety and public health grounds and that maintaining a prestigious image does not qualify as a legitimate aim for limiting competition. The CJEU also found that the measures under review could not benefit from the VBER. A general Internet ban operates as a limitation on active and passive sales within the meaning of Article 4(c) VBER.

The CJEU nonetheless left it open whether such measures could benefit from the individual exemption under Article 101(3) TFEU. Online sales restrictions also constitute a high priority for national enforcers.

A vertical agreement between a supplier and distributor must not restrict the latter's commercial freedom. In particular, the reseller must remain free to set its own resale prices. The direct or indirect imposition of a minimum retail price (resale price maintenance – RPM) is traditionally considered to be a serious infringement of the competition rules. The RPM clause constitutes a restriction of competition by object and cannot in principle be exempted. A supplier therefore engages in anticompetitive behavior when it imposes the setting of resale or discount prices at a specific level.

Article 101(1)(a) TFEU specifically prohibits agreements that 'directly or indirectly fix purchase or selling prices or any other trading conditions'. Moreover, Article 4(a) of the new VBER specifically excludes from the block exemption agreements that include: *"the restriction of the buyer's ability to determine its sale price, without prejudice to the possibility of the supplier to impose a maximum*

[557] European Commission, Antitrust: Commission opens three investigations into suspected anti-competitive practices in e-commerce (2 February 2017). Available at: https://ec.europa.eu/commission/presscorner/detail/en/IP_17_201

sale price or recommend a sale price, provided that they do not amount to a fixed or minimum sale price as a result of pressure from, or incentives offered by, any of the parties."

This covers all behaviour on the part of the seller intended to constrain the buyer to resell the contract products at or above a certain price. Paragraph 187 of the new Vertical Guidelines gives a non-exhaustive list of practices that are tantamount to price maintenance. The EC further refers to practices, the combination of which tends to indicate price maintenance, such as coupling a resale price recommendation with incentives to apply a certain price level. The new Vertical Guidelines also provide specific guidance on setting minimum advertised prices that is considered a form of RPM.

Paragraph 196 of the new Vertical Guidelines explains how RPM restricts intra-brand or inter-brand competition by setting out the anticompetitive effects following from RPM practices[558]. The new Vertical Guidelines also recognise that there are situations where RPM restrictions may lead to efficiencies and be justified pursuant to Article 101(3) TFEU[559]. By way of example, it can be legitimate to impose RPM for a short period in the context of the promotion of a new product.

Algorithms and other electronic surveillance technologies further facilitate RPM practices in online sales and exacerbate the anticompetitive impact resulting therefrom. The relevant technologies:

- allow prices to be automatically adopted and adjusted, ensuring that the imposed RPM is followed at all times; and

[558] The Vertical Guidelines identify that RPM practices may, among other things:
- facilitate collusion between suppliers by enhancing price transparency in the market, thereby making it easier to detect whether a supplier deviates from the collusive equilibrium by cutting its price;
- eliminate intra-brand price competition and facilitate collusion between the buyers (i.e., at the distribution level);
- soften competition between manufacturers or between retailers, in particular when manufacturers use the same distributors to distribute their products and RPM is applied by all or many of them;
- pressure on the margin of the manufacturer, in particular where the manufacturer has a commitment problem;
- be implemented by a manufacturer with market power to foreclose smaller rivals; and prevent price competition between distributors, therefore reducing innovation at the distribution level.

[559] New Vertical Guidelines, Paragraph 197. For example, fixed resale prices may be necessary to organize a coordinated short-term, low price campaign; or a minimum resale price can be used to prevent a distributor from using the product of a supplier as a loss leader since regularly reselling a product below the wholesale price could damage the brand image of that product and overtime reduce overall demand for it and undermine supplier's incentives to invest in quality and brand image.

- render monitoring compliance with any imposed RPM practices easier and, therefore, increase any corresponding sanctioning. This explains why RPM practices in the e-commerce field have recently come under the enforcers' spotlight.

On 24 July 2018, the EC closed its investigation on consumer electronics manufacturers Asus, Denon & Marantz, Philips and Pioneer by imposing a total fine of €111 million. The EC found that the infringing parties had limited price competition among retailers 'by restricting the ability of their online retailers to set their own retail prices for widely used consumer electronics products such as kitchen appliances, notebooks, and hi-fi products', leading to an increase in consumer prices. The use of algorithms to implement and enforce the RPM practices under review was a central piece of the EC's analysis. As the EC explained at the time the investigation was opened: *"The effect of these suspected price restrictions may be aggravated due to the use by many online retailers of pricing software that automatically adapts retail prices to those of leading competitors. As a result, the alleged behaviour may have had a broader impact on overall online prices for the respective consumer electronics products."*[560]

Similarly, national competition authorities have been increasingly active in investigating and sanctioning RPM practices in online sales.

5.2 Valve case

The Commission opened formal antitrust proceedings into the bilateral agreements concluded between Valve Corporation and the five PC video game publishers on 2 February 2017. On 5 April 2019 the Commission sent Statement of Objections to Valve and the five videogame publishers on "geo-blocking" of PC video games.

Article 101 of the Treaty on the Functioning of the European Union and Article 53 of the Agreement on the European Economic Area prohibit agreements between companies that prevent, restrict or distort competition within the EU's Single Market.

The European Commission has fined Valve, owner of the online PC gaming platform "Steam", and the five publishers Bandai Namco, Capcom, Focus Home, Koch Media and ZeniMax € 7.8 million for breaching EU antitrust rules.

Valve and the publishers restricted cross-border sales of certain PC video games on the basis of the geographical location of users within the European Economic Area ('EEA'), entering into, the so called "geo-blocking" practices.

[560] Case C-439/09, Pierre Fabre Dermo-Cosmétique SAS, ECLI:EU:C:2011:649 (Pierre Fabre).

The fines for the publishers, totalling over €6 million, were reduced due to the companies' cooperation with the Commission. Valve chose not to cooperate with the Commission and was fined over €1.6 million.

Steam is one of the world's largest online PC video gaming platforms offering more than 35 000 games worldwide. It allows users, upon authentication, to directly download or stream PC video games. It also allows users who buy PC video games outside Steam, such as in brick-and-mortar shops (e.g. on DVDs) or digitally through downloads from third-party websites, to activate and play video games on Steam.

Valve provides to video game publishers the technical means to activate and play games on Steam, including those games bought outside Steam, through the so-called, "Steam activation keys". Publishers include those keys in their PC video games for user authentication/activation. The PC video games are then sold by third party distributors across the EEA. Valve also offers to the publishers a territory control function, which enables the setting up of geographical restrictions upon activation. The combination of Steam activation keys with the territory control function enables the "geo-blocking" of PC video games based on the geographical location of the user.

The video game publishers granted Valve a non-exclusive license to exploit specified PC video games on a worldwide basis, including the entirety of the EEA. In turn, the publishers obtained from Valve a license for the use of Steam activation keys for distribution of those PC video games outside Steam. The publishers requested Valve to set up geographical restrictions and to provide geo-blocked Steam activation keys. The publishers provided those keys to their distributors for sale and distribution of the PC video games in the Member States concerned. As a result, users located outside a designated Member State were prevented from activating a given PC video game with Steam activation keys.

The Commission found that by bilaterally agreeing to geo-block certain PC video games from outside a specific territory, Valve and each publisher partitioned the EEA market in violation of EU antitrust rules. In particular, today's Decisions conclude that Valve and the publishers engaged in the following geo-blocking practices:

- Bilateral agreements and/or concerted practices between Valve and each of the five PC video game publisher implemented by means of geo-blocked Steam activation keys which prevented the activation of certain of these publishers' PC video games outside Czechia, Poland, Hungary, Romania, Slovakia, Estonia, Latvia and Lithuania, in response to unsolicited consumer requests (so-called "passive sales"). These lasted between one and five years and were implemented, depending on the cases, between September 2010 and October 2015.

- Geo-blocking practices in the form of licensing and distribution agreements concluded bilaterally between four out of the five PC video game publishers (i.e. Bandai, Focus Home, Koch Media and ZeniMax) and some of their respective PC video games distributors in the EEA (other than Valve), containing clauses which restricted cross-border (passive) sales of the affected PC video games within the EEA, including the above-mentioned Central and Eastern European countries. These lasted generally longer, i.e. between 3 and 11 years and were implemented, depending on each bilateral relationship, between March 2007 and November 2018.

The geo-blocking practices concerned around 100 PC video games of different genres, including sports, simulation and action games. They prevented consumers from activating and playing PC video games sold by the publishers' distributors either on physical media, such as DVDs, or through downloads. These business practices therefore denied European consumers the benefits of the EU's Digital Single Market to shop around between Member States to find the most suitable offer.

The Commission has concluded that the illegal practices of Valve and the five publishers partitioned the EEA market in violation of EU antitrust rules.

The five publishers cooperated with the Commission by providing evidence of added value to the investigation, and by expressly acknowledging the facts and the infringements of EU antitrust rules.

The Commission therefore granted reductions to the fines depending on the extent of this cooperation ranging from 10% (for Bandai, Focus Home, Koch Media and ZeniMax) and 15% (for Capcom).

The breakdown of the fines imposed on the publishers is as follows:

Videogame publisher	Reduction for cooperation	Fine (€)
Bandai Namco	10 %	340 000 EUR
Capcom	15 %	396 000 EUR
Focus Home	10 %	2 888 000 EUR
Koch Media	10 %	977 000 EUR
ZeniMax	10 %	1 664 000 EUR

Valve chose not to cooperate with the Commission. The Commission has therefore adopted a prohibition Decision against Valve under the ordinary antitrust procedure and has imposed a total fine of € 1 624 000 on Valve.

6. Conclusion

As far as the EU recognizes internal market and free movement of goods as fundamental pillars for the it`s function, digitalized trade became that tool, that totally fits in the free movement of goods and external market policy. However, due to novelty distribution practices, and vertical agreements which became *sue generis* for the existing law system, the European Commission, as main executive body of the European Union become investigating and regulating this sphere. Firstly, the research flow into E-commerce inquiry, where European Commission collected the statistics and the information of the practices. After this, the Guess case appeared, where European Commission on the basis of the collected information from the inquiry started investigation and fined Guess company for the restrictive measures on the online platforms. It`s very important due to that fact that it was reaction of the European Commission on the misconduct and infringements of the companies, resulted in the infringement. Also, the case demonstrated specific of the application of the Article 101 TFEU and Vertical Block Exemption Regulation on the e-commerce practices. Important feature of the case, is the used fine, and it`s reduction, used by European Commission.

Geo-blocking encompasses various practices through which online sellers restrict cross-border sales based on consumers' nationality, residence or place of establishment. Frequently, online sellers allow consumers to access and purchase goods or services cross-border, but nonetheless extend different terms and conditions if the customer is in a different Member State (geo-filtering).

The Geo-blocking Regulation seeks to remove unwarranted, discriminatory restrictions to users' access to cross-border trade and services and obliges online sellers to treat similarly situated EU consumers in the same manner, irrespective of their nationality, place of residence or establishment.

Especially current EC practice shows unprecedented brave preconditions on geo-blocking practice in the form of licensing and distribution agreements concluded bilaterally between four out of the five PC video game publishers.

PART IV.

CYBER SECURITY, CIVIL LIABILITY, CYBER CRIMES AND LEGAL INSTRUMENTS FOR EFFECTIVE RESILIENCE

CHAPTER ELEVEN

EU Legal Framework of Digital Security Vulnerabilities

AGNES KASPER, ANETT MÁDI-NÁTOR

1. Introduction

Code is at the heart of digital infrastructures. All code and systems (both hardware and software) contain vulnerabilities, which can be exploited in various ways. Software needs a physical medium, i.e. microprocessors, to run, however these are not perfect either. Compromises in these vectors can have cascading effects and lead to terrible consequences. The discovery of the critical Spectre and Meltdown vulnerabilities in Intel microprocessors in 2017 have affected billions of devices worldwide ever since. Desktops, laptops, cloud servers, smartphones cannot be fully fixed by software patches without redesigning and changing the faulty processors. This means that these are and probably will be around for some time, just waiting to be exploited by malicious actors.

Hardware and software vulnerabilities are technology-bound, both of which are subject to EU legislation as goods and/or services, thus vulnerabilities therein can also be addressed in the light of different existing and proposed EU laws dealing with the quality of products, standards, market practices, etc. This chapter starts off by briefly discussing the Spectre and Meltdown vulnerabilities case, also elaborating on key concepts and governance frameworks in place. Then we map the current EU legal framework that applies to such security vulnerabilities down the supply chain, and provide a brief analysis of some of the legal issues relevant to the case at hand. This will include consideration of criminal law instruments, consumer laws, as well as existing and proposed cybersecurity legal instruments.

As nothing is without flaws, digitalisation has brought around its vulnerabilities. Software and hardware products have flaws or vulnerabilities, some of which may be exploited. Vulnerabilities make many cyber attacks possible. Recent epic examples of the devastating consequences of cyber attacks include the 2017

Wannacry[561] and 2020 SolarWinds crisis[562], both of which have had a significant global reach and stirred up reactions from decision-makers, academia and industry. Wannacry swept the world infecting systems and locking data in over 150 countries paralyzing hospitals and critical infrastructures. SolarWinds Orion had thousands of elite customers starting from US Government to top cybersecurity firms, and it was proposed that all the compromised systems should be "burned down to the ground and rebuilt".[563] There is one thing common to both infamous cyber attacks: the attackers exploited digital security vulnerabilities.

Vulnerabilities are typically in the system from the beginning, so software and hardware products are designed, developed and marketed with vulnerabilities. These may remain hidden or be discovered at any time during the lifecycle of the product. Security researcher communities make an effort to maintain vast databases and try to systematically disclose information about some vulnerabilities. For example the MITRE Corporation's CVE database published over 20 000 CVE records in 2022, where each record corresponds to a cybersecurity vulnerability.[564] However, these lists are far from exhaustive.

None of this is new to the technical community and the industry. On the other hand, it took the regulators many devastating global cyber incidents to step up and consider intervention in the markets, where producers/manufacturers have not sufficient incentives to prioritize security over functionality, appearance and other properties of products. The authors argue that the discovery, disclosure of the Spectre and Meltdown vulnerabilities in microprocessors[565] and subsequent lawsuit against Intel Corp.[566] has been a game-changer for regulation concerning vulnerabilities. These vulnerabilities are design flaws in all microprocessors by major manufacturers since 1995, which made virtually every system on the globe affected. The scale of the problem left no choice but to seek changes, and EU legislators now explicitly address digital vulnerabilities in current and proposed legal instruments. While the exploitation of vulnerabilities fall within the scope of more generic legislation

[561] CERT-EU Advisory 2017-12 'WannaCry Ransomware Campaign Exploiting SMB Vulnerability'. Available at: https://cert.europa.eu/static/SecurityAdvisories/2017/CERT-EU-SA2017-012.pdf. See also Europol's information page on the Wannacry ransomware. Available at: https://www.europol.europa.eu/wannacry-ransomware.

[562] Detailed description of the case. Available at https://www.gao.gov/blog/solarwinds-cyberattack-demands-significant-federal-and-private-sector-response-infographic

[563] 'Hacked Networks Will Need to Be Burned 'Down to the Ground' US News 18. December 2020. Available at: https://www.usnews.com/news/business/articles/2020-12-18/hacked-networks-will-need-to-be-burned-down-to-the-ground

[564] Available at: https://www.cve.org/

[565] Available at: https://www.ncsc.gov.uk/guidance/meltdown-and-spectre-guidance

[566] City of Providence v. Intel Corp. US District Court for the Northern District of California, case nr 5:2018cv00894, filed 12 February 2018.

prohibiting misuses of information and communication technologies, the new regulatory approach is aimed at actually reducing and remedying vulnerabilities.

The following chapters will use the Spectre and Meltdown vulnerabilities, and the themes of the lawsuit against Intel Corp. to map and illustrate the developing legal landscape regulating digital vulnerabilities. Chapter 2 starts with practical insight into the mechanics of vulnerabilities and points to some of the early initiatives addressing this challenge. Chapter 3 gives an overview of the technical and the legal case concerning Spectre and Meltdown. Chapter 4 maps and analyses existing EU legislation relevant in the context, and finally Chapter 5 considers the EU newest and most targeted proposal that is expected to put an end to security-ignorant practices in each step of the product supply-chain.

2. Digital vulnerabilities

2.1 Basic concepts

According to the US National Institute of Standards and Technology (NIST) the former definition of vulnerability is "[a] flaw or weakness in the design or implementation of an information system (including the security procedures and security controls associated with the system) that could be intentionally or unintentionally exploited to adversely affect an organization's operations or assets through a loss of confidentiality, integrity, or availability".[567] The updated definition reads as "[w]eakness in an information system, system security procedures, internal controls, or implementation that could be exploited or triggered by a threat source."[568] Here weakness stands as a synonym for deficiency. Such vulnerabilities or deficiencies are primarily categorized as network vulnerabilities, operating system vulnerabilities, process or procedural vulnerabilities, and human vulnerabilities. From another perspective, vulnerabilities may occur both in the hardware or in the software that runs on the hardware or in a special combination of these that are called embed systems.

Such vulnerabilities may equally affect the overall security posture of any device regardless where a vulnerability lays due to complexity of systems and to the high level integration. Exploiting such vulnerabilities (i.e. crossing privilege boundaries or performing unauthorized actions) may result in rare cases of single effects, in more cases of combined and cascading effects and consequences. For that an adversary or attacker needs at least one applicable tool or technique

[567] NIST SP 800-37

[568] Available at: https://nvlpubs.nist.gov/nistpubs/SpecialPublications/NIST.SP.800-37r2.pdf, p.111.

that can connect to a system weakness and utilize it. In this respect, this makes vulnerabilities attack surfaces.

Academia, but mostly government and industry, has set standards and categories to better identify threats and those weaknesses that threats can exploit. Hence, when a vulnerability is discovered, it is analyzed, evaluated, identified, collected, cataloged, and tracked. As a first step, analysis and evaluation is conducted in CVE, a glossary for Common Vulnerabilities and Exposures (CVE), launched by MITRE Corporation. The CVE glossary classifies vulnerabilities in a way that it provides comparable metrics for standardized evaluation of discovered vulnerabilities for consumer hardware and software. The CVE code is often used for prioritizing vulnerabilities.[569] As a second step, when the CVE code is assigned, the vulnerability gets registered in the U.S. National Vulnerability Database (NVD), the U.S. government repository of standards-based vulnerability management data – represented using the NIST Security Content Automation Protocol (SCAP)[570]. Collecting and cataloging is also done according to SCAP[571]. As the third step, SCAP evaluates vulnerabilities and assigns a unique identifier to each. Fourth, NVD also utilizes the Common Vulnerability Scoring System (CVSS) established by FIRST (Forum of Incident Response and Security Teams). The CVSS provides a way to capture the principal characteristics of a vulnerability and produce a numerical score reflecting its severity[572]. That CVSS value evaluates the threat level of each vulnerability from low to high or even critical. However, vulnerabilities do not get published immediately after discovery and reporting (if reported), and industry good practice allows the manufacturer/producer time to fix the vulnerability. Moreover, there is clear interest in coordinating various vulnerability disclosure programs.

2.2 Coordinated Vulnerability Disclosure

Publishing discovered vulnerabilities via NVD and through CVE, and some other similar digital databases originating from the US, has become a global standard hence provides the technical background for vulnerability disclosure policies of manufacturers[573] and software developers. That includes missions of internal CERT and CSIRT units to support IT system development and maintenance

[569] Available at: https://cve.mitre.org/docs/cve-intro-handout.pdf

[570] Available at: https://nvd.nist.gov/

[571] Available at: https://nvlpubs.nist.gov/nistpubs/SpecialPublications/NIST.SP.800-126r3.pdf

[572] Available at: https://www.first.org/cvss/

[573] See for example https://www.intel.com/content/www/us/en/security/security-practices/coordinated-disclosure.html

processes, vulnerability handling and management processes, bug bounty programs and secure development processes.

While such policies may differ at each manufacturer and developer, global initiatives have also been launched that raise the need for vulnerability management to a more strategic, at some points even to political level. The aim of such initiatives is to grow transparency and establish confidence-building measures in cyberspace. The London Conference on Cyberspace in 201[574] was the first of such kind of political level discussions including nations, academia and industry, followed by the second edition in Budapest in 2012[575], the third in Seoul in 2013[576], and the fourth in The Hague in 2015[577] where the Dutch National Cyber Security Centre produced a guideline document on responsible disclosure of vulnerabilities to which the previous conferences and discussions set a solid basis. The initiative of creating a coordinated vulnerability disclosure platform was supported by the Netherlands, Hungary, and Romania and by many others from the private sphere[578], and so the evolution of the Coordinated Vulnerability Disclosure Manifesto started in 2015, also with the formulation of and supported by the Global Forum of Cyber Expertise (GFCE) then and there. This version, primarily driven by the Dutch community, vastly involves private entities representing the European industry as signatories. ENISA on the other hand declared its third party independent role in its good practice guide early in 2016[579], but it has followed suit and promotes as well as coordinates national coordinated vulnerability disclosure policies ever since.[580] The role of ENISA stays in line with its original mandate, meaning it can respond to the needs of the EU institutions, EU Member States and the business community. Nevertheless, it primarily focuses on Member States' vulnerability disclosure policies.

574 Available at: https://citizenlab.ca/cybernorms2012/BaseleyWalker2011.pdf, p. 35

575 Giles-Hagestad: Divided by a common language. NATO CCDCOE, 2013, p. 2.

576 Available at: https://repo.kinu.or.kr/bitstream/2015.oak/2308/1/0001469273.pdf#page=69, p. 83.

577 Available at: https://www.ripe.net/publications/news/industry-developments/report-on-global-conference-on-cyberspace-gccs-2015

578 Available at: https://thegfce.org/initiatives/coordinated-vulnerability-disclosure/

579 Good Practice Guide on Vulnerability Disclosure, ENISA, 2016, p. 12.

580 Available at: https://www.enisa.europa.eu/news/enisa-news/coordinated-vulnerability-disclosure-policies-in-the-eu

3. Spectre, Meltdown and Intel Corp: the Global game-changer combination

3.1 Spectre & Meltdown vulnerabilities

A computer is not a single device, but a system of amalgamated devices working together to achieve the desired tasks. As such, computers and other digital devices consist of hardware and software. The term hardware refers to the tangible components and devices a computer is made of.

Computer security issues equally affect hardware and software, but surely stem from vulnerabilities referring to the weaknesses found in the design process and implementation of hardware architecture, which can be exploited by a hacker or perpetrator to mount an attack. Hardware is usually manufactured before or during software development, but cannot be easily updated like software, yet hardware executes the software. Hence, it is often the last line of defence against potential attacks meaning that if the attack reaches the hardware, the damage may be permanent or irreversible.[581] Though neither permanent nor irreversible, a most remarkable hardware vulnerability is transient execution (a side-channel vulnerability) enabling *Spectre* and *Meltdown*, the two vulnerabilities seriously affecting Intel Corp. processors among many more, also contributing to Intel Corp. adapting its own Coordinated Vulnerability Disclosure.

CPU stands for central processing unit, otherwise known as processor or microprocessor, the "brain" of computing devices. That is the unit of electronic circuitry to execute instructions of a computer program or operations. Most modern CPUs are implemented on integrated circuit microprocessors. Such CPUs have speculative execution capabilities, which improves processor performance. It is basically an optimization technique where a processor performs some task in a parallel manner.

As hardware design and attack patterns are highly connected, depending on the design and architecture of the CPU (a hardware unit), speculative execution, which is a functional feature of processors, can introduce side-channel-attack vulnerabilities[582]. Transient execution CPU vulnerabilities are vulnerabilities in which a speculative execution optimization implemented in a microprocessor is exploited to leak data to an unauthorized party or to an adversary, potentially

---

[581] YOUNIS, Z., MAHMOOD, B. An In-Depth vision to hardware design security vulnerabilities. *Jordanian Journal of Computers and Information Technology (JJCIT).* vol. 8, no. 1, March 2022, pp. 33–44. (p. 33).

[582] Available at: https://vuls.cert.org/confluence/display/Wiki/Vulnerabilities+Associated+with+CPU+Speculative+Execution

compromising confidentiality and potentially integrity of data.[583] A classic example of a speculative execution bug is *Spectre*, a side-channel attack first discovered in 2017, but since January 2018 when it was reported as CVE-2017-5715 as CVE-2017-5753 and later as CVE-2018-3639 and CVE-2018-3665, many similar vulnerabilities have been identified[584], affecting all Intel Corp. processors or at least specific types of those, depending on variation of Spectre and type of processor.[585]

Spectre class vulnerabilities have largely remained unfixed. To fix this vulnerability CPU designers would have to disable speculative execution on hardware level, which may result in a significant performance loss of processors, which is against consumer expectation that is to suffer zero performance loss. Disabling speculative execution would also need an update in the hardware design, ie. a new iteration of hardware that is a replacement of CPU in the affected computing devices.

In order to otherwise overcome transient execution type CPU vulnerabilities methods may be conducted in the following layers. Besides replacing the affected hardware, microcode (embed program code in the processor) can also be updated, but it alters the software code that the CPU runs on and it would have to be conducted on all individual CPUs, as well as on all operating systems that run on the affected CPUs. Operating systems and virtual machines may also be updated, but this often results in significant loss of performance, again. Software recompilation is also possible, but it comes with the same result as applying mitigation measures on operating system or virtual machine layers, ie. loss of performance.[586]

A different but related attack type is *Meltdown reported as* CVE-2017-5754 and CVE-2018-3640, practically affecting millions of customers of Intel Corp. and other processor manufacturers. Meltdown is also a side-channel attack, leading to information leakage, compromising confidentiality of data.[587] Unlike in the

[583] BULCK, J., VAN, MINKIN, M., WEISSE, O., GENKIN, D., KASIKCI, B., PIESSENS, F., SILBERSTEIN, M., THOMAS, F., WENISCH, T. F., YAROM, Y., STRACKX, R. FORESHADOW: Extracting the Keys to the Intel SGX Kingdom with Transient Out-of-Order Execution. *In Proceedings of the 27th USENIX Security Symposium.* August 15–17, 2018, Baltimore, MD, USA. ISBN 978-1-939133-04-5.

[584] Available at: https://vuls.cert.org/confluence/display/Wiki/Vulnerabilities+Associated+with+CPU+Speculative+Execution

[585] Available at: https://www.intel.com/content/www/us/en/search.html?ws=typeahead#q=spectre&sort=relevancy

[586] Paul Kocher, Daniel Genkin, Daniel Gruss, Werner Haas, Mike Hamburg, Moritz Lipp, Stefan Mangard, Thomas Prescher, Michael Schwarz, Yuval Yarom: Spectre Attacks: Exploiting Speculative Execution. 3 Jan 2018. Available at: https://doi.org/10.48550/arXiv.1801.01203

[587] LIPP, M., SCHWARZ, M., GRUSS, D., PRESCHER, T., HAAS, W., FOGH, A., HORN, J., MANGARD, S., KOCHER, P., GENKIN, D., YAROM, Y., HAMBURG, M. *Meltdown: Reading Kernel Memory from User Space*. p. 2–3.

case of Spectre, there is a countermeasure available to avoid harmful effects of Meltdown, but it equally impedes the performance of the CPU. Apart from the currently available short-term mitigation method known since 2017, permanent elimination of Meltdown also needs redesigning the affected CPUs.[588]

Both Spectre and Meltdown were reported by academic and security researchers and published at various sources, including the US National Vulnerability Database and the official website of Intel Corp., simultaneously. [589, 590, 591, 592, 593] Given the ever evolving threat landscape, the research community is continuously detecting newer vulnerabilities of similar kinds. Therefore, the safest approach is to assume that Intel Corp. and several other mass-produced processors continue to be the subject to the above mentioned issue, affecting millions of devices. Mitigation and elimination measures are complex, and implementing firmware updates is not an option for the consumer in the majority of cases, due to the lack of expertise. Besides, replacing older hardware with newer hardware does not guarantee mitigation of all side-channel vulnerabilities due to the long-standing hardware design issues.

The impact of the discussed vulnerability disclosures is significant, as Spectre affects nearly all processor products to some degree while Meltdown primarily affects Intel Corp. products. On one hand it has led to rethinking hardware design, more particularly the side-effects of microcode optimization. Previously the professional community accepted these flows. Since understanding the impact of Spectre and Meltdown these and similar design flaws are considered as bugs to which the final answer is redesigning the hardware through serious technological innovation and at a high cost. The same applies to those cases when the software code is flawless, but the inbuilt features of the underlying hardware are vulnerable.[594] On the other hand Intel Corp. and some other hardware manufacturers have implemented coordinated disclosure policies and have introduced the option of coordinated reporting to minimize impact.

[588] Ibid., p. 15.

[589] Available at: https://meltdownattack.com/

[590] Available at: https://www.intel.com/content/www/us/en/developer/articles/technical/software-security-guidance/advisory-guidance/branch-target-injection.html?wapkw=cve-2017-5715

[591] Available at: https://www.intel.com/content/www/us/en/developer/articles/technical/software-security-guidance/advisory-guidance/bounds-check-bypass.html?wapkw=cve-2017-5753

[592] Available at: https://nvd.nist.gov/vuln/detail/CVE-2017-5715

[593] Available at: https://nvd.nist.gov/vuln/detail/CVE-2017-5753

[594] LIPP, M., SCHWARZ, M., GRUSS, D., PRESCHER, T., HAAS, W., FOGH, A., HORN, J., MANGARD, S., KOCHER, P., GENKIN, D., YAROM, Y., HAMBURG, M. *Meltdown: Reading Kernel Memory from User Space.* p. 15.

City of Providence vs Intel Corp

In 2018, shortly after the Spectre and Meltdown vulnerabilities were disclosed to the public, an ambitious legal action started in the US demanding 5 billion USD in various damages from Intel Corp. and which was claimed to be the result of Intel's unlawful conduct related to these vulnerabilities. The claim, a class action, was predominantly based on what we can refer to as consumer protection legislation, as well as non-contractual rules.[595] Plaintiffs claimed violation of various unfair competition laws stating, for example, that the "[d]*efendant engaged and continues to engage in unfair business practices by selling microprocessor chips it designed to consumers when it knew those microprocessor chips were designed defectively as alleged herein. Moreover, the resolution offered by Intel for Meltdown security flaw still leaves the machine vulnerable to attack and significantly reduces machine performance while also causing machine instability. Defendant's business practices were and are unscrupulous, unethical, and substantially injurious to consumers*".[596]

Plaintiffs also raised the argument of breach of implied warranties, claiming that the "[d]*efendant breached its implied warranty of merchantability. The Affected Devices sold or leased by Defendant to Plaintiff and Class Members was not fit for the ordinary purpose for which Defendant marketed its processors to be used due to the design defects (and associated security, stability, and performance issues) alleged herein*".[597]

While in 2022 the case was finally dismissed, it stirred the waters across the globe prompting policy makers to consider and respond to the underlying problem of digital security vulnerabilities and product quality. Indeed, one can be intrigued to examine how the EU's regulatory framework would perform had a similar case arose on the old continent, and more generally, what legal rules in the EU have relevance to such digital vulnerabilities.

[595] United States District Court, Northern District of California, Case No. 5:18-cv-0894, City of Providence vs Intel Corp.

[596] Ibid. Class action complaint filed 02/12/2018, p. 18.

[597] Ibid., p. 21.

4. Current regulations relevant to certain aspects of digital vulnerabilities

4.1 Regulatory attention starts to turn to digital vulnerabilities

The 2017 Cybersecurity Strategy of the EU expressly recognized the merit of 'security by design' approach and 'duty of care' principle.[598] This started to materialize, in particular, in the EU Cybersecurity Act 2019, where key element is standardization and certification frameworks for products, services and processes. This includes aspects of vulnerability management.

The case of the Intel microprocessors in 2018 and the attempts by various companies in the supply chain to mitigate the risks posed by the Spectre and Meltdown vulnerabilities have been instructive for the policy makers and the legal community, since the proclaimed duty of care principle in cybersecurity is now being clarified in recent legislative initiatives in the EU. The case also seems to be a turning point for Intel's own vulnerability management policy and practices as well, given that its public advisories start on 1st March 2018 with CVE-2017-5753 (Spectre) and CVE-2017-5754 (Meltdown), and continues with other, subsequently discovered ones.[599]

The normative framework that guides us on the questions of what to do and what not to do with digital vulnerabilities is currently shifting and becoming specialized, expressly tailored to digital vulnerabilities. Some of the legal norms, which have the effect of prohibiting or permitting certain exploitation of vulnerabilities, have been around for decades. Abstract legal concepts (in substantive criminal laws) addressed misuses of technologies in rather technology neutral terms, thus also including in their scope misuse techniques that are built on exploitation of digital vulnerabilities. However, binding rules about what ought to be (done) about vulnerabilities specifically tend to be more recent.

4.2 Norms of Prohibition

Digital vulnerabilities are not to be exploited without authorization, in other words, for example hacking into computer systems by using techniques that exploit digital vulnerabilities can amount to a criminal offence. There is clearly

[598] JOINT COMMUNICATION TO THE EUROPEAN PARLIAMENT AND THE COUNCIL Resilience, Deterrence and Defence: Building strong cybersecurity for the EU, JOIN/2017/0450 final.

[599] Software Security Advisory Guidance from Intel. Available at: https://www.intel.com/content /www/us/en/developer/topic-technology/software-security-guidance/advisory-guidance.html

relevant EU legislation addressing such cases, for example when the discovered vulnerability has already been exploited – so when, for example using the Spectre or Meltdown vulnerabilities, personal data is leaked. In the hypothetical case of such data leak, there is a likelihood that in a preceding step, unauthorized access would be gained in the target system by the attacker, which is typically a first step in committing cybercrimes. Hence, Article 3 of the Botnet Directive (2013/40/EU), which also closely follows the analogous Article 2 of the CoE Cybercrime Convention[600], on illegal access becomes relevant presuming that the attacker resorts to exploitation of a vulnerability, because (s)he does not have authorization to access the information system or its part running the targeted data stream. However, the applicability of further cybercrime legislation depends on further details and techniques applied, noting here that actual moment of stealing of data, which simply means mere copying, in itself does not amount to an offence according to the Botnet Directive nor the Cybercrime Convention.[601] To the extent the exploitation also involves unauthorized alteration, deleting, deterioration, damaging or suppression of computer data, the conduct may also qualify as illegal data interference.[602]

In a somewhat different scenario, to the extent the vulnerability allows lateral movement and thereby the attacker also illegally accesses a discernible part of an information system, the exploitation of the given vulnerability itself could amount to illegal access.

It should be noted that cybercrime laws apply regardless of whether a patch has been issued to mitigate a vulnerability, it is a zero-day or the exploitation takes place in the embargo/grace period. However, criminal laws are best suited to address conduct where exploitation of vulnerabilities has already taken place, and thus not representative of a preventive approach in cybersecurity policy.

4.3 Norms of Permission

A key difference between cybercrime and legal conduct lies in whether one is authorized to engage in that conduct. This may also entail exploitation of digital vulnerabilities. Authorization to do so can derive from two main sources, contract or in investigative processes with authorization from judge and appropriate authorities.

System owners can authorize persons to perform various test on their systems, e.g. penetration testing, which may include discovery and exploitation of

[600] ETS No. 185.

[601] National criminal laws, however, may criminalize such conduct.

[602] Art. 5 Botnet Directive; Art. 4 Cybercrime Convention.

vulnerabilities, or even vulnerability assessment. However, in these cases the intention is not nefarious, and such conduct is part of a service. A similar, specific type of arrangement can be seen in bug bounty programs, where the system owner makes a public call to reward discovery and reporting of security vulnerabilities, and of course sets the conditions and limits of the program. One large technology company for example expects that when investigating a vulnerability, the tester target his/her own account only, add attack scenarios to vulnerability reports, and not disclose vulnerabilities publicly without reasonable advance notice.[603]

Exploitation of vulnerabilities may be part of performing investigative acts, such as installing and operating spyware on suspect devices in criminal or national security investigations. Reportedly for example Pegasus spyware – a tool favored by many government agencies – exploited CVE-2016-4657 and CVE-2019-3568 vulnerabilities.[604] The second flaw enabled the installation of the spyware by simply calling the target. Relevant national laws (should) prescribe the rules, including the necessary authorizations for such covert investigative measures. One should also point out that the existence of national frameworks authorizing the use of such tools does not, in itself, guarantee that the fundamental rights of targets are respected and that agencies do not abuse these tools. However, this is a different question and human rights regimes do not *per se* rule out the interference with the right to privacy, but rather set the conditions for it. Therefore, exploitation of vulnerabilities is not inherently illegal, undesired or wrong, thus the assessment needs to go beyond the mere technical details and should focus on how technology is used.

4.4 Norms of Obligation

The timing of exploitation and whether a patch is available makes a significant difference for legal obligations of parties in the supply chain, manufacturers, vendors, service providers, as well as data processors and data controllers in the meaning of the GDPR. Moreover, EU regulators now started to directly aim at underlying causes of cyber insecurity and recent legislative proposals, such as the Cyber Resilience Act (CRA) proposal[605], which takes on to set cybersecurity benchmarks for products with digital elements, in particular regarding

[603] Available at: https://bughunters.google.com/

[604] Whattsapp Inc. and Facebook, Inc. v NSO GROUP TECHNOLOGIES LIMITED and Q CYBER TECHNOLOGIES LIMITED, Case 4:19-cv-07123-PJH, Document 1, Filed 10/29/19.

[605] European Commission, Proposal for a REGULATION OF THE EUROPEAN PARLIAMENT AND OF THE COUNCIL on horizontal cybersecurity requirements for products with digital elements and amending Regulation (EU) 2019/1020, Brussels, 15. 9. 2022, COM(2022) 454 final.

the widespread vulnerabilities and the insufficient and inconsistent provision of security updates to address them. The CRA proposal will be discussed in detail in the next chapter.

The main EU legislative instruments that are already in force and are potentially applicable in the context of the discovery and management of vulnerabilities like the Spectre and Meltdown include some consumer law directives that concern product quality (e.g. Directive 2019/771 on certain aspects concerning contracts for sales of goods), and to some extent, also the current and upcoming Network and Information Security Directives (nr 2016/1148, NIS1 and Directive (EU) 2022/2555, NIS2) and the General Data Protection Regulation (nr 2016/679). The following sections elaborate on the relevant provisions in the mentioned instruments.

Data protection rules

As previously demonstrated already with the Heartbleed bug[606] and the early case of Gloucester city data breach in 2017[607], leaving a known vulnerability unpatched (despite the availability of security update), and which is subsequently exploited leading to a personal data breach, could result in a fine under the GDPR. Article 32 of the GDPR sets security requirements for personal data processing, and states that "[t]*aking into account the state of the art, the costs of implementation and the nature, scope, context and purposes of processing as well as the risk of varying likelihood and severity for the rights and freedoms of natural persons, the controller and the processor shall implement appropriate technical and organisational measures to ensure a level of security appropriate to the risk…"*[608]

By today numerous fines were imposed for violation of this obligation, however generally it appears from the review of the decisions[609] that in order to receive a fine, an actual data breach also needs to have happened as a consequence of the data processor's or controller's failure to take appropriate technical and

606 Available at: https://www.csoonline.com/article/3223203/the-heartbleed-bug-how-a-flaw-in-openssl-caused-a-security-crisis.html

607 "Gloucester City Council fined £100,000 over Heartbleed hack – ICO issues penalty after authority leaks 30,000 employee emails" 14 June 2017. Available at: https://www.itpro.co.uk/security/28844/gloucester-city-council-fined-100000-over-heartbleed-hack

608 Regulation (EU) 2016/679 of the European Parliament and of the Council of 27 April 2016 on the protection of natural persons with regard to the processing of personal data and on the free movement of such data, and repealing Directive 95/46/EC (General Data Protection Regulation).

609 For the review the authors used the GDPR fine database. Available at: https://gdpr-fines.inplp.com/list/

organisational measures to ensure security in accordance with Art. 32. While the GDPR's enforcement regime and potential of big fines for violations may serve as a significant motivator to address vulnerabilities in one's information system – e.g. implement security updates and patches –, regulatory attention is still mainly directed on the actual misuses and security breaches, instead of the underlying causes and digital vulnerabilities. The GDPR guidance is built on ISO/IEC 27701 privacy information management standard[610] as best practice in this field, which in turn is an extension to the ISO/IEC 27001 information security standard, yet unfortunately the standard remains vague on vulnerability management. Furthermore, guidance has been issued by ENISA and Teletrust on what is the 'state of the art' in IT security, which indeed identifies the state of the art organisational security measures for secure software development and vulnerability and patch management.[611] The guidance provides important practical assistance to determine what is the objective standard and content of measures demanded by the GDPR. However, the GDPR "only" requires to take the state of the art into account, and allows deviations from it based on economic factors, contextual factors, risk assessment, etc. thus this 'state of the art' becomes an objective but relative standard with a wide margin of discretion for the implementer. To the extent the appropriateness of measures can be assessed within a range, rather on a case-by-case basis, rigorous enforcement response is likely only for extreme outlier cases. Hence, despite the significant impact of GDPR and its force to incentivize the implementation of security measures, it is not a prime example of preventive approach to cybersecurity when it comes to addressing digital vulnerabilities.

Network and Information Security (NIS) Directives

The requirement to apply cybersecurity measures is also found in the NIS directives, which does not limit its scope to the processing of personal data, but it currently applies only to designated essential entities and certain digital service operators. As of the writing of this study, the NIS1 directive is still in force, however will soon be replaced by NIS2 directive (nr 2022/2555). This also provides a good opportunity to point out the coming changes in the legal regime after transposition in second half of 2024.

[610] ISO/IEC 27701:2019 Security techniques – Extension to ISO/IEC 27001 and ISO/IEC 27002 for privacy information management – Requirements and guidelines.

[611] Chapters 3.3.3 and 3.3.5, Guideline "State of the Art" Technical and organisational measures, 2021. Available at: https://www.teletrust.de/fileadmin/user_upload/2021-09_TeleTrusT_Guideline_State_of_the_art_in_IT_security_EN.pdf

The first NIS Directive signifies a turning point in the cybersecurity policy of the EU, and it imposes security requirements and notification obligations on operators of essential services (OES) and digital service providers (DSP).[612] This scope remained modest and covered only the most critical areas in the EU. The NIS Directive also refers to 'state of the art', and therefore the same problems arise in its interpretation as under the GDPR, however it is exacerbated by the highly specific and heterogenous group of OESs. Moreover, the Commission Implementing Regulation (EU) 2018/151 addressed to DSPs goes no further than merely requiring policies and processes on identifying weaknesses and vulnerabilities in their information systems *as part of incident handling*.[613] This approach cannot be characterized as preventive either.

However, the NIS2 Directive will bring along significant changes both in scope as well in its substantive provisions. Due to space limitations, only a few of these changes are pointed out in this study.

Digital vulnerabilities take a central place in the new legislation. As evidence of heightened regulatory attention, the new directive includes a definition of 'vulnerability', which means a weakness, susceptibility or flaw of ICT products or ICT services that can be exploited by a cyber threat.[614] The directive emphasizes that since the exploitation of vulnerabilities in network and information systems may cause significant disruption and harm, swiftly identifying and remedying such vulnerabilities is an important factor in reducing risk. To this end various measures are put in place for vulnerability discovery and disclosure, and –finally – addresses manufacturers and providers of ICT products and ICT services directly.

National cybersecurity strategies will need to include policies on managing vulnerabilities,[615] national CSIRTS will be tasked with monitoring and analysing vulnerabilities and incidents at national level, but also will provide information on as well as proactively scan certain systems for vulnerabilities.[616] Moreover,

[612] Articles 14 and 16 of Directive (EU) 2016/1148 of the European Parliament and of the Council of 6 July 2016 concerning measures for a high common level of security of network and information systems across the Union.

[613] Article 2(2) of Commission Implementing Regulation (EU) 2018/151 of 30 January 2018 laying down rules for application of Directive (EU) 2016/1148 of the European Parliament and of the Council as regards further specification of the elements to be taken into account by digital service providers for managing the risks posed to the security of network and information systems and of the parameters for determining whether an incident has a substantial impact.

[614] Article 6(15) of Directive (EU) 2022/2555 of the European Parliament and of the Council of 14 December 2022 on measures for a high common level of cybersecurity across the Union, amending Regulation (EU) No 910/2014 and Directive (EU) 2018/1972, and repealing Directive (EU) 2016/1148 (NIS 2 Directive).

[615] Art. 7(2) point c.

[616] Art. 11(3).

the NIS2 directive prescribes an enhanced role for national CSIRTs, as well as for ENISA regarding information sharing on digital vulnerabilities. CSIRTs will be coordinators of and will facilitate coordinated vulnerability disclosure at EU level. A clear evolution can be observed in the role foreseen for CSIRTs, moving from that of a distant observer and advisor, towards a hands-on operational resource and tool. Giving such tasks to national CSIRTs indicates the acceptance of a greater level of responsibility by the state for cybersecurity and cyber resilience, however it also brings along state intervention in areas relying on market forces so far.

A very significant initiative in the NIS2 directive is the coordinated vulnerability disclosure and the European vulnerability database under Article 12. Designated CSIRTs will coordinate and may act as trusted parties for vulnerability disclosure, such as bug bounty programs, but more importantly also in cases where such formal programs for the particular IT product or service are not in place. A key enabler for vulnerability disclosure is that the security researcher reporting it may remain anonymous and that such disclosure does not expose them to criminal or civil liability. The NIS2 directive foresees anonymous reporting, and encourages the Member States to put in place the necessary measures to foster non-malicious vulnerability research and disclosure practices.

Finally, ENISA will establish a European vulnerability database where entities, regardless of whether they fall within the scope of the NIS2 directive, and their suppliers of network and information systems, as well as the competent authorities and the CSIRTs, can disclose and register, on a voluntary basis, publicly known vulnerabilities for the purpose of allowing users to take appropriate mitigating measures.[617] In order to avoid duplication of efforts, the cooperation opportunities with operators of other similar databases (e.g. CVE system) are explored.

Consumer contracts

Examining the claims introduced in the City of Providence vs Intel, potential causes of action may be identified based on EU law for a hypothetical scenario similar to the case of Intel and the Spectre and Meltdown vulnerabilities. Similarly to the US approach, resort to consumer protection law could be considered, and in particular the recent revision of the sale of goods directive (SGD)[618] could

[617] Preamble 62-63 of NIS2 Directive.

[618] DIRECTIVE (EU) 2019/771 OF THE EUROPEAN PARLIAMENT AND OF THE COUNCIL of 20 May 2019 on certain aspects concerning contracts for the sale of goods, amending Regulation (EU) 2017/2394 and Directive 2009/22/EC, and repealing Directive 1999/44/EC.

be instructive with its provisions on conformity of goods. The SGD's new iteration includes within its scope 'goods with digital elements', that means goods that are interconnected with digital content in such a way that the goods cannot fulfill their functions without these digital products. Therefore, in the event of a purchase by a consumer from a seller of a laptop computer – including certain type of microprocessor –, the SGD would cover both the hardware, as well as the operation system software.

The SGD provides for subjective and objective requirements for product conformity. Subjective requirements of conformity (Article 6 of the SGD) essentially mean conformity with the terms of the sales contract, including features of functionality, quality, quantity, type, etc., that is what is promised regarding the product in the sales contract. Such promises may be related to particular performance, fitness for a certain purpose, updates to be supplied, but subjective conformity is ultimately a function of that particular relationship between the seller and the consumer. Although sellers are not entirely free to set the contract terms (certain unfair terms and practices vis-à-vis consumers are certainly outlawed[619]), objective conformity requirements (Article 7 of the SGD) set standards or benchmarks that look beyond the individual sales contract terms.

Objective conformity is assessed by looking at the compliance of the product with applicable technical standards or codes of conduct (if any) or by comparison to similar products – so examining how well the product in question aligns with what may be considered 'normal' quality or reasonable expectation in the market. The marketing material, labels, ads and other public statements by or on behalf of the seller, or others in the links of the chain of transactions, including the producer, will also be taken into account. Moreover, pursuant to Article 7 (3), in case of goods with digital elements objective conformity also includes an obligation of the seller to ensure that the consumer is informed of and supplied with updates, including security updates, for a certain period.

For a hypothetical microchip security flaw in the laptop purchase scenario, the above requirements apply cumulatively. First, the conformity depends on the terms of the individual sales contract, which is a case-by-case assessment, thus will be skipped here. The second level, objective requirements allow more abstract analysis, since it concerns standards and benchmarks. Therefore, one needs to inquire into what applicable technical standards or industry good practices exists regarding security of processors, but a distinction between unknown vulnerabilities (incl. zero-days) and known vulnerabilities should be made.

---

[619] Council Directive 93/13/EEC on unfair terms in consumer contracts; Directive 2005/29/EC concerning unfair B2C commercial practices.

The consumer product conformity regime is not equipped, nor should be, to thoroughly address unknown vulnerabilities. Conformity requirements address currently known situations and compare it to reference points, but focus is at the consumer end of the supply-chain, and rather on the end product – not directly on the process of design and production. Therefore, how manufacturers, producers deal with unknown vulnerabilities, is secondary for the purposes of this legislation, however there is at least a partial presumption that there will be a security vulnerabilities/flaws in products with digital elements, and thus security updates are mandated (but only to the extent necessary to keep the goods in conformity, and only for a limited time). What we can probably establish as 'normal' regarding unknown vulnerabilities, is that they exist in all systems, thus discovering a new flaw in a microprocessor is something that can be expected from time to time. However, it is less straightforward to draw conclusions on the 'normal' frequency and criticality of new vulnerabilities. One can argue, that in case of general purpose microprocessors, transit of confidential data, as well as personal data within and through the device is foreseen by functionality design, thus confidentiality of data should be protected. Transient execution CPU vulnerabilities (discovered also in various microprocessor brands and products, not only Intel), however, allow to bypass security tools that protect confidentiality of data, and as demonstrated by Spectre, such vulnerabilities cannot always be exhaustively fixed without changing physical components. This raises the question whether such complete defeats of functionality and security features constitute the objectively 'normal' standard for the purposes of the SGD. If so, this implies a situation of market failure to ensure high level of cybersecurity in consumer products, thus calls for regulatory intervention and elaboration of obligatory security standards – which is coming in the form of the Cyber Resilience Act Proposal and relevant cybersecurity certification schemes to be established under the Cybersecurity Act.[620]

In case of known vulnerabilities and for which there is a patch or update, the analysis proceeds with a different focus, since the SGD is explicit on this point. According to Article 7(3) the seller shall ensure that for a certain time the consumer is informed of and supplied with updates, including security updates, that are necessary to keep those goods in conformity. As long as appropriate and timely security updates are issued for a product, these can be informed and supplied to consumers. However, considering the scenario of the Intel case for the Spectre and Meltdown vulnerabilities, complications can arise down the supply chain and potentially trigger the seller's liability under Article 10 of the

[620] Regulation (EU) 2019/881 of the European Parliament and of the Council of 17 April 2019 on ENISA (the European Union Agency for Cybersecurity) and on information and communications technology cybersecurity certification and repealing Regulation (EU) No 526/2013 (Cybersecurity Act).

SGD. First, at the time of writing there is no general obligation to issue security updates by producers, manufacturers or service providers, and what seems to be 'normal' for microprocessors is that they have transient execution vulnerabilities. Secondly, fixes for the Spectre and Meltdown were issued not by Intel, but for example Microsoft, which raises questions to what extent it can be expected from an independent company to fix a flaw in the product of another. Thirdly, as in the Intel case, the possibility remains that a vulnerability cannot be fixed or that simply no update is issued. A similar case has the potential to open the door for millions of claims for remedies for lack of conformity against sellers, while sellers would have the right of redress under Article 18 and would be entitled to pursue remedies against the person or persons liable in the chain of transactions.

While the SGD reverses the burden of proof for a one year period and applies a presumption of lack of conformity, there are important exceptions for cases where this would be incompatible with the nature of the goods or with the nature of the lack of conformity. It remains unclear, in the absence of clear benchmarks regarding the security requirements, if these exceptions would be applicable to future vulnerabilities similar to Spectre. However, European legislators are intensively working on setting such benchmarks and are determined to set horizontal cybersecurity requirements for products with digital elements.

5. Proposed legislation in the context of digital vulnerabilities

Cyber Resilience Act proposal

The proposed Cyber Resilience Act brings a watershed moment on global markets. It is expected to be a truly standard-setting piece of legislation that reaches beyond the borders of the EU in its effects. It also specifically addresses microprocessors, which have been the key illustrative tools throughout this study. General purpose microprocessors, and various other types of microprocessors, are listed in Annex III of the CRA as critical products with digital elements. As such, general purpose microprocessors should comply with the essential requirements for all with digital elements in order to be allowed to the European market, and will be subject to third-party conformity assessment. Crucially for this study, the CRA lays down essential requirements for the vulnerability handling processes put in place by manufacturers to ensure the cybersecurity of products with digital elements during the whole life cycle, and obligations for economic operators in relation to these processes. These essential requirements are listed in Annex I and are divided into two parts: 1) Security requirements relating to the properties of products with digital elements; and 2) Vulnerability handling requirements.

Critically for the cases like the faulty Intel microchips, an essential requirement will be that 'Products with digital elements shall be delivered without any known exploitable vulnerabilities'.[621] Considering that the Intel processors still contain the same vulnerability, and the authors have not found indications of redesign or remedy of the vulnerability at the production level, the CRA – if and when passed keeping this provision – will have far-reaching implications and force manufacturers to continuously innovate under pressure from innovation on the malicious cyber actors side.

However, as to the requirement of vulnerability handling at the manufacturers, the proposal settles for less dramatic rules and codifies many already existing practices. These include mandatory identification and documentation of vulnerabilities in products; timely remediation of vulnerabilities, including by providing security updates; disclosure of and information sharing on vulnerabilities; putting in place and enforcing coordinated vulnerability disclosure policies; secure distribution of updates and providing users with relevant information.

6. Conclusion

This study focused on the EU regulatory framework concerning digital vulnerabilities. Structured cooperation within the industry in this field originates from the US, and since global technology companies are also established in the US, it is not a surprise that the game-changer case also arose there. The Spectre and Meltdown vulnerabilities in microchips affected virtually every system in the globe and the resolutive remedy would require redesign and replacement of them, which illustrates the scale of the problem. Since the emergence of these cases the current industry practice that de-prioritizes security has been under attack and EU regulators introduce new instruments that signify a paradigm shift in building cyber resilience, moving from the risk-based approach towards preventive approach.

The Spectre and Meltdown vulnerabilities, and also the critical case of City of Providence vs Intel Corp. concerning these vulnerabilities prompted the authors to consider the developing legal landscape in the EU on what conduct is prohibited, permitted, mandated vis-a-vis digital vulnerabilities. This study mapped and briefly assessed relevant legislation that address

- exploitation of vulnerabilities as criminal offences, cybercrimes;
- exploitation of vulnerabilities as authorized investigative measures and as authorized acts under service contracts;

[621] Annex I. Part 1 point (2).

- required conduct by data controllers under GDPR (Art. 32 Security of processing) and obligations under the NIS directives concerning vulnerabilities;
- conformity of products with digital elements and seller's liability;
- and the proposed obligations of manufacturers to ensure essential requirements, including remedying all exploitable vulnerabilities in products before putting them on the market – as proposed in the Cyber Resilience Act.

With the coming of the IT security compliance scheme for hardware and software and the certification labs enabling the process properly as it is proposed through the Cyber Resilience Act, the European Union points out the need for manufacturers to improve the security of products with digital elements and to ensure that hardware and software products are placed on the market with fewer vulnerabilities in particular.[622] Thus the proposed Act aims to set a paradigm shift in building cyber resilience. Having access to certified hardware and software devices with better cybersecurity posture may lead from reactive approaches to prevention. Consequently, European consumers have a unique chance to have conditions that allow them to take cybersecurity into account when selecting and using products with digital elements, hoping to result in less societal and economic costs in the future. However, it also means the end of IT as we know it and businesses will be under significant pressure to keep up with innovation by malicious actors.

[622] Available at: https://www.european-cyber-resilience-act.com/. Update, September 2022 – Proposed Articles of the European Cyber Resilience Act (CRA).

CHAPTER TWELVE

Who is Accountable for the Algorithm? Assessing the Effectiveness of the EU's Approach towards AI Liability

PABLO MARTÍNEZ-RAMIL, TANEL KERIKMÄE

1. Introduction

The many challenges that AI systems possess for legal systems generated a wide debate in academia. The fast pace of R&D, along with the potential incorporation of these technologies into any human activity, made the list of potential challenges grow exponentially. The European Commission, seeing itself at the mercy of technological design choices taken beyond its borders, proposed in 2021 the AI Act. For the first time, part of the challenges posed by AI systems would be tackled through hard law, revolutionizing the digital regulatory landscape, and generating echoes in the legal systems of its digital counterparts.

In September 2022, a set of rules to address the civil liability of AI systems was proposed. Defined as "the two sides of the same coin", the AI Act and the AI Liability directive intended to contribute to the establishment of a digital ecosystem of trust. A compendium of safety-oriented rules aimed at reducing risks and preventing damages, accompanied by a liability regime that ensures 'effective and realistic' compensation, developed with contributions from Tatjana Evas-Peeters, who is affiliated with the TalTech Law School.

The academia had previously approached from multiple angles the issue of AI responsibility, covering questions that range from the granting legal personality to AI systems to the definition of elements that hinder the establishment of criminal liability for AI malfunctioning.

This research, while finding its grounds in the preceding academic discussion, incorporates technical aspects attached to the AI life cycle to break down the notion of liability; defining and delimiting the role of the multiple actors involved to introduce a comprehensive understanding of the issue at stake. Against this backdrop, this chapter will assess the effectiveness of the legal reforms undertaken by the EU to accommodate the civil liability regime to the technical reality of AI systems.

It should come as no surprise that contemporary societies have seen in recent times the rapid expansion of AI systems, progressively transforming more and more areas of our everyday lives and revolutionizing industries across the globe. And yet, along with its tremendous potential, these systems present complex legal and ethical challenges when facing regulatory landscapes rooted in analogue times. One core question, debated for years in the legal academic circles, reflects on the notion of liability when applied to AI systems. Who should be held accountable when an autonomous system causes harm or makes erroneous decisions?

Recognizing the urgency of the matter, the European Union (hereinafter EU) has taken proactive steps, negotiating, and drafting several legal initiatives that will shape the first comprehensive regulatory framework that will apply to AI systems deployed withing its borders.

On June 14, 2023, with an overwhelming majority of 499 votes in favor, 28 against and 93 abstentions, the European Parliament adopted its final negotiating position on the Artificial Intelligence (hereinafter AI) Act (hereinafter AIA),[623] *de facto* launching the "trilogue," the interinstitutional negotiations between the Commission, the Council, and the Parliament. Barely two weeks later, some of the largest companies across the EU raised their concerns in an open letter to the EU lawmakers.[624] The signing companies (such as Germany's Siemens or France's Airbus) claimed that, among other issues, the current approach taken by the AIA would *"jeopardize Europe's competitiveness and technological sovereignty without effectively tackling the challenges we are and will be facing"* and involved *"disproportionate compliance costs and disproportionate liability risks"*.[625]

With their words, the signing companies were not only lobbying against the current state of the AI Act but also against two newly proposed legal instruments: the AI liability Directive (hereinafter AILD) and the Product Liability Directive (hereinafter PLD), for they all constitute a whole. This type of criticism has been constant since the early beginnings of the legislative process. And very often, the never-ending debate focused on the role of innovation and

[623] EUROPEAN PARLIAMENT. *MEPs ready to negotiate first-ever rules for safe and transparent AI.* European Parliament News, Press release, June 14, 2023.

[624] TOH, M. *'Serious concerns': Top companies raise alarm over Europe's proposed AI law.* CNN Business, June 30, 2023. [online]. Available at: https://edition.cnn.com/2023/06/30/tech/eu-companies-risks-ai-law-intl-hnk/index.html. Accessed 1. 7. 2023.

[625] NO NAME. *Open letter to the representatives of the European Commission, the European Council and the European Parliament. Artificial Intelligence: Europe's chance to rejoin the technological avant-garde.* [online] Available at: https://drive.google.com/file/d/1wrtxfvcD-9FwfNfWGDL37Q6Nd8wBKXCkn/view?pli=1. Accessed 1. 7. 2023.

whether it promotes or hinders R&D. This will remain outside the scope of this chapter.[626] Instead, the following sections will shed light on the specific issue of AI liability, delimiting the approach taken by the EU, and evaluating the recent proposals.

To that end, and based on prior academic discussions, this research explores the intersection of the AI life cycle, the actors involved in it, the proposed regulatory regime, and the determination of liability. It aims to offer a comprehensive understanding of the current legislative landscape while addressing it critically. In other words, this chapter will evaluate the EU's legal reforms and the effectiveness of its overall approach towards AI liability, exploring its key components, assessing its strengths and limitations, and discussing potential implications for accountability in the era of algorithmic decision-making.

2. Methodology

Ultimately, this chapter seeks to answer – to the extent that is possible – the question that names it: "Who is accountable for the algorithm?" Given its broad formulation and the many cornerstones of the topic, it has been narrowed to answer it considering the proposed EU legislation and the technical reality attached to these systems.

A detailed examination of the upcoming regime would deserve a much more extensive analysis than what this chapter would be able to provide. Instead, it intends to serve as a roadmap that will help others to navigate and approach the upcoming regime while acknowledging potential pitfalls.

To that end, this chapter departs from the prior discussion concerning AI and liability, defining the core concepts to this discussion, and introducing some of the main legal challenges that needed urgent regulatory attention. Section 4 continues addressing the technical aspects related to the AI life cycle and the many actors that can be involved in the process, essential to provide context and understand the complexities of AI liability. Section 5 covers the EU, the scope of their competences and a brief mapping of the regulatory initiatives that aim to establish a liability regime. It also digs into the liability regime implemented by the EU and provides an overview of how it applies in practice, in relation to the technical reality previously addressed and commenting on potential pitfalls, or the areas that -to the date- remain unaddressed by harmonization instruments. Section 7 closes this chapter providing some conclusions.

[626] See, in this regard: LIU, H. Y., MAAS, M. M., DANAHER, J., SCARCELLA, L., LEXER, M., VAN ROMPAEY, L. Artificial Intelligence and Legal Disruption: A New Model for Analysis. *Law, Innovation and Technology*. vol. 12, no. 2, 2020, pp. 205–258.

3. A recap on the discussion concerning AI and liability

a) Defining AI

Even if, by now, most of the readers will be already acquainted with the concept of AI, a brief commentary is in place. The recently approved compromised position on the AIA by the EU parliament defines it as: *"a machine-based system that is designed to operate with varying levels of autonomy and that can, for explicit or implicit objectives, generate outputs such as predictions, recommendations, or decisions, that influence physical or virtual environments."*[627]

In the original proposal, the Commission had its focus on the technical reality that imbued certain types of software and made them qualify as AI systems, adopting a dynamic approach that would allow the Commission to qualify new technical developments as AI.[628] This partially obeyed to the historically loose character of its definition, often referred in the doctrine as the "AI effect." In a few words, it came to express that, ever since Alan Turing allegedly coined the term for the first time in 1950, the concept itself evolved along with the state of art of the technology. Hence, when innovative technologies become mundane, they lose the "privilege" of qualifying as AI.[629] With their latest approach, the definition took a more abstract turn, leaving aside the technical aspects and bridging the gap between the Commission's approach and the one of the Organization for Economic Cooperation and Development (OECD).

Given the purposes of this chapter, the differences between the different types of AI techniques will not be examined.[630] The definition employed here will follow the one of the EU parliament, understanding AI as a machine-based system (hence admitting both software and hardware) operating with different levels of autonomy (therefore encompassing in essence, the most widespread AI

---

[627] Amendment 165. Amendments adopted by the European Parliament on 14 June 2023 on the proposal for a regulation of the European Parliament and of the Council on laying down harmonized rules on artificial intelligence (Artificial Intelligence Act) and amending certain Union legislative acts (COM(2021)0206–C9-0146/2021–2021/0106(COD)).

[628] Art 3(1). Proposal for a Regulation of the European Parliament and of the Council laying down harmonized rules on Artificial Intelligence (Artificial Intelligence Act) and amending certain Union Legislative Acts.

[629] LIU, H. Y., MAAS, M. M., DANAHER, J., SCARCELLA, L., LEXER, M., VAN ROMPAEY, L. Artificial Intelligence and Legal Disruption: A New Model for Analysis. *Law, Innovation and Technology.* vol. 12, no. 2, 2020, pp. 215.

[630] However, they are paramount to develop a more comprehensive understanding of the issue at stake. See, in this regard, MARTÍNEZ-RAMIL, P. Discriminatory algorithms. A proportionate means of achieving a legitimate aim? *Journal of Ethics and Legal Technologies.* vol. 4, no. 1, 2022, pp. 3–24.

techniques[631] – supervised, unsupervised, deep and reinforcement learning-) that produce outputs (with effects in the digital or the analogue world, or both) based on a given set of objectives (often called inputs).

b) Navigating the notion of legal liability.

The People's Law Dictionary provides a concise yet clarifying definition of liability. In essence, it means *"legal responsibility for one's acts or omissions"*.[632] The figure below simplifies the distinction between the types of liability and the relevant legal initiatives that apply to AI in the EU:

Figure 1: Types of liability and relevant EU legal initiatives

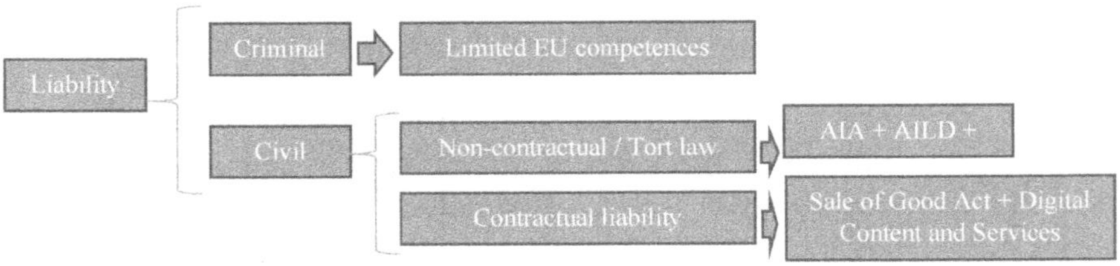

Civil and criminal liability typically reflect the responsibility arising from violations of private law (that governs relationship between people) and criminal law[633] (ultimate expression of the monopoly on the use of force by the states, and to protect the public interests of a society).[634]

Several reasons explain the slow EU harmonization in criminal matters. The Treaty on the Functioning of the European Union (hereinafter TFEU) Article 67 establishes the obligation of ensuring a high level of security in the Union through *"coordination and cooperation"* between the relevant authorities, through *"mutual recognition of judgements in criminal matters"* and *"if, necessary, through the approximation of criminal laws"*. In a similar way, Article 82 (2) empowers the Parliament and the Council to establish minimum rules on criminal matters

[631] SARKER, I. H. Machine Learning: Algorithms, Real-World Applications and Research Directions. *SN Computer Science*. vol. 2, no. 160, 2021, pp. 1–2.

[632] HILL, G. N., HILL, K. T. *The People's Law Dictionary. Taking the mystery out of the legal language*. New York: MJF Books, 2002, pp. 248–249.

[633] TURNER, J. *Robot Rules. Regulating Artificial Intelligence*. Cham: Springer Link, Palgrave Macmillan, 2019, p. 82.

[634] For the purposes of this research, this section will only refer to criminal and civil liability. Liability arising from administrative law related causes will be left aside, for the regimes are very specific to national realities.

"to the extent necessary to facilitate mutual recognition of judgments and judicial decisions and police and judicial cooperation".[635] The primary law specifically refers to this type of harmonization through the prism of "necessity" to achieve the goals set in the treaties. This has led to a cautious harmonization in this area, understanding that criminal law is an expression of the sovereignty of the Member States that needs to be respected attending to the necessity principle. In other words, *"the more intrusive harmonization measures intervene in national criminal law systems, the more important they must be for achieving the Union's objectives".*[636]

Hence, and while acknowledging the influence of EU law not only in the national legal systems but over their own interpretation, criminal law remains mostly under the control of Member States, that only need to observe obligations emanating from international law instruments that define the minimum standards (such as the European Convention on Human Rights)[637] as well as their own constitutional rules. To the date, criminal systems among the Member States still differ. A good example -and of special relevance for AI systems- is the notion of hate crimes. Specifically, those not involving racism or xenophobia. While several countries regulated hate crimes against women and LGBT+ people, others do not offer the same level of protection across the EU.[638] In absence of a specific harmonization measures in digital areas, an AI system (and specially, a general-purpose one -such as the (in)famous ChatGPT 4 or Bard-) might end up reflecting a conduct that, if it was a natural person the one committing it, would entail criminal liability. Moreover, in the context of hate crimes, the same conduct could raise legal questions in some Member States yet not in others.

As highlighted above, civil liability arises from violations of private law. Those might be (i) originated in a contractual relationship or (ii) not, also referred to as tort law. Within the meaning of tort law, several types are acknowledged across different legal regimes.

- Negligence: In a few words, the term refers to conducts that fail to perform to a required standard[639]. A conduct qualifying as a negligence presumes the

[635] Arts 67 & 82(2), Consolidated versions of the Treaty on European Union and the Treaty on the Functioning of the European Union. 2012/C 326/0.

[636] SCHROEDER, W. Limits to European Harmonization of Criminal Law. *Eurocrim.* vol. 2, 2020, p. 147.

[637] Art 52(3) identifies the Convention as the bare minimum that the Union can enhance through more extensive protection. Charter of Fundamental Rights of the European Union.

[638] STUDY REQUESTED BY THE LIBE COMMITTEE. *Hate speech and hate crime in the EU and the evaluation of online content regulation approaches.* PE 655.135, July 2020, European Parliament, [online]. Available at: https://www.europarl.europa.eu/RegData/etudes/STUD/2020/655135/IPOL_STU(2020)655135_EN.pdf. Accessed 12. 6. 2023

[639] NOLAN, D., DAVIES, J. Torts and Equitable Wrongs. In BURROWS, A. (ed.). *English Private Law.* Oxford: Oxford University Press, 2017, p. 934.

existence of a duty not to cause, or to prevent a specific harm. That duty must have been breached and that breach must constitute the cause of the produced harm. Some legal systems include an extra circumstance to consider, the foreseeability of the damage[640]. The latter is of special relevance when dealing with AI systems that are progressively learning from their interactions with the users; for new types of interactions, inputs, or data hold the potential to alter the algorithmic decision-making process and therefore bring unforeseeable consequences.

- Strict and product liability: Typically, product liability is considered a type of strict liability. The former refers to a set of rules that define liability regimes when a specific product causes harm. The origin of the harm must come from a defect in the product itself. Strict liability refers to situations where liability arises (hence entailing legal consequences) in the absence of fault or criminal intention.[641] Traditional examples involve liability arising from the harm caused by the possession of very dangerous products (even when they are carefully stored), such as explosives, or wild animals.
- Vicarious Liability: Cases of vicarious liability refer imply the existence of responsibility for one person (the so-called "principal") for actions undertaken by another (the "agent"). Typical examples involve a contractual relationship between employee and employer, or a hierarchical organization. The victim of the damage has the option to sue the principal for the actions of its agent, and later the principal will have (attending to the specific circumstances of the case) the option to act against its own agent for compensation.[642]

Contractual liability arises when there are specific provisions in a contract that outline the consequences in the event of a breach of obligations between two private parties, whether they are natural or legal persons.[643] As shown in *Figure 1*, proposed and approved EU regulatory initiatives started to shape scenarios where civil liability arises from AI systems in both tort law and contractual law. They will be analyzed below.

[640] TURNER, J. *Robot Rules. Regulating Artificial Intelligence.* Cham: Springer Link, Palgrave Macmillan, 2019, p. 86.

[641] Ibid., p. 91.

[642] Ibid., p. 100.

[643] Ibid., p. 109.

c) Questions that arise when analyzing Legal Liability originated in AI systems

In the previous section, the traditional types of liability have been delineated. Before addressing their "translation" into the EU regulatory landscape, this section will introduce some of the main elements that justified the legal discussion and the regulatory intervention.

In a nutshell, the legal liability of AI presents many challenges for contemporary legal frameworks, often rooted in analogue times. A significant one lies in determining who should be held responsible when an AI system causes harm or makes errors. Criminal liability traditionally revolves around natural persons, while civil liability affects both natural and legal persons. AI systems fall outside the scope of both definitions while holding a certain degree of autonomy. In 2017 the issue was debated in the European institutions, being finally disregarded.[644] This autonomy is amplified in complex algorithms and decision-making processes (for instance, a Deep Learning Algorithm that is receiving real-time training from its own interactions with the users), making it challenging to trace and understand the exact cause of an AI-related incident.[645] Although the issue of transparency and the black box[646] will eventually disappear,[647] the matter of accountability becomes more complicated when considering the diverse range of AI technologies and applications across various industries. In this regard, the number of liability questions that arise in healthcare contexts, or self-driving vehicles differ from the ones originated in a system designed to profile with advertisement targeting purposes.[648]

Different questions arise depending on the type of liability involved. For instance, under the prism of liability for defective products, it would not be clear *"whether the adaptive and dynamic nature of the AI through either machine-learning techniques, or updates, or revisions, may entail or create a defect"*

[644] BURRI, T. *The EU is right to refuse legal personality for Artificial Intelligence.* Euractiv, May 31, 2018 [online]. Available at: https://www.euractiv.com/section/digital/opinion/the-eu-is-right-to-refuse-legal-personality-for-artificial-intelligence/. Accessed 12. 6. 2023.

[645] MARTÍNEZ-RAMIL, P. Discriminatory algorithms. A proportionate means of achieving a legitimate aim? *Journal of Ethics and Legal Technologies.* vol. 4, no. 1, 2022, p. 7.

[646] This term refers to the complicated decision-making processes in AI systems that are difficult for humans to understand and explain.

[647] There are already strategies in place that allow to "open" the black box. See, in this regard, HACKER, P., CORDES, J., ROCHON, J. Regulating Gatekeeper AI and Data: Transparency, Access, and Fairness under the DMA, the GDPR, and Beyond. *Working Paper.* December 9, 2022, pp. 1–41.

[648] See, in this regard, WACHTER, S. Affinity profiling and discrimination by association in online behavioral advertising. *Berkeley Technology Law Journal.* vol. 35, 2020, pp. 367–430.

in the AI system.[649] If, instead, criminal liability of an AI system was the issue at stake, in addition to the problems highlighted above, the role of intentionality (*mens rea*), often core to the procedure in the definition of criminal conducts, would create questions that some consider not to be *"even* [...] *solvable by our current legal system"*.[650] Nonetheless, it should be worthy of mention that similar debates have been going on for a while in relation to the controversial notion of Criminal Corporate Liability.[651]

Lastly, it should be noted that alternative liability systems exist in the world and some authors even consider them legitimate alternative solutions for AI systems, such as the New Zealand's Accident Compensation Corporation, a no-fault compensation scheme that reimburses the damages to victims of an accident regardless of "whether anyone was at fault". It is financed through specific levies or taxes.[652] However, if such a regime were to regulate damage caused by AI systems in the EU, it could somewhat transform the internal market into a big sandbox, where the taxpayers would have to deal with the economic consequences of a harm produced by a malfunction of an AI system. Moreover, considering that AI developing companies already benefit from an unregulated landscape, where most of the data used to train the models is freely obtained through techniques such as data scraping,[653] relying on their *bona fides* would not be prudent or sufficient to ensure ethical and responsible AI developing practices.

4. The AI life cycle and the actors involved in it

Once disregarded the possibility of granting a new type of legal personality to AI systems, it becomes necessary to identify the actors involved in their development, for they will be the ones that could be held liable for potential malfunctions. The figure below simplifies the AI life cycle:

[649] KARIKMÄE, T., MÜÜRSEPP, P., PIHL, H. M., HAMULAK, O., KOCHARYAN, H. Legal Person or Agenthood of Artificial Intelligence Technologies. *Acta Baltica Historiae et Philosophiae Scientiarum.* vol. 8, 2020, p. 86.

[650] Ibid., p. 84.

[651] MARCIANO, A., BATTISTA RAMELLO, G. *Encyclopedia of Law and Economics.* Montpellier: Springer, 2019, pp. 391–392.

[652] TURNER, J. Robot Rules. *Regulating Artificial Intelligence.* Cham: Springer Link, Palgrave Macmillan, 2019, p. 102.

[653] WES, D. & LAWLER, R. *Elon Musk blames data scraping by AI startups for his new paywalls on reading tweets.* The Verge, July 1, 2023 [online]. Available at: https://www.theverge.com/2023/7/1/23781198/twitter-daily-reading-limit-elon-musk-verified-paywall. Accessed 1. 7. 2023.

Figure 2. The AI life cycle and the potential involved actors, simplified[654]

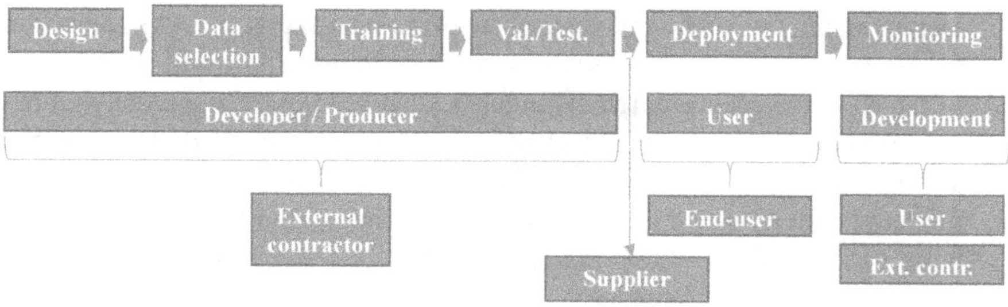

Design: In a preparatory stage, the AI system is conceptually designed. Typically, the task lies in a developing company or producer that, either at their own expenses or attending a specific commission, determines the strategic steps to develop the system, which type of data will be necessary to train it, which model or algorithmic tool must be coded in light of the data, where will it be deployed…

1. Data selection: This stage involves both (i) the collection of datasets relevant to the purposes and tasks that the AI system will perform and (ii) the data cleaning and labelling (when necessary). While data cleaning aims at ensuring a certain level of data quality and integrity, labelling refers to different methods of data classification and is necessary for the development of supervised learning AI systems. This stage is key to ensure the correct functioning of the system; for biased, unrepresentative or uncomplete data sets will be reflected in the functioning of the system.[655] It is not uncommon that these tasks are often subcontracted, being a third party the one in charge of the Data Selection phase.
2. Training and Validation: The datasets are usually divided into two groups: the training data set and the validating data set. Once the AI model has been developed and the data has been prepared, the system is trained with it. This process involves "feeding" the training data through the model, adjusting internal parameters, optimizing it to minimize errors... The model's performance is then evaluated using the validating data set, defined metrics, and validation techniques. This way, its effectiveness and capacity to establish generalizations are assessed. Typically, it is the developing company the one in charge of the training and validating stages.

Once the system has been tested and considered to be ready for deployment, either the developing company itself or a third party acting as a supplier (for

[654] For the purposes of this chapter, we will focus solely on the development of a Machine Learning system, excluding reinforcement learning due to its distinct applications.

[655] HACKER, P. Teaching Fairness to Artificial Intelligence: Existing and Novel Strategies Against Algorithmic Discrimination Under EU Law. *Common Market Law Review*. 2018, vol. 55, pp. 1146–1147.

instance, in cases where the AI is developed outside EU borders and enters the internal market) deals with the commercialization of the system.

1. Deployment: The deployment stage involves integrating the AI system into the intended environment or application. Depending on who will be in control of the AI, the literature often distinguishes between users and end users, being the latest the final user for whom the system was intended. For example, a company might acquire a license for an AI system that would allow them to implement an AI-powered chat-box for customer support. While they might be in control of the system (as "users"), the customers using the chat-box would constitute the "end-users".
2. Monitoring: After an AI system is deployed, typically engineers work on optimizing the model's performance, ensuring its compatibility with the deployment environment, and addressing any potential problems or challenges that could arise. Depending on the type of system, its complexity and its functioning, this task might be carried out by an external contractor, the developing company or the user piloting the deployment of the AI system.[656]

5. The EU approach towards regulating AI liability

5.1 Limits to the EU capacity

As is well-known, the EU draws its powers from primary law. Therefore, its capacity to regulate and harmonize is limited by the treaties.

Above, the reasons behind the limited harmonization in criminal matters were exposed. In addition, the TFEU Article 82 (2) also highlighted that any necessary harmonization on criminal matters through minimum rules must "*take into account the* differences between the legal traditions and systems of the Member States".[657] Extending criminal liability to AI systems or granting them a new type of legal personality would greatly exceed the capacities granted by primary law and could render its qualification ultra vires.

Conversely, the capacity to regulate civil liability for AI system lies in the TFEU Article 114, the legal basis for both the AIA and the AILD. The provision grants the EU the capacity to *"adopt the measures for the approximation of the provisions laid down by law, regulation or administrative action in Member States which have as their object the establishment and functioning of the internal*

[656] MARTÍNEZ-RAMIL, P. Is the EU human rights legal framework able to cope with discriminatory AI? *IDP. Internet, Law and Politics E-Journal*. vol. 34, 2022, pp 3–5.

[657] Art 82(2), Consolidated versions of the Treaty on European Union and the Treaty on the Functioning of the European Union. 2012/C 326/0.

market".[658] This provision has been broadly interpreted, facilitating the adaptation of the internal market to the digitalisation process that has been going on for years. Thus, it has been the legal basis for most of the digital regulatory initiatives promoted by the Von der Leyen Commission, such as the Digital Markets Act, or the Digital Services Act. The same provision justifies the existence of certain provision harmonizing contractual liability and product liability rules at the EU level, core to the notion of discussion on liability, as established above.

5.2 Relevant legislation

Contractual liability

Simply put, a contract constitutes a promise enforceable by law.[659] It is the maximum expression of the legal principle of *pacta sunt servanda* and the principle of freedom of contract, only limited by concrete reasons of public interest. Therefore, any liability regime will be defined on a case-by-case basis, depending on the content of a specific contract.

The TFEU Article 4 (f) recognizes consumer protection as a shared competence between the EU and the Member States. In this regard, two instruments that aim at levering the playing field between customer and seller deserve our attention, for they include provisions that limit contractual relationships and therefore influence the liability regimes included in contracts.

When AI systems are licensed through the cloud, they are referred to as Artificial Intelligence as a Service (AIaaS). The contractual relationships do not differ much from those governing Software as a Service (SaaS). The Directive (EU) 2019/770 of the European Parliament and of the Council of 20 May 2019 on certain aspects concerning contracts for the supply of digital content and digital services, includes some liability of the trader provision, establishes the burden of proof for breaches of Article 5 of the Directive on the trader (the stronger part of the contract), among other provisions.[660]

Conversely, if an AI system is sold as a good, the Directive (EU) 2019/771 of the European Parliament and of the Council of 20 May 2019 on certain aspects

[658] Art 114, Consolidated versions of the Treaty on European Union and the Treaty on the Functioning of the European Union. 2012/C 326/0.

[659] MEHREN, A. T. von. *Contract*. Encyclopedia Britannica, May 28, 2023 [online]. Available at: https://www.britannica.com/money/topic/contract-law. Accessed 15. 6. 2023.

[660] See, in this regard, Arts 11 & 12, Directive (EU) 2019/770 of the European Parliament and of the Council of 20 May 2019 on certain aspects concerning contracts for the supply of digital content and digital services (Text with EEA relevance.) PE/26/2019/REV/1 OJ L 136, 22. 5. 2019, pp. 1–27.

concerning contracts for the sale of goods would apply. If the previous directive established certain liability standards for the trader, this one does the same on the seller. As the stronger part, the seller is also granted with the burden of proof in certain cases.[661]

These two directives establish the minimum standards that contractual relationships concerning the sale of goods and the provision of services should comply with.

Non-Contractual liability: An overview of the AIA

Being at the center of the academic discussions surrounding AI regulation, the AIA constitutes the world's first comprehensive AI Law. At the time of writing this chapter, the so-called "trilogue" (EU inter-institutional negotiations) just initiated discussions, therefore rendering any in-depth examination of the proposed obligations outdated. And yet, some notes can be drafted regarding the liability system that intends to be established.

The AIA distinguishes between four types of AI systems, attending to the risk they possess:

- AI systems constituting an unacceptable risk. Considered a threat to safety and fundamental rights, the systems falling under this category are clearly banned, such as social scoring systems by governments.
- AI systems qualifying as high-risk. These systems present a high risk due to their area of deployment and the consequences of their outputs, therefore being governed by a set of obligations defined in the law.[662]
- AI systems with limited risk. These systems only need to comply with specific transparency requirements.
- AI systems presenting minimal or no risk at all. The AIA allows their free use.[663]

The figure below incorporates to the previously introduced AI life cycle the obligations imposed by the AIA to a high-risk AI system:

[661] See, in this regard, Art 10 & 11, Directive (EU) 2019/771 of the European Parliament and of the Council of 20 May 2019 on certain aspects concerning contracts for the sale of goods, amending Regulation (EU) 2017/2394 and Directive 2009/22/EC, and repealing Directive 1999/44/EC (Text with EEA relevance.) PE/27/2019/REV/1 OJ L 136, 22. 5. 2019, pp. 28–50.

[662] See, in this regard, *Figure 3*.

[663] EUROPEAN COMMISSION. *Regulatory framework proposal on artificial intelligence*. Shaping Europe's digital future. European Commission, [online]. Available at: https://digital-strategy.ec.europa.eu/en/policies/regulatory-framework-ai. Accessed 14. 6. 2023.

Figure 3. An overview of the AIA obligations for high-risk AI systems through their life cycle.

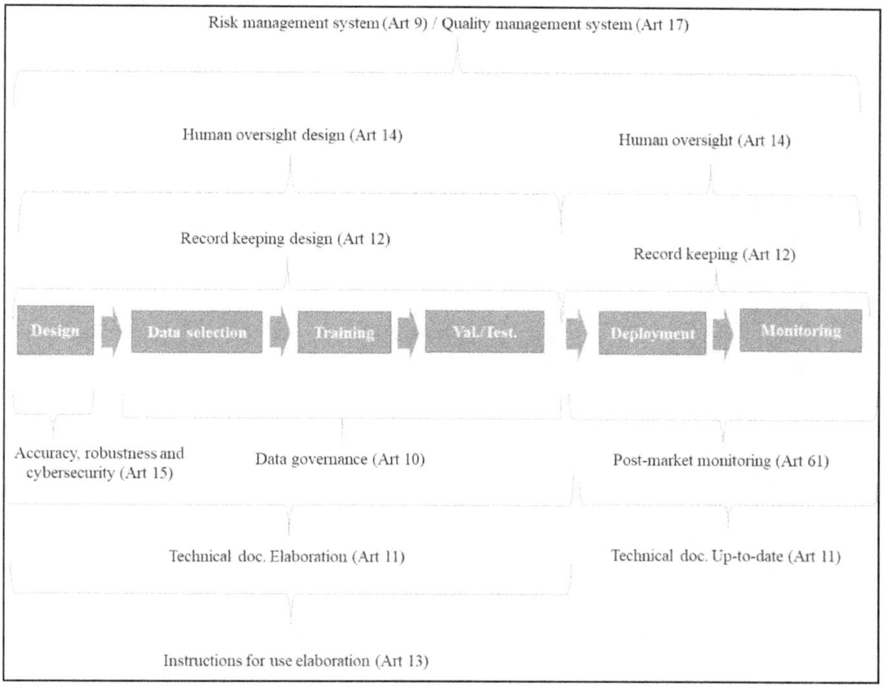

In a few words, the AIA establishes several requirements that are connected to the risk that an AI system might possess. Ultimately, these requirements must be fulfilled by natural or legal entities, who can be held responsible in cases of non-compliance.

Article 71 of the proposed AIA established the system of penalties, that are imposed to "operators". This term includes the *"provider, the user, the authorized representative, the importer and the distributor"*. They are defined in Article 3:

- Provider: means a natural or legal person, public authority, agency or other body that develops an AI system or that has an AI system developed with a view to placing it on the market or putting it into service under its own name or trademark, whether for payment or free of charge.
- Small-scale provider: means a provider that is a micro or small enterprise within the meaning of Commission Recommendation 2003/361/EC 61.
- User. Any natural or legal person, public authority, agency or other body using an AI system under its authority, except where the AI system is used in the course of a personal non-professional activity.

- Authorized representative. Any natural or legal person established in the Union who has received a written mandate from a provider of an AI system to, respectively, perform and carry out on its behalf the obligations and procedures established by this Regulation.
- Importer. Any natural or legal person established in the Union that places on the market or puts into service an AI system that bears the name or trademark of a natural or legal person established outside the Union.
- Distributor. Any natural or legal person in the supply chain, other than the provider or the importer, that makes an AI system available on the Union market without affecting its properties.[664]

The original text of the proposal reserved in its Article 71 the highest penalties for operators that:

- Did not comply with the prohibition of AI qualifying as unacceptable risk.
- Did not comply with Article 10, Data Governance in the development of a high-risk AI system.

These fines, in their current wording, would involve a maximum of 30 million euro or up to 6% of the annual worldwide turnover if the operator is a company, whichever is bigger.

The noncompliance with the rest of the measures contained in *Figure 3*[665] would entail fines of up to 20 million euro or 4% of the annual worldwide turnover if the operator is a company, whichever is bigger.

Lastly, noncompliance with Article 23 would involve fines of up to 10 million euro or 2% of annual worldwide turnover if the operator is a company, whichever is bigger.

Non-Contractual liability. The PLD and the AILD

As a stand-alone instrument, the AIA does not seem to open new paths for victims of an AI system to seek liability. The providers are the ones bound by the regulation, that need to ensure compliance in most cases through the – still controversial – self-conformity assessments.[666] In other words, it only establishes some sort of EU administrative liability for these operators when it is revealed the lack of compliance with the relevant provisions.

[664] Art 3. Proposal for a Regulation of the European Parliament and of the Council laying down harmonized rules on Artificial Intelligence (Artificial Intelligence Act) and amending certain Union Legislative Acts.

[665] In addition to Arts 19, 20, 21 & 22 of the proposed AIA.

[666] See, in this regard, HACKER, P. *The European AI Liability Directives – Critique of a Half-Hearted Approach and Lessons for the Future.* arXiv preprint arXiv:2211.13960, November 25, 2022, pp. 1–72.

However, when addressed jointly with the AILD, the approach of the AIA somewhat reflects the type of tort liability known as "negligence". In fact, the preamble to the proposed AILD refers to the term on two occasions. The AILD introduces a fault-based system that seeks to tackle the power unbalance between an end-user suffering harm from a specific AI-system and the operator of the system. It obliges the Member States to empower the courts to be able to obtain and disclose relevant evidence regarding a high-risk AI system suspected of having caused damage. Moreover, it establishes a presumption of a causal link in the case of fault if several conditions are fulfilled, opening the paths for potential victims to claim damages.

On the other hand, the proposed PLD addresses AI liability from a perspective of product liability. The key requirement for liability is the existence of a defect on the product. While the current PLD introduced many questions when facing digital assets, the newly proposed one incorporates them explicitly, listing elements that are strongly connected to the nature of AI systems. In this regard, when addressing the defectiveness of a product, references include:

- *the presentation of the product, including the instructions for installation, use and maintenance;*
- *the effect on the product of any ability to continue to learn after deployment;*
- *the moment in time when the product was placed on the market or put into service or, where the manufacturer retains control over the product after that moment, the moment in time when the product left the control of the manufacturer;*
- *product safety requirements, including safety-relevant cybersecurity requirements.*

If operated comprehensively and proportionately, these requirements can significantly improve the current standing of the product liability regime involving AI systems. But an explanation of how these elements will be measured is still missing, rendering any expectations futile at this point.

Another inclusion worth mentioning in the proposed PLD is the definition of "damage", that now includes medically recognized harm to psychological health. This is of great significance, for it leaves the door open to address the legal challenge that recommendation algorithms in social media platforms constitute and the harm they cause to their users. Especially, because that might fall outside the high-risk qualification of the AIA.

Lastly, it should be noted that the proposed PLD Article 3 imposes a somewhat stricter transposition of the Directive in comparison to the AILD.[667] And,

[667] Art 3 establishes that "*Member States shall not maintain or introduce, in their national law, provisions diverging from those laid down in this Directive, including more, or less, stringent provisions to achieve a different level of consumer protection, unless otherwise provided for in*

although they share a similar wording in their respective Articles 8 and 3, the high reliance of the AILD on the AIA will necessarily entail certain modifications before assessing its full potential.

6. Conclusions

In conclusion, the implementation of the AI Act and the legal instruments analyzed represents a significant step towards regulating Artificial Intelligence and ensuring ethical and responsible AI practices. However, it must be acknowledged that, despite the obligations outlined in these frameworks, there are still potential instances where AI wrongdoings may occur, even in full compliance with the existing legal instruments. Acknowledging this reality can only leave a bittersweet taste, for there is no concrete answer that can give a closure to the proposed question.

Who is accountable for the algorithm? Well, it depends. There are no systems of criminal liability for AI in place, and, although it is only a matter of time before we see them occupy the headlines, it is not clear whether the current legal landscape can tackle the questions that will come. The arguments exposed above reinforce this view.

In exploring non-contractual civil liability, previous research has shown that AI systems can still cause harm to users, even when complying with the AI Act. Instances such as proxy discrimination highlight this concern. In an ideal scenario of implementing the AI Act and the AI liability regime, three conditions would need to be met to establish liability: the harm must be caused by a high-risk AI system, a breach of the AI Act's obligations must be proven, and a causal connection between the breach and the harm must be demonstrated. If no breach occurs, the Product Liability Directive (PLD) may be the applicable instrument. Under the PLD, the defectiveness of an AI system will be assessed considering the listed circumstances in Article 6. How these requirements are balanced by the relevant authorities will significantly impact the outcome.

Lastly, it should be highlighted that neither the AIA, the PLD, or the AILD will keep their current wording unaffected. The results of the inter-institutional negotiations on the AIA will necessarily have an impact on the AILD, while the PLD will have to undergo its own procedure. The intention of this chapter was none other than to provide an overview of the state of the art. Only future research will be able to examine and study the established regime built upon the final form of these initiatives.

---

this Directive". Proposal for a DIRECTIVE OF THE EUROPEAN PARLIAMENT AND OF THE COUNCIL on liability for defective products. COM/2022/495 final.

CHAPTER THIRTEEN

Cyber Security of Automated and Fully Automated Vehicles – New Legal Instruments

JOZEF ANDRAŠKO

1. Introduction

Web Hackers vs. The Auto Industry: Critical Vulnerabilities in Ferrari, BMW, Rolls Royce, Porsche, and More. This is the title of a blog published by ethical hacker Sam Curry in January 2023.[668] In 2022, Sam Curry and his friends spent several months looking for all possible vulnerabilities in vehicles from different manufacturers. His findings include vulnerabilities in vehicles manufactured by Kia, Honda, Infiniti, Nissan, and Acura. By exploiting this vulnerability, it was possible to remotely lock, unlock the vehicle, start the engine, turn off the engine, determine the exact location, flash the headlights and honk the horn only with the help of the detected VIN number. In other vehicles (Mercedes-Benz), hundreds of critical internal applications could be accessed. In the case of some vehicles, it was possible to obtain a name, phone number, e-mail address (Toyota) or physical address and information about the vehicle (Jaguar, Land Rover).

There are many examples of successful cyber attacks on vehicles or their systems. In 2015, two ethical hackers Charlie Miller and Chris Valasek demonstrated a cyber attack by which they gained remote access to the internal network of a Chrysler-Jeep motor vehicle and were subsequently able to control the brakes, engine and wipers.[669]

[668] CURRY, S. Web Hackers vs. The Auto Industry: Critical Vulnerabilities in Ferrari, BMW, Rolls Royce, Porsche, and More. [online]. Available at: https://samcurry.net/web-hackers-vs-the-auto-industry/. Accessed 15. 8. 2023.

[669] SCHELLEKENS, M. Car hacking: Navigating the regulatory landscape. *Computer Law and Security Review.* 2015, vol. 32, no. 2, p. 307. Current luxury cars, such as BMW 7 series can contain up to 150 electronic control units. See CHARETTE, R. N. How Software Is Eating the Car The trend toward self-driving and electric vehicles will add hundreds of millions of lines

The Society of Motor Manufacturers and Traders stated in its position paper on connected and autonomous vehicles that failure in this area could undermine public confidence in the technology and also pose a real risk to public safety.[670]

Cyber security incidents, the result of which is taking control over the driving of the vehicle, can have fatal consequences in road traffic not only for the driver and passengers of the vehicle, but also for other road users. Road traffic safety may be impaired, damage may occur, a person may be injured or even killed. Therefore, it is more than necessary to deal with issues of cyber security of automated vehicles and fully automated vehicles, which should ensure a sufficient level of protection of automated vehicles and fully automated vehicles, or their systems against various cyber threats.

In this chapter, first of all, concepts such as automated vehicle and fully automated vehicle will be clarified. Subsequently, attention will be paid to the United Nation (hereinafter referred to as "UN") regulatory act in the field of vehicle cyber security. Furthermore, the chapter discusses the new legislation in the field of cyber security at the level of EU law, which will significantly affect vehicle manufacturers. At the end, there will be a summary of the chapter.

2. Automated and fully automated vehicles

The issue of automated and fully automated vehicles is regulated by regulation (EU) 2019/2144 of the European Parliament and of the Council of 27 November 2019 on type-approval requirements for motor vehicles and their trailers, and systems, components and separate technical units intended for such vehicles, as regards their general safety and the protection of vehicle occupants and vulnerable road users (hereinafter referred to as the "General Safety Regulation").[671]

of code to cars. Can the auto industry cope? [online]. Available at: https://spectrum.ieee.org/software-eating-car. Accessed 15. 8. 2023.

[670] Society of Motor Manufacturers and Traders. Connected and Autonomous Vehicles. Position Paper, 2017, p. 29. [online]. Available at: https://www.smmt.co.uk/wp-content/uploads/sites/2/SMMT-CAV-position-paper-final.pdf. Accessed 15. 8. 2023.

[671] Regulation (EU) 2019/2144 of the European Parliament and of the Council of 27 November 2019 on type-approval requirements for motor vehicles and their trailers, and systems, components and separate technical units intended for such vehicles, as regards their general safety and the protection of vehicle occupants and vulnerable road users, amending Regulation (EU) 2018/858 of the European Parliament and of the Council and repealing Regulations (EC) No 78/2009, (EC) No 79/2009 and (EC) No 661/2009 of the European Parliament and of the Council and Commission Regulations (EC) No 631/2009, (EU) No 406/2010, (EU) No 672/2010, (EU) No 1003/2010, (EU) No 1005/2010, (EU) No 1008/2010, (EU) No 1009/2010, (EU) No 19/2011, (EU) No 109/2011, (EU) No 458/2011, (EU) No 65/2012, (EU) No 130/2012, (EU)

The regulation in question defines an automated vehicle as: "a motor vehicle designed and constructed to move autonomously for certain periods of time without continuous driver supervision but in respect of which driver intervention is still expected or required."[672] The General Safety Regulation neither specifies the requirements for autonomous movement nor discuss this concept further. The abovementioned definition contains four basic legal requirements for an automated vehicle. First of all, the motor vehicle must be designed and constructed in such a way that it can move autonomously. Secondly, an autonomous movement is performed only for a certain time. Thirdly, the motor vehicle can move autonomously without continuous driver's supervision. This requirement can be interpreted in such a way that the driver does not have to monitor the road environment. In terms of the last requirement, the driver is expected to be required to intervene. In other words, the driver is required to take control of the vehicle under certain circumstances.

The General Safety Regulation also created the concept of fully automated vehicles. Fully automated vehicle is defined as: "a motor vehicle that has been designed and constructed to move autonomously without any driver supervision." Compared to an automated vehicle, a fully automated vehicle moves autonomously without any restrictions and does not require the driver to intervene.

Automated vehicles as well as fully automated vehicles must be equipped with specific systems pursuant to Art. 11 of the General Safety Regulation. The requirement that these vehicles move autonomously will be met mainly through systems replacing the driver's control of the vehicle, including signalling, steering, accelerating and braking.[673]

Uniform procedures and technical specifications for systems replacing the driver's control of the vehicle and other systems listed in Art. 11 of the General Safety Regulation will be regulated by implementing acts issued by the Commission. Furthermore, these implementing acts will regulate uniform procedures and technical specifications for the type-approval of automated and fully automated vehicles with regard to those systems and other items in order to ensure the safe operation of automated and fully automated vehicles on public roads.[674]

In that regard, the Commission adopted Commission Implementing Regulation (EU) 2022/1426 of 5 August 2022 laying down rules for the application of Regulation (EU) 2019/2144 of the European Parliament and of the Council as

No 347/2012, (EU) No 351/2012, (EU) No 1230/2012 and (EU) 2015/166 (Text with EEA relevance).

[672] General Safety Regulation, Art. 3 (21).

[673] General Safety Regulation, Art. 11 (1).

[674] General Safety Regulation, Art. 11 (2).

regards uniform procedures and technical specifications for the type-approval of the automated driving system (ADS) of fully automated vehicles.

Despite the fact that EU legislation in the field of automated vehicles uses the concepts related to automated vehicles known from technical standards, it does not use the levels of automation known from the SAE standard J3016_202104 Taxonomy and Definitions for Terms Related to Driving Automation Systems for On-Road Motor Vehicles users (hereinafter referred to as the "SAE Standard"). In general, SAE Standard levels primarily identify how the dynamic driving task is divided between a human driver and a system. At level 0 (no automation), it is performed entirely by a human driver, and at level 5 (full automation), entirely by an automated driving system.[675]

3. Legislative acts

In the following part, we will focus mainly on binding legislative acts that regulate social relations in the field of cyber security of automated vehicles. However, it should be mentioned that various reports or guidelines in this area are adopted at the level of the EU or some states. As an example, the report of the European Union Agency for Cyber Security (ENISA) entitled Cybersecurity challenges in the uptake of Artificial Intelligence in autonomous drivingcan be mentioned.[676] In 2017, the United Kingdom Government published the Vehicle Cyber Security Guidance for Connected and Automated Vehicles, which defines eight key principles in this area.[677] Another important document also published in United Kingdom is Code of Practice: automated vehicle trialling[678], in terms of which trialling organizations are recommended to apply the British Standards

[675] Levels of automation have been the subject of research by several authors. See GALINSKI, M. Kybernetická bezpečnosť automatizovaných vozidiel – technické aspekty. In ANDRAŠKO, J. et al. *Právne a technické aspekty kybernetickej bezpečnosti automatizovaných vozidiel.* Bratislava: Wolters Kluwer SR, 2022, pp. 14–17; HODÁS, M. *Implementácia autonómnej mobility – niektoré filozofické a (ústavno) právne aspekty a ich právne a metaprávne impliká-cie nielen pre Slovenskú republiku.* Praha: Leges, 2022, pp. 22–25.

[676] ENISA. Cybersecurity challenges in the uptake of artificial intelligence in autonomous driving. 2021, p. 10. [online]. Available at: https://www.enisa.europa.eu/news/enisa-news/cyber security-challenges-in-the-uptake-of-artificial-intelligence-in-autonomous-driving. Accessed 16. 8. 2023.

[677] UK GOVERNMENT. Guidance: The key principles of vehicle cyber security for connected and automated vehicles. Available at: https://www.gov.uk/government/publications/principles -of-cyber-security-for-connected-and-automated-vehicles/the-key-principles-of-vehicle-cyber -security-for-connected-and-automated-vehicles. Accessed 16. 8. 2023.

[678] UK GOVERNMENT. Guidance: Code of Practice: automated vehicle trialling. [online]. Available at: https://www.gov.uk/government/publications/trialling-automated-vehicle-technologi es-in-public/code-of-practice-automated-vehicle-trialling. Accessed 16. 8. 2023.

Institution (BSI) standard regarding the basic principles of automotive cyber security.[679]

3.1 UN Regulation No. 155

Threats in the form of unauthorised remote access to in-vehicle data and the illegal modification of software over the air are global in nature. This fact is also expressed in the General Safety Regulation, which in its recitals requires the mandatory application of UN Regulations or other regulatory acts on cyber security to such threats, as soon as possible after they come into force.[680]

In addition, the General Safety Regulation emphasizes the need to introduce harmonized rules and technical requirements for software modifications in accordance with type approval procedures. Automated vehicles need a system (software) for their operation, the modification of which can significantly change functionalities of the vehicle. Therefore, UN Regulations or other regulatory acts regarding software update procedures should be applied as soon as possible after they come into force.[681]

With respect to technical regulations for vehicles prepared by United Nations Economic Commission for Europe (hereinafter referred to as "UNECE"), which have been adopted as a UN regulation, they become legally binding within the EU as part of the type approval legislation following the procedure set out in the type approval regulation.[682]

At the UN level, UNECE adopted UN Regulation No. 155 – Uniform provisions concerning the approval of vehicles with regards to cyber security and cyber security management system (hereinafter referred to as "UN Regulation No. 155") in 2019. The regulation in question primarily concerns the issue of cyber security of vehicles.

UN Regulation No. 155 defines cyber security as: "the condition in which road vehicles and their functions are protected from cyber threats to electrical

[679] BSI. PAS 1885:2018 The fundamental principles of automotive cyber security. Specification. [online]. Available at: https://standardsdevelopment.bsigroup.com/projects/2017-02712#/section. Accessed 18. 8. 2023.

[680] General Safety Regulation, recital 26.

[681] General Safety Regulation, recital 27. With regard to software update, UN Regulation No. 156 – Software update and software update management system was adopted.

[682] Regulation (EU) 2018/858 of the European Parliament and of the Council of 30 May 2018 on the approval and market surveillance of motor vehicles and their trailers, and of systems, components and separate technical units intended for such vehicles, amending Regulations (EC) No 715/2007 and (EC) No 595/2009 and repealing Directive 2007/46/EC (Text with EEA relevance.), recital 48, 49 and Art. 57.

or electronic components."[683] This is the first ever legally binding definition of cyber security that can be applied in the field of vehicles.

UN Regulation No. 155 neither defines the term cyber security incident, nor mentions this term in the text of the regulation. In general, a security incident occurs when a threat exploits a vulnerability in an asset and causes some impact, e.g. in the form of data leakage, device malfunction, etc. Despite the fact that the regulation in question does not regulate this concept, in Annex No. 5 examples of the impacts of the attack are given. Possible attack impacts may include:

a) *Safe operation of vehicle affected;*
b) *Vehicle functions stop working;*
c) *Software modified, performance altered;*
d) *Software altered but no operational effects;*
e) *Data integrity breach;*
f) *Data confidentiality breach;*
g) *Loss of data availability;*
h) *Other, including criminality*

From the abovementioned attack impacts, it can be seen that in such cases the basic security requirements for the protection of information, namely confidentiality, integrity and availability, would be violated. Disruption of the safe operation of the vehicle, stopping the functions of the vehicle represent serious impacts of cyber attacks, which would endanger not only the driver and passenger, but also other road users. The result of various attacks can also be criminal activity or inferring responsibility for illegal actions. Legal regulation at the level of EU law[684], as well as the legal order of the Slovak Republic, penalizes illegal actions, which consist in illegal access to the information system, illegal system interference, illegal data interference, as well as the provision of tools for committing such offences.[685]

Despite the fact that cyber threats are mentioned in the definition of the term cyber security, the regulation in question only defines the term threat as: "a potential cause of an unwanted incident, which may result in harm to a system, organization or individual."[686] In Annex no. 5 of UN Regulation No. 155 is a list of threats and relevant mitigations. A mitigation is: "a measure that is reducing

[683] UN Regulation No. 155, point 2.2.

[684] Directive 2013/40/EU of the European Parliament and of the Council of 12 August 2013 on attacks against information systems and replacing Council Framework Decision 2005/222/JHA.

[685] In the legal order of the Slovak Republic, computer crimes are regulated primarily by Act No. 300/2005 Coll. Criminal code. See DRAŽOVÁ, P. Kybernetická kriminalita. In ANDRAŠKO, J. et al. *Právo informačných a komunikačných technológií.* 2. vydání. Bratislava: TINCT, 2021, pp. 149–194.

[686] UN Regulation No. 155, point 2.12.

risk."[687] A risk is: " the potential that a given threat will exploit vulnerabilities of a vehicle and thereby cause harm to the organization or to an individual."[688] A vulnerability is defined as: " a weakness of an asset or mitigation that can be exploited by one or more threats."[689] The list of vulnerabilities is provided in Annex 5 of UN Regulation No. 155 in Table A1.

Terms and their definitions used in UN Regulation No. 155 are based on standards in the field of information and cyber security, specifically the ISO/IEC 2700x series standards and the ISO/IEC 27032:2012 standard.

As a practical example, when a threat could exploit the vulnerability of the vehicle's systems, the following situation can be mentioned. The driver connected his tablet to the vehicle. However, the tablet was infected with a virus and the vehicle's systems may also be infected. As a mitigation security control will be applied to external interfaces.[690] In this case, the vulnerability is an irresponsible driver connecting other devices to the vehicle, the threat is an infected tablet, and the mitigation is a security check.

From the above example, it can be seen that UN Regulation No. 155 does not establish concrete specific mitigations that need to be implemented, or the way in which it needs to be implemented. The addressees of the norms, which are car manufacturers, have some freedom in the way of implementing a specific mitigation. In this case, these are norms that determine what result the vehicle manufacturer should achieve.

The vehicle manufacturer is obliged to implement measures for the vehicle type to:[691]

a) *Detect and prevent cyber-attacks against vehicles of the vehicle type;*
b) *Support the monitoring capability of the vehicle manufacturer with regards to detecting threats, vulnerabilities and cyber-attacks relevant to the vehicle type;*
c) *Provide data forensic capability to enable analysis of attempted or successful cyber-attacks.*

Another difference of the UN Regulation No. 155 compared to the regulation regarding vehicle type approval is an extension of scope to car manufacturers. While the General Safety Regulation contains requirements that must be met by the vehicle, its components and system before being placed on the market, UN Regulation No. 155 will also be applied to the certification of the car manufacturers themselves.

687 UN Regulation No. 155, point 2.8.
688 UN Regulation No. 155, point 2.9.
689 UN Regulation No. 155, point 2.13.
690 UN Regulation No. 155, Table B4 point 18.2 of the Annex 5.
691 UN Regulation No. 155, point 7.3.7.

UN Regulation No. 155 regulates the creation and certification of a Cyber Security Management System (CSMS). This system represents: "a systematic risk-based approach defining organisational processes, responsibilities and governance to treat risk associated with cyber threats to vehicles and protect them from cyberattacks."[692]

The Cyber Security Management System contains specific procedures and the vehicle manufacturer is obliged to demonstrate that the processes used in its Cyber Security Management System ensure adequate consideration of security, including the risks and mitigations listed in Annex 5. This will include e.g. the processes used to monitor for, detect and respond to cyber-attacks, cyber threats and vulnerabilities on vehicle types and the processes used to assess whether the cyber security measures implemented are still effective in the light of new cyber threats and vulnerabilities that have been identified.[693]

The vehicle manufacturer is obliged to report at least once a year, or more frequently if relevant, to the Approval Authority or the Technical Service the outcome of their monitoring activities. This will include relevant information on new cyber-attacks. The vehicle manufacturer is also obliged to report and confirm to the Approval Authority or the Technical Service that the cyber security mitigations implemented for their vehicle types are still effective and any additional actions taken.[694]

The Cyber Security Management System covers the development phase, the production phase and the post-production phase which means that this system will cover the whole life cycle of the vehicle until the end-of-life of all vehicles under the vehicle type. In other words, the manufacturer of vehicles of the given type will have to meet the requirements in accordance with UN Regulation No. 155 and it will be possible to verify whether the requirements are met even after the vehicle has been put on the market.

The reason for extending the scope of the regulation of technical requirements also to the phase after market launch is mainly the dynamic nature of threats that may not even have existed at the time of production and market launch.

The manufacturer has to have a valid Certificate of Compliance for the Cyber Security Management System relevant to the vehicle type being approved.[695] An application for a Certificate of Compliance for Cyber Security Management System is submitted by the vehicle manufacturer or by their duly accredited

692 UN Regulation No. 155, point 2.3.

693 UN Regulation No. 155, point 7.2.2.2.

694 UN Regulation No. 155, point 7.4.1.

695 UN Regulation No. 155, point 7.3.1 and 3.2.3.

representative. Approval Authority will carry out the assessment of the manufacturer and issue a Certificate of Compliance for Cyber Security Management System.[696]

When the assessment has been satisfactorily completed a certificate named Certificate of Compliance for Cyber Security Management System will be granted to the manufacturer. The Approval Authority which has granted the Certificate of Compliance for Cyber Security Management System may at any time verify that the requirements for it continue to be met.[697]

3.2 NIS 2 Directive

The first regulatory act in the field of cyber security at the level of EU law was the Directive (EU) 2016/1148 of the European Parliament and of the Council of 6 July 2016 concerning measures for a high common level of security of network and information systems across the Union (hereinafter referred to as the "NIS Directive"). However, the application practice as well as the conclusions of the Commission[698] pointed out that the goal of the NIS Directive, the achievement of a high common level of security of networks and information systems within the EU, could not be fulfilled. For these reasons was adopted Directive (EU) 2022/2555 of the European Parliament and of the Council of 14 December 2022 on measures for a high common level of cybersecurity across the Union, amending Regulation (EU) No 910/2014 and Directive (EU) 2018/1972, and repealing Directive (EU) 2016/1148 (hereinafter referred to as the "NIS 2 Directive"). The NIS 2 Directive is repealing NIS Directive and has to be transposed into legal orders of EU Members states by 17 October 2024.

3.2.1 Scope

In the field of regulation of automated vehicles, the NIS 2 Directive brings a fundamental change in comparison to the NIS Directive because the range of regulated sectors and sub-sectors is extended to the manufacturing of motor vehicles.

[696] UN Regulation No. 155, point 6.1 and 6.2.

[697] UN Regulation No. 155, point 6.5 and 6.8.

[698] Commission. Commission staff working document impact assessment report Accompanying the document Proposal for a Directive of the European Parliament and of the Council on measures for a high common level of cybersecurity across the Union, repealing Directive (EU) 2016/1148. SWD(2020) 345 final.

Entities that fall within the scope of the NIS 2 Directive are divided into two categories depending on the industry in which they operate or the type of services they provide, in particular:

- essential entities and
- important entities.

The NIS 2 Directive does not oblige Member States to identify entities that meet the criteria to act as operators of essential services (identification process) as set out in the NIS Directive. Instead, the NIS 2 Directive established a uniform criterion to determine the entities that fall within the scope of the NIS 2 Directive. This criterion consists in the application of the size-cap rule, according to which the NIS 2 Directive applies to public or private entities of a type referred to in Annex I or II which qualify as medium-sized enterprises under Article 2 of the Annex to Recommendation 2003/361/EC, or exceed the ceilings for medium-sized enterprises provided for in paragraph 1 of that Article, and which provide their services or carry out their activities within the EU.[699]

There are also exceptions to the size-cap rule and thus the directive in question will also apply to entities of the type listed in Annex I or II, regardless of their size. The exceptions in question are listed in Article 2 (2) of the NIS 2 Directive.

Annex I defines the following sectors of high criticality: energy; transport; banking; financial market infrastructures; health; drinking water; waste water; digital infrastructure; ICT service management (business-to-business); public administration and space. Compared to the sectors regulated in the NIS Directive, sectors such as waste water, public administration and space have been added.

Annex II defines the following other critical sectors: postal and courier services; waste management; manufacture, production and distribution of chemicals; production, processing and distribution of food; manufacturing; digital providers and research.

The extension of the scope of the NIS 2 Directive will also significantly affect the field of vehicles. While the NIS Directive applied only to operators of intelligent transport systems the NIS 2 Directive applies in addition to the mentioned operators also to manufacturers of motor vehicles in the sector Manufacturing and its sub-sector Manufacture of motor vehicles, trailers and semi-trailers according to Annex II of the directive in question. Within the given subsector, undertakings carrying out any of the economic activities referred to in section C division 29 of NACE Rev. 2 – Statistical classification of economic activites in the European Community (hereinafter referred to as "NACE Rev. 2") are listed as types of entities.[700]

[699] NIS 2 Directive, Art. 2 (1).

[700] NACE Rev. 2, p. 185. [online]. Available at: https://ec.europa.eu/eurostat/documents/3859598/5902521/KS-RA-07-015-EN.PDF. Accessed 20. 8. 2023.

The division in question includes the manufacture of motor vehicles for transporting passengers or freight. Furthermore, the manufacture of various parts and accessories, as well as the manufacture of trailers and semi-trailers, is included here.[701]

3.2.2 Measures

Essential and important entities are obliged to take: "appropriate and proportionate technical, operational and organisational measures to manage the risks posed to the security of network and information systems which those entities use for their operations or for the provision of their services, and to prevent or minimise the impact of incidents on recipients of their services and on other services."[702]

The measures in question are based on an all-hazards approach that aims to protect network and information systems and the physical environment of those systems from incidents, and include at least the following:[703]

a) *policies on risk analysis and information system security;*
b) *incident handling;*
c) *business continuity, such as backup management and disaster recovery, and crisis management;*
d) *supply chain security, including security-related aspects concerning the relationships between each entity and its direct suppliers or service providers;*
e) *security in network and information systems acquisition, development and maintenance, including vulnerability handling and disclosure;*
f) *policies and procedures to assess the effectiveness of cybersecurity risk-management measures;*
g) *basic cyber hygiene practices and cybersecurity training;*
h) *policies and procedures regarding the use of cryptography and, where appropriate, encryption;*
i) *human resources security, access control policies and asset management;*
j) *the use of multi-factor authentication or continuous authentication solutions, secured voice, video and text communications and secured emergency communication systems within the entity, where appropriate.*

In order to establish technical, methodological as well as sectoral requirements for measures, the Commission may adopt implementing acts.[704]

[701] NACE Rev. 2, p. 185.
[702] NIS 2 Directive, Art. 21 (1).
[703] NIS 2 Directive, Art. 21 (2).
[704] NIS 2 Directive, Art. 21 (5).

3.2.3 Incident reporting

Essential and important entities are obliged to notify, without undue delay, its CSIRT or, where applicable, its competent authority of any incident that has a significant impact on the provision of their services (significant incident).[705]

The following requirements must be met for the notification obligation to arise:

a) it must be an incident within the meaning of Art. 6 (6) of the NIS 2 Directive
b) the incident must be serious within the meaning of Art. 23 (3) of the NIS 2 Directive.

Ad a)

The definition of the term "incident" used in the NIS 2 Directive is significantly changed compared to the definition used in the NIS Directive. The NIS 2 Directive defines an incident as: "an event compromising the availability, authenticity, integrity or confidentiality of stored, transmitted or processed data or of the services offered by, or accessible via, network and information systems."[706]

The first part of the definition of the term "incident" does not specify what data it is. Data in question must be interpreted in connection with the definition of the concept of networks and information systems in the sense of Article 6 (1) of the NIS 2 Directive. In terms of the provision in question, it will be data that is stored, processed, retrieved or transmitted by electronic communications network or any device or group of interconnected or related devices, one or more of which, pursuant to a programme, carry out automatic processing of digital data for the purposes of their operation, use, protection and maintenance. With regard to networks and information systems, only networks and information systems are considered that entities use for their operations or for the provision of their services, and to prevent or minimise the impact of incidents on recipients of their services and on other services. This conclusion can be reached based on the interpretation of Article 21 (1) of the NIS 2 Directive.

Networks and information systems in the case of automated vehicles could be considered networks and information systems that ensure the manufacturing of automated vehicles. Therefore, it can be concluded that the incident in the meaning of the NIS 2 Directive concerns the systems that ensure the manufacture of the vehicle.

Where appropriate, essential and important entities are obliged to notify, without undue delay, the recipients of their services of significant incidents that are likely to adversely affect the provision of those services.[707]

---

705 NIS 2 Directive, Art. 23 (1).
706 NIS 2 Directive, Art. 6 (6).
707 NIS 2 Directive, Art. 23 (1).

Furthermore, essential and important entities are obliged to report, inter alia, any information enabling the CSIRT or, where applicable, the competent authority to determine any cross-border impact of the incident.[708]

Ad b)

According to the second requirement, the incident must be considered as significant. Pursuant to Article 23 (3) of NIS 2 Directive, an incident is considered to be significant if:

a) it has caused or is capable of causing severe operational disruption of the services or financial loss for the entity concerned;
b) it has affected or is capable of affecting other natural or legal persons by causing considerable material or non-material damage.

Aforementioned requirements do not have to be met cumulatively. Such a conclusion can be justified by recital 101 of the NIS 2 Directive, in terms of which: "In that regard, this Directive should include the reporting of incidents that, based on an initial assessment carried out by the entity concerned, could cause severe operational disruption of the services or financial loss for that entity or affect other natural or legal persons by causing considerable material or non-material damage."

Essential and important entities are obliged to submit to the CSIRT or, where applicable, the competent authority:

a) without undue delay and in any event within 24 hours of becoming aware of the significant incident, an early warning,[709]
b) without undue delay and in any event within 72 hours of becoming aware of the significant incident, an incident notification,[710]
c) upon the request of a CSIRT or, where applicable, the competent authority, an intermediate report on relevant status updates,[711]
d) a final report not later than one month after the submission of the incident notification under point (b).[712]

In the event of an ongoing incident at the time of the submission of the final report, entities concerned provide a progress report at that time and a final report within one month of their handling of the incident.[713]

[708] NIS 2 Directive, Art. 23 (1).
[709] NIS 2 Directive, Art. 23 (4) (a).
[710] NIS 2 Directive, Art. 23 (4) (b).
[711] NIS 2 Directive, Art. 23 (4) (c).
[712] NIS 2 Directive, Art. 23 (4) (d).
[713] NIS 2 Directive, Art. 23 (4) (e).

The Commission may adopt implementing acts specifying the cases in which an incident will be considered to be significant.[714]

Where applicable, essential and important entities communicate, without undue delay, to the recipients of their services that are potentially affected by a significant cyber threat any measures or remedies that those recipients are able to take in response to that threat. Where appropriate, the entities will also inform those recipients of the significant cyber threat itself.[715]

When defining the term cyber threat, the NIS Directive 2 refers to the definition used in Article 2 (8) of the regulation (EU) 2019/881 of the European Parliament and of the Council of 17 April 2019 on ENISA (the European Union Agency for Cybersecurity) and on information and communications technology cybersecurity certification and repealing Regulation (EU) No 526/2013 (Cybersecurity Act). In terms of this definition, a cyber threat is: "any potential circumstance, event or action that could damage, disrupt or otherwise adversely impact network and information systems, the users of such systems and other persons." A significant cyber threat is within the meaning of Article 6 (11) of the NIS 2 Directive: "cyber threat which, based on its technical characteristics, can be assumed to have the potential to have a severe impact on the network and information systems of an entity or the users of the entity's services by causing considerable material or non-material damage."

4. Conclusion

Without achieving a sufficient level of cyber security of automated vehicles, fully automated vehicles and their systems so that they do not pose a threat to road users, such vehicles cannot be successfully deployed on public roads. However, in the context of automated vehicles and fully automated vehicles, not only the safety of its individual components is important, but especially the cyber security of these vehicles, or their systems.

By adopting UN Regulation No. 155, specific obligations are imposed on vehicle manufacturers in the context of vehicle type approval with regard to cyber security. Vehicle manufacturers are required to demonstrate that the procedures used in their Cyber Security Management System ensure adequate consideration of security, including risks and mitigations in accordance with UN Regulation No. 155. These procedures include procedures used for processes used to monitor for, detect and respond to cyber-attacks, cyber threats and vulnerabilities on

[714] NIS 2 Directive, Art. 23 (11).
[715] NIS 2 Directive, Art. 23 (2).

vehicle types. Part of the response to a cyber attack, cyber threat or vulnerability will be reporting them. The vehicle manufacturer is obliged to report at least once a year, or more frequently if relevant, to the Approval Authority or the Technical Service the outcome of their monitoring activities. This will include relevant information on new cyber-attacks. The vehicle manufacturer is also obliged to report and confirm to the Approval Authority or the Technical Service that the cyber security mitigations implemented for their vehicle types are still effective and any additional actions taken.

Compared to the General Safety Regulation, which applies to the vehicle and its components and systems, UN Regulation No. 155 also applies to the certification of vehicle manufacturers themselves. Another factor that will improve the cyber security of vehicles is the extension of the scope of application of the technical requirements for vehicles to the phase after the launch of the vehicle. In that regard these requirements will apply to the entire life cycle of the vehicle, which starts with development, continues with production and launch on the market and ends by stopping production until the end-of-life of all vehicles under the vehicle type.

The NIS 2 Directive will strengthen the cyber security of traditional vehicles as well as automated vehicles and fully automated vehicles. Vehicle manufacturers will be obliged to implement security measures that will include, e.g. risk analysis, incident handling, supply chain security, policies and procedures to assess the effectiveness of cybersecurity risk-management measures, basic cyber hygiene practices and cybersecurity training. Vehicle manufacturers will also be obliged to notify, without undue delay, its CSIRT or, where applicable, its competent authority of any incident that has a significant impact on the provision of their services. However, it must be noted that the incident must concern networks and information systems that ensure the production of vehicles.

CHAPTER FOURTEEN

The European Union's Strategic Sovereignty – Legal Implications in the Light of Modern Threats

PETER-CHRISTIAN MÜLLER-GRAFF

The European Union's Strategic Sovereignty[716] has suddenly become a current topic on the political scene since Russia's civilisation-breaking imperial crime of warfare against Ukraine. The Union asks itself whether and to what degree it is fully aware of elementary challenges to its existence and sufficiently equipped for surviving in a hostile world. The Council of the European Union has published "The Strategic Compass of the EU" not later than one month after Russia's full invasion.[717] Since then, the public discussion has increasingly opened the eyes for the threats to the Union arising from dependencies from third countries in essential matters as well as for the permanent necessity to realistically reflect on the Union's international leeway capabilities and on its capacity to autonomously and effectively act in its own interest on the planetary scene. Recently the French President accentuated this ambition when returning from China – although with a rather counterproductive formulation on Taiwan.[718]

For a legal scholar who ponders on the legal web and on the role of the EU as a legally constituted transnational polity[719] of 27 states the *very first* question which comes to mind in this issue is the simple issue of constitutional competence. Or in other words: Which Treaty based constitutional powers does

---

[716] This text is based on the presentation of the author at the Jean Monnet Scientific Conference "The European Union's Response on the Challenges of Modern Society" at Palacky University Olomouc on April 26, 2023.

[717] See Council of the European Union, The Strategic Compass of the European Union, March 21, 2022.

[718] KOUTSOKOSTA, E. Die Woche in Europa: Macrons Taiwan-Aussagen spalten die EU. Available at: https://de.euronews.com/my-europe/2023/04/14/die-woche-in-europa-macrons-taiwan-aussagen-spalten-die-eu

[719] For this qualification of the EU see MÜLLER-GRAF, P.-Ch. Verfassungsziele der Europäischen Union, in Manfred Dauses/Markus Ludwigs (Hrsg.), Handbuch des EU-Wirtschaftsrechts, EL 49 (November 2019), A I Rn. 58 et seq., 61 et seq.

the Union hold to act autonomously in its own interest? Three issues shall be looked upon: First: What is the substantive *meaning* of the objective "strategic sovereignty"? Second: What are the *general links* of the conditions of strategic sovereignty to the *primary law* of the Union? Third: What are *are* the constitutional conditions for the Union's aim to successfully strive for sovereignty in *energy, trade and defence*?

1. Strategic Sovereignty as a General Objective?

What is the meaning of "strategic sovereignty" as a general objective? I understand this idea as the *willingness* and *factual capability* to *continuously* upholding the *self-defined concept* of living in relation to others. In this sense it is a permanent task and has many *prerequisites*: first for the *self-defined concept* the *spiritual* prerequisite of self-determination on the basis of intellectual clarity; second for the *willingness* the *mental* virtues of political decisiveness, willpower and persistence; and third for the *capabilities* the *factual* requirements of economic resources, the citizens' internal democratic and social support, diplomatic skills and effective military defence capacities.

2. The Links to the Union's Treaty Based Constitutional Law?

What are the links of these three prerequisites (concept, willingness, capability) to the European Union as a transnational polity constituted by law and bound by its constitutional law?

2.1 Links of the Self-Defined Strategic Concept to the Union's Constitutional Law

For the prerequisite of a self-defined *concept* of living in relation to others the Union is constitutionally bound by Article 3 para 5 TEU "in its relations with the wider world (to) uphold and promote its values and interests and contribute to the protection of its citizens. It shall contribute to peace, security, the sustainable development of the Earth, solidarity and mutual respect among peoples, free and fair trade, eradication of poverty and the protection of human rights…". Article 21 para 1 TEU unfolds it even more ambitious: "The Union's action on the international scene shall be guided by the principles which have inspired its own creation, development and enlargement, and which it seeks to advance in the wider world: democracy, the rule of law, the universality and indivisibilty of human rights and fundamental freedoms, respect for human dignity, the principles of equality and solidarity, and respect for the principles of the United Nations Charter and international law." More specific aims are listed for the Union's approach to neighbouring countries. With them "the Union shall develop a special relationship…, aiming to establish an area of prosperity and good neighbourliness, founded on the values of the Union and characterised by close and peaceful relations based on cooperation" (Article 8 TEU).

Hence, the *substantive narrative* of the Union's self-understanding can be seen in upholding and promoting its intended (and widely practiced) *enlightened European way of life* as laid down in its constitutional value and objective orientation (Article 2 TEU: "respect for human dignity, freedom, democracy, equality, the rule of law, respect for human rights"). It can be understood as the conceptual core for what is meant with the sometimes used word of a "narrative" or "vision" for the so called "survival of the West".

2.2 Links of Strategic Willingness to the Union's Constitutional Law

What about the link of *strategic willingness* to the Union's constitutional law? Law cannot substitute real willpower. But the Union's constitutional law can continuously remind the necessity to muster political decisiveness, willpower and persistence for pursuing the track of its genuine *Article 2-narrative*. Strategic sovereignty requires its translation into a coherent strategy: more concrete into a *comprehensive strategy* to define and realize its adequate geopolitical place as well as into fitting *sub-strategies*, in particular into *regional* sub-strategies and *subject-matter-policy* sub-strategies. *Regional* sub-strategies concern in particular those towards the Mediterranean, the Balcans and the very East of Europe. Currently the question is at hand as to whether this orientation should include, e.g., a sub-strategy of the Union to support the transformation of Russia's historically inherited autocratic and violent system of power into an order that is not threatening the Union and its Member States as proposed by *Alexei Nawalny* in the Frankfurter Allgemeine Sonntagszeitung some times ago.[720] In any case, the Union's sub-strategy of self-assertion in the "system rivalry" needs to be concretized and pursued. Among the essential *subject-matter policy areas* for realizing "strategic sovereignty" rank in particular reliable energy and raw material availability, economic clout in relation to other global actors and sufficient self-defence capabilities – and internal unity.

[720] *Alexej Nawalny.* Wie Putin besiegt werden kann. Frankfurter Allgemeine Sonntagszeitung, October 2, 2022, p. 2.

2.3 Links of Strategic Capability to the Union's Constitutional Law

What about the links to *strategic capabilities* to the Union's constitutional law*?* Law cannot substitute factual capability either. But due to the Union's constitutional principle of conferral (Article 5 para 2 TEU) the Union is empowered to contribute to the three mentioned factual requirements, although only on the basis of the corresponding competences.

3. Constitutional Conditions of the Union's Striving for Autonomy in Energy, Trade and Defence?

3.1 Constitutional Challenges to the Union's Energy Sovereignty

Concerning *energy sovereignty* the questions of competences, of the principle of consistency, of the relation to the Energy Community and to the European Atomic Energy Community arise.

3.1.1 Competences

In the area of energy Article 194 para 2 TFEU in conjunction with its para 1 lit. b empower the Union to legislatively "establish the measures necessary to achieve the objective", "to … *ensure security of energy supply* in the Union". Ensuring security of energy supply is not necessarily self-sufficiency, but does not exclude this form of security (if feasible at all for the Union). *However*, this objective stands in *tension* with the Treaty's provision that the Union's measures "shall not affect a Member State's right to determine the conditions for exploiting its energy resources, its *choice* between different energy sources and the general structure of its energy supply" (current example: Hungary's gas supply policy[721]). *But* this statement is qualified by the wording "without prejudice" to the EU's *environmental protection* policy competence "to adopt measures significantly affecting" such a choice (Article 192 par 2 lit. c TFEU). *Hence* the promotion of the so called *"green"* conversion of the modes of all economic activities in production, distribution and consumption in order to achieve climate neutrality until 2050, as it is pursued by the incumbent Commission,[722] can also comprise

[721] International Energy Ageny, Hungary National Gas Security Policy, Report of 10 August 2022. Available at: https://www.iea.org/articles/hungary-natural-gas-security-policy

[722] *Ursula von der Leyen.* A Union that strives for more. My agenda for Europe. Political Guidelines for the Next European Commission 2019–2024, Brussels, 2018.

a concept of ensuring the security of energy supply based on *"green energy resources"*. Insofar the Union is empowered to pursue an *environmental* policy which overrides the restrictions of the energy policy competence. This even matches one of the objectives to be pursued on the basis of the *"pure" energy policy*, namely to "promote ... the development of ... renewable forms of energy" (Article 194 para 1 lit. c TFEU). These efforts are, e.g., factually fostered by the Ostend Declaration of nine North Sea riparian states to turn the North Sea into the world's biggest wind power production plant.[723]

3.1.2 The Obligation of Consistency

An additionally relevant constitutional aspect for energy sovereignty is the Union's obligation to ensure "consistency between its policies and activities, taking all its objectives into account" (Article 7 TFEU). At least one group of them has to be addressed in the energy context: namely the general guiding line for the adoption of an *economic policy* "which is based ... on the *internal market* ... and conducted in accordance with the principle of an *open market economy with free competition*" (Article 119 para 1 TFEU) and its ramifications into a system that competition is not distorted in the internal market (Protocol No. 27), the basic incompatibility of state aid that distorts competition (Article 107 para 1 TFEU), the prohibition of distortions of competition by industrial policy (Article 173 para 3 sub-para 2 TFEU) and the pursuit of the harmonious development of world trade (Article 206 TFEU). The *consequences* of the obligation of Article 119 para 1 TFEU should not be overrated,[724] but also not underestimated.[725] The obligation *requires* a steady basic policy orientation towards upholding the free coordination of free preferences of offer (including free production) and demand, *but* it does not contain an absolute prohibition of any regulatory measure that interfers with the free production and the free dealing and wheeling on the market. *Indeed*, the Union's constitutional order of the economy is also marked by provisions for protecting specific public goods such as, e.g, health (Article 168 TFEU) and by provisions for transforming the economy into sustainability and climate neutrality (Article 191 TFEU) as well as provisions for reaching certain sectoral or regional economic results (e.g. in agriculture Article 39 TFEU and for regional cohesion Article 174 TFEU) and by those for reaching macroeconomic goals such as, e.g., price stability (Article 127 TFEU). *Nevertheless*, the principle of an open market

[723] Ostend Declaration of Energy Ministers on the North Sea as Europe's Green Power Plant, April 24, 2023.

[724] No direct applicability: CJEU, Case C-9/99 (Échirolles), ECLI:EU:C:2000:532, note 25.

[725] The CJEU, Case C-9/99, note 8 (supra) labels it as "a general principle".

economy with free competition requires that any of the Union's measures on the basis of a shared competence complies with the principles of *subsidiarity* and *proportionality* and, if a regulatory measure restricts a fundamental right such as the freedom to conduct a business (Article 16 CFR), also with this principle of *proportionality*. And as far as such an energy-environmental policy can be qualified as "industrial policy" (Article 173 TFEU) it must *not distort competition* (Article 173 para 3 sub-sec. 3 TFEU). Hence, when restricting the markets of fossil energy market-conform measures (such as certificates) should to be preferred.

The principle of an open market economy with free competition has also an *external* dimension. This is underlined by Article 206 TFEU, which aims at "the progressive abolition of restrictions on international trade". *However* this does not exclude *protective* measures (Article 207 para 1 TFEU) for *supporting* internal policies to converse the energy mode of production and consumption.

3.1.3 The Role of the European Atomic Energy Community

A third aspect in view of achieving the Union's self-sufficiency in energy supply relates to the European Atomic Energy Community (EAEC). Despite its character as an independent international organisation[726] all and only Member States of the Union are its members and it is connected to the EU by the identical institutional framework (Article 106 EAEC-Treaty). Its constitutional task "to contribute to the standard of living … by creating the conditions necessary for the speedy development and growth of nuclear industries" poses no obstacle to a European strategy, if politically wanted, to secure its "energy sovereignty" by way of promoting nuclear industries within the Union. Nor is the primary law of the Union a roadblock.

3.1.4 The Role of the Energy Community

Eventually the Union's primary law does not bar the potential of the Energy Community as an independent international organisation founded by the EU and nine Balkan States in 2005[727] to legally and factually contribute to the Union's energy sovereignty.

[726] GRUNWALD, J. Europäische Atomgemeinschaft. In Armin Hatje/Peter-Christian Müller-Graff (Hrsg.). Europäisches Organisations- und Verfassungsrecht (Enzyklopädie Europarecht, Band 1), 2. Aufl., 2022, p. 1247 et seq.

[727] For the text of the Energy Community Treaty see OJEU 2025 L 198/15.

3.2 Constitutional Challenges to Economic, Trade and Development Assistance Sovereignty

In view of the perspective of economic, trade and development assistance sovereignty, its backbone can be seen in the Union's stable economic prosperity as the Treaty-indended well-being of its peoples (Article 3 TEU) and as the Union's and its Member States' capacity for financing the material prerequisites of its sovereignty: in particular for paying the necessary essential imports (such as energy, rare earth, semiconductors or medicaments as long as self-sufficiency is not achieved), for funding the transformation of the economy into a sustainable and climate-neutral mode, for fostering the economic and social development in third countries and for funding the personal power and the physical and digital equipment for reliable defence (" si vis pacem, para bellum"). Again there are internal and external aspects in Union law.

3.2.1 Functioning Internal Market Within the Union's Constitutional (Economic) Order

The essential basis of any solid realization of concepts of the Union's sovereignty depends upon the good functioning of the *internal market* within the Union's constitutional order. The question is at hand as to whether the Union is *constitutionally endowed* with the necessary power to keep the legal framework of the internal market in step with the developing economic, social, environmental and other challenges to the objective of a prosperous economy. It can be submitted that the Union disposes of a *wide legal maneuvering space*,[728] in particular the competences for approximating relevant national laws (e.g. Article 114 TFEU) as well as for industrial, technological and environmental policy (Articles 173, 179 et seq., 191 et seq. TFEU). Insofar, in particular, the promotion of raw material exploitation and semiconductor promotion within the Union, will play an important role. Whether the continuation of Europe's economic prosperity will succeed depends less on the Union's competences than on their factual and careful use to let the market economy generate economic welfare in view of changing challenges.

[728] See, e.g., MÜLLER-GRAF, P.-Ch. Europäisches Binnenmarkt- und Wirtschaftsordnungsrecht, Das System. In Peter-Christian Müller-Graff (Hrsg.), Europäisches Binnenmarkt- und Wirtschaftsordnungsrecht (Enzyklopädie Europarecht Band 4), 2. Aufl., 2021, p. 53, 112 et seq.; MÜLLER-GRAF, P.-Ch. Festigkeits- und Elastizitätsproben des Europäischen Wirtschaftsordnungsrechts. In Florian Bien/Joachim Jickeli/Peter-Christian Müller-Graff (Hrsg.), Maß- und Gradfragen im Wirtschaftsrecht, 2021, p. 211, 219 et seq., 232.

3.2.2 Trade and Development Cooperation Policies in Relation to Third Countries

On the other side the Union's strategic sovereignty is intertwinned with its *export/import* and *related policies* (development co-operation). For promoting *trade* the Union holds the *exclusive* competence (Article 206 TFEU). It is well known that the Union uses this power for its global outreach with a view to increasing the density of rules in the content of its agreements.[729] The so called "comprehensive" trade agreements[730] with their regulatory framework for free trade (shaped along the lines of regulatory topics and rules of the internal market) can be understood as the expression of a *double-headed strategy*: on the one hand promoting a regulatory level playing field for competition with imported goods and services (thereby also protecting consumers in the Union), on the other hand easening exports of European enterprises to the respective third countries. As an international *side effect* of the Union's intensive creation of legal standards for the protection of diverse public goods within the internal market (such as health, consumers' self-determination, labour protection, environment, climate) an increasing voluntary adaptation to these standards by third countries is reported.[731] *Anu Bradford* assesses the Union as a standard-setting world power.[732] This, however, does *not* seem to apply to *financial* transactions and the banking sector, where the Union is adapting to standards[733] set elsewhere (in particular IFRS issued by the IASB[734]).

The Union's new *"Global Gateway" strategy*[735] fits into this strategy of *linking commerce and politics*. According to its own definition it is "an EU plan for major investment in infrastructure around the world" aiming "to forge links and not create dependencies".[736] This programme can be based on the Union's *competence* for development cooperation (Article 208 TFEU). It takes on the challenge posed by China's "One Belt One Road" strategy.[737] In view of the "Global South"

[729] See, e.g., MÜLLER-GRAF, P.-Ch. Unionsrechtliche Europäisierung außerhalb der Europäischen Union. In Wolfram Hilz/Antj. Nötzold (Hrsg.), Die Zukunft Europas in einer Welt im Umbruch, 2018, p. 185, 192 et seq.

[730] See, e.g., Comprehensive Economic And Trade Agreement between Canada, of the one part, and the European Union and its Member States, of the other part, OJEU 2017 L 11/23.

[731] BRADFORD, A. The Brussels Effect: How the European Union Rules the World, 2021.

[732] Ibid.

[733] See Regulation (EC) No 1606/2002 of the European Parliament and the Council of 19 July 2002 on the application of international accounting standards, OJEU 2002 L 243/1.

[734] International Financial Reporting Standards (IFRS), Wiley-VCH, Weinheim, 2023.

[735] European Union, Joint Communication JOIN(2021) 30 final, EU, Brussels 2021.

[736] Ibid.

[737] See, e.g., MORITZ, R. Chancen und Risiken der Seidenstraßeninitiative. In MÜLLER-GRAFF P.-Ch. (Hrsg.) Die Beziehungen zwischen der Europäischen Union und China, 2017, p. 69 et seq.

it may also serve to mitigate lingering pains caused by the former colonialism of European states. Whether it will reach its objectives, is an open question.

3.2.3 Protection Against Foreign Economic Interference

Shaping the economic dimension of strategic sovereignty has also to consider *unwanted* foreign economic interferences. On the level of *politics* the Union is faced in particular with the task of countering divisive effects of China's Road and Belt strategy in Europe (headword: "16+1"[738]) and with the task of overcoming dependencies of its economy from single providers, in particular from a hostile autocratic state such as Russia. In view of *competences* Article 207 para 1 TFEU (with its mention of "measures to protect trade") confers the relevant power upon the Union. Headwords are: defence against *dumping*[739]; *screening of foreign direct investments* in the Union[740] with the intriguing question of whether restrictions are required by strategic sovereignty or are counterproductively jeopardizing it by barring timely imports of newest innovations (e.g. 5G); avoiding state aids to European enterprises which distort competition in the internal market;[741] establishing restrictive measures of imports in order to promote and establish *self-sufficiency* in essential sectors such as semiconductors, rare earth exploitation, active substances, medicaments, energy and nutrition; *investment restrictions* of European enterprises in critical third countries.[742] However, tensions to the principle of an open market economy and to a competitive market order (Article 3 para 3 TEU, Article 173 para 3 TFEU) are inherent.

3.3 Constitutional Challenges to Defence Sovereignty

The third aspect of strategic sovereignty to be looked upon are effective defence capabilities. Obviously, the European Union, in its present shape, is no

[738] VANGELI, A. China's Engagement with the Sixteen Countries of Central, East and Southeast Europe under the Belt and Road Initiative, 25 China and World Economy, 2017, issue 5, p. 101 et seq.

[739] Regulation (EU) 2016/1036, OJEU 2016 L 176/21.

[740] Regulation (EU) 2019/452, OJEU 2019 L 79I/1. For the increase of regulatory controls of foreign direct investments by the MemberStates and an assessment of Regulation (EU) 2019/452. See *Jean-François Bellis/Isabelle Van Damme.* General Report. In Alexander Kornezov (ed.). The New Geopolitical Domension of the EU Competition and Trade Policies (volume 2 of the XXX Congress in Sofia), Sofia 2023, p. 41, 71 et seq.

[741] Regulation (EU) 2022/2560, OJEU 2022 L 330/1.

[742] European Commission, COM(2022) 548 final, Commission work programme 2023, p. 9 ("additional tools ... in respect of outbound strategic investment controls").

military power. The security of its Member States basically depends on their own capabilities and their NATO-membership – the latter in the hope that the deterrence and defence commitment of the USA to succour its European allies is reliable. Is this potentially fragile situation due to the Union's constitutional configuration?

3.3.1 The Status Quo of the Union's Constitutional Law on Security and Defence

The Union has a security and defence dimension (Articles 42 to 46 TEU) as "an integral part of the common foreign and security policy" – and rightly so. Upholding its prosperity, life style and external trade connections is not feasible without effective defence in hostile surroundings. But while energy, economy, trade and economic assistance competences rest on supranational primary law, the security and defence competences are *traditional international law*. The Union is capable to act, in principle, only on the basis of *unanimous* decisions of its members in the European Council and the Council (Articles 31, 42 TEU). This mirrors the fact that the monopoly on the use of force ("Gewaltmonopol") lies with each Member States in its territory.

3.3.2 Constitutional Starting Points for the Union's Defence Strategy

Nevertheless, the Union Treaty contains *starting points* for developing a common defence strategy. Article 42 TEU mandates the common defence and security policy to "provide the Union with an operational capacity drawing on civilian and military assets". The Union even "may use them on missions outside the Union for peace-keeping, conflict prevention and strengthening international security in accordance with the principles of the United Nations Charter". But these assets come from the *Member States*. They "shall make civilian and military capabilities available to the Union" and "shall undertake progressively to improve their military capabilities". Consequently, the Treaty also provides for a specialized Agency, the "European Defence Agency", with the focus on "defence capabilities development, research, acquisition and armaments".[743]

Moreover the Treaty also empowers the Council "to entrust the execution of a task ... to a *group of Member States* in order to protect the Union's values und serve its interests" (Article 42 para 5 TEU). And, even farer reaching,

[743] Art. 42 para 3 TEU.

the Council is also entitled to establish (by qualified majority) a "permanent *structured cooperation*" (PESCO) on notification by Member States "whose military capabilities fulfil higher criteria and which have made more binding commitments to one another in this area with a view to the most demanding missions" (Article 46 para 2 TEU). The establishment of *PESCO* happened in 2017 – viewed with skepticism by the USA at that time.[744] Today PESCO runs 60 projects with different member compositions, structured in 7 thematic groups (Training, Enabling, Land, Maritime, Air Systems, Space, Cyber), among them 10 projects in the *Cyber* Group (e.g. Electronic Warfare Capability, Cyber Rapid Response System, Secure Software-Defined Radio, Cyber Threats and Incident Response Information Sharing Platform).[745]

Eventually the Treaty also contains a *solidarity clause* for the case that "a Member State is the victim of armed aggression on its territory". Then "the other Member States shall have towards it an obligation of aid and assistance by all the means in their power, in accordance with Article 51 of the United Nations Charter" (Article 42 para 7 TEU). But it can hardly be seen or is rather speculative that currently the degree of credibility and the deterrence effect of this obligation comes close to or could substitute that of the solidarity clause of Article 5 NATO-Treaty.

The repeatedly demanded *Treaty amendment* of transforming the unanimity requirement of decisions of the Council and European Council in the common foreign, security and defence policy into the possibility of qualified majority decisions[746] seems out of touch with the reality of the national willingness to keep the state monopolies of the use of force. Even more dubious appears the idea of establishing a fully integrated European army – as envisaged and failed seven decades ago.[747] Supranationalizing the military is far more ambitious than the security architecture of the NATO. Instead of this the *potential* of the existing primary law should be seriously used and, in particular, the already existing options of constructive abstention (Article 31 para 1 TEU) and structured cooperation (Article 46 para 2 TEU) should be brought to life and, last not least, a self defined comprehensive defence compass of the EU should be developed as – for the time being – to the collective EU *assistance* to the security structure provided by NATO.

[744] BERKER, M. 23 EU-Staaten gründen Militärunion, Spiegel Online, 13 November 2017.

[745] See the detailed overview under "PESCO" in Wikipedia.

[746] E.g. Conference on the Future of Europe, Report on the Final Outcome, Brussels, 2022, Proposal 21.

[747] E.g. HOFER, G. Europäische Armee. Vision und Utopie, 2008.

4. Conclusion

The final conclusion of this short overview is fourfold: First: The Union's current constitutional powers *do not imply a defence policy* based on autonomous operative capacities, though there are starting points. But as long as the Union cannot muster credible defence capacities, its Member States are well advised to anchor their security in the collective defence structure of NATO. Second: The Union's *energy supply security* and even *self-sufficency* can be constitutionally promoted by the Union. Third: The Union's strategic sovereignty essentially depends on the competence to *promote a powerful economy*. Here, huge tasks exist: the transition into a sustainable and climate neutral mode of doing business, into digitalisation, into self-suffiency in essential commodities and into reliable trade relations. It is the task of a transition to be generated by the conviction of the majority of the citizens, by human ingenuity, by *law* and by *funds*. Fourth and last: The very basis for the Union's strategic sovereignty is the requirement of *willpower in for unity in the Union* around its values and institutions – in permanent global awareness and strategic thinking with a view to shape a comprehensive smart neighbourhood policy and a far-sighted geopolitical strategy and to forge suitable economic, diplomatic and defence tools for concept-led actions in order to uphold the Union's orientation to the enlightened mode of the well-being of its peoples.

CHAPTER FIFTEEN

EU-NATO Cooperation in Cyber Security and Cyber Defence

ONDŘEJ FILIPEC

Introduction

The partnership between the EU and NATO is crucial for the security of Europe. In many respects, this premise are valid also for the area of cybersecurity and cyber defence. Despite both actors developing their own policies, their primary focus varies, and mutual cooperation is providing valuable benefits. The main aim of this chapter is to explore the different natures of cybersecurity and cyber defence policy of the EU and NATO and highlight the most important aspects of cooperation. The contribution goes beyond a basic overview of existing instruments by showing the complexity of tools associated with cybersecurity and cyber defence, including a different understanding of the issue by both actors. While in the EU cybersecurity is built mainly around the civilian domain of the single market, NATO from the early beginning associated cybersecurity with the military domain and hard power. Due to the different focus of both actors, their cooperation is more than necessary, especially in the context of increasingly blurring lines between the civilian and military domain and the hybrid threats.

The recent two decades were characterized by the rapid development of cyberspace which become a natural environment for various human and later also non-human activities.[748] In the history of mankind, it is hard to find another domain experiencing such fast growth and progress. Moreover, the increased complexity of the environment, together with the development of new technologies including Artificial Intelligence, supercomputers, and quantum cryptography are presenting new challenges. Cyberspace is also increasingly becoming an arena of conflict involving countries and non-state actors. Cyberspace becomes another

[748] TATNALL, A. The Internet of Things and Beyond: Rise of the Non-Human Actors. *International Journal of Actor-Network Theory and Technological Innovation*. 2015, vol. 7, no. 4, pp. 56–67.

significant domain of security at times when boundaries between the civilian and military are more blurring and increasingly shadowed by the hybrid conflict.

The main aim of this chapter is to review and assess EU initiatives and activities in the areas of cyber security and cyber defence, especially in relation to cooperation with NATO and reveal the potential for strengthening cooperation between both actors. This is a particularly relevant issue in the context of the Russian full-scale invasion of Ukraine, which is having important implications for cyberspace. At the same time, it is a challenging task for the EU and NATO, mainly due to the different genealogy of both actors, aims, or structure, and a rather sensitive area of cooperation strongly linked to national sovereignty. Any international cooperation in sensitive matters characterized by a strong intergovernmental form of cooperation is challenged by the quality of implementation within a diverse environment split among several sovereign states. Despite cyberspace is not demarcated by state borders, the states are responsible for implementing policies and security standards. Also in this regard, the EU and NATO represent important platforms for stimulating the development of national capacities and capabilities in cyberspace as states alone have difficulties in responding to large-scale cyber incidents.

This chapter is focuses mainly on cybersecurity and cyber defence, which are not understood as a synonym and may have problematic connotations.[749] According to the EU Cybersecurity Act (2019) the term cybersecurity *"means the activities necessary to protect network and information systems, the users of such systems, and other persons affected by cyber threats"*[750]. Regarding cyber defence, there is no explicit definition. However in the Joint Communication to the European Parliament and the Council entitled "EU Policy on Cyber Defense", the European Commission understand behind the term: *"the ability to prevent, detect, defend against, recover from, and deter cyberattacks aimed at the EU and its Member States using all means available"*.[751] In some aspects including resilience or prevention, both definitions overlap. Nonetheless, it is evident, that defence may be understood in the context of an attack as there

[749] FLOWERS, A., ZEADALLY, S. UP Policy on Active Cyber Defense. *Journal of Homeland Security and Emergency Management*. 2014, vol. 11, no. 2, pp. 289–308. Available at: https://doi.org/10.1515/jhsem-2014-0021

[750] REGULATION (EU) 2019/882 of the European Parliament and the Council of 17 April 2019 on ENISA (the European Union Agency for Cybersecurity) and on information and communications technology cybersecurity certification and repealing Regulation (EU) No 526/2013 (Cybersecurity Act). Available at: https://eur-lex.europa.eu/legal-content/EN/TXT/HTML/?uri=CELEX:32019R0881&from=EN#d1e1357-15-1. Accessed 5. 3. 2023.

[751] EUROPEAN COMMISSION. *Joint Communication to the European Parliament and the Council. EU Policy on Cyber Defence*. Brussels, 10. 11. 2022 [online]. Available at: https://www.eeas.europa.eu/sites/default/files/documents/Comm_cyber%20defence.pdf. Accessed 5. 3. 2023.

is an active element of response. Despite the fact, that the EU's definition of security is focused mainly on and built around "protection", as shown later the EU initiatives go far beyond this scope and contribute to the cultivation of cyber ecosystem.

The chapter is divided into three parts. The first part is explores the development of EU cyber security and cyber defence policy, its main pillars, and its focus. The second part is dedicated to NATO's relevant activities in cyber security and cyber defence and finally, the third part is about the cooperation of both actors. Hopefully, the chapter will contribute to a better understanding of activities conducted by the EU and NATO within the area of cyber security and cyber defence. Also, it will help to understand the different natures of cyber policies with implications for possible future cooperation.

EU cybersecurity and cyber defence policy

The EU is not having an official cybersecurity policy. However, over the years EU created a dense and robust environment characterized by strategic documents, tools, and initiatives, which are having significant policy dimensions. It is very hard to track the origins of this policy because at the beginning in 1990s, the agenda was related mainly to the security of information[752] and computer-related crime. A probably most important milestone was the adoption of the Maastricht treaty (in force since 1st November 1993), transforming existing platforms of security cooperation (namely European Political Cooperation and TREVI[753]) into a separate inter-governmental pillar, dedicated to Common Foreign and Security Policy (second pillar) and Justice and Home Affairs (third pillar). Adoption of the Maastricht treaty provided the EU legal capacity to develop later initiatives within areas later linked to cybersecurity. As a result of the strongly inter-governmental nature of both pillars, the 1990s, and early 2000s are linked mainly to non-binding initiatives aimed at a shared perception of the threat. As concluded by Helena Carrapico and André Barrinha (2017), cybersecurity was not at the top of EU security priorities and the real change is coming after 2004 when the EU realized, that cyberspace is a vulnerable domain having a real impact on daily life.[754] As a result

[752] Here was a strong influence of the Council of Europe. For example Council of Europe Convention of 28 January 1981 for the protection of individuals with regard to the automatic processing of personal data.

[753] TREVI was informal cooperation between EC countries established in 1975 aimed at Terrorism, Radicalism, Extremism, Violence, and Information Exchange.

[754] CARRAPICO, H., BARRINHA, A. The EU as a Coherent (Cyber)Security Actor?. *JCMS: Journal of Common Market Studies*. 2017, vol. 55, no. 6, pp. 1254–1272. Available at: https://doi.org/10.1111/jcms.12575

of environmental transformation marked by the growing complexity of threats and tools available to the attackers, the EU approach to cybersecurity was reshaped.

Since 2004 the EU approach was marked by the departure from legally non-binding policy tools to a more comprehensive approach using also legally binding acts aimed to "bridge the gap" between various levels of cybersecurity measures as operated by the Member States. European Commission and European Parliament repeatedly attempted to push for a more centralized approach and despite the fact, that cyber defence and cyber security belonged merely to the intergovernmental approach, both institutions pushed for centralization, common EU approaches and common standards.[755] A noticeable example from this start of a new era is the Council Framework Decision on attacks against information systems which is improving cooperation among judicial authorities and relevant authorities, for example, by defining and requiring measures to criminalize illegal access to information systems, illegal system interference, or illegal data interference.[756] However, EU activities slowly started to grow and spread also other areas which included also the creation of specialized institutions and adapting the structure of existing ones.

In relation to cybercrime, Europol is playing a key role. In 2013 Europol established European Cybercrime Centre (EC3) to strengthen law enforcement to cybercrime, support training, and capacity building, create awareness campaigns, contribute relevant information to the decision-making, and provide non-stop operational and technical support to law enforcement agencies in the Member States. Moreover, the centre is acting to support other EU-related institutions including Eurojust, European External Action Service, The European Network and Information Security Agency (ENISA), The Computer Security Incident Response Team (ERT-EU), and the European Commission. Moreover, Europol is operating Joint Cybercrime Action Taskforce (J-CAT) for combating cybercrime, also including online child sexual exploitation, transnational payments fraud, etc.[757] To sum up, cybercrime focus might be characterized as one of the EUs pillars of cybersecurity.

Another pillar is the security of networks. Within this area, the most relevant institution is the European Network and Information Security Agency (ENISA), established on 10 March 2004, to ensure a high and effective level of network

[755] STASZCZYK, A. European Parliament Position on EU Cyber Security and Defense Policy. *Reality of Politics*. 2019, vol. 10, pp. 122–133.

[756] COUNCIL OF THE EUROPEAN UNION. *Council Framework Decision 2005/222/JHA of 24 February 2005 on attacks against information systems.* 2005 [online]. Available at: https://eur-lex.europa.eu/legal-content/EN/ALL/?uri=celex:32005F0222. Accessed 5. 3. 2023.

[757] EUROPOL. *Joint Cybercrime Action Taskforce (J-CAT) – Fighting cybercrime around the world.* [online]. Available at: https://www.europol.europa.eu/operations-services-and-innovation/services-support/joint-cybercrime-action-taskforce. Accessed 5. 3. 2023.

and information security within the Community.[758] Since then the mandate of the agency has been extended in 2008, 2011, and 2013.[759] Today, ENISA provides complex services that enhance the trustworthiness and safety of ICTS products and services. It processes with certification schemes, contributes to the rise of awareness, contributes to education, facilitates cybersecurity policy development, manages incident reporting and response, ICT crisis management, research and innovation, and many other activities in the civilian domain.[760] In total, there are nine operation activities and two corporate activities to meet strategic goals within the mandate of ENISA.[761] In regard to cybersecurity, a cornerstone is the NIS2 Directive from 2022[762] which is extending high-security standards on private and public actors, including medium and large enterprises or supply chains with the energy sector, transportation, baking, finance, healthcare, pharmaceuticals, water management, digital infrastructure, cloud computing, data centres, etc.

Finally, the third pillar is aimed at cyber defence. The principal initiative was adapted on 18th November 2014 when the European Council adopted the EU Cyber Defense Policy Framework,[763] which was based on Council conclusions on CSDP from November and December 2013.[764] This non-legislative document

[758] REGULATION (EC) No 460/2004 OF THE EUROPEAN PARLIAMENT AND OF THE COUNCIL of 10 March 2004 establishing the European Network and Information Security Agency (Text with EEA relevance).

[759] REGULATION (EC) No 1007/2008 OF THE EUROPEAN PARLIAMENT AND OF THE COUNCIL of 24 September 2008 amending Regulation (EC) No 460/2004 establishing the European Network and Information Security Agency as regards its duration. Compare with: REGULATION (EU) No 580/2011 OF THE EUROPEAN PARLIAMENT AND OF THE COUNCIL of 8 June 2011 amending Regulation (EC) No 460/2004 establishing the European Network and Information Security Agency as regards its duration; and REGULATION (EU) No 526/2013 OF THE EUROPEAN PARLIAMENT AND OF THE COUNCIL of 21 May 2013 concerning the European Union Agency for Network and Information Security (ENISA) and repealing Regulation (EC) No 460/2004.

[760] ENISA (European Union Agency for Cybersecurity). *A Trusted and Cyber Secure Europe – Activities, What we do, Mission.* [online]. Available at: https://www.enisa.europa.eu/. Accessed: 21. 2. 2023.

[761] ENISA (European Union Agency for Cybersecurity). *ENISA Single Programming Document 2022–2024. Including multiannual planning, 2022 work programme and multiannual staff planning.* 2022. [online]. Available at: https://www.enisa.europa.eu/publications/corporate-documents/enisa-single-programming-document-2022-2024. Accessed 21. 2. 2023.

[762] DIRECTIVE (EU) 2022/2555 OF THE EUROPEAN PARLIAMENT AND OF THE COUNCIL of 14 December 2022 on measures for a high common level of cybersecurity across the Union, amending Regulation (EU) No 910/2014 and Directive (EU) 2018/1972 and repealing Directive (EU) 2016/1148 (NIS 2 Directive) (Text with EEA relevance). [online]. Available at: https://eur-lex.europa.eu/eli/dir/2022/2555. Accessed 21. 2. 2023.

[763] COUNCIL OF THE EUROPEAN UNION. *EU Cyber Defence Policy Framework.* 2014 [online]. Available at: https://ccdcoe.org/uploads/2018/11/EU-141118-EUCyberDefencePolicyFrame-2.pdf. Accessed 27. 2. 2023.

[764] COUNCIL OF THE EUROPEAN UNION. *Council Conclusions on Common Security and Defense Policy.* 2023a. [online] Available at: https://www.consilium.europa.eu/uedocs/cms_da

laid down the foundations for countering threats in cyberspaces and implementation of the EU Cyber Security Strategy.[765] Later on, in 2018 the framework was updated with the aim to strengthen cyber resilience. Simply said, within the framework, cybersecurity is considered a fifth domain of operations (together with defence of land, sea, air, and space) with six priorities set under the EU Cyber Defence Policy Framework: 1) Support in the development of cyber defence capabilities in the EU Member States; 2) Enhancing the protection of CSDP communication and information systems used by EU entities; 3) Promotion of civil-military cooperation; 4) Research and technology; 5) Improve education, training and exercises opportunities and 6) Enhancing cooperation with relevant international partners (including NATO, which is dealt later).

It is necessary to note, that next to the above-mentioned instruments, there are many tools of the EU that are horizontally developing the above-mentioned pillars or target selected cybersecurity and cyber defence aspects in setting obligations and responsibilities, clarifying roles of actors, regulating relevant areas, providing minimal standards or generally optimizing functions in cyberspace. For example, for both cybersecurity and cyber defence, resilience is a key issue. Here, the EU adopted The Critical Entities Resilience Directive (CER); the Digital Operational Resilience Act (DORA), or the more general European Cyber Resilience Act (CRA)[766]. While CRA is aimed at the development of secure products with digital elements including toys or baby monitors, CER is replacing the European Critical Infrastructure Directive of 2008 and strengthening the resilience of the critical infrastructure, which gained new momentum after attacks against the Nord Stream pipeline and risk associated with the Russian aggression against Ukraine.[767] Finally, DORA is aimed improving the financial regulation of the EU by setting rules on ICT risk management, incident reporting, testing, etc.[768]

ta/docs/pressdata/En/foraff/139719.pdf. Accessed 3. 3. 2023; COUNCIL OF THE EUROPEAN UNION. *Council Conclusions*. 2023b. [online] Available at: https://www.consilium.europa.eu/uedocs/cms_data/docs/pressdata/en/ec/140214.pdf. Accessed 3. 3. 2023.

[765] JOINT COMMUNICATION TO THE EUROPEAN PARLIAMENT, THE COUNCIL, THE EUROPEAN ECONOMIC AND SOCIAL COMMITTEE AND THE COMMITTEE OF THE REGIONS. *Cybersecurity Strategy of the European Union: An Open, Safe and Secure Cyberspace.* [online]. Available at: https://eur-lex.europa.eu/legal-content/EN/TXT/?uri=celex%3A52013JC0001. Accessed 3. 3. 2023.

[766] CYBER RISK GMBH. *The Articles of the Cyber Resilience Act.* [online]. Available at: https://www.european-cyber-resilienceact.com/Cyber_Resilience_Act_Articles_(Proposal_15.9.2022).html. Accessed 27. 2. 2023.

[767] DIRECTIVE (EU) 2022/2557 OF THE EUROPEAN PARLIAMENT AND OF THE COUNCIL of 14 December 2022 on the resilience of critical entities and repealing Council Directive 2008/114/EC (Text with EEA relevance).

[768] REGULATION (EU) 2022/2554 OF THE EUROPEAN PARLIAMENT AND OF THE COUNCIL of 14 December 2022 on digital operational resilience for the financial sector and

Considerable attention is aimed at the proper functioning of the digital market in the EU. In this regard, several initiatives might be mentioned including The Digital Markets Act (DMA), The Digital Services Act (DSA), or The European Chips Act, which is now (March 2023) coming to the final stage of the legislative process. The Chips Act shall stimulate technology development and ensure the security of the supply chain in relation to semiconductors as some European companies suffer from a lack of chips.[769] Moderation and optimization of the market in much general sense is the subject of the Digital Markets Act which is aimed to solve the issue of "gatekeeper platforms" and potential misuse of the dominant position on the digital market.[770] However, similarly important for protecting consumer rights and preventing illegal content[771] is the Digital Services Act (DSA). That is why both acts are often considered items belonging to the same package.

Digital market regulation would be incomplete without data regulation, which is another complex area covered by general regulations and specific segment regulations. The EU adopted in February 2020 a European strategy for data in with the aim to become a leader in the data-driven society.[772] As a part of its implementation, the European Data Governance Act was adopted together with the European Data Act, which is revising a database directive.[773] The Data Governance Act of 2020 facilitates data sharing across sectors in the EU Member States and the Data Act (2022) clarifies, who can create value from data and the conditions for that. Both tools are aimed at the cultivation of "Ten European Common Data Spaces" covering various sectors including industry, transportation, energy, or health, a critical sector in the terms of security. However, there are

---

amending Regulations (EC) No 1060/2009, (EU) No 648/2012, (EU) No 600/2014, (EU) No 909/2014 and (EU) 2016/1011 (Text with EEA relevance).

769 CYBER RISK GMBH. *The European Chips Act.* [online]. Available at: https://www.european-chips-act.com/. Accessed 21. 2. 2023.

770 CYBER RISK GMBH. *The Digital Markets Act (DMA).* [online]. Available at: https://www.eu-digital-markets-act.com/. Accessed 21. 2. 2023.

771 CYBER RISK GMBH. *The Digital Services Act (DSA).* [online]. Available at: https://www.eu-digital-services-act.com/. Accessed 21. 2. 2023.

772 EUROPEAN COMMISSION. *Communication from the Commission to the European Parliament, the Council, the European Economic and Social Committee, and the Committee of the regions: A European strategy for data.* [online]. Available at: https://eur-lex.europa.eu/legal-content/EN/TXT/?uri=CELEX%3A52020DC0066. Accessed 3. 3. 2023.

773 EUROPEAN COMMISSION. *Proposal for a Regulation of the European Parliament and of the Council on European data governance (Data Governance Act).* Brussels, 25. November 2020. [online]. Available at: https://eur-lex.europa.eu/legal-content/EN/TXT/?uri=celex%3A52020PC0767. Accessed 3. 3. 2023; EUROPEAN COMMISSION. *Data Act: Commission proposes measures for a fair and innovative data economy.* Brussels, 23 February 2022. [online]. Available at: https://ec.europa.eu/commission/presscorner/detail/en/ip_22_1113. Accessed 3. 3. 2023.

also other relevant acts strengthening security in specific domains. For example, in the area of health, very relevant is the European Health Data Space (EHDS) aimed at creating safe ecosystem of rules, standards and practices empowering patients, fostering single market for health record systems and regulates use of health data.[774] EHDS is thereby building on General Data Protection Regulation (GDPR) which is having a position as "lex generalis" in health data regulation, and the NIS 2 Directive, mentioned above.[775]

The position of GDPR is very special in relation to cyber security, as it covers the protection of personal data, which might be misused in the hybrid conflict, for example in targeting disinformation campaigns through social networks and manipulation of citizens. As the general regulation it is in many aspects developed within "lex specialis" entitled The European ePrivacy Regulation – a remake of the 2002 ePrivacy directive. The regulation is, among other things, aimed at preventing misuse of sensitive information by user behaviour tracking webs and services.[776] The area of user data protection well demonstrates changes in the attitude of the EU towards cyber security. First, the adoption of the GDPR proves that the protection of personal data is understood in its complexity as a multi-sectoral issue. Second, GDPR sets basic standards and principles, which are in various sectors strengthened by specialized regulations, reflecting the different nature of the sectors and challenges posed by the technologies used. Finally, the nature of regulation itself reflects the increasing significance of the challenge: from non-binding tools to directives and from directives to regulations.

In relation to security and defence, there are more salient areas and challenges, which might have a much greater security impact and cause "an earthquake" or even the "black swan effect".[777] This is mainly the area of Artificial Intelligence, whose elements are being applied in daily use in various sectors. It is expected, that fully developed Artificial Intelligence will be the most important milestone in human history, which has many security implications. On 25th November 2022 the Council of the EU approved a compromise version of the proposed Artificial

[774] EUROPEAN COMMISSION. *Proposal for a Regulation of the European Parliament and of the Council on the European Health Data Space*. Strasbourg, 3. May 2022. [online]. Available at: https://eur-lex.europa.eu/legal-content/EN/TXT/?uri=CELEX%3A52022PC0197. Accessed 3. 3. 2023.

[775] REGULATION (EU) 2016/679 OF THE EUROPEAN PARLIAMENT AND OF THE COUNCIL of 27 April 2016 on the protection of natural persons with regard to the processing of personal data and on the free movement of such data, and repealing Directive 95/46/EC (General Data Protection Regulation) (Text with EEA relevance). [online]. Available at: https://eur-lex.europa.eu/legal-content/EN/TXT/?uri=celex%3A32016R0679. Accessed 3. 3. 2023.

[776] CYBER RISK GMBH. *The European ePrivacy Regulation.* [online]. Available at: https://www.european-eprivacy-regulation.com/. Accessed 21. 2. 2023.

[777] TALEB, N. N. *The Black Swan: The impact of the Highly Improbable*. New York: Penguin Books, 2010.

Intelligence Act, and the European Parliament is expected to vote on the proposal by the end of March 2023.[778] As expected, the regulation is laying down basic standards for the use of AI, including the prohibition of certain practices. However, Article 2 of the regulation makes the exclusion of national security and dense and military purposes from the scope of the Act. In other words, Article 2 sets boundaries between civilian and military use, which is fortifying the sovereignty of Member States on one hand, and the role of the EU as a mainly civilian actor on the other.

To sum up, the EU builds its cyber security and defence mainly around the internal market and tries to use its soft power also in the external dimension. Cyber security is an important part of the dialogue with candidate countries and EU partners in the EU neighbourhood and beyond. This is for example the case of cyber security dialogues with India, South Korea or Japan.[779] In this sense, the EU is trying to utilize its position as an economic actor in promoting cyber security in its environment with soft tools. In 2017, the EU adopted "Cyber Diplomacy Toolbox" in order to increase the cohesiveness of the EU's actions in relation to both: partners and potentially problematic states.[780] In this regard, the EU may use its foreign policy and diplomatic experience to prevent security incidents and foster cyber security partnerships through effective cyber diplomacy.[781] Nonetheless, EU's reluctance to create strong and centralized cyber defence might be well interpreted in the context of patch dependency and the guarantees of NATO. For that purpose, it is worth exploring NATO cybersecurity and cyber defence policy.

NATO cybersecurity and cyber defence policy

While the first steps of the EU cyber security were linked to the internal market and securing safe use of products (internal aims), cybersecurity in the context of NATO was from the early beginning linked to defence and protection

[778] EUROPEAN COMMISSION. *Proposal for a Regulation of the European Parliament and of the Council laying down harmonised rules on artificial intelligence (artificial intelligence act) and amending certain union legislative acts.* Brussels, 21. April 2021. [online]. Available at: https://eur-lex.europa.eu/legal-content/EN/TXT/?uri=celex%3A52021PC0206. Accessed 3. 3. 2023.

[779] BARRINHA, A. Virtual Neighbors: Russia and the EU in Cyberspace. *Insight Turkey.* 2018, vol. 20, no. 3, pp. 29–42. Available at: https://doi.org/10.1515/jhsem-2014-0021.

[780] COUNCIL OF THE EUROPEAN UNION. *Council Conclusions on a Framework for a Joint EU Diplomatic Response to Malicious Cyber Activities ("Cyber Diplomacy Toolbox").* 2017. [online] Available at: https://data.consilium.europa.eu/doc/document/ST-10474-2017-INIT/en/pdf. Accessed 3. 3. 2023.

[781] In this regards, see for example: FORD, Ch. A. Conceptualizing Cyberspace Security Diplomacy. *The Cyber Defense Review.* 2022, vol. 7, no. 2, pp. 35–54.

with a strong military dimension. NATO as a military pact always protected its communications and information systems, which is in contrast with civilian use of the Internet, where protection standards were naturally lower. It was at the NATO Summit in Prague (2002) that cyber defence become stressed as a part of the political agenda.[782] However, the main catalyst came in the years 2006 to 2008 which are marked by the increasing significance of the area. NATO Summit in Riga (2006) highlighted the need for cyber security improvement and the need was further supported by large scale cyber-attack against Estonian institutions in 2007.[783] During the 2008 Russian aggression against Georgia it was evident, that in the future cyber-attacks will be a separate component to conventional warfare and may be considered as the fifth force (after ground, water, air and space). This potential was acknowledged in the NATO's new Strategic Concept adopted on NATO Summit in Lisbon (2010).[784] Following the summit, cyber defence become part of NATO Defence Planning Process with clear prospect to centralize effort to strengthen cyber defence. As a result of this process NATO Communications and Information Agency was established and during the NATO Summit in Chicago Member States expressed the need to create centralised protection.[785]

From the practical perspective, significant progress was reached in 2014. First, the NATO structure was adapted, and new bodies were established – including Cyber Defense Committee. The establishment of a specialized committee highlighted the significance of the agenda and potentially improved NATO's deterrent capability by enhancing its decision-making process. Also, the summit in Wales recognized cyber defence as part of NATO's core agenda linked to collective defense.[786] As a result, a cyber-attack against one member state may provide grounds to invoke Article 5 of the Washington treaty and become a reason for collective response. This step was unprecedented, because it expressed the view, that international law and the concept of state sovereignty applies also in cyberspace and raised many questions about the terms including cyber *Ius in Bello*, cyber aggression etc.[787]

---

782 NATO. *Prague Summit Declaration.* 2002 [online]. Available at: https://www.nato.int/cps/en/natohq/official_texts_19552.htm. Accessed 3. 3. 2023.

783 NATO. *Riga Summit Declaration.* 2006 [online]. Available at: https://www.nato.int/cps/en/natohq/official_texts_37920.htm?selectedLocale=en. Accessed 3. 3. 2023.

784 NATO. *Strategic Concept for the Defence and Security of the Members of the North Atlantic Treaty Organization.* 2010 [online]. Available at: https://www.nato.int/lisbon2010/strategic-concept-2010-eng.pdf. Accessed 3. 3. 2023.

785 NATO. *Chicago Summit Declaration.* 2012 [online]. Available at: https://www.nato.int/cps/en/natohq/official_texts_87593.htm?selectedLocale=en. Accessed 3. 3. 2023.

786 NATO. Wales *Summit Declaration.* 2014 [online]. Available at: https://www.nato.int/cps/en/natohq/official_texts_112964.htm. Accessed 3. 3. 2023.

787 See for example FIDLER, D. P., PREGENT, R., VARDURME, A. NATO, Cyber Defense, and International Law. *Journal of International and Comparative Law*. 2013, vol. 4, no. 1,

Since then NATO developed several tools, which are aimed to strengthen inter-operability and increase the capacities and capabilities of its members. Among them are for example yearly Cyber Coalition exercises including simulation of attacks against NATO critical infrastructure.[788] Among other practical results is the establishment of the NATO Cooperative Cyber Defense Centre of Excellence in Tallinn which is aimed at research and training in the area of cyber defence education but also provides strategic and conceptual input into NATO decision-making. The centre serves as the NATO headquarters for cyber defence and is located at the Signal battalion base in Tallinn. As of January 2023, the centre consisted of 25 NATO allies and 4 cooperating nations (including for example Japan or South Korea) with prospects to be enlarged by Ukraine.[789]

It shall be noted that apart from the Centre of Excellence, NATO operates infrastructure in over 60 different locations. Also, NATO is home to approx. 200 members of the special cyber team which is defending NATO networks. Among other important bodies is the NATO Computer Incident Response Capability (NCIRS) which is based at Supreme Headquarters Allied Powers Europe in Mons. The NCIRS is part of the NATO Communications and Information Agency, supportive of NATO operations. Next to it is also Cyberspace Operation Centre in Mons providing mainly situational awareness to inform military commanders about the actual situation. As the development of IT experts working for NATO is the issue of specialized training and education, NATO operates NATO School in Oberammergau (Germany) and NATO Communications and Information Academia in Oeiras (Portugal). Part of the cyber defence education related to strategic thinking and politico-military decision making is possible to obtain in Rome at the NATO Defense College.[790] It is evident that education and training are essential in NATO's approach to defence and security. This approach is supportive of the idea, that technology itself is limited in defence without people with proper training and that technology itself will not solve the issue of security.[791]

---

pp. 1–25; VALUCH, J., GÁBRIŠ, T., HAMUĽÁK, O. Cyber Attacks, Information Attacks, and Postmodern Warfare. *Baltic Journal of Law & Politics*. 2017, vol. 10, no. 1, pp.63–89. Available at: https://doi.org/10.1515/bjlp-2017-0003.

788 MILLER, M. *NATO prepares for cyber war.* [online]. Available at: https://www.politico.com/news/2022/12/03/nato-future-cyber-war-00072060. Accessed 3. 3. 2023.

789 STATE SITES OF UKRAINE. *Ukraine has signed an agreement on accession to the NATO Cooperative Cyber Defence Centre of Excellence.* [online]. Available at: https://cip.gov.ua/en/news/ukrayina-pidpisala-ugodu-pro-priyednannya-do-ob-yednanogo-centru-peredovikh-tekhnologii-z-kiberoboroni-nato. Accessed 3. 3. 2023.

790 NATO. *Factsheet: NATO Cyber Defence*. [online]. Available at: https://www.nato.int/nato_static_fl2014/assets/pdf/2021/4/pdf/2104-factsheet-cyber-defence-en.pdf. Accessed 3. 3. 2023.

791 See for example PEÑA, J., GARCIA-SEGURA, L. A. The Critical Role of Education in Every Cyber Defense Strategy. *Northern Kentucky Law Review.* 2014, vol. 41, no. 3, pp. 459–469.

To sum up, the NATO in the last two decades succeeded to create a very dense environment covering a relatively new domain of warfare and provide adequate protection to its members against cyber-attacks. Despite NATO is reluctant to specify under what conditions or scale of a cyber-attack would be activated Article 5, it is possible to expect that some "red line" exists. This is probably the most important element of NATO cyber defence strategy: that cyber defence is part of collective defence and large-scale attacks in the cyber domain may result even in military retaliation. In another word, NATO effectively connected cyber defence (which is mainly virtual) with well-visible hard power. A power, which is the EU lacking, but thanks to the close partnership with NATO, felt in presence.

EU-NATO cooperation

Cooperation between EU and NATO is essential for ensuring security on the European continent, which is envisaged also in the most actual strategic documents of both actors: EU's Strategic Compass and NATO's 2022 Strategic Concept. Despite the EU and NATO cooperation facing structural challenges including different membership structures or *raison d'être,* they share a basic vision of security. Since the EU started its integration of the Common Foreign and Security Policy and later also the Common Security and Defence Policy, new opportunities were opened for the cooperation of both organizations. From the theoretical perspective, it was a vital match: while the EU lacked operational capacities and was focusing mainly on civilian aspects of security, NATO represented hard power with relevant military capacities. However, changing nature of the security environment, including increasingly blurring lines between civilian and military created a need for closer cooperation and mutual learning, including in the area of cyber defence.

European Union is having its own cyber defence policy based on the Cyber Defence Policy Framework of 2014, in which one of the pillars mentions cooperation with NATO.[792] However, it is necessary to note, that real cooperation started much earlier than the official foundations of the EU cyber defence policy were laid down. The EU-NATO cooperation in cybersecurity dates back to 2010 when both entities started with staff-to-staff cyber defence consultations and annual meetings on an informal basis.[793] On a more practical level cooperation

[792] COUNCIL OF THE EUROPEAN UNION. *EU Cyber Defence Policy Framework.* 2014 [online]. Available at https://ccdcoe.org/uploads/2018/11/EU-141118-EUCyberDefencePolicyFrame-2.pdf. Accessed 27. 2. 2023.

[793] EUROPA.EU (THE OFFICIAL WEBSITE OF THE EUROPEAN UNION). *EU and NATO cyber defence cooperation.* [online]. Available at: https://www.eeas.europa.eu/node/3667_en. Accessed 3. 3. 2023.

was developed one year later, when the newly established CERT-EU started to cooperate with NCIRC (NATO Computer Incident Response Capability) and the EU received observing status on NATO's annual cyber defence exercise "Cyber Coalition". Also, European union agencies become included in the cooperation with the NATO Cooperative Cyber Defence Centre of Excellence.[794]

The adoption of the EU Cyber Defence Policy Framework indicated the direction of future cooperation with NATO in several lines. For example (1) in exploring the possibility of creating joint cyber defence training programmes between the European Security and Defence College and NATO Defence College with the aim to foster a shared cybersecurity culture; (2) in inviting NATO to EU's cyber security exercises; (3) establish regular staff-to-staff consultations, cross-briefings, and meetings between Politico-Military Group with NATO committees; (4) Utilise European Defense Agency liaison agreement with NATO Cooperative Cyber Defence Centre of Excellence; and (5) Reinforce cooperation between CERT-EU and other relevant EU cyber defence bodies with NATO Computer Incident Response Capability).[795]

A very important milestone in mutual cooperation between the EU and NATO was the adoption of the Warszaw (2016) and Brussels (2018) Joint declaration. In the declaration from Warszaw, the EU and NATO declared an urgent need (among others) to *"expand our coordination on cyber security and defence including in the context of our missions and operations, exercises and on education and training"*.[796] The dedication was repeated two years later with reference to the implementation of the bound.[797] It is important to mention, that various documents in the area stress the issue of synergy, interoperability, and complementarity in the policies of both actors and the need to avoid duplicity.[798] In doing so, communication between the EU and NATO is the key – not only in the area

[794] EUROPA.EU (THE OFFICIAL WEBSITE OF THE EUROPEAN UNION). *EU and NATO cyber defence cooperation.* [online]. Available at: https://www.eeas.europa.eu/node/3667_en. Accessed 3. 3. 2023.

[795] COUNCIL OF THE EUROPEAN UNION. *EU Cyber Defence Policy Framework...* 2014. op. cit.

[796] JOINT DECLARATION BY THE PRESIDENT OF THE EUROPEAN COUNCIL, THE PRESIDENT OF THE EUROPEAN COMMISSION, AND THE SECRETARY GENERAL OF THE NORTH ATLANTIC TREATY ORGANIZATION. [online]. Available at https://www.europarl.europa.eu/cmsdata/121580/20160708_160708-joint-NATO-EU-declaration.pdf. Accessed 27. 2. 2023.

[797] JOINT DECLARATION ON EU-NATO COOPERATION BY THE PRESIDENT OF THE EUROPEAN COUNCIL, THE PRESIDENT OF THE EUROPEAN COMMISSION, AND THE SECRETARY GENERAL OF THE NORTH ATLANTIC TREATY ORGANIZATION. [online]. Available at https://www.consilium.europa.eu/media/36096/nato_eu_final_eng.pdf. Accessed 27. 2. 2023.

[798] EUROPEAN COMMISSION. *Joint Communication to the European Parliament and the Council. EU Policy on Cyber Defence.* Brussels, 10. November 2022 [online]. Available at:

of information exchange and planning the events, but also on the more practical level. For example, in 2016 the EU and NATO signed a "Technical Arrangement" between CERT-EU and NCIRC aimed at better incident prevention, detection, and response of both organizations while respecting decision-making autonomy and procedures. From both: theoretical and practical perspectives it is great progress, as information sharing between organizations regarding cyber incidents may be prevented by many factors that undermine cooperation effectiveness.[799]

Russian full-scale invasion of Ukraine in 2022 stimulated area of cyber cooperation. All aspects of the contemporary policy are well summarized in the Joint Communication to the European Parliament and the Council entitled "EU Policy on Cyber Defence" from 10th November 2022.[800] However, from the document it is evident, that EU cyber defence cooperation with NATO is built up mainly on cyber defence training, education, situational awareness, and exercises, on foundations laid down more than 10 years ago or focuses on a cyber element in the missions conducted under the umbrella of EU Common Security and Defense Policy.[801]

Despite great progress over the years, there are still limits of cooperation that are inherent also to other areas dealing with security. The diverging position of Member States in the EU often prevented greater development of cyber defence. For example, as noted by Luukas et al. (2016), there were always Member States like Germany or the Netherlands viewing cyber security as the issue of homeland security in opposition to more progressive countries like Estonia or Denmark, with a vision of common defence, which is also contrary to Italy and Finland, seeing cybersecurity as the issue of commerce and communication.[802] It is important to note, that often diverging positions were adjusted and moderated by the EU institutions, leading to compromises covering various fields of cyber security, as demonstrated by various regulations adopted in the last years. Moreover, it is evident that Russian aggression against Ukraine in 2022 succeeded to change the attitudes of countries built for decades (e.g. hesitance of Germany) or even centuries (e.g. neutrality of Finland and Sweden). This provides a new

---

https://www.eeas.europa.eu/sites/default/files/documents/Comm_cyber%20defence.pdf. Accessed 3. 3. 2023.

[799] SKOPIK, F., SETTANNI, G., FIEDLER, R. (2016) A problem shared is a problem halved: A survey on the dimensions of collective cyber defense through security information sharing. *Computers & Security.* 2016, vol 60, pp. 154–176, ISSN 0167-4048. Available at: https://doi.org/10.1016/j.cose.2016.04.003.

[800] EUROPEAN COMMISSION. *Joint Communication to the European Parliament and the Council. EU Policy on Cyber Defence…2022*: op. cit.

[801] Ibid., p. 20.

[802] LUUKAS, S., EVANS, T., CILLUFFO, F., NADEAU, A. European Union and NATO Global Cybersecurity Challenges: A Way Forward. *PRISM.* 2016, vol. 6, no. 2, pp. 126–41. [online]. Available at: http://www.jstor.org/stable/26470452. Accessed 3. 3. 2023.

opportunity for strengthening the EU element of cyber defence and closer co-operation with NATO.

However, it is important to mention, that obstacles to closer cooperation in cyber defence are not only political but also organizational and administrative. For example, Sergei Boeke (2017) highlighted that computer security incident response teams can be embedded inside or outside the intelligence community and at the same time centralized units or spread across different sectors. Taking into count only these two dichotomies, a variety of systems is created. For example, Denmark adopted a lead-agency model, while the Netherlands is using the participant-governed network, and the Czech Republic or Estonia is using a network of administrative organizations with the enforcement role of the national cyber security centre.[803] In other words, cyber defence is strongly linked to administrative and organizational practices, including different cultures, creating diversity in cyber defence organizations. This logic is valid also for cooperation that takes place between international organizations.

Conclusion

From the short overview above it is evident that NATO is much more focused on cyber defence as a part of hard power while the EU is focusing mainly on the "internal" dimension of cyber security, which is developed in a very complex way around the single market. However, both actors are cooperating in the areas which are allowing the EU to keep its status as a civilian and regulatory superpower and NATO as a main guardian of European security. Internal links between both actors and overlapping membership ensure a joint perception of threats. The existing setting is allowing greater flexibility to countries, which are not part of NATO but keep the focus on the civilian dimension of cybersecurity and those, who are members of NATO, but do not share EU regulatory ambitions and push for greater supra-nationalization of the policy. In other words, both organizations are developing their own capacities, setting the minimum standards, and providing new opportunities to the Member States. However, the implementation and the level of participation are merely on the individual Member States. Due to the binding character of some measures and the enforcement role of the actors (e.g. in the case of regulations or directives or political pressure), both EU and NATO contribute to increased cybersecurity of its members who can rely on robust defence in the case of an

[803] BOEKE, S. National cyber crisis management: Different European approaches. *Governance*. 2018, vol. 31, pp. 449–464. Available at: https://doi.org/10.1111/gove.12309

attack. In this regard, the EU and NATO are strongly interconnected entities, both characterized by the collective defence.

The limits of cooperation between the EU and NATO are inherent to the character of both actors and the political divergencies of the Member States. However, as discussed above, even the basics of cyber security and cyber defence in the EU are perceived differently by the Member States, and political divergence is further undermined by varying administrative-organizational environments among the Member States. It is questionable, whether the current setting in which the EU sets minimum standards and cyber defence is merely the issue of Member States (with NATO guarantee) is an optimal setting. On one hand, variability, diversity, and certain flexibility is allowing Member States to maintain the required level of sovereignty and respect natural differences among Member States, on the other hand, it may be associated with vulnerability in case of policy laggards. In the contemporary Word, the advantage might be on actors with strong central capacities who can assemble huge resources to connect high ICT technologies with expert human capital. The rise of China or USA, together with emerging AI will create further pressure for closer cooperation with NATO and possibly also centralization and supra-nationalization of cyber security and cyber defence policy in the EU, as protecting citizens and companies will be associated with increased costs for countries, willing to rely on sovereign approach.

CHAPTER SIXTEEN

Legal Regulation of Cybersecurity in the European Union: New Challenges and Prospects of Development

VOLODYMYR DENYSOV, LIUDMYLA FALALIEIEVA

Introduction

Along with the spread and development of digital legal relations, the number of cyber threats is increasing. They are directed both against individuals and legal entities, as well as against critical infrastructure, security and defence systems. The chapter analyses the state of legal and institutional provision of cybersecurity in the European Union (hereinafter referred to as the EU). The private and public components of cyber security are defined. They relate to different legal relationships in cyberspace, but must be considered in combination and interrelation. The authors revealed the need to update the catalogue of fundamental rights guaranteed by the EU by supplementing it with a right to cybersecurity. In the process of researching the legal basis of cyber security regulation at the EU level, it was established that the integration association still does not have a unified cyber protection system. The implementation of such a system is extremely urgent and extremely important, as it will enable the full implementation of the ideas that are the basis of the EU's digital single market.

Digitization of everyday human life, economic relations, activities of the state apparatus, as well as public and private legal relations is obvious. It is aimed at improving living conditions, facilitating economic activity, especially international activity, and increasing the efficiency of public service provision. This also applies to the functioning of the EU internal market, which is in constant evolutionary development. The inevitable digitization of the EU internal market is discussed in A Digital Single Market Strategy for Europe, published in 2015.[804] The objectives of the digital single market are: better access of consumers and

[804] Communication from the Commission to the European Parliament, the Council, the European Economic and Social Committee and the Committee of the Regions. A Digital Single Market

businesses to online goods and services throughout Europe; creation of proper conditions for the prosperity of digital networks and services; maximizing the growth potential of the European digital economy.

These trends require not only the introduction of legal frameworks for the development of the digital economy, but also the effective protection of all participants in digital legal relations. Every minute of using information and communication technologies (hereinafter referred to as ICT) is connected with cyber threats that require a timely and adequate response and permanent work on the formation of a safe cyber environment. Failure to do so may endanger the existence of the EU internal market and the integration association itself. As stated in the preamble to Regulation (EU) 2019/881 of the European Parliament and of the Council of 17 April 2019 on ENISA (the European Union Agency for Cybersecurity) and on information and communications technology cybersecurity certification and repealing Regulation (EU) No 526/2013 (hereinafter referred to as Cybersecurity Act), cyber threats have no borders and are a global problem.[805] Large-scale incidents can disrupt the provision of essential services across the whole EU. This convincingly shows that the creation of national mechanisms only for ensuring cyber security is obviously insufficient.

As of 2023, EU law has a fairly extensive system of legal acts aimed at ensuring EU control over safety in the digital environment and designed to unite the efforts of Member States in this direction. However, the question arises whether the existing legal and institutional framework of the EU corresponds to the today's challenges? Thus, Europol reports on the growth of the level of cybercrime, as well as the emergence of new violations. Its most common forms are: online fraud, theft of personal data, laundering of traditional and virtual currencies.[806] As is well known, the purpose of such crimes is to enrich at the expense of private users. This is a negative but natural consequence of the development and dissemination of ICT. However, criminal interference in public legal relations is becoming increasingly threatening in scale. In most cases, it is associated with the activities of the Russian Federation, including, in the context of armed aggression, a full-scale invasion of Ukrainian territory. The EU and its Member States, although not parties to the conflict, are nevertheless systematically experiencing

Strategy for Europe. COM/2015/0192 final. [online]. Available at: https://eur-lex.europa.eu/legal-content/EN/TXT/?uri=celex%3A52015DC0192

[805] Regulation (EU) 2019/881 of the European Parliament and of the Council of 17 April 2019 on ENISA (the European Union Agency for Cybersecurity) and on information and communications technology cybersecurity certification and repealing Regulation (EU) No 526/2013 (Cybersecurity Act), OJ L 151, 7. 6. 2019, pp. 15–69. [online]. Available at: https://eur-lex.europa.eu/eli/reg/2019/881/oj

[806] Europol report. Cybercrime areas. [online]. Available at: https://www.europol.europa.eu/crime-areas-and-statistics/crime-areas/cybercrime

pressure on their own cybersecurity system. The National Cyber Security Centre and the Regional Cyber Defence Centre in Lithuania have reported an increase in the number of DDoS attacks on state institutions, the banking system, and the communication system.[807] Poland has also reported constant attacks on the Internet resources of government agencies. A special investigation showed that an attack on the website of the Polish Sejm was carried out by a pro-Russian hacker group[808], which can be treated as "cyber terrorism". Obviously, all this requires effective and coordinated response, as well as crisis management at the EU level.

Threats to public and private legal relations concern various aspects of human life, yet are equally dangerous to the legal, social, economic, and political systems of the EU. Therefore, it is important to thoroughly investigate the existing EU legal approaches to cybersecurity, as well as to search for acceptable procedures and mechanisms for creating a secure cyber environment that would ensure the development of the EU's digital single market.

EU Cybersecurity: From Theory to Practice

In 2013, the EU Cybersecurity Strategy was published as Joint Communication to the European Parliament, the Council, the European Economic and Social Committee and the Committee of the Regions (hereinafter referred to as the First Cyber Security Strategy).[809] It outlined the main priorities and directions on the path to a unified European cybersecurity system. In it, instead of the term "network and information security" which was common at that time, the term "cybersecurity" is used for the first time. Admittedly, the authors of the Strategy did not dare to give a clear definition to this term. Most likely, this is due to the fact that at that time, EU institutions were not ready to give preference to one of the many conceptual approaches to the essence of cybersecurity and cyber threats. In addition, hasty formulations would not have been decisive in any case, considering that communications as a legal instrument are not mentioned in the Treaties.

Regulation (EU) 2019/881 of the European Parliament and of the Council of 17 April 2019 on ENISA (the European Union Agency for Cybersecurity) and

807 Regional Cyber Defence Centre. 3rd quarter report, 2022, p. 10. [online]. Available at: https://www.nksc.lt/doc/rkgc/CTAC_2022_3rd_Quarter_Report.pdf

808 Service of the Republic of Poland. Russian cyberattacks. [online]. Available at: https://www.gov.pl/web/sluzby-specjalne/rosyjskie-cyberattacks (in Polish)

809 Joint communication to the European Parliament, the Council, the European economic and social committee and the Committee of the regions. Cybersecurity Strategy of the European Union: An Open, Safe and Secure Cyberspace, JOIN/2013/01 final. [online]. Available at: https://eur-lex.europa.eu/legal-content/EN/TXT/?uri=celex%3A52013JC0001

on information and communications technology cybersecurity certification and repealing Regulation (EU) No 526/2013 (hereinafter referred to as Cybersecurity Act) became a fundamental legal act that formed the basic institutional and legal guarantees of security for participants in digital legal relations. No less important is the fact that Article 2 of the Cybersecurity Act defines cybersecurity as the activities necessary to protect network and information systems, the users of such systems, and other persons affected by cyber threats.[810] The latter include any potential circumstance, event or action that could damage, disrupt or otherwise adversely impact network and information systems, the users of such systems and other persons. Apparently, the rather detailed definition of cybersecurity in EU law did not put an end to discussions about its essence and significance for the EU internal market, private legal relations of EU citizens, the security of Member States, and the integration association itself as an actor of international relations and a subject of international law. One of the reasons for this is that the Cybersecurity Act is primarily the founding document of the European Union Agency for Cybersecurity (hereinafter referred to as ENISA) and the basis for the European cybersecurity certification scheme, rather than systematizing rights and obligations, as might have been expected, given the "loud" name of the legislative act.

It is worth considering that providing a comprehensive, exhaustive, and all-encompassing characterization of cybersecurity is almost impossible. Scholars have developed too many diverse conceptual approaches to understanding it. This, to some extent, also applies to the approaches of Member States, embodied in domestic legislation, as well as national cybersecurity strategies adopted following the approval of the First Cybersecurity Strategy.

Doctrinal differences have led to the fact that cybersecurity can be considered from at least three perspectives: as measures and actions aimed at protecting information systems; as the state of security in the cyber environment; and finally, as the ability to defend and resist existing and potential threats.[811] For example, the Cambridge dictionary proposes to consider cyber security as things that are done to protect a person, organization, or country and their computer information

[810] Regulation (EU) 2019/881 of the European Parliament and of the Council of 17 April 2019 on ENISA (the European Union Agency for Cybersecurity) and on information and communications technology cybersecurity certification and repealing Regulation (EU) No 526/2013 (Cybersecurity Act), OJ L 151, 7.6.2019, pp. 15–69. [online]. Available at: https://eur-lex.europa.eu/eli/reg/2019/881/oj

[811] PAPAKONSTANTINOU, V. Cybersecurity as Praxis and as a State: the EU Law Path Towards Acknowledgement of a New Right to Cybersecurity? *Computer Law & Security Review*. 2022, vol. 44, p. 3. [online]. Available at: https://www.sciencedirect.com/science/article/pii/S0267364922000012?via%3Dihub

against crime or attacks carried out using the Internet.[812] Looking at cyber security from a "state" rather than a "measures/actions" perspective gave reasons to some scientists to conclude that it consists in the protection of systems connected to the Internet, including hardware, software and data, from cyberattacks.[813] However, we share the position of V. Papakonstantinou, who leans towards the dichotomy of cyber security as a state of security and measures aimed at such security.[814] The current legislative definition of cyber security at the EU level fully corresponds to this concept. Cybersecurity Act considers it both as a state of protection, since all subjects have the right to protection against "potential circumstance, event or action" that may have an adverse effect, and as a practice ("activities necessary to protect" subjects or objects, which are threatened by cyber threats). Admittedly, such ideas have not found further development in EU legislation, although they logically follow from the basic ideas and principles of cybersecurity laid down in the Cybersecurity Act. The Joint Communication: The EU's Cybersecurity Strategy for the Digital Decade published in December 2020[815] (hereinafter referred to as the Second Cybersecurity Strategy) also does not contain tasks and objectives that fit into the outlined paradigm.

The state of being secured in cyberspace can exist exclusively in combination with the human right to cyber security. Such a right is exercised through legal and institutional guarantees of protection of the rights of participants in digital legal relations. However, Cybersecurity Act, as well as the First and Second Cyber Security Strategies, emphasize the importance of cyber security to ensure the functioning of the EU internal market, rather than the protection of human rights. The digital world is viewed mostly through an economic prism from the standpoint of view of free trade. Directive (EU) 2016/1148 of the European Parliament and of the Council of 6 July 2016 concerning measures for a high common level of security of network and information systems across the Union (hereinafter

[812] Cambridge Dictionary. [online]. Available at: https://dictionary.cambridge.org/dictionary/english/cybersecurity

[813] SEEMMA, P. S., NANDHINI, S., SOWMIYA, M. Overview of Cyber Security. *International Journal of Advanced Research in Computer and Communication Engineering.* 2018, vol. 7, issue 11, p. 125. [online]. Available at: https://www.researchgate.net/publication/329678338_Overview_of_Cyber _Security

[814] PAPAKONSTANTINOU, V. Cybersecurity as Praxis and as a State: the EU Law Path Towards Acknowledgement of a New Right to Cybersecurity? *Computer Law & Security Review.* 2022, vol. 44, p. 3. [online]. Available at: https://www.sciencedirect.com/science/article/pii/S0267364922000012?via%3Dihub

[815] European Commission and the High Representative of the Union for Foreign Affairs and Security Policy. The EU's Cybersecurity Strategy for the Digital Decade, 2020. [online]. Available at: https://digital-strategy.ec.europa.eu/en/library/eus-cybersecurity-strategy-digital-decade-0

referred to as NIS Directive),[816] which aims, according to paragraph 1 of Article 1, to improve the functioning of the EU internal market, is critical. Undoubtedly, any security gaps can have uncontrollable consequences for the internal market of the EU, undermining the basis of the functioning of this integration association. However, viewing the protection of human rights and freedoms as a secondary component of cybersecurity cannot be considered justified.

It is evident that the EU's legislative approaches to cybersecurity are quite broad and leave room for interpretation. For example, Pablo A. Mazurier links the adoption of EU cybersecurity legislation to the fact that the constant risk undermines public trust in digital devices, making the digital transformation and enrichment of people's everyday life stressful and problematic.[817] In fact, the argument is that ensuring the proper functioning of the EU internal market fully meets the interests of EU citizens, as it contributes to meeting their economic and social needs.

Focusing on the need to ensure the functioning of the internal market also has a fairly logical legal, and possibly political, rationale. In accordance with the principle of subsidiarity, in areas which do not fall within its exclusive competence, the Union shall act only if and in so far as the objectives of the proposed action cannot be sufficiently achieved by the Member States, either at central level or at regional and local level, but can rather, by reason of the scale or effects of the proposed action, be better achieved at Union level (Article 5 (paragraph 3) of the Treaty on European Union as amended by the Treaty of Lisbon in 2007).[818] The protection of human rights mostly remains within the scope of the powers of the Member States, while the legal regulation of the EU internal market requires consolidated efforts at the Union-wide level. The formulations used in the NIS Directive mainly indicate not the neglect of the necessity of protecting the individual in cyberspace, but rather the justification of the need for legal regulation of this area at the EU level.

To a large extent, the above is confirmed by the evolution of EU approaches to the legal basis of regulation of the outlined issues. In the Second Cybersecurity Strategy, it is recognized that people deserve to use available amenities with the

[816] Directive (EU) 2016/1148 of the European Parliament and of the Council of 6 July 2016 concerning measures for a high common level of security of network and information systems across the Union, OJ L 194, 19. 7. 2016, pp. 1–30. [online]. Available at: https://eur-lex.europa.eu/eli/dir/2016/1148/oj

[817] MAZURIER, P. A. Cybersecurity Landscape: Technological Perspectives and Certification Framework, Products, and Services. European Cybersecurity in Context A Policy-Oriented Comparative Analysis. 2022, p. 2. [online]. Available at: https://liberalforum.eu/wp-content/uploads/2022/08/European-Cybersecurity-in-Context_ELF-Study_Techno-Politics.pdf

[818] Consolidated version of the Treaty on European Union. OJ C 326, 26. 10. 2012, pp. 13–390. [online]. Available at: https://eur-lex.europa.eu/legal-content/EN/TXT/?uri=celex%3A12012M%2FTXT

confidence that they are reliably protected from cyber threats.[819] In the preamble to Directive (EU) 2022/2555 of the European Parliament and of the Council of 14 December 2022 on measures for a high common level of cybersecurity across the Union, amending Regulation (EU) No 910/2014 and Directive (EU) 2018/1972, and repealing Directive (EU) 2016/1148 (hereinafter referred to as NIS 2 Directive), the importance of regulation at the EU level is explained not only by the security of the Union, but also by the protection of its citizens, businesses and institutions from incidents and cyber threats. Attention is focused on the need to promote and protect a global, open, free, stable and secure cyberspace based on human rights, fundamental freedoms, democracy and the rule of law.[820] The implementation of the above may indicate the growth of consensus among Member States and the beginning of a rethinking of the essence of cyber security. This is the first step towards the formation of real legal and institutional guarantees of cyber security within the EU. In the context of the above, V. Papakonstantinou rightly notes that although state security and criminal law may lie outside the competence of the EU, this does not prevent the EU legislator from introducing protective regulatory provisions on cyber security in the interests of Europeans.[821]

Thus, cybersecurity can be viewed from the perspective of individual security of EU citizens in cyberspace. The right to individual security is one of the fundamental human rights, guaranteed by Article 3 of the Universal Declaration of Human Rights, Article 5 of the European Convention on Human Rights, and Article 6 of the Charter of Fundamental Rights of the European Union. Private legal relationships in cyberspace are becoming everyday occurrences, so their protection from infringements is one of the fundamental human rights in today's realities. This provides a basis for discussing the existence of a private level of cybersecurity. It is related to the implementation of fundamental rights and freedoms by EU citizens, as well as ensuring their economic, social, and political interests.

Many cyber threats are aimed at the functioning of public institutions of the EU and its Member States, as well as critical sectors of the economy, energy, and

[819] European Commission and the High Representative of the Union for Foreign Affairs and Security Policy. The EU's Cybersecurity Strategy for the Digital Decade, 2020. [online]. Available at: https://digital-strategy.ec.europa.eu/en/library/eus-cybersecurity-strategy-digital-decade-0

[820] Directive (EU) 2022/2555 of the European Parliament and of the Council of 14 December 2022 on measures for a high common level of cybersecurity across the Union, amending Regulation (EU) No 910/2014 and Directive (EU) 2018/1972, and repealing Directive (EU) 2016/1148 (NIS 2 Directive), OJ L 333, 27. 12. 2022, pp. 80–152. [online]. Available at: https://eur-lex.europa.eu/eli/dir/2022/2555/oj

[821] PAPAKONSTANTINOU, V. Cybersecurity as Praxis and as a State: the EU Law Path Towards Acknowledgement of a New Right to Cybersecurity? *Computer Law & Security Review.* 2022, vol. 44, p. 14. [online]. Available at: https://www.sciencedirect.com/science/article/pii/S0267364922000012?via%3Dihub

banking systems. This is undoubtedly an infringement on the national interests of Member States and the collective interests of the EU as an integration association. Considering the nature of the dangers and the objects of infringement, this pertains to the public level of cybersecurity, which requires an appropriate legal framework and an extensive institutional system of cyber defence.

Cyber defence is a component of cybersecurity according to the First Cybersecurity Strategy, Section 2 of which states that one of the strategic priorities of cybersecurity is developing cyber defence policy and capabilities related to the Common Security and Defence Policy (hereinafter referred to as CSDP).[822] Further research under the auspices of the European Defence Agency (hereinafter referred to as EDA) confirmed the critical importance of cybersecurity for the defence sector.[823] A similar approach is reflected in the national strategies of EU Member States.

According to the provisions of Estonia's Cybersecurity Strategy for 2019-2022, cybersecurity is defined as an integral part of the functioning of the state, economy, internal and external security.[824] The Czech Republic's National Cybersecurity Strategy for 2021–2025[825] also links the functioning of the cybersecurity system to ensuring national security. Latvia's Cybersecurity Strategy for 2019-2022 recognized cybersecurity as an element of a comprehensive national defence system. At the same time, cybersecurity policy is aimed at creating a safe, open, free, and trusted cyberspace where individual human rights are respected in both physical and virtual environments.[826] The authors of the French National Digital Security Strategy also see a direct connection between cybersecurity and national security.[827]

Taking into account the above, we have grounds to assert that cybersecurity has both private and public components. The first one relates to ensuring the

[822] Joint communication to the European Parliament, the Council, the European economic and social committee and the Committee of the regions. Cybersecurity Strategy of the European Union: An Open, Safe and Secure Cyberspace, JOIN/2013/01 final. [online]. Available at: https://eur-lex.europa.eu/legal-content/EN/TXT/?uri=celex%3A52013JC0001

[823] See RÖHRIG, W., SMEATON, W. C. R. Cyber security and cyber defence in the European Union opportunities, synergies and challenges. Cyber security and cyber defence in the EU, 2022, pp. 23-27. [online]. Available at: https://eda.europa.eu/docs/default-source/documents/23-27-wolfgang-r%C3%B6hrig-and-j-p-r-smeaton-article.pdf

[824] See Cybersecurity strategy. Republic of Estonia. 2019–2022. p. 72. [online]. Available at: https://www.mkm.ee/media/703/download

[825] See National Cyber Security Strategy of the Czech Republic for the period from 2021 to 2025. p. 23. [online]. Available at: https://nukib.cz/en/cyber-security/strategy-action-plan/

[826] See Informatīvais ziņojums. Latvijas kiberdrošības stratēģija 2019–2022 gadam. p. 27. (in Latvian). [online]. Available at: https://www.mod.gov.lv/sites/mod/files/document/kiberstrategija.pdf

[827] See French national digital security strategy. 40 p. [online]. Available at: https://www.enisa.europa.eu/topics/national-cyber-security-strategies/ncss-map/France_Cyber_Security_Strategy.pdf

rights of EU citizens to a secure cyber environment and, as a result, unhindered access to social benefits and free economic activity within the EU's internal market. The second one involves ensuring the security of Member States and the EU as a whole, constituting an important component of their defence activities carried out within the framework of the EU Common Security and Defence Policy.

Legal and Institutional Framework of the Private Component of EU Cybersecurity

The private component of cybersecurity covers an extremely broad range of legal relationships. At least a part of them is intended to be regulated by the Cybersecurity Act. As already mentioned, this legal act has an extraordinary significance for the formation of a unified EU cybersecurity system, as it defines the concepts of cybersecurity and cyber threats for the first time at the EU legislative level. At the same time, its regulatory impact is limited only to the objectives, tasks, and organizational issues related to ENISA, as well as establishing the framework for EU cybersecurity certification schemes (Article 1).[828]

ENISA was established back in 2004, but the Cybersecurity Act fundamentally changed the authority, structure, and most importantly, the objectives and tasks of this agency. It was founded with the aim of promoting the exchange of best practices among Member States and private stakeholders, making policy proposals to the European Commission and EU Member States, initiating EU sectoral policy initiatives on cybersecurity, and fostering operational cooperation both among Member States and between institutions, bodies, services, and agencies of the EU. The Cybersecurity Industrial, Technology and Research Competence Centre and Network of Coordination Centres (CCCN) are recognized as playing a crucial role in strengthening technological sovereignty through joint investment in strategic cybersecurity projects.[829]

Legal guarantees of cybersecurity, established by the Cybersecurity Act, are focused on setting up certification schemes. Their purpose is to ensure that ICT products, services, and processes meet established security requirements. As cybersecurity is inherently linked to all digital products, services, and processes, EU certification has the potential to become a key instrument in supporting the

[828] Regulation (EU) 2019/881 of the European Parliament and of the Council of 17 April 2019 on ENISA (the European Union Agency for Cybersecurity) and on information and communications technology cybersecurity certification and repealing Regulation (EU) No 526/2013 (Cybersecurity Act), OJ L 151, 7. 6. 2019, pp. 15–69. [online]. Available at: https://eur-lex.europa.eu/eli/reg/2019/881/oj

[829] European Commission and the High Representative of the Union for Foreign Affairs and Security Policy. The EU's Cybersecurity Strategy for the Digital Decade, 2020. [online]. Available at: https://digital-strategy.ec.europa.eu/en/library/eus-cybersecurity-strategy-digital-decade-0

strategic autonomy of the European cyberspace.[830] It aims to ensure its stable functioning and foster public trust in it. At the same time, an effective certification system can require foreign providers and other states to comply with schemes for access to the EU internal market.

The Regulation (EU) 2022/2554 of the European Parliament and of the Council of 14 December 2022 on digital operational resilience for the financial sector (hereinafter referred to as Regulation (EU) 2022/2554)[831] is an extremely important legal act with direct effect, which regulates the private component of cybersecurity. It forms the legal basis for cybersecurity in financial legal relations, as it establishes the legal principles of regulation, uniform requirements for the security of network and information systems that support the business processes of financial organizations.

The most significant achievement of Regulation (EU) 2022/2554 is imposing an obligation on financial organizations to establish internal management and risk control in the ICT sphere. In addition, this legal act sets up a rather clear system of supervision over third-party providers of critical ICT services at the EU level. The leading role in supervision and control is given to the European Supervisory Authorities (European Banking Authority, European Insurance and Occupational Pensions Authority, European Securities and Markets Authority).

We believe that in this way, the basic level of cybersecurity at the EU level in the financial sector has been regulated. This is a significant step in protecting the rights and interests of participants in financial legal relations within the EU's internal market. However, an analysis of the preamble and main text of Regulation (EU) 2022/2554 suggests that the authors do not consider it a logical continuation of the Cybersecurity Act and generally avoid the term "cybersecurity". Instead, they use formulations like "security of the network and information systems". It is evident that this term is narrower than "cybersecurity", but such a conclusion is the result of logical analysis rather than a direct indication of the norms of the Cybersecurity Act and Regulation (EU) 2022/2554. Moreover, none of the European Supervisory Authorities is essentially an authority responsible for ensuring (or controlling) cybersecurity. ENISA is given the role of an auxiliary

[830] MAZURIER, P. A. Cybersecurity Landscape: Technological Perspectives and Certification Framework, Products, and Services. European Cybersecurity in Context A Policy-Oriented Comparative Analysis, 2022, p. 3. [online]. Available at: https://liberalforum.eu/wp-content/uploads/2022/08/European-Cybersecurity-in-Context_ELF-Study_Techno-Politics.pdf

[831] Regulation (EU) 2022/2554 of the European Parliament and of the Council of 14 December 2022 on digital operational resilience for the financial sector and amending Regulations (EC) No 1060/2009, (EU) No 648/2012, (EU) No 600/2014, (EU) No 909/2014 and (EU) 2016/1011, OJ L 333, 27. 12. 2022, pp. 1–79. [online]. Available at: https://eur-lex.europa.eu/eli/reg/2022/2554/oj

body that assists the European Supervisory Authorities in developing draft regulatory technical standards. It is doubtful that such a situation contributes to the formation of a logically structured EU cybersecurity system.

We have reason to believe that the adoption of Cybersecurity Act and Regulation (EU) 2022/2554 are only the first, rather cautious and limited step towards the formation of a unified EU cybersecurity system, as the mentioned legal acts are not without some shortcomings. They are criticized for not very effective legal mechanisms for protecting the rights of participants in private legal relations using ICT.

Under the strategic guidance of the European Commission and the technical supervision of ENISA, the cybersecurity framework established by the Cybersecurity Act currently remains voluntary (Article 56).[832] Analysts expect it to become mandatory after a four-year trial period, which ends on December 31, 2023.[833]

In addition, this legal act avoids addressing the responsibility (or at least its principles) of certification bodies in case of non-compliance with legislative standards. However, while the issue of liability enforcement may be resolved by EU Member States, a real gap in the Cybersecurity Act is that it does not outline the scope of rights or means of protection for individuals whose rights would be violated in such cases.

A significant step forward in this regard was made with the adoption of Regulation (EU) 2022/2554, which defines a supervisory system for ICT service providers. However, the scope of this legal act is extremely limited and only covers the main aspects of financial activities using ICT. For example, it pays minimal attention to legal relations related to cryptocurrencies (issuance, circulation, investment activities, exchange, etc.). Considering that the market capitalization of cryptocurrencies exceeds 1 trillion US dollars, its impact on the private financial relations of EU citizens and the internal EU market cannot be overlooked. It could very well become the basis for the functioning of the EU's digital single market. At the same time, the cryptocurrency market exists exclusively in cyberspace, and any interference with the security of cryptocurrency operations is nothing less than cyber threats. In most cases, Regulation

[832] Regulation (EU) 2019/881 of the European Parliament and of the Council of 17 April 2019 on ENISA (the European Union Agency for Cybersecurity) and on information and communications technology cybersecurity certification and repealing Regulation (EU) No 526/2013 (Cybersecurity Act), OJ L 151, 7. 6. 2019, pp. 15–69. [online]. Available at: https://eur-lex.europa.eu/eli/reg/2019/881/oj

[833] MAZURIER, P. A. Cybersecurity Landscape: Technological Perspectives and Certification Framework, Products, and Services. European Cybersecurity in Context A Policy-Oriented Comparative Analysis, 2022, p. 2. [online]. Available at: https://liberalforum.eu/wp-content/uploads/2022/08/European-Cybersecurity-in-Context_ELF-Study_Techno-Politics.pdf

(EU) 2022/2554 gives preference to referral legal norms, which delegate legal regulation to the Regulation of the European Parliament and of the Council on Markets in Crypto-assets, and amending Directive (EU) 2019/1937 (MiCA Regulation Proposal).[834] Ultimately, the adoption of this regulation has been delayed and, as of March 15, 2023, is still is not finally adopted.

The analysis of the MiCA Regulation Proposal indicates that it only partially addresses cybersecurity issues and is more focused on financial control over the activities of crypto-asset issuers. They are obliged to act honestly and professionally, maintain all their systems and security access protocols according to the relevant Union standards, return any collected funds to buyers in case of issuance cancellation, etc. At the same time, as Ágnes Horváth points out, these obligations are more general commercial duties of common sense with little noticeable applicability – their deeper scope and applicability will likely be determined by courts and primarily by the European Union Court.[835] In this regard, supervisory and control functions over the legality of legal relations with crypto-assets are entrusted to the European Banking Authority and ESMA.

One of the most progressive legal acts that allows speaking about the unconditional positive dynamics of the EU legislative process regarding cryptosecurity is the NIS 2 Directive. It obliges Member States to implement a system of control and supervision over cybersecurity, introduces more precise rules concerning the incident reporting process, the content of reports, and the deadlines for their submission. In addition, it aims at harmonizing sanction regimes in EU Member States. The NIS 2 Directive has confirmed that cybersecurity should be understood in accordance with the provisions of the Cybersecurity Act, i.e., aimed not only at protecting information systems but also at protecting the rights and interests of subjects that use ICT.[836] However, like the legal acts mentioned earlier, the NIS 2 Directive does not provide for any individual legal protection measures.

Thus, EU law does not directly define, but recognizes the private component of cybersecurity. At the same time, it does not establish mechanisms for the protection of private entities at the EU level, mainly regulating financial relationships.

[834] Proposal for a Regulation of the European Parliament and of the Council on Markets in Crypto-assets, and amending Directive (EU) 2019/1937, COM/2020/593 final. [online]. Available at: https://eur-lex.europa.eu/legal-content/EN/TXT/?uri=CELEX%3A52020PC0593

[835] HORVATH, A. Protection of consumers provided in the proposal for a regulation of markets in crypto assets. *Zaštita kolektivnih interesa potrošača*. 2021, p. 435. [online]. Available at: https://doi.org/10.18485/union_pf_ccr.2021.ch21

[836] Directive (EU) 2022/2555 of the European Parliament and of the Council of 14 December 2022 on measures for a high common level of cybersecurity across the Union, amending Regulation (EU) No 910/2014 and Directive (EU) 2018/1972, and repealing Directive (EU) 2016/1148 (NIS 2 Directive), OJ L 333, 27. 12. 2022, pp. 80–152. [online]. Available at: https://eur-lex.europa.eu/eli/dir/2022/2555/oj

Legal and Institutional Support of the Cybersecurity's Public Component

The public component of cybersecurity is implemented through the cyber defence of Member States and the Union as a whole. However, the Cybersecurity Act and NIS 2 Directive do not pay attention to cyber defence and the characteristic threats to public legal relations. The Cybersecurity Act contains a kind of disclaimer, stating that the regulation does not limit the competence of Member States regarding activities related to public safety, defence, national security, and state activities in the field of criminal law. Considering that the public aspect of cybersecurity is inextricably linked to defence activities and is based on the protection of national security, the security of critical sectors of Member States and the EU, it is evident that this legal act focuses exclusively on the private level of cybersecurity. The NIS 2 Directive is somewhat more progressive, as it introduces the concept of active cyber defence, which is part of the defence strategy. This does not give grounds to believe that the NIS 2 Directive extends its scope to the public component of cybersecurity, but confirms the recognition of the importance of cyber defence for its guaranteeing.

Legal regulation of the public component of cybersecurity has a much less systematized nature compared to the private component. Unfortunately, in this case, we don't mean a single legal act or legal acts united by a common subject of legal regulation. A striking example of this is the absence of a legislative definition of the concept of "cyber defence" and, moreover, highlighting the relationship between cyber defence and cybersecurity.

Cyber defence in the EU has been established over the past years exclusively as a component of the CSDP. This approach was once again reaffirmed in the Joint Communication to the European Parliament and the Council "EU Policy on Cyber Defence" dated November 10, 2022 (hereinafter referred to as EU Policy on Cyber Defence). Updated approaches to policy were adopted specifically in connection with "the return of war in Europe, with Russia's unjustified and unprovoked military aggression against Ukraine."[837] Scholars from EU Member States pay considerable attention to the issue of systematizing the legal regulation of cyber defence and confirm that although the EU's moderate mandate to develop cyber defence projects within the CSDP has recently gained some political momentum, these areas are still largely regulated at the national level.[838]

[837] Joint communication to the European Parliament and the Council. EU Policy on Cyber Defence. JOIN/2022/49 final. [online]. Available at: https://eur-lex.europa.eu/legal-content/EN/TXT/?uri=CELEX%3A52022JC0049&qid=1668204173348

[838] BENDIEK, A., MAAT, E. P. The EU's Regulatory Approach to Cybersecurity. *Stiftung Wissenschaft und Politik.* 2019, p. 4. [online]. Available at: https://www.swp-berlin.org/publications/

Assessing the real role of EU institutions in the CSDP, some scientists admit to a rather sharp assessment, indicating that the EU can only exhort, facilitate, and incentivise.[839]

The EU Policy on Cyber Defence is somewhat belated but extremely relevant response to the current situation. It recognizes that there is currently very limited interaction between Member States in the field of cyber defence and proposes a number of progressive ideas aimed at both ensuring proper legal and institutional support for cyber defence within the EU and forming a unified cybersecurity system.[840] Member States tend to cooperate not within the EU, but within NATO, aiming to improve their cyber defence potential.[841]

Critically important for the implementation of the EU Policy on Cyber Defence are bodies/entities such as the EDA, ENISA, Europol's European Cybercrime Centre (EC3), Computer Emergency Response Teams, and others. However, the scope of imperative powers of these bodies/entities is extremely limited, and the content of the EU Policy on Cyber Defence does not indicate any substantial expansion. For example, the EDA is to be assigned many new coordination and organizational functions, but they are aimed at improving communication between Member States and information centralization. This in no way changes the essence of this institution, which remains purely a coordination platform for security and defence. Some potential powers of the EDA include: assisting Member States in developing recommendations that do not have mandatory legal force for the defence community; annually informing Member States about the state of new technologies, including those applicable to cyber defence; and supporting Member States in choosing long-term strategic directions, identifying synergies, and opportunities for cooperation. Furthermore, there is a task to expand cooperation with all relevant entities regarding defence-related standards within the functioning of the European Defence Standardization Committee.[842]

The outlined approach will indeed help to increase readiness for cyber threats, regardless of whether they are directed against a Member State or the EU as

products/arbeitspapiere/WP_Bendiek_Pander_Maat_EU_Approach_Cybersecurity.pdf

839 BISCOP, S. Oratio pro pesco. Egmont paper 91, 2017, p. 3. [online]. Available at: https://www.egmontinstitute.be/app/uploads/2017/01/ep91.pdf?type=pdf

840 Joint communication to the European Parliament and the Council EU. Policy on Cyber Defence. JOIN/2022/49 final. [online]. Available at: https://eur-lex.europa.eu/legal-content/EN/TXT/?uri=CELEX%3A52022JC0049&qid=1668204173348

841 Cybersecurity in the EU. Common Security and Defence Policy (CSDP). Challenges and risks for the EU. European Parliamentary Research Service Scientific Foresight Unit (STOA), 2017, p. 8. [online]. Available at: https://www.europarl.europa.eu/RegData/etudes/STUD/2017/603175/EPRS_STU(2017)603175_EN.pdf

842 Joint communication to the European Parliament and the Council EU. Policy on Cyber Defence. JOIN/2022/49 final. [online]. Available at: https://eur-lex.europa.eu/legal-content/EN/TXT/?uri=CELEX%3A52022JC0049&qid=1668204173348

a whole. In fact, establishing an effective mechanism for responding to such threats remains the responsibility of the Member States within their national strategies and policies.

The EU Policy on Cyber Defence does not aim to establish a unified EU cyber security system and, accordingly, to strengthen the role of its bodies, although it acknowledges that the current model of cyber defence is not very effective. As for the coordination measures that are the main focus, their importance cannot be diminished in any way. The EU Policy on Cyber Defence proposes a fairly detailed plan for their further improvement, which provides grounds for discussing potential positive changes. However, considering the nature and intensity of threats, this can hardly be considered sufficient.

Another feature of the EU Policy on Cyber Defence is the transformation of the approach to understanding cyber defence. As indicated in the briefing by European Parliamentary Research Service, initially, the emphasis was mainly on protecting military resources, but the implementation of this policy extended its reach to cover the civilian sector as well. This enlargement is due to the reliance of both military and civilian sectors on a secure cyberspace to defend crucial infrastructure, including electrical grids, water supply systems, banking and transportation systems, communication channels, and the circulation of goods and services[843]. This once again confirms that public and private cyber security components are two sides of the same coin and must be considered comprehensively and interconnected. The EU Policy on Cyber Defence touches on the issue of critical infrastructure protection only tangentially, specifically in the context of its importance for military purposes. Such a militaristic bias creates two problems at once. Firstly, it limits the role and importance of cyber defence. Secondly, it creates artificial barriers to forming a unified EU cyber security system. In particular, the EU is exclusively concerned with cyber self-protection and guaranteed access to cyberspace to ensure normal military operations. No offensive cyber capabilities are deployed under the EU flag.[844] Notably, due to the significant threats posed by cyberattacks to state security, scholars qualify cyber war as an armed conflict, with all the legal consequences, including the right to self-defence, and cyberattacks as a modern form of aggression.[845] Therefore, any excessive militaristic bias in the

[843] LAȚICI, T. Understanding the EU's approach to cyber diplomacy and cyber defence. *European Parliamentary Research Service.* 2020, p. 3. [online]. Available at: https://www.europarl.europa.eu/RegData/etudes/BRIE/2020/651937/EPRS_BRI(2020)651937_EN.pdf

[844] RÖHRIG, W., SMEATON, W. C. R. Cyber security and cyber defence in the European Union opportunities, synergies and challenges. Cyber security and cyber defence in the EU, 2022, p. 24. [online]. Available at: https://eda.europa.eu/docs/default-source/documents/23-27-wolfgang-r%C3%B6hrig-and-j-p-r-smeaton-article.pdf

[845] VAYTSEHOVSKA, O. R. The principle of non-interference in the internal affairs of states and non-use of force or threat of force in international financial law. Actual problems of domestic

EU cyber defence paradigm may conflict with the principle of non-use of force or threat of its use, established be Article 2 (paragraph 4) of the UN Charter[846], as well as the Declaration on Principles of International Law concerning Friendly Relations and Cooperation among States in accordance with the UN Charter; the Helsinki Final Act of the Conference on Security and Cooperation in Europe (CSCE). In addition, the issue of joint defence activities of EU Member States within the CSDP remains quite toxic. It is extremely important to maintain a fragile balance between the sovereignty of Member States and the competence and responsibilities of the EU.[847] Prioritizing cyber defence of infrastructure relevant to military needs over general civilian critical infrastructure may undermine internal consensus in the EU.

Thus, despite the fact that the EU Policy on Cyber Defence aims to establish functional compatibility and unification, the legal basis for regulating the public component of cyber security clearly lacks sufficient systematization. Much of this is related to a certain military bias in understanding the essence of cyber defence, and therefore, the priority role of national regulation over regulation at the EU level. This provides another basis for contemplating the prospects of forming a unified cyber security system within the integration association.

Prospects for the Formation of a Unified Cyber Security System in the EU

The dynamics of EU law development, as well as the content of existing projects and strategies, indicate a clear awareness of the pervasive digitalisation of private and public legal relations, as well as the seriousness of the threats arising from it. However, this has not significantly brought the creation of a unified cyber security system in the EU closer, which would combine comprehensive legal regulation at the level of the integration association, institutions with imperative powers, and platforms for operational communication among EU Member States. The most likely reasons for this appear to be political barriers related to the demarcation of sovereignty between the EU and its Member States, as well as the absence of a comprehensive understanding of the essence of cyber security.

jurisprudence, N 2, 2019, p. 206 (in Ukrainian). [online]. Available at: http://apnl.dnu.in.ua/2_2019/49.pdf

[846] United Nations Charter (full text). [online]. Available at: https://www.un.org/en/about-us/un-charter/full-text

[847] Cybersecurity in the EU. Common Security and Defence Policy (CSDP). Challenges and risks for the EU. European Parliamentary Research Service Scientific Foresight Unit (STOA), 2017, p. 7. [online]. Available at: https://www.europarl.europa.eu/RegData/etudes/STUD/2017/603175/EPRS_STU(2017)603175_EN.pdf

Nevertheless, this does not indicate the EU and its Member States' unwillingness to reconsider approaches to the legal foundations of cyber security regulation.

There is no point in analysing in detail the external factors (cyber threats) that stimulate the reform of the European cyber security system. The danger from private cyber attacks and aggressive cyber activities in the public domain is evident and not disputed by either scholars or politicians. Regarding the EU's internal readiness to change the legal and institutional paradigm in the field of cybersecurity, there are many facts that sometimes go unnoticed.

EU Member States' scientists point out that cybersecurity, as a new area of policy, has proven capable of providing relatively broad political support for joint actions, including the expansion of provisions of the Treaty on European Union as amended by the Lisbon Treaty in 2007, concerning the EU's Common Foreign and Security Policy. Notably, there is much more consensus among Member States regarding the legal regulation of cyberspace than it may seem at first glance.[848] The critical level of cyber threats has become an unexpected but entirely logical cementing factor that restores trust within the EU and activates integration processes. Bushra Al Blooshi and Angelika Eksteen, analysing national cyber strategies of EU Member States, have noted that most of them prioritize mutual cooperation within the EU and the establishment of management mechanisms.[849] Cybersecurity has an all-encompassing nature and affects almost all legal relations. This indicates that its legal and institutional provision may fall entirely under the competence of EU law. This primarily concerns harmonization within the EU internal market and ensuring the proper protection of fundamental rights and freedoms guaranteed at the level of the integration association, among other things.

Despite this, in today's realities, individual EU Member States are responsible for their own cyber potentials. It is quite evident that they have very different levels of cyber maturity and the ability to proportionally respond to cyber threats. This is directly related to the level of digitalisation, economic, and political situation in the respective states. This complicates the build-up of cyber potential in the EU but once again highlights the acute need for coordinated and systematic efforts in this direction. Ultimately, the EU recognizes the need to implement a more unified approach to cyber defence across all sectors and to find ways to adapt

[848] OSULA, A. M., KASPER, A., KAJANDER, A. EU Common Position on International Law and Cyberspace. *Masaryk University Journal of Law and Technology.* 2022, vol. 16, p. 114. [online]. Available at: https://journals.muni.cz/mujlt/article/view/20668/16944

[849] AL BLOOSHI, B., EKSTEEN, A. Cyber Governance in the EU. *European Cybersecurity in Context A Policy-Oriented Comparative Analysis*, 2022, p. 22. [online]. Available at: https://liberalforum.eu/wp-content/uploads/2022/08/European-Cybersecurity-in-Context_ELF-Study_Techno-Politics.pdf

it to changing geopolitical conditions (paragraph 3.1 of the EU Policy on Cyber Defence).[850]

The need for a unified cybersecurity system in the EU is related not only to a certain lack of coordination within the Union but also to the rather complex and unsystematic legal regulation within the national law of many Member States. For example, in Germany, France, Sweden, and some other countries, there are no specific laws on cybersecurity. In most cases, the sources of legal regulation are laws on information, information security, and personal data protection. Of course, they cover only a small part of the legal relations related to the protection against cyber threats of various levels.

In this context, the experience of Ukraine is worth noting as a country that has not only achieved an extremely high level of digitalisation but also permanently counteracts cyber threats that affect both private and public legal relations. As early as 2018, the Law "On the Basic Principles of Ensuring Cybersecurity of Ukraine"[851] was adopted in Ukraine. In 2022, it was updated, taking into account the full-scale invasion of the Russian Federation into Ukraine's territory. In our opinion, the conceptual aspect of this Law is essential.[852] It effectively forms a new branch of law and becomes the basis for further legal regulation of narrower aspects of cybersecurity.

Ukraine's cybersecurity legislation, including the Cybersecurity Strategy of Ukraine and its implementation plan, is based on the EU's Cybersecurity Strategy. Paradoxically, it appears more structured and logical than in the EU. It encompasses a comprehensive view of cybersecurity and cyber threats. In particular, Article 1 of the mentioned Law of Ukraine defines cybersecurity as the protection of vital interests of human beings and citizens, society, and the state during the use of cyberspace, ensuring the sustainable development of the information society and the digital communicative environment, timely detection, prevention, and neutralization of real and potential threats to Ukraine's national security in cyberspace. Ukrainian scientists also emphasize that the implementation of national cybersecurity legislation should be aimed at ensuring the safe functioning of cyberspace and its use for the benefit of people, society, and the state.[853] This testifies to the existence of a cybersecurity concept, which includes

[850] Joint communication to the European Parliament and the Council. EU Policy on Cyber Defence. JOIN/2022/49 final. [online]. Available at: https://eur-lex.europa.eu/legal-content/EN/TXT/?uri=CELEX%3A52022JC0049&qid=1668204173348

[851] Pro osnovni zasady zabezpechennia kiberbezpeky Ukrainy: Zakon Ukrainy vid 05.10.2017 r. No 2163-VIII. [online]. Available at: https://zakon.rada.gov.ua/laws/show/2163-19#Text

[852] Ibid.

[853] STEFANCHUK, R., KOPILENK, O., BERSHEDA, E., KLIMENKO, O. «Cyfrova Ukraina»: konstytucijno-pravova model. Instytut zakonodavstva Verhovnoi Rady Ukrainy, 2021, p. 121 (in Ukrainian).

both private and public components. The former pertains to the protection of the rights and interests of individuals and legal entities, while the latter addresses issues of state defence and the protection of critical infrastructure, regardless of its purpose. At the same time, most EU Member States do not consider cyber defence as a component of cybersecurity.[854]

We believe that the division of cybersecurity into private and public components is the conceptual foundation for a unified EU cybersecurity system. The theoretical-legal basis for this has already been laid. The first and foremost change we propose is the unequivocal recognition of the right to cybersecurity, guaranteed at the EU level. Such a right, being fundamental, embodies the private component of cybersecurity. The importance of its codification in normative form lies in the fact that it recognizes the right of an individual to protect themselves against cyber threats and imposes a duty on all others not to infringe upon it. This will also enable the EU to resolve the issue of priority cybersecurity goals, which has not yet been unequivocally addressed at the official level.

V. Papakonstantinou believes that one of the first steps in the EU law-making process could be the recognition of the right to cybersecurity by amending the Cybersecurity Act. An alternative method of regulating the right to cybersecurity, according to the scholar, is by including it as a special subcategory of the general right to security in the EU, through amendments to Article 6 of the EU Charter of Fundamental Rights.[855] We believe that this is not only an alternative option for the legislative process but also an extremely important step towards forming the EU's cybersecurity system. The EU Charter is a progressive document that enshrines many rights not typically guaranteed by other international organizations. Furthermore, the EU Charter forms a unified concept of the quality of human life.[856] Considering that the security of the cyber environment is an integral characteristic of the quality of life in modern society, the catalogue of rights defined in the EU Charter cannot be complete without the right to cybersecurity. At the same time, as it seems to us, including this right in the Charter does not imply its automatic provision by EU institutions[857] but enables the definition of the vector for further policy on cybersecurity.

[854] BENDIEK, A., MAAT, E. P. The EU's Regulatory Approach to Cybersecurity. Stiftung Wissenschaft und Politik, 2019, p. 21. [online]. Available at: https://www.swp-berlin.org/publications/products/arbeitspapiere/WP_Bendiek_Pander_Maat_EU_Approach_Cybersecurity.pdf

[855] PAPAKONSTANTINOU, V. Cybersecurity as Praxis and as a State: the EU Law Path Towards Acknowledgement of a New Right to Cybersecurity? *Computer Law & Security Review.* 2022, vol. 44, p. 13. [online]. Available at: https://www.sciencedirect.com/science/article/pii/S0267364922000012?via%3Dihub

[856] ŠIŠKOVÁ, N. Regulace lidských práv na úrovni EU – vývoj a perspektivy. *International and Comparative Law Review.* 2004, no. 10, p. 31. (in Czech)

[857] See HAMULAK, O. The Variations of Judicial Enforcement of EU Charter of Fundamental Rights vis-á-vis Union Institutions and Bodies. *The Review of European Law, Economics and*

A unified EU cybersecurity system requires a developed institutional basis that guarantees realization of the rights and interests of private entities and the security of the EU's and its Member States' critical infrastructure. The existing dispositive model of institutional guarantees is aimed at standardization (the private component of cybersecurity) or communication and experience exchange (the public component of cybersecurity). We agree with L. Martino and N. Gamal's position that it is impossible (and dangerous) to replicate solutions that were effective for old phenomena to manage the new dynamics of cyberspace.[858] The EU should recognize that cybersecurity is a separate global sector requiring specific legal regulation and authorities with special powers.

We believe that the many years of positive experience of ENISA's functioning give grounds to consider the possibility of expanding the powers of this agency. Its structure could include departments responsible for the security of crypto-assets, departments with certain supervisory powers, as well as departments authorized to respond to violations by obliged entities. The possibility of granting ENISA authority over cyber defence issues is not so clear-cut. In any case, this body should be involved in ensuring the public component of cybersecurity, but the specifics of such a component indicate the need to establish a separate specialized agency. For example, the existing mechanism does not allow for the implementation of a common active cyber defence system within the EU, the need for which became urgent after Russia's aggression against the civilized world. In particular, this method of countering cyber threats was first introduced in the Law of Ukraine "On the Fundamental Principles of Ensuring Cybersecurity of Ukraine"[859] by making amendments in 2022.[860]

Active cyber defence is defined as actions aimed at enhancing the level of cyber protection by neutralizing cyberattacks of the aggressor state, its systems and networks, as well as sources of cyber threats and cyberattacks used to harm national security. The system of active counteraction to aggression in cyberspace consists of a set of organizational, legal, scientific, and technical measures aimed at increasing the level of cyber defence of the state by influencing the information (automated), electronic-communication, and information-communication

Politics. 2018, pp. 98–112. [online]. Available at: https://papers.ssrn.com/sol3/papers.cfm?abstract_id=3436791

[858] MARTINO, L., GAMAL, N. Editorial: European Cybersecurity in Context. European Cybersecurity in Context. A Policy-Oriented Comparative Analysis, 2022, p. 8. [online]. Available at: https://liberalforum.eu/wp-content/uploads/2022/08/European-Cybersecurity-in-Context_ELF-Study_Techno-Politics.pdf

[859] Pro osnovni zasady zabezpechennia kiberbezpeky Ukrainy: Zakon Ukrainy vid 05.10.2017 r. No 2163-VIII. [online]. Available at: https://zakon.rada.gov.ua/laws/show/2163-19#Text

[860] Pro vnesennia zmin do deiakykh zakoniv Ukrainy shchodo zabezpechennia formuvannia ta realizatsii derzhavnoi polityky u sferi aktyvnoi protydii ahresii u kiberprostori: Zakon Ukrainy vid 28. 7. 2022 r. No 2470-IX. [online]. Available at: https://zakon.rada.gov.ua/laws/show/2470-20#n21

systems of the aggressor state, sources of cyber threats and cyberattacks. To implement it, according to Article 3 of the Law of Ukraine "On the State Service of Special Communication and Information Protection of Ukraine", the Centre for Active Counteraction to Aggression in Cyberspace is established.[861]

The norms of the UN Charter, which prohibit aggression and intervention, are also applicable to international cybersecurity law.[862] At the same time, both the UN Charter and the Declaration on the Principles of International Law, based on it, interpret aggressive actions extremely broadly. They can recognize any actions that actually or potentially threaten the maintenance of international peace and security. Therefore, it is extremely important that the content of active cyber defence indicates that it is an element of self-defence, and the actions of authorized entities are directed exclusively against the sources of cyber threats. It is also worth noting that the EU Policy on Cyber Defence has already laid the foundation for the introduction of such a mechanism. In particular, the introduction to the EU Policy on Cyber Defence states that general prevention and detection are an important part of the EU's defence capabilities.[863] It must be able to detect attacks at an early stage. Such detections must be converted into useful information that can contribute to ensuring cybersecurity. Thus, a similar model of countering aggression in cyberspace fits both within the framework outlined by the UN Charter and the modern EU defence policy, as it does not provide for offensive operations, but allows for the prevention of critical cyber threats. Implementation of such preventive mechanisms within the EU is possible only with an effective unified cybersecurity system.

Therefore, we consider it justified and timely to move from a dispositive to an imperative nature of the powers of special authorities, which will significantly expand the protection of the rights and interests of EU citizens, and enable effective counteraction to cyber threats. Of course, a more detailed list of imperative powers should be considered at a joint conference of Member States, given the sensitivity of the issue of national sovereignty. However, we have no doubt that the Member States are ready for such a dialogue, considering the nature of the current cyber threats. This provides grounds to assert that the formation of a single EU cybersecurity system is a realistic goal that corresponds to the objectives of the Union's founding and the interests of all its citizens.

---

[861] Pro Derzhavnu sluzhbu specialnogo zvyazku ta zahystu informacii Ukrainy: Zakon Ukrainy vid 23. 2. 2006 r. No 3475-IV. [online]. Available at: https://zakon.rada.gov.ua/laws/show/3475-15#Text

[862] KETTEMANN, M. C. Ensuring cybersecurity through international law. Revista Española de Derecho Internacional. vol. 69/2, 2017, p. 284. [online]. Available at: http://www.revista-redi.es/wp-content/uploads/2017/08/11_foro_kettemann_ensuring-cybersecurity.pdf

[863] Joint communication to the European Parliament and the Council. EU Policy on Cyber Defence. JOIN/2022/49 final. [online]. Available at: https://eur-lex.europa.eu/legal-content/EN/TXT/?uri=CELEX%3A52022JC0049&qid=1668204173348

Thus, we consider it justified and timely to transition from discretionary to imperative powers of special authorities, which will significantly expand the protection of rights and interests of EU citizens and enable effective counteraction to cyber threats. Of course, a more detailed list of imperative powers should be discussed at a joint conference of Member States, considering the sensitivity of the national sovereignty issue. However, we have no doubt that Member States are ready for such a dialogue, given the nature of current cyber threats. This provides grounds to assert that the formation of a unified EU cybersecurity system is a realistic goal that corresponds to the objectives of the Union's founding and the interests of all its citizens.

Conclusion

The digitalisation of social relations has a pervasive nature. It affects both private and public spheres in the EU. At the same time, cyber threats are growing, which can have both local and global character. The EU is taking gradual steps to provide full legal certainty to legal relations in cyberspace. These steps allow for a positive assessment of the prospects for ensuring the overall security of users and the expansion of the internal market's capabilities. However, current legal and institutional guarantees do not allow for the presence of an effective cybersecurity system in the EU.

EU law does not directly define, but it allows to distinguish the private and public components of cyber security. The former is related to the protection of the rights and interests of individuals and legal entities from encroachments on their social, economic, and other private legal relations. The latter concerns the protection against cyber threats aimed at the national interests of Member States, the interests of the EU as a whole, and critical infrastructure. Such a concept of cybersecurity requires proper legal fixation, as Member States have not only different approaches to its legal regulation but also different capabilities for its real provision. This clearly does not contribute to the formation of a secure cyber environment within the EU.

The use of ICT becomes part of everyday life in society. The EU Charter, as a relevant catalogue of rights and freedoms guaranteed by the integration association, does not take into account this peculiarity of modern realities. In this context, it is extremely important for the EU to recognize the right to cybersecurity. This requires certain efforts to update EU law, primarily the EU Charter of Fundamental Rights. The result will be opening the way to new fundamental shifts in creating effective legal and institutional guarantees of the rights of EU citizens.

In contrast to the private component of cybersecurity, the public component raises many controversies since it is associated with defence and military activity. This has led to the exclusively discretionary nature of legal regulation of cyber defence within the EU. In fact, cyber defence covers not only military objects but also civil critical infrastructure.

Institutional guarantees of cybersecurity are based on the work of several important EU bodies, the most significant of which is ENISA. Establishing the right to cybersecurity requires a transformation of the agency's structure and powers. In addition to coordination functions, ENISA must receive basic control functions and mechanisms for responding to violations of the right to cybersecurity. Also, this agency must necessarily receive a number of powers aimed at protecting the rights and interests of crypto asset users. The scope of their use in the modern economy indicates that they are gradually becoming an essential component of the internal market.

In the process of reforming the concept of cybersecurity in the EU, the experience of Ukraine, a country with a high level of digitalisation and experience in fighting aggression, is of particular interest. Ukrainian legislation is characterized by a comprehensive vision of cybersecurity, including the recognition of the priority of human rights and interests in cyberspace. In addition, Ukraine is in the process of building a cyber defence system against the aggression of the Russian Federation. Introduced innovations, such as active counteraction to aggression in cyberspace (active cyber defence), can become part of the European cyber defence system, as they fit into the paradigm of EU defence policy and comply with the principle of non-use of force or the threat of its use.

The outlined transformations will make it possible to form a unified EU cybersecurity system, which will include legal and institutional guarantees for the rights and interests of private individuals, as well as the protection of the security of Member States and the EU as a whole. The need for such a system has been long overdue and has become even more relevant over the past few years, contributing to the formation of a consensus on the outlined issues among EU Member States.

CHAPTER SEVENTEEN

Energy Sector Digitalisation: Issues of Cybersecurity in the EU and Ukraine

YULIIA VASHCHENKO

1. Introduction

Energy sector is one of the strategic industries of each country. Sustainable, reliable, affordable, and clean energy is essential for functioning of economy and active participation of citizens in economic and social life. Energy security is a crucial part of the national security. In the recent years, the energy sector faces significant increase of digitalisation. These processes bring both benefits and challenges. Digitalisation of energy services contributes to the protection of energy consumer rights. Recent EU policy targets the digitalization of the energy sector. The European Commission pays attention that legislative frameworks on this matter shall encourage the right balance between the general frameworks for European data spaces and the energy sector-specific rules and pre-existing or planned investments[864].

However, vulnerability of smart energy systems to cyber-attacks requires efficient mechanisms of protection of consumers of digitalized energy services, both economic entities and households, due to the rise of interconnected and smart devices (smart meters, smart thermostats, distributed energy resources, etc[865]). The consequences, which can be severe and will also be felt immediately, as well as multiplying effect, when the problems in one network can easily cascade to other networks have been defined among the key challenges related to cybersecurity in the energy sector[866].

---

[864] EU policy supporting the digital and green transformation of the energy system. [online]. Available at: https://digital-strategy.ec.europa.eu/en/policies/eu-policy-digitalisation-energy

[865] GENTZOGLANIS, E. Cybersecurity in the energy sector: what does it mean for network regulation? [online]. Available at: https://www.cepa.co.uk/news-insights/view/cybersecurity-in-the-energy-sector-what-does-it-mean-for-network-regulation

[866] Bird&Bird. *NIS Directive and the energy sector: a patchwork of national implementations.* [online]. Available at: https://www.twobirds.com/en/insights/2020/global/nis-directive-and-the-energy-sector-a-patchwork-of-national-implementations

The encouragement of cybersecurity in the energy sector became crucial due to the Russian Federation war in Ukraine. After the first large cyberattacks on the energy infrastructure in Ukraine in 2015, the cyber security issues in the energy sector have been placed among the key directions of the cybersecurity policy worldwide. Government officials and representatives of the IT sector pay attention to the cyberattacks on Ukrainian civilian digital targets, including the energy sector companies[867]. Sapharov, F., the Deputy Minister for energy of Ukraine, points out that the number of cyber-attacks on the energy infrastructure objects of Ukraine increased from the beginning of the large-scale war by a third – to more than 1,2 million – in comparison with 0.9 million of cyber-attacks during the whole 2021 year[868]. The distribution and transmission system operators are among the key objects of cyber-attacks of the enemy[869]. Considering that Ukrainian energy system has been operating synchronously with the European continental network ENTSO-E since 16 March 2022 and now is part of the European energy space cyber attacks on the energy infrastructure objects in Ukraine can negatively influence other elements of the European energy system. Therefore, the EU Member States and Ukraine, with the support of international community, shall joint their efforts in the protection of European energy system from cyber-attacks. The effective legal mechanisms for the cyber security in the energy sector is crucial for European energy system as a whole.

Some organizational and legal issues of the cyber security of critical infrastructure in general and in the selected sectors have been analyzed by scientists. In particular, Yermenchuk, O. explored the legal aspects of critical infrastructure protection in Ukraine[870] and analyzed the international approaches to the protection of critical infrastructure in European countries (the Great Britain, France, Germany, Spain, and Denmark), and expressed the author vision on the possible organizational and legal national model of the critical infrastructure protection[871]. Bakalinska, O., Bakalinsky, O. analyzed the

[867] SMITH, B. *Digital technology and the war in Ukraine*. [online]. Available at: https://blogs.microsoft.com/on-the-issues/2022/02/28/ukraine-russia-digital-war-cyberattacks/

[868] ZHARIKOVA, A. *The number of attacks on energy infrastructure increased in a third.* [online]. Available at: https://www.epravda.com.ua/news/2022/11/21/694084/

[869] Cyberprotection of the energy sector: in 2022 bore than 1,5 million attacks on the industry were blocked. [online]. Available at: https://www.mev.gov.ua/novyna/kiberzakhyst-enerhosektoru-u-2022-rotsi-zablokovano-ponad-15-mln-sprob-atakuvaty-haluz

[870] YERMENCHUK, O. Normative and legal regulation of the procedure of the objects of critical infrastructure detection at the strategic level of the normative legal regulation as the guarantee for the organization of their effective protection. *Bulletin of the Ministry of Justice of Ukraine.* 2019/1, no 6, pp. 37–41.

[871] YERMENCHUK, O. The main approaches to the organization of the critical infrastructure protection in the countries of Europe: an experience for Ukraine: a monograph. *Dnipro State University of Internal Affairs*. 2018, 180 p.

development of the legislation of Ukraine in the field of cybersecurity, detected the main problems, and defined the perspectives for the enhancement of Ukrainian legislation in this field, including the ways of the adaptation of the legislation of Ukraine to the EU legislation in frames of the realization of the EU-Ukraine Association Agreement[872]. An analysis of the certain organizational and legal aspects of the protection of the critical infrastructure was presented in the analytical report prepared by the researchers of the National Institute for Strategic Development in 2019[873]. The characteristics of the development of the EU legislation in the field of protection of the critical infrastructure in the sphere of energy supply presented in this analytical report is of high interest in the light of the present research. Gankevych, K., Levchuk, V., Korolyov, S. analyzed the development of the critical infrastructure in the system of the Ministry of Defense of Ukraine[874]. Experience of the USA, the UK, and Poland in the field of cybersecurity of the critical infrastructure was analyzed by Pyadyshev, V.[875] The cybersecurity of the energy sector was specifically targeted in the research conducted by Stezhko, S., Fitsa, V.[876] However, organizational and legal issues of the cybersecurity in the energy sector have not been deeply explored yet.

In the recent years, the legislation in the EU Member States and in Ukraine in the field of cybersecurity protection in general and in the fuel and energy complex in particular was changed; new threats appeared. Public administration needs a comprehensive theoretically proven solutions in order to elaborate the adequate responses.

Therefore, it is planned to analyse the EU legislation regarding the cybersecurity protection in the field of the energy sector, best practices on cybersecurity strategies in the energy sector from certain EU Member States, the recent developments of Ukrainian legislation in the field, and elaborate the recommendations regarding improvement of organizational and legal mechanisms of cybersecurity protection of consumers in the energy sector.

---

[872] BAKALINSKA, O., BAKALINSKY, O. The Legal encouragement of the cyber security in Ukraine. *Administrative Law and Process*. 9/2019, pp. 100–108.

[873] BOBRO, D. et al. Organizational and legal aspects of the encouragement of security and stability of the critical infrastructure of Ukraine: analytical report. K., *НІСД*, 2019, 224 p.

[874] GANKEVYCH, K., LEVCHUK, V., KOROLYOV, S. (2021). Critical Infrastructure Facilities of Ukraine in the System of the Ministry of Defense of Ukraine. Legal scientific electronic journal, 2021, №11, c. 79–82. [online]. Available at: http://www.lsej.org.ua/11_2021/17.pdf

[875] PYADYSHEV, V. Cyber Security of the Critical Infrastructures: Foreign Experience and Ukrainian realities. *Theoretical and practical aspects of the encouragement of the national security.* 4-2022, ч. 3, pp. 229–234.

[876] STEZHKO, S., FITSA, V. Cyber Security as an Important Factor for the encouragement of the Life Sustenance of the Domestic Energy Industry/. *Information and Law.* 2021, 4 (39), pp. 113–120.

For the purpose of this research a wide range of scientific methods was used. In particular, the dialectic method was used in order to analyse the development of the legislation in the field of the cybersecurity protection. The methods of the systematic and structural analysis were used for the purpose of the characteristics of the system of the public administration entities in the field of the cyber protection in the energy sector. The method of comparative legal research enabled to detect the best practices of targeting the energy sector peculiarities in the cybersecurity strategies of the EU Member States.

2. Cyber security in the energy sector in the light of the EU legislation and functions of energy regulatory authorities

2.1 The EU legislative requirements and the EU Member States strategic documents on cybersecurity in the energy sector

Digitalisation of the energy sector is one of the key directions of the EU energy policy. The encouragement of cybersecurity refers to the most important tasks of the EU institutions.

At the EU level, relations in the field of cybersecurity in the energy sector are regulated by legal acts on the protection of the critical infrastructure, on cybersecurity, and special acts of the EU energy legislation.

One of the first strategic documents related to the protection of the critical infrastructure is the Green Paper on a European Programme for Critical Infrastructure Protection of 17. 11. 2005[877]. The energy sector is included in the list of the critical infrastructure sectors in this document. In 2008, Council Directive 2008/114/EC of 8 December 2008 on the identification and designation of European critical infrastructures and the assessment of the need to improve their protection[878] was approved. It should be noticed that the energy sector (electricity, oil, and gas) is in the focus of this Directive.

In 2013, the Cybersecurity Strategy of the European Union: An Open, Safe and Secure Cyberspace[879] was announced. The energy sector belongs to the key sectors in the light of cybersecurity issues according to this act.

[877] Green Paper on a European Programme for Critical Infrastructure Protection of 17. 11. 2005. [online]. Available at: https://eur-lex.europa.eu/legal-content/EN/TXT/PDF/?uri=CELEX:52005DC0576

[878] Council Directive 2008/114/EC of 8 December 2008 on the identification and designation of European critical infrastructures and the assessment of the need to improve their protection. OJ L 345, 23. 12. 2008, pp. 75–82.

[879] Joint Communication of the European Commission and the High Representative of the Union for Foreign Affairs and Security Policy to the European Parliament, the Council, the European

In 2017, the Joint Communication of Cybersecurity[880] was presented. It stresses the importance of sector specific considerations and requirements at EU level, including in the energy sector.

On 16 December 2020, the European Commission and the High Representative of the Union for Foreign Affairs and Security Policy presented a new EU Cybersecurity Strategy[881]. In this Strategy, the energy sector again is among the key sectors that require cybersecurity protection measures. The importance of cybersecurity protection in frames of transition to cleaner energy under the European Green Deal through cross-border grids and smart meters and avoiding unnecessary duplication of data storage is specifically targeted. Energy technologies embedding digital components and the security of the associated supply chains are important for the continuity of essential services and for the strategic control of critical energy infrastructure. The Commission will therefore propose measures, including a "network code" setting rules for cybersecurity in cross-border electricity flows for adoption by end 2022. The main emphasis is made on cybersecurity of electricity grids in this Strategy.

The Regulation (EU) 2019/881 of the European Parliament and of the Council of 17 April 2019 on ENISA and on information and communication technology cybersecurity certification and repealing Regulation (EU) No 526/2013 (Cybersecurity Act)[882] that establishes a European cybersecurity framework for the certification of products, processes and services that will be valid throughout the Union covers also the energy sector.

The energy sector is one of the strategic sectors in frames of the Directive (EU) 2016/1148 of the European Parliament and of the Council of 6 July 2016 concerning measures for a high common level of security (NIS 1). According to Art. 7 of this Directive the EU Member States shall approve the National strategy on the security of network and information systems. This Directive will be repealed with effect from 18 Oct. 2024 by Directive (EU) 2022/2555

Economic and Social Committee and the Committee of the regions. Cybersecurity Strategy of the European Union: An Open, Safe and Secure Cyberspace of 7. 2. 2013. [online]. Available at: https://eur-lex.europa.eu/legal-content/EN/TXT/PDF/?uri=CELEX:52013JC0001

[880] Joint Communication to the European Parliament and the Council: Resilience, Deterrence and Defense: Building strong cybersecurity for the EU. 13. 9. 2017. [online]. Available at: https://eur-lex.europa.eu/legal-content/en/TXT/?uri=CELEX:52017JC0450

[881] Joint Communication of the European Commission and the High Representative of the Union for Foreign Affairs and Security Policy to the European Parliament and the Council. The EU's Cybersecurity Strategy for the Digital Decade of 16. 12. 2020. [online]. Available at: https://digital-strategy.ec.europa.eu/en/library/eus-cybersecurity-strategy-digital-decade-0

[882] Regulation (EU) 2019/881 of the European Parliament and of the Council of 17 April 2019 on ENISA (the European Union Agency for Cybersecurity) and on information and communication technology cybersecurity certification and repealing Regulation (EU) No 526/2013 (Cybersecurity Act). OJ L 151, 7. 6. 2019, pp. 15–69.

of the European Parliament and of the Council of 14 Dec. 2022 on measures for a high common level of cybersecurity across the Union, amending Regulation (EU) No 910/2014 and Directive (EU) 2018/1972, and repealing Directive (EU) 2016/1148 (NIS 2). According to this Directive (in particular, Article 7) the EU Member States shall adopt the National cybersecurity strategy, which means a coherent framework of a Member State providing strategic objectives, priorities, the resources required to achieve those objectives, and appropriate policy and regulatory measures in the area of cybersecurity and the governance with the view to achieving and maintaining a high level of cybersecurity in that Member State.

It should be noticed that the energy sector is addressed by both Directives, however, the NIS-2 covers more subsectors (please see in the table below):

Table 1. The energy sector under the NIS 1 and NIS2

NIS 1	NIS 2
electricity	electricity
oil	oil
gas	gas
	district heating and cooling
	hydrogen

As was noticed by specialists, several EU Member States have already identified operators of essential services beyond the scope of the NIS 1, "including undertakings in thermal industry, heat supply, mining, radioactive waste management as well as supply of research equipment and services to the energy sector"[883].

Bases on the analysis of the cybersecurity strategies of the EU Member States the following approaches to targeting the energy sector are selected: special provisions related to the energy sector are included; the energy sector has been mentioned among the critical infrastructure objects; critical infrastructure and essential services provision are targeted in general (without specification of industries, including the energy sector). The second approach is the most popular (please see in the table below):

[883] Bird&Bird. *NIS Directive and the energy sector: a patchwork of national implementations.* [online]. Available at: https://www.twobirds.com/en/insights/2020/global/nis-directive-and-the-energy-sector-a-patchwork-of-national-implementations

Table 2. The energy sector in the focus of the Cyber Security Strategies of the EU Member States and the UK[884]

Energy sector is specifically targeted	Energy sector is mostly mentioned within the critical infrastructure objects	Critical infrastructure and essential services provision are targeted in general
Germany	Latvia	Czech Republic
Sweden	Lithuania	Slovakia
Estonia	Finland	Netherlands
UK (still an EU member at the time of NIS implementation)	Belgium	Croatia
	Bulgaria	France
	Denmark	Portugal
	Luxembourg	Spain
	Poland	Malta
	Slovenia	Iceland
	Ireland	
	Switzerland	
	Italy	
	Austria	
	Finland	
	Norway	

Energy sector has been specifically targeted in the Cybersecurity Strategy of Germany of 2021. Electricity supply is mentioned among the critical infrastructures that are essential for private, economic and public life and are significantly dependent on IT infrastructure and its cyber protection. According to this Strategy the PKI for smart metering, as a key infrastructure component for digitalising the energy transformation, will be operated successfully for growing user numbers. It is also stated that the Federal Ministry for Economic Affairs and Energy/BSI roadmap for developing technical cornerstones for the areas of application smart grid (controlled consumption and production facilities), smart mobility (integration of the charging infrastructure of electric vehicles), and smart/sub metering

[884] The information is based on the analysis of the Cybersecurity Strategies presented on the web page of ENISA Available at: https://www.enisa.europa.eu/topics/national-cyber-security-strategies

(cross-sector measurement for electricity, gas, water, and heating or heat) has been implemented through several standardisation projects.[885]

The energy sector has been mentioned as one of the key objects for the cyberattacks in the Cybersecurity Strategy of Estonia for 2019–2022 It is stressed that the specialists being hired must ideally get their specialized cyber skills from formal education (e.g., energy and communication engineers, healthcare professionals and others)[886].

National Cybersecurity Strategy of Sweden stresses that electricity distribution is based on digital information and control systems that continuously handle large quantities of sensitive information in order to control. It is stated in the Strategy that both the report on Cybersecurity in Sweden and the report on a new Protective Security Act stress the critical infrastructures' dependence on industrial information and control systems and the importance of maintaining a strong national expertise in the area of control systems. Concerning the control systems, the importance of preventive work and of management of disruptions for central societal functions, including the electricity supply, is emphasized[887].

The energy sector has been specifically targeted in the National Cybersecurity Strategy of the United Kingdom for 2016–2021. It is stressed that the energy sector is among the key objects for cyber-attacks. The Ukrainian case (cyber-attack on western Ukrainian electricity distribution company Prykarpattya Oblenergo and Kyiv Oblenergo on 23 December 2015) is mentioned in this Strategy. It is pointed out that this Ukraine incident is the first confirmed instance of a disruptive cyber-attack on an electricity network. It is concluded that the UK shall be ready to prevent similar incidents occurring in the UK. The "rapid implementation of connectivity in industrial control processes in critical systems, across a wide range of industries such as energy, mining, agriculture and aviation, has created the Industrial Internet of Things. This is simultaneously opening up the possibility of devices and processes, which were never vulnerable to such interference in the past, being hacked and tampered with, with potentially disastrous consequences"[888].

[885] Federal Ministry of the Interior, Building and Community. Cyber Security Strategy for Germany 2021. [online]. Available at: https://www.bmi.bund.de/SharedDocs/downloads/EN/themen/it-digital-policy/cyber-security-strategy-for-germany2021.pdf;jsessionid=D19AB68CB792BAC36AD2A28598363958.1_cid364?__blob=publicationFile&v=4

[886] Cyber Security Strategy. Rebuplic of Estonia. [online]. Available at: https://webcache.googleusercontent.com/search?q=cache:pleeSu2Zc9cJ:https://www.mkm.ee/media/703/download&cd=1&hl=uk&ct=clnk&gl=sk

[887] Government offices of Sweden. Ministry of Justice. A National Cyber Security Strategy 2016. [online]. Available at: https://www.enisa.europa.eu/topics/national-cyber-security-strategies/ncss-map/national-cyber-security-strategies-interactive-map?selected=Sweden

[888] HM Government. National Cyber Security Strategy 2016–2021. [online]. Available at: https://www.enisa.europa.eu/topics/national-cyber-security-strategies/ncss-map/national-cyber-security-strategies-interactive-map?selected=United%20Kingdom

The National Cybersecurity Centre (NCSC) launched on 1 October 2016. It is continuing to provide expert sectoral advice to Government and critical sectors like energy, and providing cybersecurity advice across the UK. Also, special attention is paid to the development of the long-term skills strategy. This includes, in particular, creating higher and degree-level apprenticeships, in particular, within the energy sector, to address skills gaps in essential areas[889].

Considering that cyber security strategies target the complex aspects of cyber security protection mechanisms in different EU Member States they are subject to analysis by representatives of different fields of science. In particular, Tvaronavičienė, M., Plėta, T., Silvia Della Casa, S., Juozas Latvys, J. evaluated the national cyber security strategies of the UK, the USA, France, Estonia and Lithuania for their managerial solutions in terms of critical energy infrastructure[890]. Interdisciplinary approach is necessary to elaborate the effective mechanisms for cyber security protection of the critical infrastructure of the energy sector.

Cybersecurity issues are targeted in the EU special energy legislation. In particular, the Energy Efficiency Directive[891] requests that the EU Member States shall fully explore the potential for energy savings through the use of smart technologies and processes (p. 22 of the preamble to this Directive). According to the Directive, the EU Member States shall promote cybersecurity and ensure the privacy and data protection of final users in accordance with applicable Union Law (Art. 10a, part 2, "d").

Special requirements on cybersecurity protection of data in the energy market are included in the Electricity Directive[892]. This Directive stresses the importance of ensuring the highest level of cybersecurity and data protection (para 57 of the preamble). Member States shall install smart metering systems following the legislative requirements on the security of the smart metering systems and data communication, "having due regard of the best available techniques for ensuring the highest level of cybersecurity protection while bearing in mind the costs and the principle of proportionality" (p. "b", Art. 20 of the Directive).

[889] HM Government. National Cyber Security Strategy 2016–2021. [online]. Available at: https://www.enisa.europa.eu/topics/national-cyber-security-strategies/ncss-map/national-cyber-security-strategies-interactive-map?selected=United%20Kingdom

[890] Manuela Tvaronavičienė, Tomas Plėta, Silvia Della Casa, Juozas Latvys. Cyber security management of critical energy infrastructure in national cybersecurity strategies: cases of USA, UK, France, Estonia and Lithuania. *Insights into Regional Development*. 2020, 2 (4), pp. 802–813. [online]. Available at: https://hal.science/hal-03298796

[891] Directive 2018/2022 of the European Parliament and the Council of 11 December 2018 amending Directive 2012/27/EU on energy efficiency. OJL 328, 21. 12. 2018, pp. 210–230.

[892] Directive 2019/944 of the European Parliament and of the Council of 5 June 2019 on Common Rules for the Internal Market for Electricity and Amending Directive 2012/27/EU (recast) OJ L 158, 14. 6. 2019, pp. 125–199.

Also, the privacy of final customers and the protection of their data shall comply with relevant Union data protection and privacy rules (p. "c", Article 20 of the Directive). According to Art. 40 of the Electricity Directive cybersecurity and data protection belong to the main tasks of the transmission system operators. In Annex II to this Directive it is stated that the Member States shall ensure the deployment of smart metering systems in their territories that may be subject to an economic assessment of all of the long-term costs and benefits to the market and the individual consumer or which form of smart metering is economically reasonable and cost-effective and which time frame is feasible for their distribution. Such assessment shall take into consideration, in particular, the best available techniques for ensuring the highest level of cybersecurity and data protection.

According to Art. 30 (p. 2, "n") of Regulation (EU) 2019/943 of the European Parliament and of the Council of 5 June 2019 on the internal market for electricity[893] the ENTSO for Electricity (the European Network of Transmission System Operators for Electricity) shall promote cybersecurity and data protection in cooperation with relevant authorities and related entities. As referred to in Art. 55 of this Regulation, supporting the development of data management, cybersecurity and data protection in cooperation with relevant authorities and regulated entities belongs to the tasks of the entity of distribution system operators in the Union (EU DSO entity) (p. 1, "e", Article 55). Important provisions related to cybersecurity are included in Art. 59, para 2 (e) of this Regulation. It is stated that the Commission is empowered to adopt network code on sector-specific rules for cybersecurity aspects of cross-border electricity flows, including rules on common minimum requirements, planning, monitoring, reporting and crisis management.

It should be noticed that the Gas Directive[894] lacks such provisions on cybersecurity and data protection, despite the recommendations to Member States (their regulatory authorities) to introduce intelligent metering systems or smart grids (p. 8, Article 3). The legal acts on the regulation of security of supply in the electricity and natural gas sectors – Regulation (EU) 2019/941 of the European Parliament and of the Council of 5 June 2019 on risk-preparedness in the electricity sector[895] and repealing Directive 2005/89/EC and Regulation (EU) 2017/1938 of the European Parliament and of the Council of 25 October 2017 concerning measures to safeguard the security of gas supply and repealing Regulation (EU)

[893] Regulation (EU) 2019/943 of the European Parliament and of the Council of 5 June 2019 on the internal market for electricity. OJ L 158, 14. 6. 2019, pp. 54–124.

[894] Directive 2009/73/EC of the European Parliament and the Council of 13 July 2009 concerning common rules for the internal market in natural gas and repealing Directive 2003/55/EC. OJL 211, 14. 8. 2009, pp. 94–136.

[895] Regulation (EU) 2019/941 of the European Parliament and of the Council of 5 June 2019 on risk-preparedness in the electricity sector. OJ L 158, 14. 6. 2019, pp. 1–21.

No994/2010[896] – define the cyber-attacks among the key technological risks for the regulated sectors.

As to the risks for the electricity supply it is stressed that the cyberattacks may affect entire regions at the same time (p. 2 of the Preamble to the Regulation 2019/941 mentioned above). Regulation 2019/941 complements Directive (EU) 2016/941 by ensuring that cyber-incidents are properly identified as a risk, and that the measures taken to address them are properly-reflected in the risk-preparedness plans.

The European Commission in its Recommendation (EU) 2019/553 of 3 April 2019 on cybersecurity in the energy sector[897] aims at helping stakeholders keep in mind the specific requirements of the energy sector when implementing internationally recognised cybersecurity standards. The European Commission suggests the EU Member States to include the recommendations into their national cybersecurity framework via strategies, laws, regulations and other administrative provisions.

Thus, at the EU level, the cyber security issues in the energy complex are subject to strategic documents, regulations, directives and recommendations both related to the cyber security and critical infrastructure, and special energy legislation. EU Member States, based on EU legislative requirements, adopt and periodically review the cyber security strategies applicable to the energy sector in particular. Preventive control measures and development of cyber security skills among of employees and public officials are among the most common measures related to the cyber security issues in the energy sector.

2.2 Cybersecurity in the focus of the EU and EU Member States energy regulatory authorities

The European Union Agency for Cooperation of Energy Regulators (ACER) makes its input into encouragement of the cyber security in the European Union via providing the advises on EU legislative requirements, sharing information among national energy regulatory authorities and capacity building, and collaboration with the EU and international organizations on the cyber security issues[898].

[896] Regulation (EU) 2017/1938 of the European Parliament and of the Council of 25 October 2017 concerning measures to safeguard the security of gas supply and repealing Regulation (EU) No994/2010. OJ L 280, 28. 10. 2017, pp. 1–56.

[897] Recommendation (EU) 2019/553 of 3 April 2019 on cybersecurity in the energy sector. OJ L 96, 5. 4. 2019, pp. 50–54. [online]. Available at: https://eur-lex.europa.eu/legal-content/EN/TXT/PDF/?uri=CELEX:32019H0553

[898] ACER and Cybersecurity. [online]. Available at: https://www.acer.europa.eu/electricity/about-electricity/clean-energy-package/acer-and-cybersecurity

Pursuant to mentioned above Article 59, paragraph 2(e) of Regulation (EU) 2019/943 of the European Parliament and of the Council of 5 June 2019 on the internal market for electricity, the ACER adopted in 2021 Framework Guideline on sector-specific rules for cybersecurity aspects of crossborder electricity flows[899]. This is a document of a non-binding character that defines the core principles for future legally binding Cybersecurity Network Code. The Framework Guideline covers governance, cross-border risk assessment and management, a common electricity cybersecurity framework, information sharing and essential information flows, incident handling and crisis management (including data collection), and electricity cybersecurity exercise framework, protection of information exchange in the context of data processing, monitoring, benchmarking and reporting[900]. The drafting procedure on the Cybersecurity Network Code was started in July 2021 by ENTSO-E[901] and EU DSO[902] Entity. The ACER revised draft Code based on Framework Guideline and submitted the revised draft to the European Commission on 14 July 2022[903]. The European Commission shall review the draft Code and initiate its procedure for the adoption. When adopted by Member States, it becomes legally binding across the EU[904].

Starting from 2015, ACER and national energy regulatory authorities cooperate and exchange the information within a cybersecurity task force co-chaired by ACER and CEER[905]. In particular, they cooperate on such issues as cybersecurity preparedness, response, recovery planning, and regulatory approaches to drive prudent risk reduction effort. They share resources, reports and recommendations. This task force, together with CEER training courses help ongoing capacity building with the aim to prevent, detect, respond, and recover from cyberattacks[906].

[899] Framework Guideline on sector-specific rules for cybersecurity aspects of crossborder electricity flows of 22 July 2021. [online]. Available at: https://acer.europa.eu/Official_documents/Acts_of_the_Agency/Framework_Guidelines/Framework%20Guidelines/Framework%20Guideline%20on%20Sector-Specific%20Rules%20for%20Cybersecurity%20Aspects%20of%20Cross-Border%20Electricity%20Flows_210722.pdf

[900] ACER and Cybersecurity. [online]. Available at: https://www.acer.europa.eu/electricity/about-electricity/clean-energy-package/acer-and-cybersecurity

[901] ENTSO-E – European association for the cooperation of transmission system operators. [online]. Available at: http://entsoe.eu

[902] EU DSO Entity – the Association for all sizes of Distribution System Operators in Europe. [online]. Available at: http://eudsoentity.eu

[903] Network Code on sector-specific rules for cybersecurity aspects of crossborder electricity flows (NCCS) July 6, 2022 –V2.3. [online]. Available at: https://www.acer.europa.eu/Recommendations/Revised%20Network%20Code%20on%20Cybersecurity%20(NCCS)_1.pdf

[904] ACER submits to the European Commission the revised Network Code on electricity cybersecurity. 14 July 2022. [online]. Available at: https://acer.europa.eu/news-and-events/news/acer-submits-european-commission-revised-network-code-electricity-cybersecurity

[905] CEER – Council of European Energy Regulators. [online]. Available at: https://www.ceer.eu

[906] ACER and Cybersecurity. [online]. Available at: https://www.acer.europa.eu/electricity/about-electricity/clean-energy-package/acer-and-cybersecurity

Since 2016, the CEER has arranged an annual training on cybersecurity for national energy regulatory authorities that aim not only on obtaining the knowledge on cyber security issues and solution and their role, but also to provide a platform for connection and establishment of useful relationship between national regulatory authorities' staff[907].

The importance of the cooperation of the ACER and energy regulators with the experts from the USA institutions, such as NERC[908], EPRI[909] and NARUC[910] shall be emphasized. Such cooperation aims at sharing expertise and experience on issues such as standards, strategy and prudency of investment. In particular, after the cyberattacks on the energy infrastructure in Ukraine in 2015, the NARUC and the USAID[911] launched the Europe and Eurasia Energy Sector Cybersecurity Initiative (ESCI) aimed at helping tackling cyberthreats via building resilience and expertise within energy regulators in the Black Sea region and beyond. Within this project, in particular, taking into consideration the USA best practices the work began in form of assisting national energy regulatory agencies in such countries as Armenia, Georgia, Moldova, and Ukraine in drafting the strategic documents on the cybersecurity for such authorities. It was stressed that despite the fact that energy regulators are not at the frontline of the tackling the cybersecurity issues in the energy sector, *"but the leadership and vision they articulate in a strategy are essential first steps to safeguarding the energy sector from cybersecurity threats"*[912]. Such document can emphasize the importance of cybersecurity issues for energy sector companies, public officials, inform that cybersecurity-related costs (e.g., training, infrastructure, staff) are acceptable, initiate a communication between all stakeholders regarding the readiness of the energy sector to new cyberthreats and to eliminate its vulnerabilities[913].

---

907 CEER. Training on Cybersecurity: Risk Management and Preparedness, Legal and Policy Developments. 31 May–2 June 2022. [online]. Available at: https://www.ceer.eu/training-on-cybersecurity-risk-management-and-preparedness-legal-and-policy-developments

908 NERC – the North American Electric Reliability Corporation. [online]. Available at: https://www.nerc.com/AboutNERC/Pages/default.aspx

909 EPRI – Electric Power Research Institute. [online]. Available at: https://www.epri.com/

910 NARUC – National Association of Regulatory Utility Commissioners. [online]. Available at: https://www.naruc.org/

911 USAID – United States Agency for International Development. [online]. Available at: https://www.usaid.gov/

912 NARUC. The Regulatory Cybersecurity Strategy: a Key Building Block for an Energy Sector's Cybersecurity Policy Framework. October, 2018. [online]. Available at: https://www.naruc.org/international/news/the-regulatory-cybersecurity-strategy-a-key-building-block-for-an-energy-sector-s-cybersecurity-policy-framework/

913 NARUC. The Regulatory Cybersecurity Strategy: a Key Building Block for an Energy Sector's Cybersecurity Policy Framework. October, 2018. [online]. Available at: https://www.naruc.org/international/news/the-regulatory-cybersecurity-strategy-a-key-building-block-for-an-energy-sector-s-cybersecurity-policy-framework/

European energy regulators contribute to the cybersecurity issues via different instruments. As presented in CEER's report on Europe's Electricity and Gas Sectors[914], national regulatory authorities (NRA) in the EU Member States, in particular, decide upon the acceptability of cybersecurity costs, manage threats to security of supply (e.g., Austrian E-Control), set out a catalogue of obligations for OES referring to cybersecurity (e.g., German regulator Bundesnetzagentur – BNetzA). Moreover, in some EU Member States (e.g., ILR in Luxembourg) the energy NRA was designated as the national competent authority and single contact point under the NIS Directive.

The UK energy regulator Ofgem approved the NIS Guidance for Downstream Gas and Electricity Operators of Essential Services in Great Britain (v. 2.0 published on 1st of April 2022)[915]. This Guidance aims at outlining the Ofgem's expectations for the operators of essential services, and it underpins the collaborative engagement approach sought between the Ofgem and operators of essential services community to ensure compliance with the NIS Regulations. Operators of essential services should engage with the Ofgem when interpreting this Guidance to seek clarifications and support where needed (p. 1.6. of this Guidance). According to page 1.4. of this Guidance operators of essential services have a duty to notify Ofgem as the designated competent authority in writing about any incident which has a significant impact on the continuity of the essential service which the operator of essential services provides (a NIS Incident).

Therefore, national energy regulatory authorities in the EU can and should contribute a lot to the cyber security protection mechanism via different instruments, including strategic outlines, tariff regulation, cyber threats management, and even executing the powers of the competent authority and single contact point under the NIS Directive.

[914] CEER. Cyber Security Work Stream. Cybersecurity Report on Europe's Electricity and Gas Sectors (26 October 2018). [online]. Available at: https://www.ceer.eu/cybersecurity-report-on-europe-s-electricity-and-gas-sectors

[915] NIS Guidance for Downstream Gas and Electricity Operators of Essential Services in Great Britain (v. 2.0 published on 1st of April 2022. [online]. Available at: https://www.ofgem.gov.uk/publications/nis-directive-and-nis-regulations-2018-ofgem-guidance-operators-essential-services

3. Ukrainian legislation and public administration in the field of cybersecurity and cyber protection in the energy sector

3.1 Ukrainian legislation in the field of cybersecurity of the energy sector

Ukraine, in frames of its obligations under the EU-Ukraine Association Agreement[916] and as a full-pledged member of the Energy Community[917] since February 2011, shall put its legislation on cybersecurity in the energy sector in accordance with the EU legislative requirements mentioned above. In the last years, Ukraine made significant steps in this direction. The development of legislative framework has been catalyzed because of the increase of the cyber threats in the conditions of the war started by the Russian Federation in Ukraine.

Strategic documents in Ukraine related to the cybersecurity in the energy sector include:

- National Security Strategy of Ukraine approved by Decree of the President of Ukraine of 14. 9. 2020 No 392/2020;
- Energy Strategy of Ukraine for the period until 2035 "Security, energy efficiency, and competitiveness (approved by CMU Regulation of 18 August 2017 No605-p) (replaced by the Energy Strategy of Ukraine for the period until 2050);
- Energy Strategy of Ukraine for the period until 2050 (approved by CMU Regulation of 21. 4. 2023 No373-p)[918];
- Cybersecurity Strategy of Ukraine approved by the Decision of the NSDCU of 14. 5. 2021 (entered into force by Decree of the President of Ukraine of 26. 8. 2021 No447/202);
- Draft Cybersecurity Strategy of Ukraine for the period until 2025 (approved by the working group under the National Cybersecurity Coordination Centre of the National Security and Defense Council of Ukraine).

The Concept on the Introduction of the "Smart Networks" in Ukraine until 2035 and the medium-term Action Plan in introduction of "smart networks" in Ukraine until 2035 are approved by CMU Regulation of 14 of October 2022 No 908-p.

[916] Association Agreement between the European Union and the European Atomic Energy Community and their Member States, of the one part, and Ukraine, of the other part OJ L 161, 29. 5. 2014, p. 3–2137.[online]. Available at: https://eur-lex.europa.eu/legal-content/EN/TXT/?uri=CELEX%3A02014A0529%2801%29-20230424

[917] Energy Community is an international organization aims at extending the EU internal energy market rules and principles to countries in South East Europe, the Black Sea region and beyond on the basis of a legally binding framework.

[918] The text of the Energy Strategy of Ukraine until the period of 2050 is not currently accessible for public (as of 28. 7. 2023).

There are general and special laws related to the cyber security in the energy sector of Ukraine. General laws include, in particular, the Law of Ukraine "On Framework for Internal and External Policy" of 1 July 2010 No2411-VI, the Law of Ukraine "On National Security of Ukraine" of 21 June 2018 № 2469-VIII. Law of Ukraine "On Critical Infrastructure" No 1882-IX of 16 November 2021 and the Law of Ukraine "On the Main Framework for the Encouragement of the Cybersecurity of Ukraine" of 5 October 2017 No 2163-VIII shall be considered as special ones.

Law of Ukraine "On Critical Infrastructure" regulates the relations in the field of functioning and protection of critical infrastructure in peace-time, whereas during the state of martial law that is currently in place in Ukraine the peculiarities of protection of critical infrastructure are regulated by the Law of Ukraine "On the State of Martial Law". As to the cyber protection of objects of critical infrastructure, the relations in this field shall be regulated by the law on cyber protection and cybersecurity (part 3, Art. 3 of the Law of Ukraine "On Critical Infrastructure"). Energy supply (including heating supply) is among vital functions and/or services which interruption leads to negative consequences for the national security of Ukraine.

Law of Ukraine "On the Main Framework for the Encouragement of the Cybersecurity of Ukraine" is a special Law of Ukraine in the field of cybersecurity. This Law does target the energy sector among other sectors of critical infrastructure.

Special provisions devoted to the encouragement of the cybersecurity in the energy sector related to the introduction of the smart grids are included in Law of Ukraine "On Energy Efficiency" of 21 of October 2021 No1818-IX.

Based on the laws mentioned above the CMU, Minenergo, and the State Service of Special Communications and Information Protection of Ukraine approved a significant number of regulations on different procedures in the field of cybersecurity of critical infrastructure, including the energy sector. In particular, the CMU approved the General requirements on the Cyber Protection of the Objects of Critical Infrastructure (Regulation of 19 June 2019 No518), as well as the Regulations on the organizational and technical model of cybersecurity (CMU Regulation of 29. 12. 2021 No1426). Based on these requirements, the Minenergo approved the Requirements on the Cybersecurity of the Fuel and Energy Sector of the Critical Infrastructure (Order of the Minenergo of 15 December 2022 No 417).

3.2 Public administration entities in the field of energy cybersecurity in the energy sector of Ukraine

The realization of the cyber policy in the energy sector requires the efficient system of public administration. In Ukraine, the organization of the realization and/or realization of this policy is performed by general authorities (like the President of Ukraine, CMU, local public administrations, self-government authorities) and special public administration entities (authorities specialized in cyber security protection – State Service of Special Communications and Information Protection of Ukraine, the authorities specialized in the field of national security and defence, like NSDCU, SSU, and sectoral authorities, like industrial ministries (Minenergo, Ministry for Infrastructure), NEURC and SAEE.

The State Service of Special Communications and Information Protection of Ukraine is a state authority responsible for the development and realization of the state policy in the fields of cyber protection of critical information infrastructure (Art. 22 of the Law of Ukraine "On National Security of Ukraine"). During the state of martial law and 12 months after its termination or annulation it also executes powers of the responsible authority in the field of protection of critical infrastructure of Ukraine stipulated by the Law of Ukraine "On Critical Infrastructure". The Minenergo is a special body in the field of critical infrastructure protection of the fuel and energy complex of Ukraine.

It should be noticed that the legislative provisions regarding the powers of special authorities in the field of energy sector sometimes are not clear and require improvement. In particular, According to the Law of Ukraine "On Energy Efficiency" the Concept on the Introduction of the "Smart Networks" in Ukraine and the medium-term Action Plan in introduction of "smart networks" in Ukraine are developed by the central body of executive power responsible for the development of the state policy in the field of efficient use of fuel and energy resources, energy savings, renewable energy sources and alternative types of fuel. Previously these functions were performed by the Minenergo; however, according to Regulation of the CMU "On certain issues of optimization of the activity of the central bodies of executive power in the field of energy efficiency" of 14 February 2023 No153 they are distributed between two ministries: the Minenergo is responsible for the development of the state policy in the field of renewable energy sources and alternative types of gas fuel, whereas the functions of the development of the state policy in the field of efficient use of fuel and energy resources, energy efficiency and energy savings, and alternative types of liquid and solid fuel were transferred to the Ministry of Infrastructure. The Ministry of Infrastructure also obtained the functions of the realization of the state policy in the field of efficient use of fuel and energy resources, alternative types of liquid and solid fuel, and energy savings. However, these functions are also performed by another central body of executive power – SAEE according to CMU Regulation of 26 November 2014, No 676. Such legislative changes can cause the conflict of powers between above mentioned authorities and need to be revised and improved.

The next issue related to the powers of the NEURC in the field of energy cybersecurity. The Law of Ukraine "On National Energy and Utility Regulatory Commission" does not include special provisions regarding the powers of the energy regulator in the field of cyber security. Only in the Law of Ukraine "On Energy Efficiency" it is stated that the NEURC in frames of its competence encourages the promotion of the introduction of "smart networks" via the system of economic stimulation for the electricity transmission system operators. The introduction of "smart networks" is conducted with the consideration of the Concept on the Introduction of the "Smart Networks" in Ukraine and the medium-term Action Plan in introduction of "smart networks" in Ukraine. Certain provisions regarding the cyber security are included in the Transmission System Code approved by Regulation of the NEURC of 14. 3. 2018 No309. Taking into consideration the experience of the EU Member States, the best practice of the USA regarding the role of the energy regulators in the field of energy cyber security it is recommended to amend the Law of Ukraine "On NEURC" with provisions regarding the powers of NEURC in the field of cyber security protection and to develop the regulatory cyber security strategy in the energy sector of Ukraine.

4. Conclusion

Based on the analysis conducted, in particular, the following conclusions have been made and the following recommendations have been developed.

1. In the recent years, digitalisation became one of the trends in the development of the energy sector in many countries, including the EU Member States, that brought both benefits and challenges. Cybersecurity threats are among the most dangerous ones that lead to arbitrary disconnections of energy services supply and cause significant problems for citizens, economic entities, and the state. Therefore, the adequate organizational and legal mechanism of the cybersecurity in the energy sector introduced on the basis of scientifically proven concept is requested.
2. Cybersecurity policy in the energy sector is based on the following directions of the public policy – energy policy and cybersecurity policy. The energy sector belongs to the critical infrastructure that require special protection in frames of the national security.

3. The issues on cybersecurity in the energy sector shall reflected in such strategic acts at the national level as National Security Strategy, National Cybersecurity Strategy, National Energy Strategy, and the National Security Strategy in the Energy Sector. The energy sector shall be specifically targeted in the national cybersecurity strategy (including the definition of the key threats and the possible solutions). The cybersecurity issues shall be targeted in the energy strategy (with targets, solutions, and distribution of responsibilities among public administration entities and regulated companies across the sectors). The importance of the special strategic document on cyber security in the energy sector in frames of emergency situations, including armed conflicts is vital.
4. In the recent years, legislation on cybersecurity in the energy sector was significantly developed at the EU level and in the EU Member States. These processes have been accelerated due to the increase of the cyberthreats in the conditions of the war in Ukraine started by the Russian Federation. The legal framework in this field consists of strategic documents, regulations, directives and recommendations on cybersecurity in general and in the sectors of critical infrastructure in particular (including the energy sector). Special provisions on the cybersecurity are included in the energy legislation as well. EU Member States, bases on EU legislative requirements, adopt and periodically review the cyber security strategies applicable to the energy sector in particular. Preventive control measures and development of cyber security skills among of employees and public officials are among the most common measures related to the cyber security issues in the energy sector.
5. In Ukraine, the development of organizational and legal mechanisms of the cyber protection of the critical infrastructure of the energy sector has been intensified in the recent years. The main laws and regulations in the field have been approved. They shall be subject to periodical review on their performance (effectiveness).
6. The efficiency of cybersecurity protection in the energy sector depends on the adequate public administration. Currently, there are many public administration entities that have powers in the realization of the cyber security policy in the energy sector, both intersectoral and sectoral. Their powers stipulated by different laws and regulations approved in the recent years. The adequate distribution of powers between sectoral authorities in the energy sector is necessary. National energy regulatory authorities in the EU can and should contribute a lot to the cyber security protection mechanism via different instruments, including strategic outlines, tariff regulation, cyber threats management, and even executing the powers of the competent authority and single contact point under the NIS Directive. Regulatory cybersecurity strategy in the energy sector is considered as a useful tool.

7. In Ukraine, the distribution of powers between sectoral bodies in the energy sector (including the issues of cybersecurity) have been recently changed. The legislative provisions shall be revised in order to exclude risks of the conflict of powers and to encourage the adequate coordination between all public administration entities. The role of the energy regulator (NEURC) in the field of cybersecurity shall be strengthened.
8. Cybersecurity action plans in the energy sector shall include both preventive and management of disruptions solutions, efficient control measures, professional education and trainings on cybersecurity issues for the staff of energy public administration and energy companies and to elaborate the best solutions. Special attention shall be paid to the development of special skills of citizens on cybersecurity issues.
9. The cooperation between the public administration entities in the field of cybersecurity in the energy sector, both inside and outside the EU (e.g., UK, Ukraine, USA), as well as their cooperation with EU institutions (e.g., ENISA, ACER), European and international organizations (e.g., CEER, NARUC) in order to regular exchange the best practices (in particular, regarding the introduction of "smart networks") and elaborate the most appropriate solutions is crucial.
10. Public-private cooperation in the field of cyber security of the energy sector, involvement of civil society institutions in the decision-making processes in this field, the development of the system of independent audit of cybersecurity of the energy sector, the role of energy regulators in the cyber security protection, liability for violations of legislative requirements in the field of cybersecurity of the energy sector are defined as priority directions for further research in this field.

CHAPTER EIGHTEEN

New Cybersecurity Rules for Markets in Crypto-Assets in the EU Law

BOHDAN STRILETS

1. Introduction

Considering digitalisation trends and subsequently occurring new threats for crypto-asset consumers' rights, the European Union (the EU) has to develop an ultimate approach to the crypto-economy in general and the cybersecurity on the cryptocurrency market in particular. The Article aims to analyze existing EU legislative acts and newest act proposals related to the cybersecurity on the cryptocurrency (crypto-asset) market. The contemporary practice and doctrinal views on the issue discussed are examined. Certain shortcomings in the existing legal approach to cybersecurity in the EU in general are identified. It is also revealed that in the current EU legislation there is an unreasonable lack of attention to cybersecurity of crypto-assets consumers and investors. Conclusions regarding possible pathways of improving legal regulation of cybersecurity for markets in crypto-assets in the EU are made.

The effective functioning of the internal market of the European Union (hereinafter referred to as the EU) is conditioned by a high level of economic, political and legal integration. In addition to the opportunity for EU Member States and citizens to use the advantages of the EU internal market, this actualizes the need for a more active joint response to today's challenges. The development of information and communication technologies (hereinafter referred to as ICT) and their penetration into private and public legal relations requires the creation of effective cybersecurity mechanisms. This relates to both everyday threats to individuals and global threats that could harm the EU's financial system. The first ones are related to the spread of fraudulent schemes of using ICT for profit. The second ones are real and potential global threats, which arose after the full-scale military aggression of the Russian Federation against Ukraine. The EU, not being formally a party to the armed conflict, has also become the victim of a criminal attack, at least in the cyber sphere. For example, the National Cyber Security Centre of

Lithuania recorded an increase in the number of DDoS attacks in its 2022 3rd quarter report. They were mainly aimed at government organizations, the banking system and the communication system. The provision of certain government and banking services was temporarily limited in connection with these attacks.[919] At the same time, the EU Member States have not yet reached a consensus on the definition of the concept of "cyberattack" and on whether the presence of physical damage is required for a cyber action to be classified as a cyberattack.[920] The complexity of unification in this area does not contribute to ensuring the rights and interests of participants in digital legal relations. In the context of the EU internal market's functioning, any security gaps can have uncontrollable cascading consequences. This especially applies to the financial sphere, which was emphasized by the European Systemic Risk Board (ESRB) back in 2020.[921]

The stability of the EU financial system is absolutely necessary for the proper functioning of the internal market. The markets in crypto-assets are gradually becoming its full-fledged component. It includes the emission of tokens, crypto-asset trading and exchange, P2P trading (trade between users without intermediaries), the operation of crypto exchanges and other platforms that allow the use of crypto-assets, the creation of stablecoins (crypto-assets tied to an asset with a stable price) for conducting settlements, etc. This digital market is becoming increasingly important in the global financial system and needs proper legal regulation.

Circulation and any use of crypto-assets is primarily based on distributed ledger and blockchain technologies. There is a widespread opinion among crypto-asset users about the high level of safety of these latest technologies. However, in a February 2021 report, The European Union Agency for Cybersecurity (hereinafter referred to as ENISA) noted that the hype around such technologies creates unrealistic expectations about what problems they can solve.[922] Indeed, these technologies cannot by themselves guarantee a safe cyber environment for economic activity and require additional institutional and legal guarantees from the EU. Moreover, while classic financial markets can somehow function

919 Regional Cyber Defence Centre. 3rd quarter report, 2022, p. 10. [online]. Available at: https://www.nksc.lt/doc/rkgc/CTAC_2022_3rd_Quarter_Report.pdf

920 OSULA, A-M., KASPER, A., KAJANDER, A. EU Common Position on International Law and Cyberspace. *Masaryk University Journal of Law and Technology*. 2022, vol. 16, p. 110. [online]. Available at: https://journals.muni.cz/mujlt/article/view/20668/16944

921 European Systemic Risk Board. Systemic cyber risk. Executive summary, 2020, p. 2. [online]. Available at: https://www.esrb.europa.eu/pub/pdf/reports/esrb.report200219_systemiccyberrisk~101a09685e.en.pdf

922 European Union Agency for Cybersecurity. Crypto Assets: Introduction to Digital Currencies and Distributed Ledger Technologies, 2021, p. 2. [online]. Available at: https://www.enisa.europa.eu/publications/crypto-assets-introduction-to-digital-currencies-and-distributed-ledger-technologies

outside the cyber environment, all forms of circulation of crypto-assets take place exclusively online. Therefore, with the gradual increase in the popularity of crypto-assets, the problem of guaranteeing the safety of their consumers and investors arises. Only the presence of mechanisms to protect this market from cyber threats can protect the EU financial system from the negative consequences of external interference.

In 2020, together with the submission to the European Parliament of the Proposal for a Regulation of the European Parliament and of the Council on Markets in Crypto-assets, and amending Directive (EU) 2019/1937 COM/2020/593 final[923] (hereinafter referred to as MiCA Regulation Proposal) the stage of systemic legal regulation of the circulation of cryptocurrencies in the EU began. However, it is far from the logical end, as the issues of ensuring cybersecurity and protecting the rights of consumers of services in markets in crypto-assets still remain open. Therefore, legal science cannot stop on the way of researching possible options for ensuring legal certainty of economic activity related to crypto-assets. The scientific community faces the task of finding the most acceptable models of legal and institutional guarantees of the rights and interests of crypto-assets' consumers and investors.

2. Current legal regulation of cryptocurrencies in the EU

The EU Member States are constantly working on the formation of a legal framework that would allow the state to control the legality of the use of crypto-assets and protect the rights of investors and other participants in legal relations. However, this does not contribute to the unification of legal regulation in different states.

For example, representatives of Federal Bank of Germany (Bundesbank) stated that cryptocurrencies cannot be classified as digital currency *("Digitalwährung")*, as they do not perform the function of currency and are not part of the financial system of the Federal Republic of Germany.[924] At the same time, the Resolution of the Italian Tax Service 72/E dated September 2, 2016 "Tax treatment applicable to companies providing services related to virtual currencies" defined that profits and losses arising from exchange transactions

[923] Proposal for a Regulation of the European Parliament and of the Council on Markets in Crypto-assets, and amending Directive (EU) 2019/1937, COM/2020/593 final. [online]. Available at: https://eur-lex.europa.eu/legal-content/EN/TXT/?uri=CELEX%3A52020PC0593

[924] HÖNIG, M. *Initial Coin Offering. Studie zu Kryptowährungen und der Blockchain-Technologie.* 2018, p. 11, 12. [online]. Available at: https://www.frankfurt-university.de/fileadmin/standard/Hochschule/Fachbereich_3/Kontakt/Professor_inn_en/Hoenig/20180502_Bitcoin_Studie_fra_uas_Hoenig_V1.0.pdf. (in German)

converting cryptocurrency to traditional currency and vice versa, are subject to corporate income tax.[925]

The EU law reacts to the modern challenges not as quickly as the national law of the Member States. However, only a unified legal regulation of crypto-assets at the EU level can eliminate the discrepancies between the national law of the Member States.[926] Elaborating uniform approaches in the EU legal order and common game rules for crypto-assets users is extremely important for ensuring the safe use of these assets. Changes in this direction have already begun.

The first attempt at legal regulation of decentralized financial activities with tokenized assets built on blockchain technology was the inclusion of the concept of virtual currencies, by which cryptocurrencies are actually meant, in the EU legislation. The corresponding changes were made by Directive (EU) 2018/843 of the European Parliament and of the Council of 30 May 2018 amending Directive (EU) 2015/849 on the prevention of the use of the financial system for the purposes of money laundering or terrorist financing, and amending Directives 2009/138/EC and 2013/36/EU[927] (hereinafter referred to as AMLD5). It was not about the adoption of a special act that would solve all urgent issues of cryptocurrencies' circulation. Nevertheless, AMLD5 was a step towards the harmonization and unification of the EU legislation in the field of cryptocurrencies. First, the Directive defined virtual currencies as a digital representation of value that is not issued or guaranteed by a central bank or a public authority, is not necessarily attached to a legally established currency and does not possess a legal status of currency or money, but is accepted by natural or legal persons as a means of exchange and which can be transferred, stored and traded electronically. Secondly, cryptocurrency exchanges were classified as "obliged entities", which are required to carry out comprehensive monitoring of customers and provide regulators with reports on suspicious activity.

As of the end of 2022, the aforementioned MiCA Regulation Proposal remains in the status of a draft with great prospects. We would like to draw attention to some long-awaited innovations that it brings to the EU legal field. The MiCA

[925] Risoluzione Ministeriale 72/E del 2 settembre 2016, Interpello ai sensi dell'art. 11, legge 27 luglio 2000, n. 212, Trattamento Fiscale Applicabile alle Societa che Svolgono Attivita di Servizi Relativi a Monete Virtuali. [online]. Available at: https://www.agenziaentrate.gov.it/portale/documents/20143/302984/Risoluzione+n.+72+del+02+settembre+2016_RISOLUZIONE+N.+72+DEL+02+SETTEMBRE+2016E.pdf/8e057611-819f-6c8de168-a1fb487468d6. (in Italian).

[926] STRILETS, B. Suchasnyi stan ta perspektyvy pravovoho rehuliuvannia kryptovaliut u Yevropeiskomu Soiuzi. *Aktualni problemy pravoznavstva.* 2022, no. 2 (30), p. 74. (in Ukrainian)

[927] Directive (EU) 2018/843 of the European Parliament and of the Council of 30 May 2018 amending Directive (EU) 2015/849 on the prevention of the use of the financial system for the purposes of money laundering or terrorist financing, and amending Directives 2009/138/EC and 2013/36/EU, OJ L 156, 19. 6. 2018, pp. 43–74. [online]. Available at: https://eur-lex.europa.eu/legal-content/EN/TXT/?uri=celex%3A32018L0843

Regulation Proposal sets requirements for all crypto-asset service providers, such as: an obligation to act honestly, fairly and professionally; organizational requirements; rules for ensuring customer safety. Requirements for specific services are established: storage of crypto-assets; trading platforms for crypto-assets; exchange of crypto-assets for fiat currency or other crypto-assets; execution of orders; reception and transmission of orders orders on behalf of third parties and even advising on crypto-assets.[928] This indicates that the MiCA Regulation Proposal should really become a revolutionary act that will provide legal certainty to a significant amount of economic legal relations (including but not limited to marketing communications regarding the offer of crypto-assets, issuance of crypto-assets, admission of crypto-assets to trading on special platforms, etc.). Further delay in its adoption may create obstacles in its future application.

It seems for us to be obvious that this proposal is not an ideal and universal means of solving all problems of legal regulation of markets in crypto-assets. When it comes to its shortcomings, one of them is that a significant part of tokenized assets are not subject to the MiCA Regulation Proposal. Also, in the proposal, there is almost no attention paid to the cybersecurity in markets in crypto-assets. This is a serious legal gap. The fact is that any crypto-asset exist thanks to blockchain technology. Blockchain is a distributed database or a publicly available ledger of transactions or electronic actions (events). Changes to this ledger are made based on the consensus of the majority of its participants. At the same time, any information that got into such a collection can no longer be removed from it.[929] Thus, crypto-assets exist exclusively in the cyber environment. However, they are able to be a reason of real legal relations and, in case of illegal interference in them, cause significant losses to market participants. Hence, the problem of theoretical understanding of cyber security in markets in crypto-assets and finding ways of its legal support at the EU level arises.

3. Theoretical aspects of cybersecurity with regards to crypto-assets

For a long time, the term "network and information security" rather than "cybersecurity" prevailed in the EU law. This found its vivid expression in the

[928] Proposal for a Regulation of the European Parliament and of the Council on Markets in Crypto-assets, and amending Directive (EU) 2019/1937, COM/2020/593 final. [online]. Available at: https://eur-lex.europa.eu/legal-content/EN/TXT/?uri=CELEX%3A52020PC0593

[929] CROSBY, M., PATTANAYAK, P., VERMA, S., KALYANARAMAN, V. *BlockChain technology beyond Bitcoin.* 2015, p. 3. [online]. Available at: https://scet.berkeley.edu/wp-content/uploads/BlockchainPaper.pdf

name of the special supervisory body – ENISA – which was created back in 2004. According to Regulation (EC) No 460/2004 of the European Parliament and of the Council of 10 March 2004 establishing the European Network and Information Security Agency[930] network and information security was defined as the ability of a network or an information system to resist, at a given level of confidence, accidental events or unlawful or malicious actions that compromise the availability, authenticity, integrity and confidentiality of stored or transmitted data and the related services offered by or accessible via these networks and systems. The reason why the term "cybersecurity" was not used in EU law for a long time remains unknown. This seems especially strange considering the fact that both this term itself and the actual need for protection against cyber threats existed long before the adoption of special legal acts.

The evolutionary transformation of network and information security into a more global cybersecurity concept was first established in 2013 after the publication of the Cybersecurity Strategy of the European Union.[931] However, only in 2019 with the adoption Regulation (EU) 2019/881 of the European Parliament and of the Council of 17 April 2019 on ENISA (the European Union Agency for Cybersecurity) and on information and communications technology cybersecurity certification and repealing Regulation (EU) No 526/2013[932] (hereinafter referred to as the Cybersecurity Act), the meaning of the concept of "cybersecurity" was clearly defined at the legislative level in the EU. This, without a doubt, is an extremely important step towards the formation of legal and institutional guarantees of a safe cyber environment. However, is the existing theoretical and conceptual approach to cybersecurity sufficiently comprehensive and thorough and is it supported by an appropriate theoretical foundation?

In accordance with Article 2 of the Cybersecurity Act, cybersecurity means the activities necessary to protect network and information systems, the users of such systems, and other persons affected by cyber threats. At the same time, cyber threats are any potential circumstances, events or actions that can cause

[930] Regulation (EC) No 460/2004 of the European Parliament and of the Council of 10 March 2004 establishing the European Network and Information Security Agency, OJ L 77, 13. 3. 2004, pp. 1–11. [online]. Available at: https://eur-lex.europa.eu/legal-content/EN/TXT/?uri=celex%3A32004R0460

[931] Joint communication to the European Parliament, the Council, the European economic and social committee and the Committee of the regions. Cybersecurity Strategy of the European Union: An Open, Safe and Secure Cyberspace, JOIN/2013/01 final. [online]. Available at: https://eur-lex.europa.eu/legal-content/EN/TXT/?uri=celex%3A52013JC0001

[932] Regulation (EU) 2019/881 of the European Parliament and of the Council of 17 April 2019 on ENISA (the European Union Agency for Cybersecurity) and on information and communications technology cybersecurity certification and repealing Regulation (EU) No 526/2013 (Cybersecurity Act), OJ L 151, 7. 6. 2019, pp. 15–69. [online]. Available at: https://eur-lex.europa.eu/eli/reg/2019/881/oj

damage, disrupt functioning or otherwise adversely affect network and information systems, users of such systems and other persons.[933]

Undoubtedly, referring not only information systems, but also any persons who have been harmed, to objects of protection, is a positive step. However, this does not change a certain one-sidedness in the understanding of cybersecurity from the point of view of EU law. V. Papakonstantinou identified modern approaches to understanding cybersecurity. Thus, cybersecurity can be considered as measures and actions aimed at protecting information systems, as a state of security of the cyber environment, as the ability to defend and resist threats, as well as a certain set of goals. The scientist himself is inclined to the dichotomy "praxis" and "state" (condition), which, in his opinion, not only fully characterize cybersecurity, but also allow to talk about the formation of the right to it.[934] However, the practice of legal regulation is not as progressive as the doctrinal views of scientists. Currently, EU law is limited to only the first of these approaches.

How the European Parliament and the Council of the EU see cybersecurity is also revealed in the preamble to the Cybersecurity Act. There, in particular, attention is focused on the fact that cybersecurity is not only a problem related to technologies, but also an issue in which human behavior is no less important. The preamble also aims to actively promote "cyber hygiene", namely simple, routine measures implemented and regularly implemented by citizens, organizations and businesses to minimize their exposure to cyber threat risks.[935] This actually results in a certain shift in emphasis from the formation of legal and institutional guarantees to the creation of an appropriate technical base and the formation of an appropriate level of digital culture among private individuals. At the same time, the preamble repeatedly emphasizes the fact that ensuring cybersecurity is very important for the proper functioning of the EU internal market. In this connection, the criticism of some researchers (V. Papakonstantinou[936], G. G. Fuster, L.

[933] Ibid.

[934] PAPAKONSTANTINOU, V. Cybersecurity as Praxis and as a State: the EU Law Path Towards Acknowledgement of a New Right to Cybersecurity? *Computer Law & Security Review.* 2022, vol. 44. p. 2. [online]. Available at: https://www.sciencedirect.com/science/article/pii/S0267364922000012?via%3Dihub

[935] Regulation (EU) 2019/881 of the European Parliament and of the Council of 17 April 2019 on ENISA (the European Union Agency for Cybersecurity) and on information and communications technology cybersecurity certification and repealing Regulation (EU) No 526/2013 (Cybersecurity Act), OJ L 151, 7. 6. 2019, pp. 15–69. [online]. Available at: https://eur-lex.europa.eu/eli/reg/2019/881/oj

[936] See PAPAKONSTANTINOU, V. Cybersecurity as Praxis and as a State: the EU Law Path Towards Acknowledgement of a New Right to Cybersecurity? *Computer Law & Security Review.* 2022, vol. 44, pp. 1–15 [online]. Available at: https://www.sciencedirect.com/science/article/pii/S0267364922000012?via%3Dihub

Jasmontaite[937]) seems to be reasonable, as they consider the chosen approach too limited, and aimed more at improving the operation of information networks with the aim of improving market environment in Europe, rather than at protecting users' rights. Extending the scope of protection to an unlimited number of persons is an obvious step forward, but it still does not give a possibility to talk about creating a foundation for the existence of the right to cybersecurity.

At the same time, the European Parliament and the Council of the EU do not always seem to call a spade a spade. Thus, in particular, preamble to Cybersecurity Act mentions Directive (EU) 2016/1148 of the European Parliament and of the Council of 6 July 2016 concerning measures for a high common level of security of network and information systems across the Union as a legal act that was adopted for the better protection of Internet users.[938] In fact, it is about providing users with the right to cyber protection. However, the actual provisions of this Directive constitute a set of legal rules aimed at solving some technical problems in the operation of networks and information systems.[939] This Directive actually do not contain provisions that guarantee certain rights and freedoms and create a mechanism for their protection. On the other hand, such rhetoric, combined with the gradual improvement of the legal framework, indicates a sufficiently broad interpretation of cybersecurity, and therefore the possibility of further positive developments.

The updated EU's Cybersecurity Strategy for the Digital Decade presented in 2020[940] gives grounds for such considerations regarding approaches to understanding the essence and meaning of cybersecurity. In particular, it states that improving cybersecurity is necessary to protect fundamental rights and freedoms, including the right to privacy and to the protection of personal data, as well as freedom of expression and information. The practice of legislative changes has

---

[937] See FUSTER G.G., JASMONTAITE L. Cybersecurity Regulation in the European Union: The Digital, the Critical and Fundamental Rights. *The Ethics of Cybersecurity*. 2020, p. 97–115 [online]. Available at: https://www.researchgate.net/publication/339161315_Cybersecurity_Regulation_in_the_European_Union_The_Digital_the_Critical_and_Fundamental_Rights

[938] Regulation (EU) 2019/881 of the European Parliament and of the Council of 17 April 2019 on ENISA (the European Union Agency for Cybersecurity) and on information and communications technology cybersecurity certification and repealing Regulation (EU) No 526/2013 (Cybersecurity Act), OJ L 151, 7. 6. 2019, pp. 15–69. [online]. Available at: https://eur-lex.europa.eu/eli/reg/2019/881/oj

[939] Directive (EU) 2016/1148 of the European Parliament and of the Council of 6 July 2016 concerning measures for a high common level of security of network and information systems across the Union, OJ L 194, 19. 7. 2016, pp. 1–30. [online]. Available at: https://eur-lex.europa.eu/eli/dir/2016/1148/oj

[940] European Commission and the High Representative of the Union for Foreign Affairs and Security Policy. The EU's Cybersecurity Strategy for the Digital Decade, 2020. [online]. Available at: https://digital-strategy.ec.europa.eu/en/library/eus-cybersecurity-strategy-digital-decade-0

shown that outlined in the previous Strategy of 2013[941] goals are not abstract categories, but real tasks for law-making activity. Thus, it can be argued that prospects of cybersecurity transformation from a technical category to a legal category, which encompasses fundamental digital rights and freedoms, are quite real.

It may be important from a legal point of view to include the right to cybersecurity in the catalog of rights provided by the EU Charter of Fundamental Rights[942]. The importance of this document lies in the fact that it also contains new rights, which are not typically ensured by international organizations and integration associations, with the exception of the EU. As Professor N. Šišková stated, the EU Charter of Fundamental Rights emphasizes the equal status of all rights, expressing "a unified concept of the quality of human life..."[943] "On the contrary to the European Convention, which protects a relatively limited number of rights..., the EU Charter regulates the rights of four generations, including economic, social and so-called modern rights."[944] Given the constant digitization of everyday life, its quality directly depends on the level of cybersecurity. The concept embedded in the EU Charter should be updated accordingly. This will make it possible to start a fundamental shift in the conceptual approach to cybersecurity and, as a result, to the formation of the corresponding legal framework.

It is worth paying attention to the fact that, in our opinion, the existing paradigm of cybersecurity is quite abstract. On the one hand, it makes it possible to move away from specific cyber threats and technical aspects of the functioning of the cyber environment, and therefore to cover all possible problems and ways to solve them. On the other hand, the prospects for proper legal regulation of some legal relations that are completely dependent on the use of ICT look rather bleak. First of all, we are talking about the circulation, storage and issuance of crypto-assets.

---

[941] Joint communication to the European Parliament, the Council, the European economic and social committee and the Committee of the regions. Cybersecurity Strategy of the European Union: An Open, Safe and Secure Cyberspace, JOIN/2013/01 final. [online]. Available at: https://eur-lex.europa.eu/legal-content/EN/TXT/?uri=celex%3A52013JC0001

[942] Charter of Fundamental Rights of the European Union, OJ C 202, 7. 6. 2016, pp. 389–405. [online]. Available at: https://www.europarl.europa.eu/charter/pdf/text_en.pdf
See HAMULAK, O. The Variations of Judicial Enforcement of EU Charter of Fundamental Rights vis-á-vis Union Institutions and Bodies. *The Review of European Law, Economics and Politic.* 2018, pp. 98–112. [online]. Available at: https://papers.ssrn.com/sol3/papers.cfm?abstract_id=3436791

[943] ŠIŠKOVÁ, N. Regulace lidských práv na úrovni EU – vývoj a perspektivy. *International and Comparative Law Review*. 2004, no. 10, p. 31. [online]. Available at: http://iclr.upol.cz/wp-content/uploads/2011/03/10_Siskova_Nadezda-28-45.pdf (in Czech)

[944] ŠIŠKOVÁ, N. New Challenges for the EU in the Field of Human Rights (Focusing on the Mechanism of the Charter). *European Studies. The Review of European Law, Economics and Politics.* 2014, no 1, p. 14.

The features of blockchain technology by themselves allow for a certain basic level of protection against third-party interference. However, this does not reduce cyber threats, and sometimes even increases their risk, due to the negligence of crypto-asset owners. The most unprotected categories of subjects using crypto-assets are individuals and private law legal entities that carry out investment activities. In most cases, cyberattacks in this area are aimed specifically at taking over other people's funds by using phishing software or fraudulent schemes.

The legislative definition of cyber threats under the aforementioned Article 2 of the Cybersecurity Act as "any potential circumstance, event or action" allows to include even fraud with financial resources in such threats, if it concerns cyberspace. Crypto-assets cannot be used outside the digital environment, so any encroachment on them should be considered a cyber threat. However, EU law tends to adapt classic mechanisms of protection and control to this category of modern digital legal relations instead of creating new ones. In 2022, the European Supervisory Authorities (European Banking Authority, European Securities and Markets Authority and European Insurance and Occupational Pensions Authority) made a joint statement on the threats that can be faced when using crypto-assets.[945] At the same time, ENISA gives priority in its work to the description of the technical aspects of the cryptocurrency market functioning.[946] This shows that, despite the purely digital nature of interaction with crypto-assets, EU authorities seem do not directly consider threats to crypto market participants to be cyber threats.

It may be quite acceptable for the EU legal system to use Ukraine's experience in legislative approaches to understanding cybersecurity. Ukraine is characterized by a significant level of digitization of many spheres of social, political and economic life. Thus, the Law of Ukraine "On the Basic Principles of Ensuring Cybersecurity of Ukraine" No. 2163-VIII dated October 5, 2017 defines cybersecurity as the protection of the vital interests of a person and citizen, society and the state during the use of cyberspace, which ensures the sustainable development of the information society and digital communication environment, timely detection, prevention and neutralization of real and potential threats to the national security of Ukraine in cyberspace.[947] As we can see, with such a legislative approach, the

945 European Supervisory Authorities (EBA, ESMA and EIOPA). EU financial regulators warn consumers on the risks of crypto-assets, 2022, p. 2. [online]. Available at: https://www.esma.europa.eu/sites/default/files/library/esa_2022_15_joint_esas_warning_on_crypto-assets.pdf

946 See: European Union Agency for Cybersecurity. Crypto Assets: Introduction to Digital Currencies and Distributed Ledger Technologies, 2021. [online]. Available at: https://www.enisa.europa.eu/publications/crypto-assets-introduction-to-digital-currencies-and-distributed-ledger-technologies

947 *Pro osnovni zasady zabezpechennia kiberbezpeky Ukrainy*: Zakon Ukrainy vid 5. 10. 2017 r. No 2163-VIII. [online]. Available at: https://zakon.rada.gov.ua/laws/show/2163-19#Text

interests of the person and citizen, society and the state are put first, not functioning of network and information systems, as is the case of EU law.

Thus, there is an urgent need for the formation of the theoretical and legal foundations of the right to cybersecurity in the EU. In this case, it will be inevitable to create a system of legal and institutional guarantees of protection against cyber threats, as well as remedy mechanisms for violated rights. This will make it possible to specify cyber threats, including including in their list any forms of intrusion on crypto-assets. Does this indicate that the existing legal and institutional guarantees are not able to ensure the safety of crypto-asset markets' participants?

4. Protection of crypto-asset consumers' and investors' rights

Fragmentary legal regulation of crypto-assets and legal relations related to them does not contribute to legal certainty and guaranteeing the rights and interests of consumers and investors in markets in crypto-assets. In recent years, the issue of real and potential cyber threats has become particularly relevant. At the same time, the reason for many external cyber threats is precisely the lack of a legal basis for the use of decentralized ledger technology. We believe that the complete legal protection of the rights of consumers and investors in crypto-assets directly influences the quality of cyber protection. The legislation of the EU and its Member States on crypto-assets still remains unsystematized, and therefore the assessment of the security of crypto-assets markets participants should begin with the analysis of risks and the search for legal mechanisms to respond to them.

The European Supervisory Authorities, in the abovementioned joint statement, systematized the risks that users and investors may face. Seven main threats that may violate the rights and interests of crypto market participants are named: extreme price movements; misleading information; absence of protection; product complexity; fraud and malicious activities; market manipulation, lack of price transparency and low liquidity; hacker attacks, operational risks and security issues.[948]

We believe that this list fully corresponds to the essence and nature of legal relations with crypto-assets. The creation of legal mechanisms that would protect against these risks should become the main law-making direction. However, it should be recognized that neither the EU nor its Member States are capable of covering each of these risks with legal regulation. In particular, extreme price

[948] European Supervisory Authorities (EBA, ESMA and EIOPA). EU financial regulators warn consumers on the risks of crypto-assets, 2022, p. 2. [online]. Available at: https://www.esma.europa.eu/sites/default/files/library/esa_2022_15_joint_esas_warning_on_crypto-assets.pdf

fluctuations and technological complexity of crypto-assets are primarily their feature, and only then a risk factor. Users and investors who become participants in the crypto markets voluntarily are solely responsible for potential losses. However, there are still many potential factors that, without proper legal regulation, make consumers and investors virtually defenseless.

Fighting misleading information should become quite effective immediately after the adoption of the MiCA Regulation Proposal. The draft Regulation, in particular in Articles 5 and 7, imposes on crypto-asset issuers the obligation to prepare and publish a technical document (white paper) on crypto-assets that would provide consumers with complete and reliable information about the project, rights and obligations attached to crypto-assets, and risks associated with them.[949] Currently, one of the possible ways to protect against misleading information is the use of mechanisms provided by Directive 2006/114/EC of the European Parliament and of the Council of 12 December 2006 concerning misleading and comparative advertising[950] and relevant national legislation of EU Member States. However, it is obvious that the cases where advertising legislation can be effectively applied to crypto projects are significantly limited.

Fraud is one of the types of criminal offenses. Legal protection against criminal encroachments on property and monetary assets is carried out at the level of national legislation of EU Member States. However, only a unified approach to understanding the nature of crypto-assets can provide full protection against their illegal possession. The classification of virtual currencies (cryptocurrencies) provided by AMLD5 as a digital representation of value really contributes to the application of criminal law norms to cases of fraudulent possession of them. However, AMLD5 itself does not aim to protect the rights of consumers and investors, and therefore application of this Directive to such legal relations is not obvious.

In our view, given the nature of crypto-asset transactions, various types of fraudulent activities are covered by the term "cyber threat" within the meaning of the Cybersecurity Act. Taking crypto-assets in any case occurs with the use of ICT. Sometimes actions having signs of fraud are committed by officials of cryptocurrency exchanges. Thus, in 2022, the U.S. The Securities and Exchange Commission charged Samuel Bankman-Fried, one of the founders of the online platform for trading cryptoassets FTX, which was also available to EU citizens and residents, with fraud. The charge is based on the fact that Samuel

[949] Proposal for a Regulation of the European Parliament and of the Council on Markets in Crypto-assets, and amending Directive (EU) 2019/1937, COM/2020/593 final. [online]. Available at: https://eur-lex.europa.eu/legal-content/EN/TXT/?uri=CELEX%3A52020PC0593

[950] Directive 2006/114/EC of the European Parliament and of the Council of 12 December 2006 concerning misleading and comparative advertising (codified version) OJ L 376, 27. 12. 2006, pp. 21–27. [online]. Available at: https://eur-lex.europa.eu/legal-content/EN/ALL/?uri=celex:32006L0114

Bankman-Fried used the digital ecosystem of the crypto exchange to fraudulently raise investors' funds.[951] In fact, there is an encroachment on the cybersecurity of investors who were counting on the absence of any interference in the platform's operation by its founders or third parties.

A similar situation arose with protection against market manipulation. Any manipulations, including pump-and-dump schemes (manipulative increase in the price of a crypto-asset with the aim of its further sale), are impossible without at least minimum level of operational intervention in the work of digital platforms for trading and exchange of crypto-assets. Classic markets are protected from this due to Regulation (EU) No 596/2014 of the European Parliament and of the Council of 16 April 2014 on market abuse (MAR)[952] along with Directive 2014/57/EU of the European Parliament and of the Council of 16 April 2014 on criminal sanctions for market abuse (CS MAD).[953] However, markets in crypto-assets do not currently fall under the scope of these legal acts. At the same time, fraudulent manipulations take place precisely in the cyber environment and are impossible outside it. It is quite logical that adequate protection should be guaranteed through cyber defence mechanisms.

One of the threats that is not mentioned in the abovementioned statement by the European Supervisory Authorities[954] there is a global threat from state-sponsors of terrorism, for example, to which the Russian Federation actually belongs.[955] Interference with the work of global information systems that ensure the circulation of crypto-assets harms not only private, but also public interests. Possible attacks allow offenders to accumulate funds that can later be used to finance terrorist activities. It also causes losses to investors, who lose the opportunity to fill the EU economy with financial resources (taxes, etc.). In this aspect,

[951] The United States Securities and Exchange Commission. SEC Charges Samuel Bankman-Fried with Defrauding Investors in Crypto Asset Trading Platform FTX. [online]. Available at: https://www.sec.gov/news/press-release/2022-219

[952] Regulation (EU) No 596/2014 of the European Parliament and of the Council of 16 April 2014 on market abuse (market abuse regulation) and repealing Directive 2003/6/EC of the European Parliament and of the Council and Commission Directives 2003/124/EC, 2003/125/EC and 2004/72/EC, OJ L 173, 12. 6. 2014, pp. 1–61. [online]. Available at: https://eur-lex.europa.eu/legal-content/EN/TXT/?uri=celex%3A32014R0596

[953] Directive 2014/57/EU of the European Parliament and of the Council of 16 April 2014 on criminal sanctions for market abuse (market abuse directive) OJ L 173, 12. 6. 2014, pp. 179–189. [online]. Available at: https://eur-lex.europa.eu/legal-content/EN/TXT/?uri=CELEX%3A32014L0057

[954] European Supervisory Authorities (EBA, ESMA and EIOPA). EU financial regulators warn cнonsumers on the risks of crypto-assets, 2022. [online]. Available at: https://www.esma.europa.eu/sites/default/files/library/esa_2022_15_joint_esas_warning_on_crypto-assets.pdf

[955] Joint motion for a resolution on recognising the Russian Federation as a state sponsor of terrorism. (2022-2896(RSP). [online]. Available at: https://www.europarl.europa.eu/doceo/document/RC-9-2022-0482_EN.html

innovations in Ukrainian legislation that were adopted in 2022[956] are of particular interest. For the first time, preventive measures regarding cybersecurity were regulated. They make it possible to prevent cyber threats and, therefore, the violation of fundamental rights of persons concerned. The Law of Ukraine "On the Basic Principles of Ensuring Cybersecurity of Ukraine" No. 2163-VIII dated October 5, 2017 included the concept of "active countermeasures against aggression in cyberspace". These are actions aimed at increasing the level of cyber defence by neutralizing cyber attacks of the aggressor state, its systems and networks, as well as the sources of cyber threats and cyber attacks that are used to harm the national security of Ukraine.[957] Similar preventive measures can be used in the EU. In the case of crypto-assets, active countermeasures can be carried out in partnership with digital service providers, such as crypto exchanges.

What protection mechanisms can special legislation on crypto-assets offer to consumers? The Cybersecurity Act does not contain law remedies to protect the rights and interests of private individuals. It establishes clear mechanisms for cybersecurity certification and standardization. The Cybersecurity Act also gave ENISA fairly broad supervisory powers. However, some scientists[958] ask a valid question, what are the possible ways to protect the rights and interests of private individuals in case of infringement of obligations by the obliged entities? The Cybersecurity Act recognizes the need to protect all individuals from any events or actions, but does not provide a specific answer to the question. At the same time, the certification has signs of voluntariness. Its mechanisms become a means of increasing user trust by confirming compliance with established cybersecurity thresholds and "assurance levels".[959]

This once again proves that in the event that individuals and legal entities are adversely affected by the use of ICT, other branches of law shall be applied that provide protection to persons concerned. Moreover, this applies not only participants in markets of crypto-assets, but also to any other users.

---

[956] *Pro vnesennia zmin do deiakykh zakoniv Ukrainy shchodo zabezpechennia formuvannia ta realizatsii derzhavnoi polityky u sferi aktyvnoi protydii ahresii u kiberprostori:* Zakon Ukrainy vid 28. 7. 2022 r. No 2470-IX. [online]. Available at: https://zakon.rada.gov.ua/laws/show/2470-20#n21

[957] *Pro osnovni zasady zabezpechennia kiberbezpeky Ukrainy:* Zakon Ukrainy vid 5. 10. 2017 r. No 2163-VIII. [online]. Available at: https://zakon.rada.gov.ua/laws/show/2163-19#Text

[958] PAPAKONSTANTINOU, V. Cybersecurity as Praxis and as a State: the EU Law Path Towards Acknowledgement of a New Right to Cybersecurity? *Computer Law & Security Review.* 2022, vol. 44, pp. 8, 12. [online]. Available at: https://www.sciencedirect.com/science/article/pii/S0267364922000012?via%3Dihub

[959] CHIARA, P. G. The IoT and the new EU cybersecurity regulatory landscape. *International Review of Law, Computers & Technology.* 2022, vol. 36, no. 2, pp. 120, 121. [online]. Available at: https://www.tandfonline.com/doi/epdf/10.1080/13600869.2022.2060468?needAccess=true&role=button

It is clear that legal protection can be a universal way of protection against real threats. The most common type of harm that consumers and investors can face is financial loss. They can be assessed and levied by the court from the guilty party. However, A. Horvath draws attention to the low efficiency of individual judicial protection. A feature of offences related to crypto-assets is the accumulation of significant amounts of funds. If courts assess damages taking into account individual consumer losses, the amount of the sanctions will not be the same as the amount by which the fraud itself can enrich the fraudster[960], for example, in cases where illegal actions concern the crypto exchange as a whole. That is why we agree with the importance of applying mechanisms of collective legal protection. Directive (EU) 2020/1828 of the European Parliament and of the Council of 25 November 2020 on representative actions for the protection of the collective interests of consumers and repealing Directive 2009/22/EC[961] could provide such an opportunity. However, it does not contain any mention of crypto-assets.

It is important that the European Parliament and the European Commission have an understanding about the need for the gradual formation of special legislation on the crypto-assets markets and the cybersecurity of their users and investors. In Proposal for a Regulation of the European Parliament and of the Council on a pilot regime for market infrastructures based on distributed ledger technology COM/2020/594 final[962] it was in particular recognized that the majority of crypto-assets fall outside of the scope of EU legislation and raise, among others, challenges in terms of investor protection, market integrity and financial stability. Hence, they require a special regime at Union level. However, the real steps towards guaranteeing the rights of consumers and investors are significantly lagging behind the declared goals. In particular, Directive (EU) 2022/2555 of the European Parliament and of the Council of 14 December 2022 on measures for a high common level of cybersecurity across the Union, amending Regulation (EU) No 910/2014 and Directive (EU) 2018/1972, and repealing Directive (EU) 2016/1148 (NIS 2 Directive)[963] designed

960 HORVATH A. Protection of consumers provided in the proposal for a regulation of markets in crypto assets. *Zaštita kolektivnih interesa potrošača*. 2021, pp. 439, 443. [online]. Available at: https://doi.org/10.18485/union_pf_ccr.2021.ch21

961 Directive (EU) 2020/1828 of the European Parliament and of the Council of 25 November 2020 on representative actions for the protection of the collective interests of consumers and repealing Directive 2009/22/EC, OJ L 409, 4. 12. 2020, pp. 1–27. [online]. Available at: https://eur-lex.europa.eu/legal-content/EN/TXT/?uri=CELEX%3A32020L1828

962 Proposal for a Regulation of the European Parliament and of the Council on a pilot regime for market infrastructures based on distributed ledger technology, COM/2020/594 final. [online]. Available at: https://eur-lex.europa.eu/legal-content/EN/TXT/?uri=CELEX%3A52020PC0594

963 Directive (EU) 2022/2555 of the European Parliament and of the Council of 14 December 2022 on measures for a high common level of cybersecurity across the Union, amending Regulation

to fill many gaps in the legal regulation of cybersecurity. However, this legal act contains a reference to cryptocurrencies only in the context of recognizing the fact of the existence of relevant cyber threats (clause 54 of the preamble).

It can be stated that there is a strong need to change approaches to cybersecurity regulation. EU law should be based on the inalienable right to cybersecurity. Ensuring this right is possible only by establishing effective protection mechanisms, from sanctions for non-compliance with cybersecurity standards to special measures to compensate for the damage caused. This also applies to the protection of the rights of participants in crypto-asset markets as subjects, the security of which completely depends on the proper level of cybersecurity. Only special legislation can guarantee legal certainty, and, accordingly, the effectiveness of the protection of consumers and investors' rights.

5. Crypto-assets in the EU: institutional guarantees of cybersecurity

Institutional guarantees are an important component of ensuring the real protection of the rights and interests of participants in crypto-asset markets in any legal relationship. For cryptoassets consumers of and investors, this has an additional importance due to considerable gaps in legal regulation. Such guarantees are implemented through a system of special bodies empowered with a complex of control and supervisory powers, as well as authorized to protect violated rights in any other way.

MiCA Regulation Proposal in Chapter 4 of Title VII[964] provides fairly broad powers of the European Banking Authority. They consist in the control of compliance with the legislation by crypto-asset issuers, as well as in performing investigations of committed violations. Strengthening obligations with real sanctions for their non-fulfillment is an important step on the way to guaranteeing the rights and interests of participants in crypto-asset markets. However, in this case, obliged persons are limited to issuers of crypto-assets (legal entities that offer any type of crypto-assets to the public or seek to list such cryptoassets on a crypto trading platform). Moreover, financial supervision by the European

(EU) No 910/2014 and Directive (EU) 2018/1972, and repealing Directive (EU) 2016/1148 (NIS 2 Directive), OJ L 333, 27. 12. 2022, pp. 80–152. [online]. Available at: https://eur-lex.europa.eu/eli/dir/2022/2555/oj

964 Proposal for a Regulation of the European Parliament and of the Council on Markets in Crypto-assets, and amending Directive (EU) 2019/1937, COM/2020/593 final. [online]. Available at: https://eur-lex.europa.eu/legal-content/EN/TXT/?uri=CELEX%3A52020PC0593

Banking Authority, in our opinion, has little to do with cybersecurity, even with a broad approach to its understanding.

This approach to legal regulation shows that the European Parliament and the European Commission are more focused on the financial aspect of crypto-assets than on their digital nature. This creates some unjustified imbalance between financial and cybernetic security. Also, it causes even more concern if we consider that the financial security of crypto market participants, as a rule, directly depends on cybersecurity.

Control over the activities of crypto-asset service providers, which include crypto-exchanges (including decentralized ones) and P2P trading platforms, according to the MiCA Regulation Proposal, should be carried out by special competent authorities of Member States. However, the powers proposed by Article 82 of the MiCA Regulation Proposal do not seem to include those directly related to cybersecurity. Moreover, the imperative powers of these authorities are supported by a rather limited range of sanctions. For example, point (g), part 1 of Article 82 gives special authorities the right to suspend or require a crypto-asset service provider to suspend the provision of crypto-asset services for some period.[965] The effectiveness of this kind of sanctions is questionable, especially if they concern crypto exchanges or platforms registered in offshore jurisdictions.

The main EU agency responsible for cybersecurity is ENISA, established in 2004 under Regulation (EC) No 460/2004 of the European Parliament and of the Council as the European Network and Information Security Agency.[966] Cybersecurity Act in 2019, significantly expanded the scope of ENISA's powers and updated its name to the European Union Agency for Cybersecurity (although the abbreviation ENISA remained in use). In the preamble to Regulation (EU) No 2019/881, the ENISA's tasks are defined in a general form as facilitating the exchange of best practices between Member States and private stakeholders, making policy suggestions to the European Commission and EU Member States, acting as a reference point for EU cybersecurity sectoral policy initiatives, as well as promoting operational cooperation both between the Member States and between the Member States and EU institutions, bodies, offices and agencies.[967]

[965] Ibid.

[966] Regulation (EC) No 460/2004 of the European Parliament and of the Council of 10 March 2004 establishing the European Network and Information Security Agency, OJ L 77, 13. 3. 2004, pp. 1–11. [online]. Available at: https://eur-lex.europa.eu/legal-content/EN/TXT/?uri=celex%3A32004R0 460

[967] Regulation (EU) 2019/881 of the European Parliament and of the Council of 17 April 2019 on ENISA (the European Union Agency for Cybersecurity) and on information and communications technology cybersecurity certification and repealing Regulation (EU) No 526/2013 (Cybersecurity Act), OJ L 151, 7. 6. 2019, pp. 15–69. [online]. Available at: https://eur-lex.europa.eu/eli/reg/2019/881/oj

In February 2021, ENISA launched a series of report studies on information security in the field of crypto-assets to support EU policy and raise awareness of security and data protection issues that may arise.[968] This is fully in line with the Cybersecurity Act's concept of cyber hygiene and cyber education as conditions for ensuring cybersecurity. The work carried out is really important for increasing user awareness of the features of blockchain technology and the presence of significant security gaps. However, such an approach is more like an incentive to self-protection than forming a basis for protection by special EU bodies/agencies.

Despite ENISA's interest in crypto-assets, the MiCA Regulation Proposal text does not mention this agency. For the first time, ENISA was granted a possibility to really impact on the crypto-asset market only after adoption of Regulation (EU) 2022/2554 of the European Parliament and of the Council of 14 December 2022 on digital operational resilience for the financial sector and amending Regulations (EC) No 1060/2009, (EU) No 648/2012, (EU) No 600/2014, (EU) No 909/2014 and (EU) 2016/1011[969] (hereinafter referred to as Regulation 2022/2554). This legal act establishes uniform requirements for the security of network and information systems of entities, working in the financial sector, such as investment firms and payment institutions, as well as critically important third parties that provide them with ICT-related services. It covers, among others, crypto-asset service providers as they are defined in MiCA Regulation Proposal, that is, any persons whose activities or business is to provide one or more services using crypto-assets to third parties on a professional basis.

Regarding institutional cybersecurity guarantees, Article 5 of Regulation 2022/2554[970] obliges financial entities to implement a system of internal management and control that ensures effective and prudent risk management in the ICT field to achieve a high level of digital operational resilience. In addition, article 6 of this Regulation requires financial entities to have a sound, comprehensive and well-documented ICT risk management system as part of their overall risk management system that enables them to respond quickly, efficiently and comprehensively to ICT risks, including but not limited to conducting post-incident

[968] See: European Union Agency for Cybersecurity. Crypto Assets: Introduction to Digital Currencies and Distributed Ledger Technologies, 2021. [online]. Available at: https://www.enisa.europa.eu/publications/crypto-assets-introduction-to-digital-currencies-and-distributed-ledger-technologies

[969] Regulation (EU) 2022/2554 of the European Parliament and of the Council of 14 December 2022 on digital operational resilience for the financial sector and amending Regulations (EC) No 1060/2009, (EU) No 648/2012, (EU) No 600/2014, (EU) No 909/2014 and (EU) 2016/1011, OJ L 333, 27. 12. 2022, pp. 1–79. [online]. Available at: https://eur-lex.europa.eu/eli/reg/2022/2554/oj

[970] Ibid.

reviews related to ICT. Based on internal audit findings, these entities should establish a formal follow-up process, including rules for in-time reviewing and remediating of critical ICT audit findings.

Thus, Regulation 2022/2554 takes out part of the protective functions from EU institutions and Member States and transfers them to private structures. Private-public partnership is quite a positive practice, however, given the potential consequences of cyber threats, the EU should take a more balanced approach to the redistribution of powers concerning the protection of the cyber environment.

Regulation 2022/2554 in Article 15 provides that the European Supervisory Authorities shall, through the Joint Committee, in consultation with ENISA, develop common draft regulatory technical standards.[971] However, as we have already noted, the establishment of standards in itself is not sufficient to protect the rights and interests of consumers without monitoring their compliance, preventive measures, as well as damage compensation mechanisms.

Compliance with this Regulation 2022/2554 by crypto-asset service providers and token issuers must be ensured by a competent authority designated in accordance with the provisions of the MiCA Regulation Proposal. The latter in Chapter 1 of Title VII (Articles 81-91)[972] obliges Member States to designate one or more competent authorities for the purposes of this Regulation, including one competent authority as a single contact point. It also contains detailed provisions on the powers of national competent authorities, their cooperation with each other, as well as with EBA and ESMA.

We believe that the absence of ENISA in this list, as well as special national bodies for cybersecurity, is a significant drawback of the chosen approach to institutional support for the circulation of crypto-assets. We fully agree with the idea, laid down in the MiCA Regulation Proposal, about the importance of creating new special regulatory bodies by EU Member States. This seems to be justified given the specifics of the crypto-asset market. However, without similar measures at the EU level, the proposed legal regulation looks incomplete. We consider the most optimal option (in order to preserve the existing EU institutional system) to expand the powers of ENISA and create a special department within its structure, which shall be authorized to work with crypto market participants.

The expansion of ENISA's powers may lead to some disputes about interference in the sovereignty of EU Member States. However, as A.-M. Osula et al. have noted in their study of the legal positions of EU Member States regarding the legal regulation of cyberspace, there is much more consensus between states

[971] Ibid.

[972] Proposal for a Regulation of the European Parliament and of the Council on Markets in Crypto-assets, and amending Directive (EU) 2019/1937, COM/2020/593 final. [online]. Available at: https://eur-lex.europa.eu/legal-content/EN/TXT/?uri=CELEX%3A52020PC0593

than it seems at first sight.[973] It can be argued that the urgency of the cybersecurity problem is capable of consolidating efforts within the EU. The creation of appropriate legal and institutional guarantees for the protection of cyberspace participants fully corresponds to both the internal and external interests of the Member States. Therefore, we see no reason for delays in improving the legal framework for regulating cybersecurity in general and crypto-asset market security in particular.

Thus, institutional cybersecurity guarantees in EU law, especially in the field of crypto-asset use, need further improvement. Updating ENISA's powers appears to be an acceptable option.

6. Conclusion

Digitalisation of the economy creates additional opportunities for expanding the EU internal market and strengthening European integration processes. At the same time, cyberthreats that can cause significant damage to both private and public interests are being activated. EU citizens are increasingly using crypto-assets that exist solely thanks to ICT. They use them as a means of payment, accumulation, object of investment, collection, etc. Markets in crypto-assets are gradually becoming a significant part of the world economy, which cannot be ignored. Its participants need adequate protection against unauthorized interference in their economic activities.

In the EU, the process of creating a more effective legal framework has begun, which would allow combining the freedom and decentralization of the circulation of crypto-assets with national and EU control over the safety and legality of their use. However, the cybersecurity of consumers and investors of crypto-assets is given unreasonably little attention. The existing legal regulation is based on a too narrow approach to cybersecurity as such, which does not allow us to talk about a high level of protection of the rights of people using crypto-assets.

Among the possible approaches to understanding the essence of cybersecurity (including in the field of using crypto-assets), we prefer a broad approach. In such a case, the formation of the right to cybersecurity is possible, which includes not only the state of technical security, but also the appropriate legal and institutional guarantees of protection and compensation for damages. Perhaps it would be appropriate to include such a right into the EU Charter of Fundamental Rights. In our opinion, this is fully justified given the fact that many social relations are

[973] OSULA A-M., KASPER A., KAJANDER A. EU Common Position on International Law and Cyberspace. *Masaryk University Journal of Law and Technology.* 2022, vol. 16, p. 114. [online]. Available at: https://journals.muni.cz/mujlt/article/view/20668/16944

moving into the digital sphere. It is now impossible to talk about guaranteeing the proper quality of life, human rights and freedoms without ensuring a high level of protection against cyber threats.

The protection of the rights of crypto-assets' consumers and investors must be carried out on the basis of cyber protection mechanisms, since the use of crypto-assets occurs exclusively with the help of ICT. The application of legislation regulating classic financial markets is not always able to take into account all the features of the new digital market. This problem can be solved by the development and adoption of a special legal act in the EU, which would take into account the cybersecurity model proposed above.

In order to establish proper control over cybersecurity and protect the rights of users when using crypto-assets, it is important not only to create special bodies both at the level of the EU and at the level of its Member States, but also to strengthen the powers of the existing ones. In this context, the powers of ENISA would need to be improved. However, its effective activity in this direction is possible only after the expansion of its powers. The creation of a special structural unit (department) of ENISA, which would focus its activities on cybersecurity in the field of crypto-assets, seems to be fully justified.

The general dynamics of the development of EU law indicate positive developments in the legal regulation of crypto-assets in general, and cybersecurity in this market in particular. However, the development of the legal framework obviously does not keep up with the rapid development of ICT. The scientific community should join in the search for the most acceptable conceptual models of cybersecurity in markets of crypto-assets.

CONCLUSIONS

Internet seriously affects both the very nature of the person and his/her rights, in many ways even modifying them. In this context, the Internet is not just a means of exercising already existing human rights, but rather a benefit that requires careful and peculiar legal regulation. In particular, the peculiarity of the Internet is that, unlike other means of communication and/or information exchange (hereinafter referred to as "means of communication"), where a person, as a rule, retains his/her connection with the offline world, for example, in the case of a telephone or radio, the Internet access brings a person into an information space separate from the offline world, previously unknown to humans, where completely different rules and principles of functioning operate. The usage of Internet cause also a lot of legal problems, it is not going too far to say that the tension between data use and data protection is one of the defining features of the new millennium, also known as the digital age.

The doctrine of data protection and privacy in relation to technology development is not new and has been evolving for a long time, while the first data protection laws in Europe have been passed in 70s. For a long time, the right to personal data protection was in the shadow of the right to privacy, but gradually the right to personal data protection has become fully independent. This is also clear from the GDPR wording. Nevertheless, the relationship between data protection and privacy continues to exist in various forms, this is a complex and multi-layered relationship. A more broadly conceived and readily available data protection framework can in some cases directly or indirectly support the right to privacy.

The GDPR has significantly strengthened and refined the legal framework for the protection of personal data, although it is still based on the original principle expressed in in the Directive 95/46/EC and Council of Europe Convention 108 of 1981. The strengthening and refinement of the GDPR rules has also been made possible through the interpretation of the data protection principles contained in the CJEU case law which preceded the adoption of the GDPR.

Currently, the CJEU case law in data protection field is one of the most dynamically developing areas of the CJEU activities in general, fully reflecting the complexity of the relationship between technologies and processing of personal data. The main contribution of the CJEU case law can be seen in relation to the interpretation of the GDPR principles and concepts.

In any case, EU law has set up a unique, yet very complex multi-dimensional system of personal data protection pursuing more objectives.

Nevertheless, there are number of shortcomings in the enforcement of data protection law in practice and there are inconsistencies in the procedures before supervisory authorities. Different national procedures of supervisory authorities in the course of proceedings before they are considered to be an obstacle to the enforcement and enforceability of the GDPR, leading to considerations on the need to harmonise the procedural rules of EU Member States, although these rules usually remain within the competence of the Member States. In any case, further reflection on the GDPR in the near future could be conducted in the area of procedural rules reform, at least for cross-border cases.

The European Union by regulation of the right to be forgotten (which is embodied in GDPR) had taken a significant step towards the better protection of the personal sphere of the individual, acting as a pioneer in this field.

Nevertheless, in the current form the right to be forgotten couldn't be considered as a really effective instrument, which always serves for the benefits of the citizens and prevents in all the cases the spreading of their personal data via Internet, to some extent it still remains an illusory entitlement, due to the several factors:

1) Due to the design and the concept of this entitlement which despite its title doesn't count on the complete erasure or deletion of relevant information, but only with its being hidden in the territory of the EU by the technique known as geo-blocking, so the data still exists, as geo-blocking counts on their retention; 2) Due to the limits of the territorial scope of this entitlement, which reflects the *ratione loci* of EU law and thus isn't valid over the borders of the European Union. In this sense paradoxically the EU citizens and other entities with the domaine in the Member States are at a disadvantage in comparison with their counterparts in the rest of the world, because their personal data in fact are not deleted and are still available for the entities beyond the Union. This information asymmetry concerning the accessibility of information in the EU and in the rest of the world is obvious; 3) Third, due to the nature of Internet itself, which never ensures the definite removal of undesirable (from the point of view of the individual) private information. Besides the so-called trickledown effect and the circulation of the uploaded before content there is also a fact that controllers always have at their disposal all the data, which were officially erased. This gives the controllers the enormous power over the citizens and the government, that can be easily abused in the future. Therefore, the very concept of the unlimited data retention in its essence is flawed and must be changed; 4) Due to the threats and jeopardizing by the eventuality of the Streisand effect, when, despite the intention to erasure, the access to the private information from the side of the general

public is not reduced, but vice versa it is multiplied greatly. In this respect it can be considered as a double-edged sword.

So the right to be forgotten as a non-absolute entitlement which counts on a number a number of exceptions and is greatly influenced by some negative factors cannot guarantee the protection of personal data of the individual in all the cases. Nevertheless its regulation creates a step in the right direction, but in the current form is not a sufficient one.

The real effectiveness of it in the optimal way can be reached only, if this entitlement would be applicable in the global scope; if it would count on the complete erasure of data without their retention and if it would be regulated by the international legal instruments of the universal character. This course of action nevertheless strikes with the different approaches of the particular states to the correlation between the right to be forgotten and the freedom of expression.

Therefore in reality the right to be forgotten as a legally binding and invokable entitlement in a global scope cannot be ensured in the near future. On the other hand, it is worth considering the creation of at least a worldwide digital catalogue of entitlements of the individual, which will be conceived and designed at the beginning as "principles". The right to be forgotten will be a part of this catalogue.

Consumer protection in the digital world is a complex and evolving area of law that poses unique challenges and opportunities. The digitisation and technology within the innovative digital economy is accelerating. The digital sector is no longer just a specific subdivision of the market, but the basis of all innovative economic systems. Data and information collection and its analyses have become a specific commodity. On the one hand, the consumers may benefit from this fast development – they have access to specific goods and services that make their everyday lives easier. At the same time, the instant development of the digital technologies are raising novel legal issues in the field of consumer protection, such as transparency and fairness of contractual terms, access to and the use of data, liability, warranties, ethics, etc.

In the digital world, consumers often face challenges in obtaining accurate and complete information about the products or services they are purchasing online. This can include misleading product descriptions, fake reviews, hidden fees, and unclear terms and conditions. Information transparency and understanding of contractual conditions are necessary prerequisites also for sustainable consumption but consumers face the complex and often impossible task of assembling and then analysing relevant information.

Furthermore, with the increasing use of automated decision-making systems, such as recommendation algorithms and personalized pricing algorithms, consumers may not fully understand how their data is being used and how decisions are being made. This lack of transparency and understanding can lead to consumer confusion, loss of privacy, and potential discrimination.

The challenge for consumer protection in the online space is not only information asymmetry, information overload (or information anxiety and technostress) also plays an important role, as consumers can be so overwhelmed by the amount of information about products, businesses and consumer rights that they are unable to navigate it and assess their options in a relevant way. Some of the earlier studies show that more information tends to decrease the quality of consumer decision performance. This has been confirmed by more recent studies which showed that the "combination of number of attributes and distribution of attribute levels is a better predictor of information overload than the number of alternatives or attributes alone".

Automated decision-making, powered by Artificial Intelligence (AI) and machine learning algorithms, is increasingly being used in various aspects of the digital world, such as personalized pricing, product recommendations, credit scoring, and content filtering. While these technologies offer benefits such as efficiency, convenience, and personalization, they also raise concerns in terms of consumer protection. For example, there is reason to believe that profiling, automated decision-making, and credit-scoring are not declared as often as they are used.

One of the challenges associated with automated decision-making is the lack of transparency and explainability. Consumers may not fully understand how decisions are made by algorithms and may not be able to challenge or appeal against unfair or discriminatory decisions. For example, personalized pricing algorithms may result in discriminatory pricing based on factors such as location, browsing history, or demographic information, leading to price discrimination. Some authors even claim that the consumer has a right to impersonal prices under the GDPR legal provisions.

European consumer law protection should address these challenges by ensuring transparency, explainability and fairness in automated decision-making, since the requirements of the GDPR are too vague and leave substantial room for interpretation. Although the GDPR is the most advanced legislation on data protection we have, the guidance that it provides on how companies should inform data subjects about AI and automated decision-making appears to be too superficial and too vague for interpretation. Regulations should mandate businesses to disclose when decisions are made by algorithms and provide explanations to consumers. There should also be mechanisms for consumers to challenge or appeal against decisions made by algorithms. Additionally, consumer protection laws should require that algorithms are trained on unbiased and representative data, and that businesses are held accountable for the outcomes of automated decision-making processes. This may include establishing liability frameworks that clarify the responsibilities of businesses, manufacturers, and developers in cases of harm caused by automated decision-making.

In many cases, consumers are not paying for the services with subscription fees or any kind of monetary payment, but with their personal data. Consumers' personal data represents value which is exchanged for certain services, often implicitly, without users knowing which data they actually provide and what the value of their personal data is to these data controllers.

The digital world has facilitated cross-border transactions, allowing consumers to access products and services from different countries. However, this has also resulted in challenges related to consumer protection. Consumers may face difficulties in asserting their rights when dealing with businesses from different jurisdictions. Disputes may arise regarding issues such as contract enforcement, product quality and liability. Additionally, the complexity of cross-border transactions may create information asymmetry, leaving consumers vulnerable to scams, fraud, and unfair practices.

Technology can also enable greater transparency in the digital marketplace, allowing consumers to access accurate and comprehensive information about products, services, prices, and terms and conditions. For example, online reviews, comparison websites, and rating systems can empower consumers to make informed choices and hold businesses accountable for their products or services. However, information does not equal transparency because information must be read, decoded and understood and consumers must make a vast number of decisions every day based on goals, preferences, experience and available information. In general, efficient decisions rely on consumers' ability to overcome the searching costs, switching costs (the cost of changing providers and testing new brands or products) and bounded rationality (biases and heuristics in human decision making). Thus, the European consumer law protection could leverage technological tools to promote transparency in the digital world and empower consumers to make informed decisions.

Technology can enable innovative dispute resolution mechanisms, such as online mediation, online arbitration, and blockchain-based dispute resolution. These mechanisms can provide efficient, cost-effective, and accessible ways for consumers to resolve disputes with businesses in the digital world. European consumer law protection should keep pace with technological innovations in dispute resolution and explore the potential of such mechanisms to enhance consumer protection in the digital world. It should also promote the use of technology to improve access to justice for consumers, particularly in cross-border disputes and complex digital transactions.

Enforcement mechanisms should be strengthened to effectively address violations of consumer protection laws in the digital world. This may involve empowering consumer protection agencies with adequate resources and authority to investigate and prosecute wrongdoers. Digital platforms should also be held accountable for the actions of third-party sellers or service providers operating on their platforms. Cooperation among EU Member States and international cooperation in cross-border cases should be enhanced to tackle jurisdictional challenges. Consumer awareness and education play a crucial role in empowering consumers and protecting their rights in the digital world. As it was stressed before, many consumers lack awareness about their rights and responsibilities when using digital services, including issues related to data privacy, online transactions, and dispute resolution mechanisms. Therefore, efforts should be made to educate consumers about their rights and responsibilities in the digital world and equip them with the necessary knowledge and skills to make informed decisions. In this regard, European consumer law protection tries to implement consumer education programs that provide resources and information on digital platforms, data privacy, and online transactions. This involves collaborations between consumer protection agencies, educational institutions and other stakeholders to develop and disseminate educational materials, conduct workshops and seminars, and promote digital literacy among consumers.

In the last decade, competition authorities have been focusing their attention on digital markets, and in particular, digital platform services. As these markets exhibit some characteristics believed to make application of "classical" competition law especially difficult, a consensus began to form in the EU that a new regulatory approach to these markets might be necessary. The EU decided to adopt a specific regulatory framework concerning the digital markets, specifically, the "gatekeeper" platforms. The economic significance of digital markets is enormous, and it continues to grow. Even before the pandemic of COVID-19, which enabled an unprecedented expansion of some digital services, it was estimated that the digital economy stands for 15.5 % of the world's GDP.

New market definitions therefore need to be found for digital platforms. This is however complicated by the multi-sided nature of these markets, uncommon to traditional competition law, and by the fact that the services of the platforms are frequently not paid for by final consumers; conversely, in traditional competition law, market definitions are based on price-related tests.

At the first sight, DMA is not a part of competition law. It expressly tells so in its preamble. Many scholars support this view, while others oppose it. It nonetheless needs to be observed that there are significant differences between "classic" competition law and the DMA. Whereas the competition law decides in principle ex post whether competition rules had been broken, DMA imposes ex ante obligations. Arguably, DMA also pursues different objectives than the competition law.

The logic of intervention is thus completely different: whereas the key obligation of undertakings under competition law is not to engage in behaviour capable of distorting competition and the competition authority assesses ex post whether there had been an infringement, in case of DMA, it is for the undertakings to define *ex ante* how they intend to comply with the obligations set by the DMA, and for the enforcement authority to check whether they adhere to these rules.

Even though the DMA pursues similar objectives as the competition law – a functioning competition – they aim to protect the competition from different dangers: whereas the competition law aims at preventing the distortion of competition by market power of the undertakings concerned, the DMA is not limited in this way. Thus, the scope of the DMA is broader, and, arguably, the objectives of the two sets of regulation differ.

The question whether the DMA is a specific competition law or not is however mostly an academic one, without specific practical consequences. It is however clear that the DMA brings more obligations than the "traditional" competition law would. The next question, therefore is, whether these new obligations are justified.

Concerning the competition law, we have suggested above that the objectives of the DMA and competition law are not identical. The DMA envisages parallel proceedings and sets specific rules for the cooperation and coordination with NCAs. We put forward that in this regard, the post-test may be met.

The DMA is a brand-new piece of legislation, designed to remedy specific problems in digital markets dominated by the providers of core platform services. Its regulatory characteristics differ significantly from both the competition law and sector-specific regulation. Crucially, these three sets of regulation seem to have different objectives and employ different tools to achieve them.

At the first sight, the tools introduced by the DMA seem to be adequate to address the specific problems associated with the regulation of digital markets; only the future practice of the Commission may however confirm this presumption.

The application of the DMA is not exclusive, the same conduct of the same undertakings might be investigated also by competition authorities or, more exceptionally, by national regulatory authorities. Even though specific circumstances of individual cases would be decisive to assess it, we believe that in principle, such a parallel application would be in line with the *ne bis in idem* principle, as interpreted by the CJEU.

The enforcement regime is 'Commission-centric' – Art. 16 to 36 DMA provide a comprehensive system of investigation and sanction powers of the European Commission and only "residual" powers to enforce national laws [Art. 38(1) to (3) DMA] and to support the European Commission's investigation [Art.

38(6) and (7) DMA] are left to NCAs. Moreover, the DMA stresses multiple times that the European Commission is the sole enforcer of the DMA.

Thus, the DMA explicitly restricted the manoeuvring space of other measures of public enforcement of the DMA than the European Commission.

Although the DMA itself is silent on subjective rights of individuals that are counterparts to the obligations of gatekeepers stipulated by the DMA, by the reference Directive (EU) 2020/1828 collective rights of consumers under the EU law are identifiable. In the event of infringement of the DMA by a gatekeeper (as a trader in law on consumers protection), qualified entities are entitled to seek at least injunctive measures and redress measures. Thus, the DMA is not completely "silent" on private claims.

Without explicit rules stipulating possible individual rights, the private law claims under the DMA shall be construed on a basis of combination of several sets of rules: (1) EU law – the TEU and the TFEU, the CJEU's case law, and the DMA; and (2) national law in application of the principle of procedural autonomy, subject to the usual limits established by the principles of effectiveness and equivalence. Therefore, claims are based rather on national law than EU law (the DMA) and apparent violation of an obligation stipulated in the DMA is "merely" a vehicle for proving a wrongful act as an element of liability for damage under national law.

The aim of the DMA was to remove obstacles caused by possibly different national regulation and the EU lawmaker saw "preventive harmonization" under Art. 114 TFEU as a sufficient legal basis (although it has been criticized, or at least discussed). In these aspects, the DMA failed to achieve this objective in the terms of private enforcement and created new sets of possible tensions between regulations of the Member States that can lead to underenforcement or overenforcement.

The use of algorithms is making the liability becoming more subjective. The intention of the undertakings may prove to be crucial from the enforcement perspective.

In our view, the competition authority in the model situation might focus on evidence on the reasonability of the purchase of the same pricing algorithm and evidence on the input and use of the pricing algorithm. However, if the purchase of the algorithm was rational and if the possibility to influence the input and use of the algorithm is very limited, the competition authority will arguably not be able to prove that there was a concerted practice, especially if there is no evidence of prior contact among undertakings.

However, if the supra-competition prices were reached precisely due to the fact that a database used by each undertaking were "on display" and the algorithm worked also with the databases of the other undertakings, such a red flag might be present. One can even say that this appears to be an exchange of information between undertakings, which is a prohibited practice in itself.

Pricing algorithms as a challenge for competition law has been discussed for several years. Article 101 TFEU is capable of capturing pricing algorithms with certain limits.

Unsurprisingly, the core stone of the problem lies in distinguishing the mere parallel use of algorithms on the one hand, and concerted practice on the other. As we demonstrated, certain traditional pieces of evidence, such as price development, are fruitless in these situations. None the less, there are other types of evidence which might be used, such as evidence on the rationality of the purchase of the algorithm and evidence on the use of the algorithm, including data used as input for the algorithm.

The concept of "Geo-blocking" could be described in several ways. According to European Commission staff working document, "geo-blocking refers to commercial practices whereby online providers prevent users from accessing and purchasing consumer goods/digital content services offered on their website based on the location of the user in a Member State different from that of the provider." Basically, the same meaning was referred by the European Parliament in it`s briefing papers: "Geo-blocking usually refers to discriminatory practices that prevent online customers from accessing and purchasing a product or a service from a website based in another Member State, automatically re-route them to a local site, and refuse delivery or payment based on the location or place of residence of the user".

Generally, this makes the context of geo-blocking wider, than just rerouting. It includes the concept of declining of payments, from those whose payment provided registered in the area, chosen for geo-blocking by provider of goods or services. In this meaning, we shall conclude, that geo-blocking, consists of all actions, directly or indirectly aimed at restricting access of customer from the specific geographical place to the goods, services or content proceeded through the Internet.

In general, the condition of price parity obliges the supplier to provide a product or service at a price not lower and / or on terms no less favorable than those already provided to other consumers. The essence of this approach stems from the vertical relationships established between online platforms and providers of goods and services sold on them. By setting price parity conditions, online platforms eliminate the risk of free use of their infrastructure by suppliers who can use the "name" of the platform to advertise their product but sell it through other channels.

With the development of e-commerce, the establishment of conditions on price parity has been repeatedly criticized by antitrust authorities in Sweden, Germany, France, Italy, Japan and the United States.

In the context of hotel reservations, there are two options for establishing price parity. In a broad interpretation, the condition of price parity requires the accommodation facility to provide rooms on the booking portal on terms no less favorable than those that already exist for any online or offline distribution channels, including the official website of the accommodation facility. In a narrow sense, the condition of price parity gives the hotel the opportunity to offer to read the terms through any other sales channels other than its official website.

As part of the investigation, the EC concluded that the agreements between Amazon and e-book providers contain provisions on the conditions for price parity. Amazon required e-book providers to notify the establishment of more attractive terms and prices for the sale of e-books on other sites, and to offer the same or similar conditions to Amazon.

By giving priority only to its own shopping comparison service and lowering the level of competitors, Google has gained a significant advantage over competitors.

There are high barriers to entry into these markets, in part because of network effects: the more consumers use a search engine, the more attractive it becomes to advertisers. The profits can be used to attract even more consumers, and the data that the search engine collects about consumers can also be used to improve their business.

Geo-blocking encompasses various practices through which online sellers restrict cross-border sales based on consumers' nationality, residence or place of establishment. Frequently, online sellers allow consumers to access and purchase goods or services cross-border, but nonetheless extend different terms and conditions if the customer is in a different Member State (geo-filtering).

The Geo-blocking Regulation seeks to remove unwarranted, discriminatory restrictions to users' access to cross-border trade and services and obliges online sellers to treat similarly situated EU consumers in the same manner, irrespective of their nationality, place of residence or establishment. Especially current EC practice shows unprecedented brave preconditions on geo-blocking practice in the form of licensing and distribution agreements concluded bilaterally between four out of the five PC video game publishers.

Computer security issues equally affect hardware and software, but surely stem from vulnerabilities referring to the weaknesses found in the design process and implementation of hardware architecture, which can be exploited by a hacker or perpetrator to mount an attack. Hardware is usually manufactured before or during software development, but cannot be easily updated like software, yet hardware executes the software.

The 2017 Cybersecurity Strategy of the EU expressly recognized the merit of "security by design" approach and "duty of care" principle. This started to materialize, in particular, in the EU Cybersecurity Act 2019, where key element is standardization and certification frameworks for products, services and processes. This includes aspects of vulnerability management.

Digital vulnerabilities are not to be exploited without authorization, in other words, for example hacking into computer systems by using techniques that exploit digital vulnerabilities can amount to a criminal offence. There is clearly relevant EU legislation addressing such cases, for example when the discovered vulnerability has already been exploited – so when, for example using the Spectre or Meltdown vulnerabilities, a personal data is leaked. In the hypothetical case of such data leak, there is a likelihood that in a preceding step, unauthorized access would be gained in the target system by the attacker, which is typically a first step in committing cybercrimes. Hence, Article 3 of the Botnet Directive (2013/40/EU), which also closely follows the analogous Article 2 of the CoE Cybercrime Convention, on illegal access becomes relevant presuming that the attacker resorts to exploitation of a vulnerability, because (s)he does not have authorization to access the information system or its part running the targeted data stream.

It should be noted that cybercrime laws apply regardless of whether a patch has been issued to mitigate a vulnerability, it is a zero-day or the exploitation takes place in the embargo/grace period. However, criminal laws are best suited to address conduct where exploitation of vulnerabilities has already taken place, and thus not representative of a preventive approach in cybersecurity policy.

Exploitation of vulnerabilities may be part of performing investigative acts, such as installing and operating spyware on suspect devices in criminal or national security investigations. Reportedly for example Pegasus spyware –a tool favored by many government agencies – exploited CVE-2016-4657 and CVE-2019-3568 vulnerabilities. The second flaw enabled the installation of the spyware by simply calling the target.

National cybersecurity strategies will need to include policies on managing vulnerabilities, national CSIRTS will be tasked with monitoring and analysing vulnerabilities and incidents at a national level, but also will provide information on as well as proactively scan certain systems for vulnerabilities.

With the coming of the IT security compliance scheme for hardware and software and the certification labs enabling the process properly as it is proposed through the Cyber Resilience Act, the European Union points out the need for manufacturers to improve the security of products with digital elements and to ensure that hardware and software products are placed on the market with fewer vulnerabilities in particular. Thus the proposed Act aims to set a paradigm shift in building cyber resilience. Having access to certified hardware and software devices with better cybersecurity posture may lead from reactive approaches to prevention. Consequently, European consumers have a unique chance to have conditions that allow them to take cybersecurity into account when selecting and using products with digital elements, hoping to result in less societal and economic costs in the future. However, it also means the end of IT as we know it and businesses will be under significant pressure to keep up with innovation by malicious actors.

One core question, debated for years in the legal academic circles, reflects on the notion of liability when applied to AI systems. Who should be held accountable when an autonomous system causes harm or makes erroneous decisions?

The implementation of the AI Act and the legal instruments analyzed represents a significant step towards regulating Artificial Intelligence and ensuring ethical and responsible AI practices. However, it must be acknowledged that, despite the obligations outlined in these frameworks, there are still potential instances where AI wrongdoings may occur, even in full compliance with the existing legal instruments. Acknowledging this reality can only leave a bittersweet taste, for there is no concrete answer that can give a closure to the proposed question.

In exploring non-contractual civil liability, previous research has shown that AI systems can still cause harm to users, even when complying with the AI Act. Instances such as proxy discrimination highlight this concern. In an ideal scenario of implementing the AI Act and the AI liability regime, three conditions would need to be met to establish liability: the harm must be caused by a high-risk AI system, a breach of the AI Act's obligations must be proven, and a causal connection between the breach and the harm must be demonstrated. If no breach occurs, the Product Liability Directive (PLD) may be the applicable instrument. Under the PLD, the defectiveness of an AI system will be assessed considering the listed circumstances in Article 6. How these requirements are balanced by the relevant authorities will significantly impact the outcome.

There are many examples of successful cyber attacks on vehicles or their systems.

Cyber security incidents, the result of which is taking control over the driving of the vehicle, can have fatal consequences in road traffic not only for the driver and passengers of the vehicle, but also for other road users. Road traffic safety may be impaired, damage may occur, a person may be injured or even killed. Therefore, it is more than necessary to deal with issues of cyber security of automated vehicles and fully automated vehicles, which should ensure a sufficient level of protection of automated vehicles and fully automated vehicles, or their systems against various cyber threats.

The NIS 2 Directive will strengthen the cyber security of traditional vehicles as well as automated vehicles and fully automated vehicles. Vehicle manufacturers will be obliged to implement security measures that will include, e.g. risk analysis, incident handling, supply chain security, policies and procedures to assess the effectiveness of cybersecurity risk-management measures, basic cyber hygiene practices and cybersecurity training. Vehicle manufacturers will also be obliged to notify, without undue delay, its CSIRT or, where applicable, its competent authority of any incident that has a significant impact on the provision of their services. However, it must be noted that the incident must concern networks and information systems that ensure the production of vehicles.

According to the EU Cybersecurity Act (2019) the term cybersecurity "means the activities necessary to protect network and information systems, the users of such systems, and other persons affected by cyber threats". Regarding cyber defence, there is no explicit definition. However in the Joint Communication to the European Parliament and the Council entitled "EU Policy on Cyber Defence", the European Commission understand behind the term: "the ability to prevent, detect, defend against, recover from, and deter cyberattacks aimed at the EU and its Member States using all means available". In some aspects including resilience or prevention, both definitions overlap. Nonetheless, it is evident, that defence may be understood in the context of an attack as there is an active element of response. Despite the fact, that the EU's definition of security is focused mainly on and built around "protection", the EU initiatives go far beyond this scope and contribute to the cultivation of the cyber ecosystem.

The EU is not having an official cybersecurity policy. However, over the years EU created a dense and robust environment characterized by strategic documents, tools, and initiatives, which have significant policy dimensions.

Despite great progress over the years, there are still limits of cooperation that are inherent also to other areas dealing with security. The diverging position of Member States in the EU often prevented greater development of cyber defence. For example, as noted by Luukas et al. (2016), there were always Member States like Germany or the Netherlands viewing cyber security as the issue of homeland security in opposition to some other countries countries like Estonia or Denmark, with a vision of common defence, which is also contrary to Italy and Finland, seeing cybersecurity as the issue of commerce and communication.

The limits of cooperation between the EU and NATO are inherent to the character of both actors and the political divergencies of the Member States. However, as discussed above, even the basics of cyber security and cyber defence in the EU are perceived differently by the Member States, and political divergence is further undermined by varying administrative-organizational environments among the Member States. It is questionable, whether the current setting in which the EU sets minimum standards and cyber defense is merely the issue of Member States (with NATO guarantee) is an optimal setting. On the one hand, variability, diversity, and a certain flexibility is allowing Member States to maintain the required level of sovereignty and respect natural differences among

Member States, on the other hand, it may be associated with vulnerability in the case of policy laggards. In the contemporary world, the advantage might be on actors with strong central capacities who can assemble huge resources to connect high ICT technologies with expert human capital. The rise of China or USA, together with emerging AI will create further pressure for closer cooperation with NATO and possibly also centralization and supra-nationalization of cyber security and cyber defence, policy in the EU, as protecting citizens and companies will be associated with increased costs for countries, willing to rely on the sovereign approach.

Doctrinal differences have led to the fact that cybersecurity can be considered from at least three perspectives: as measures and actions aimed at protecting information systems; as the state of security in the cyber environment; and finally, as the ability to defend and resist existing and potential threats. For example, the Cambridge dictionary proposes to consider cyber security as things that are done to protect a person, organization or country and their computer information against crime or attacks carried out using the Internet.

EU law does not directly define, but it allows to distinguish the private and public components of cyber security. The former is related to the protection of the rights and interests of individuals and legal entities from encroachments on their social, economic, and other private legal relations. The latter concerns the protection against cyber threats aimed at the national interests of Member States, the interests of the EU as a whole, and critical infrastructure. Such a concept of cybersecurity requires proper legal fixation, as Member States have not only different approaches to its legal regulation but also different capabilities for its real provision. This clearly does not contribute to the formation of a secure cyber environment within the EU.

In contrast to the private component of cybersecurity, the public component raises many controversies since it is associated with defence and military activity. This has led to the exclusively discretionary nature of legal regulation of cyber defence within the EU. In fact, cyber defence covers not only military objects but also civil critical infrastructure.

Institutional guarantees of cybersecurity are based on the work of several important EU bodies, the most significant of which is ENISA. Establishing the right to cybersecurity requires a transformation of the Agency's structure and powers. In addition to coordination functions, ENISA must receive basic control over functions and mechanisms for responding to violations of the right to cybersecurity. Also, this Agency must necessarily receive a number of powers aimed at protecting the rights and interests of crypto asset users. The scope of their use in the modern economy indicates that they are gradually becoming an essential component of the internal market.

In the process of reforming the concept of cybersecurity in the EU, the experience of Ukraine, a country with a high level of digitalisation and experience in fighting aggression, is of particular interest. Ukrainian legislation is characterized by a comprehensive vision of cybersecurity, including the recognition of the priority of human rights and interests in cyberspace. In addition, Ukraine is in the process of building a cyber defence system against the aggression of the Russian Federation. Introduced innovations, such as active counteraction to aggression in cyberspace (active cyber defence), can become part of the European cyber defence system, as they fit into the paradigm of EU defence policy and comply with the principle of the non-use of force or the threat of its use.

The EU Member States are constantly working on the formation of a legal framework that would allow the state to control the legality of the use of crypto-assets and protect the rights of investors and other participants in legal relations. However, this does not contribute to the unification of legal regulation in different states.

It can be stated that there is a strong need to change approaches to cybersecurity regulation. EU law should be based on the inalienable right to cybersecurity. Ensuring this right is possible only by establishing effective protection mechanisms, from sanctions for non-compliance with cybersecurity standards to special measures to compensate for the damage caused. This also applies to the protection of the rights of participants in crypto-asset markets as subjects, the security of which completely depends on the proper level of cybersecurity. Only special legislation can guarantee legal certainty, and, accordingly, the effectiveness of the protection of consumers and investors' rights.

Among the possible approaches to understanding the essence of cybersecurity (including in the field of using crypto-assets), we prefer a broad approach. In such a case, the formation of the right to cybersecurity is possible, which includes not only the state of technical security, but also the appropriate legal and institutional guarantees of protection and compensation for damages. Perhaps it would be appropriate to include such a right into the EU Charter of Fundamental Rights. In our opinion, this is fully justified given the fact that many social relations are moving into the digital sphere. It is now impossible to talk about guaranteeing the proper quality of life, human rights and freedoms without ensuring a high level of protection against cyber threats.

In order to establish proper control over cybersecurity and protect the rights of users when using crypto-assets, it is important not only to create special bodies both at the level of the EU and at the level of its Member States, but also to strengthen the powers of the existing ones. In this context, the powers of ENISA would need to be improved. However, its effective activity in this direction is possible only after the expansion of its powers. The creation of a special structural unit (department) of ENISA, which would focus its activities on cybersecurity in the field of crypto-assets, seems to be fully justified.

These conclusions summarise the key ideas of the research which was done in the several directions and on different issues of the new born branch of the EU law.

Nevertheless, it is obvious that the real value and main asset, which must be protected in priority, is the human being itself and its dignity. As it was already stated by the leading contemporary author: "biotechnology and Artificial Intelligence now seek to change the very meaning of humanity (Harari, Y.N.: 21 lessons for the 21st century, Vintage London 2018, p. 247)".

In this respect the usage of modern technologies must be accompanied (and even preceded) by special guarantees of the human rights nature, which are applicable just in the field of digitalisation, robotisation and cybesecurity and which willl reflect the peculiarities of those. We are speaking of the digital entitlements (rights) of the individual which can be declared in the form of a separate catalogue or can be incorporated into the Charter of Fundamental Rights of the EU as the autonomous right to digital integrity, including these entitlements as its integral parts. The catalogue of digital rights could consist of both already declared rights, as well as entirely new entitlements of the individual such as, for instance:

- Right to the access to Internet;
- Right to the communication in cyber space (via email, social media, chats);
- Right to be forgotten (right to erasure);
- Right for information, clear explanation and truthful information in e-commerce;
- Right to communication with a human operator and not to be the subject of the automated decision;
- Prohibition of discriminatory conditions in the transactions made online, especially in e-commerce (personalized pricing, geo-blocking etc.);
- Right to cybersecurity.

This coherent catalogue (first in the form of declaration) can become in future a proper basis and an eligible platform for formulation of new autonomous rights and their regulation by the universal legal instruments.

TABLE OF CASES

I. Judgements of the Court of Justice of the EU and Tribunal

C- 41/69 ACF Chemiefarma v Commission, ECLI:EU:C:1970:71.

C-48/69 Imperial Chemical Industries Ltd. v Commission of the European Communities, ECLI:EU:C:1972:70.

C-114/73 Coöperatieve Vereniging "Suiker Unie" UA and others v Commission of the European Communities, ECLI:EU:C:1975:174.

C-33/76 Zentralfinanz eG and Rewe-Zentral AG v Landwirtschaftskammer für das Saarland, ECLI:EU:C:1976:188.

C-209/78 to 215/78 and 218/78 Heintz van Landewyck SARL and Others v Commission of the European Communities, ECLI:EU:C:1980:248.

C-107/82 AEG v Commission, ECLI:EU:C:1983:293.

C-25/84 and 26/84 Ford and Ford Europe v Commission, ECLI:EU:C:1985:340.

T-7/89 SA Hercules Chemicals NV v Commission of the European Communities, ECLI:EU:T:1991:75.

C-234/89 Stergios Delimitis v Henninger Bräu AG, ECLI:EU:C:1991:91.

T-43/92 Dunlop Slazenger v Commission, ECLI:EU:T:1994:79.

C-199/92 P Hüls AG v Commission of the European Communities, ECLI:EU:C:1999:358.

C-92/09 and C-93/09, Volker und Markus Schecke and Eifert, ECLI:EU:C:2010:662.

T-41/96 Bayer AG v Commission of the European Communities, ECLI:EU:T:2000:242.

C-377/98 Kingdom of the Netherlands v European Parliament and Council of the European Union.

C-344/98 Masterfoods and HB, ECLI:EU:C:2000:689.

C-403/98 Azienda Agricola Monte Arcosu Srl v Regione Autonoma della Sardegna, Organismo Comprensoriale n° 24 della Sardegna and Ente Regionale per l'Assistenza Tecnica in Agricoltura (ERSAT), ECLI:EU:C:2001:6.

C-194/99 P Thyssen Stahl v Commission, ECLI:EU:C:2003:527.

C-453/99 Courage Ltd v Bernard Crehan and Bernard Crehan v Courage Ltd and Others, ECLI:EU:C:2001:465.

C-2/01 P Bundesverband der Arzneimittel-Importeure eV and Commission of the European Communities v Bayer AG, ECLI:EU:C:2004:2.

C-105/04 P Nederlandse Federatieve Vereniging voor de Groothandel op Elektrotechnisch Gebied v Commission, ECLI:EU:C:2006:592.

C-295/04 to C-298/04 Vincenzo Manfredi v Lloyd Adriatico Assicurazioni SpA (C-295/04), Antonio Cannito v Fondiaria Sai SpA (C-296/04) and Nicolò Tricarico (C-297/04) and Pasqualina Murgolo (C-298/04) v Assitalia SpA, ECLI:EU:C:2006:461.

C-432/05 Unibet (London) Ltd and Unibet (International) Ltd v Justitiekansler, ECLI:EU:C:2007:163.

C-501/06 P, C-513/06 P, C-515/06 P a C-519/06 P GlaxoSmithKline Services Unlimited v Commission of the European Communities (C-501/06 P) and Commission of the European Communities v GlaxoSmithKline Services Unlimited (C-513/06 P) and European Association of Euro Pharmaceutical Companies (EAEPC) v Commission of the European Communities (C-515/06 P) and Asociación de exportadores españoles de productos farmacéuticos (Aseprofar) v Commission of the European Communities (C-519/06 P), ECLI:EU:C:2009:610.

C 209/07 Beef Industry Development Society and Barry Brothers, ECLI:EU:C:2008:643.

C 8/08 T Mobile Netherlands and Others, ECLI:EU:C:2009:343.

T-587/08 Fresh Del Monte Produce, Inc. v European Commission, ECLI:EU:T:2013:129.

C-92/09 and C-93/09, Volker und Markus Schecke and Eifert, ECLI:EU:C:2010:662, paragraph 48.

Decision no. 2009-580 DC of 10 June 2009 Act furthering the diffusion and protection of creation on the Internet.

C-32/11 Allianz Hungária Biztosító Zrt. and Others v Gazdasági Versenyhivatal, ECLI:EU:C:2013:160.

C-131/12, Google Spain SL and Google Inc. v. Agencia Española de Protección de Datos (AEPD) and Mario Costeja González, ECLI:EU:C:2014:317.

C-382/12 P MasterCard Inc. and Others v European Commission, ECLI:EU:C:2014:2201.

C-67/13 P Groupement des cartes bancaires (CB) v European Commission, ECLI:EU:C:2014:2204.

C-634/13 P Total Marketing Services v Commission, [EU:C:2015:614.

C-74/14 "Eturas" UAB and Others v Lietuvos Respublikos konkurencijos taryba, ECLI:EU:C:2016:42, C-807/18. C-373/14 P Toshiba Corporation v European Commission, ECLI:EU:C:2016:26.

C-469/15 P FSL Holdings and Others v European Commission, ECLI:EU:C:2017:308.

C-524/15 Criminal proceedings against Luca Menci, ECLI:EU:C:2018:197.

C-637/17 Cogeco Communications Inc v Sport TV Portugal SA and Others, ECLI:EU:C:2019:263.

C-228/18 Gazdasági Versenyhivatal v Budapest Bank Nyrt. and Others, ECLI:EU:C:2020:265.

C-132/19 Groupe Canal + v European Commission, ECLI:EU:C:2020:1007.

C-151/20 Bundeswettbewerbsbehörde v Nordzucker AG and Others, ECLI:EU:C:2022:203.

C-117/20 bpost SA v. Autorité belge de la concurrence, ECLI:EU:C:2022:202, C-306/20 SIA "Visma Enterprise" v Konkurences padome, ECLI:EU:C:2021:935.

C-460/20 Google (Déréférencement d'un contenu prétendument inexact), ECLI:EU:C:2022:962.

II. Judgements of the European Court of Human Rights

Case of Loizidou v. Turkey (Application no. 15318/89).

Case of Leyla Şahin v. Turkey (Application no. 44774/98).

Case of Cengiz and Others v. Turkey (Applications no. 48226/10 and 14027/11).

Case of Kalda v. Estonia (Application No. 17429/10).

Case of Jankovskis v. Lithuania (Application no. 21575/08).

SELECTED BIBLIOGRAPHY

AKERLOF, G. A. The market for "lemons": Quality uncertainty and the market mechanism. *The Quarterly Journal of Economics.* 1970, vol. 84, no. 3, pp. 488–500.

AL BLOOSH, I. B., EKSTEEN, A. Cyber Governance in the EU. European Cybersecurity in Context A Policy-Oriented Comparative Analysis. 2022, pp. 19–26. Available at: https://liberalforum.eu/wp-content/uploads/2022/08/European-Cybersecurity-in-Context_ELF-Study_Techno-Politics.pdf

AL-YOUZBAKY, B. A., HANNA, R. D. The Effect of Information Overload, and Social Media Fatigue on Online Consumers Purchasing Decisions: The Mediating Role of Technostress and Information Anxiety. *Journal of System and Management Sciences.* 2022, vol. 12, no. 2, pp. 195–220.

AMARO, R. Weaving Penelope's Shroud … Some Comments on the Private Enforcement of the DMA. *Competition Forum.* 2022, no. 0042, pp. 1–6. Available at: https://competition-forum.com

ANDRIYCHUK, O. Do DMA obligations for gatekeepers create entitlements for business users? *Journal of Antitrust Enforcement.* 2023, vol. 11, no. 1, pp. 123–132.

ANGWIN, J. The web's new gold mine: Your secrets: A journal investigation finds that one of the fastest-growing businesses on the internet is the business of spying on consumers. *The Wall Street Journal.* 2010. Available at: http://www.wsj.com/articles/SB10001424052748703940904575395073512989404

BAKALINSKA, O., BAKALINSKY, O. The Legal encouragement of the cyber security in Ukraine. *Administrative Law and Process.* 2019, vol. 9, pp. 100–108.

BARRINHA, A. Virtual Neighbors: Russia and the EU in Cyberspace. *Insight Turkey.* 2018, vol. 20, no. 3, pp. 29–42.

BEKE, F. T., EGGERS, F., VERHOEF, P. C., WIERINGA, J. E. Consumers' privacy calculus: The PRICAL index development and validation. *International Journal of Research in Marketing.* 2022, vol. 39, no. 1, pp. 20–41.

BENDIEK, A., MAAT, E. P. The EU's Regulatory Approach to Cybersecurity. Stiftung Wissenschaft und Politik. 2019. 30 p. Available at: https://www.swpberlin.org/publications/products/arbeitspapiere/WP_Bendiek_Pander_Maat_EU_Approach_Cybersecurity.pdf

BERGER, E. Österreichs Allgemeines Bürgerliches Gesetzbuch (ABGB): Eine europäische Privatrechtskodifikation. Band III: Das ABGB außerhalb Österreichs. Schriften zur Europäischen Rechts- und Verfassungsgeschichte, vol. 57, Wien: Duncker & Humblot GmbH, 2010.

BERNAL, P. A. A Right to Delete? *European Journal of Law and Technology.* 2011, vol. 2., issue 2.

BLAŽO, O. Bypassing Competition Law, Bypassing through Competition Law. *EU ANTITRUST: HOT TOPICS & NEXT STEPS.* Proceedings of the International Conference. Prague: 2022, s. 372–382. ISBN 9788076300217.

BLAŽO, O. The Digital Markets acts: Between market regulation, competition rules and unfair trade practices rules. *Strani pravni zivot*. 2022, vol. 66, no. 1, s. 117–136.

BLOCKX, J. Antitrust in Digital Markets in the EU: Policing Price Bots. Available at: https://papers.ssrn.com/sol3/papers.cfm?abstract_id=2987705

BOEKE, S. National cyber crisis management: Different European approaches. *Governance*. 2018, vol. 31, pp. 449–464. Available at: https://doi.org/10.1111/gove.12309

BOGDAN, M. The New EU Regulation on Online Resolution for Consumer Disputes. *Masaryk University Journal of Law and Technology*. 2015, vol. 9, no. 1, p. 155.

BOTTA, M., WIEDEMANN, K. Exploitative conducts in digital markets: Time for a discussion after the facebook decision. *Journal of European Competition Law and Practice*. 2019, vol. 10, no. 8, pp. 465–478.

BOTTA, M., WIEDEMANN, K. The interaction of EU competition, consumer, and data protection law in the digital economy: The regulatory dilemma in the facebook odyssey. *Antitrust Bulletin*. 2019, vol. 64, no. 3, pp. 428–446.

BOTTA, M. Sector Regulation of Digital Platforms in Europe: Uno, Nessuno e Centomila. *Journal of European Competition Law & Practice*. 2021, vol. 12, no. 7, pp. 500–512.

BUBLITZ, CH. The body of law: boundaries, extensions, and the human right to physical integrity in the biotechnical age. *Journal of law and the biosciences*. 2022, vol. 9, no. 2, pp. 1–26. DOI:10.1093/jlb/lsac032

CAFORIO, V. Algorithmic tacit collusion: a regulatory approach. Available at: https://ssrn.com/abstract=4164905

CAILLAUD, B., DE NIJS, R. Strategic loyalty reward in dynamic price discrimination. *Marketing Science*. 2014, vol. 33, no. 5, pp. 725–742.

CANETTI, D., SHANDLER, R. A Reality of Vulnerability and Dependence: Internet Access as a Human Right. *Israel Law Review*. 2019, vol. 52, no. 1, pp. 77–98.

CARRAPICO, H., BARRINHA, A. The EU as a Coherent (Cyber) Security Actor? *Journal of Common Market Studies*. 2017, vol. 55, no. 6, pp. 1254-1272. Available at: https://doi.org/10.1111/jcms.12575

CARUGATI, Ch. The 2017 facebook saga: A competition, consumer and data protection story. *European Competition and Regulatory Law Review*. 2018, vol. 2, no. 1, pp. 4–10.

CAUFFMAN, C., GOANTA, C. A new order: The digital services act and consumer protection. *European Journal of Risk Regulation*. 2021, vol. 12, no. 4, pp. 758–774. ISSN 21908249. DOI: 10.1017/err.2021.8

CAUFFMAN, C. The impact of Article 101(2) TFEU Nullity on Private Law. In MICKLITZ, H., SIEBURGH, C. (eds.). *Primary EU law and Private Law Concepts*. Cambridge: Intersentia, 2017, pp. 165–205.

CEER. Cyber Security Work Stream. Cybersecurity Report on Europe's Electricity and Gas Sectors (26 October 2018). Available at: https://www.ceer.eu/cybersecurity-report-on-europe-s-electricity-and-gas-sectors

CEER. Training on Cybersecurity: Risk Management and Preparedness, Legal and Policy Developments. 31 May–2 June 2022. Available at: https://www.ceer.eu/training-on-cybersecurity-risk-management-and-preparedness-legal-and-policy-developments

COHEN, J. E. Law for the Platform Economy. *Georgetown Law Technology Review*. 2018, vol. 2, pp. 191–196.

COLANGELO, G. The European Digital Markets Act and Antitrust Enforcement: A Liaison Dangereuse. *European Law Review.* 2022, vol. 47, no. 5, pp. 597–621.

CREMER, J., MONJOYE, Y., SCHWEITZER, H. Competition Policy for the Digital Era. Available at: https://ec.europa.eu/competition/publications/reports/kd0419345enn.pdf. Accessed 10. 5. 2023.

CROSBY, M., PATTANAYAK, P., VERMA, S., KALYANARAMAN, V. BlockChain technology beyond Bitcoin. Available at: https://scet.berkeley.edu/wp-content/uploads/BlockchainPaper.pdf

CROXSON, K., FROST, J., GAMBACORTA, L., VALLETTI, T. Platform-based business models and financial inclusion. *Journal of Competition Law and Economics.* 2022, vol. 19, no. 6, pp. 75–102.

CURRY, S. Web Hackers vs. the Auto Industry: Critical Vulnerabilities in Ferrari, BMW, Rolls Royce, Porsche, and More. Available at: https://samcurry.net/web-hackers-vs-the-auto-industry/.

CUSTERS, B., MALGIERI, G. Priceless data: why the EU fundmental right to data protection is at odds with trade in personal data. *Computer Law & Security Review.* 2022, vol. 45, 2022, 105683.

CUSTERS, B., Alan, M., DECHESNE, F., GEORGIEVA, I., TANI, T., VAN DER HOF, S. Introduction – The Netherlands. *EU Personal Data Protection Policy and Practice.* Asser Press: The Hague, The Netherlands, 2019, vol. 29.

DE FRANCESCHI, A., SCHULZE, R. (eds.). *Harmonizing Digital Contract Law. The Impact of EU Directives 2019/770 and 2019/771 and the Regulation of Online Platforms.* A Handbook. Baden-Baden: Hart/Nomos, 2023.

DE HERT, P., KLOZA, D. Internet (access) as a new fundamental right. Inflating the current rights framework? *European Journal of Law and Technology.* 2012, vol. 3, no. 3. Available at: https://ejlt.org/index.php/ejlt/article/view/123/268

DENEMARK, J. *Právo být zapomenout v kontextu moderního pojetí ochrany osobních údajů.* Wolters Kluwer, Prague: 2021.

DEWISPELAERE, J., GHYSELS, T. The Duplication of Proceedings and Penalties under Sectoral Rules and Competition Law Recast: Toshiba Is Dead, Long Live Bpost? *European Competition and Regulatory Law Journal.* 2022, vol. 6, no. 3, pp. 278–283.

DI DOMENICO, G., SIT, J., ISHIZAKA, A., NUNAN, D. Fake news, social media and marketing: A systematic review. *Journal of Business Research.* 2021, vol. 124, pp. 329–341.

DI DOMENICO, G., VISENTIN, M. Fake news or true lies? Reflections about problematic contents in marketing. *International Journal of Market Research.* 2020, vol. 62, no. 4, pp. 409–417.

DRAŽOVÁ, P. Kybernetická kriminalita. In ANDRAŠKO, J. (ed.). *Právo informačných a komunikačných technológií.* 2. vydání. Bratislava: TINCT, 2021, pp. 149–194.

EASTERBROOK, F. H. Cyberspace and the Law of the Horse. *University of Chicago Legal Forum.* 1996, vol. 207, pp. 207–2016.

ESKENS, S. A right to reset your user profile and more: GDPR-rights for personalized news consumers. *International Data Privacy Law.* 2019, vol. 9, no. 3, pp. 153–17.

ESPOSITO, F. The GDPR enshrines the right to the impersonal price. *Computer Law & Security Review.* 2022, vol. 45, 105660.

ESTRADA, M. Revisiting access to internet as a fundamental right in times of COVID-19. *UNIO – EU Law Journal*. 2020, vol. 6, no. 2, pp. 15–24. Available at: https://doi.org/10.21814/unio.6.2.2753

EU policy supporting the digital and green transformation of the energy system. Available at: https://digital-strategy.ec.europa.eu/en/policies/eu-policy-digitalisation-energy

EVANS, D. S. The Antitrust Economics of Multisided Platform Markets. *Yale Journal on Regulation.* 2023, vol. 20, no. 2, pp. 325–381.

EVANS, D. S. The Economics of Attention Market. Available at: https://ssrn.com/abstract=3044858. Accessed 10. 05. 2023.

EZRACHI, A., STUCKE, M. E. ARTIFICIAL INTELLIGENCE & COLLUSION: WHEN COMPUTERS INHIBIT COMPETITION. Available at: https://papers.ssrn.com/sol3/papers.cfm?abstract_id=2591874. Accessed 23. 2. 2023.

EZRACHI, A., STUCKE, M. E. Sustainable and Unchallenged Algorithmic Tacit Collusion. *Northwestern Journal of Technology and Intellectual Property.* vol. 17, no. 2, 2020.

EZRACHI, A., STUCKE, M. E. *Virtual Competition.* First Edition. Cambridge, Massachusetts: Harvard University Press, 2016.

EZRACHI, A. The Goals of EU Competition Law and the Digital Economy. Available at: https://www.beuc.eu/publications/beuc-x-2018-071_goals_of_eu_competition_law_and_digital_economy.pdf

FARHAAN, A. Right to Be Forgotten: a critique of the post Costeja Gonzalez paradigm. *Computer and Telecommunications Law Review.* 2015.

FAINMESSER, I. P., GALEOTTI, A., MOMOT, R. Digital Privacy. *Management Science.* 2022, vol. 69, no. 6, pp. 3157–3173.

FIDLER, D. P., PREGENT, R., VARDURME, A. NATO, Cyber Defense, and International Law. *Journal of International and Comparative Law.* 2013, vol. 4, no. 1, pp. 1–25.

FLOWERS, A., ZEADALLY, S. UP Policy on Active Cyber Defense. *Journal of Homeland Security and Emergency Management.* 2014, vol. 11, no. 2, pp. 289–308. Available at: https://doi.org/10.1515/jhsem-2014-0021

FORD, CH. A. Conceptualizing Cyberspace Security Diplomacy. *The Cyber Defense Review.* 2022, vol. 7, no. 2, pp. 35–54.

FRANCK, J., MONTI, G., STREEL, A. Legal Opinion commissioned by the Federal Ministry for Economic Affairs and Energy concerning Article 114 TFEU as a Legal Basis for Strengthened Control of Acquisitions by Digital Gatekeepers. In., s. 74. Available at: https://www.bmwi.de/Redaktion/EN/Publikationen/Wirtschaft/article-114-tfeu-as-a-legal-basis-for-strengthened-control-of-acquisitions-by-digital-gatekeepers.pdf?__blob=publicationFile&v=5

FROSINI, T. E. Access To Internet As A Fundamental Right. *Italian Journal of Public Law.* 2013, vol. 5, no. 2, pp. 226–234. Available at: https://www.ijpl.eu/wp-content/uploads/2022/10/7.Frosini.pdf.

FUSTER, G. G., JASMONTAITE, L. Cybersecurity Regulation in the European Union: The Digital, the Critical and Fundamental Rights. *The Ethics of Cybersecurity.* 2020, pp. 97–115. Available at: https://www.researchgate.net/publication/339161315_Cybersecurity_Regulation_in_the_European_Union_The_Digital_the_Critical_and_Fundamental_Rights

GAL, M. ALGORITHMS AS ILLEGAL AGREEMENTS. Available at: https://papers.ssrn.com/sol3/papers.cfm?abstract_id=3171977

GALINSKI, M. Kybernetická bezpečnosť automatizovaných vozidiel – technické aspekty. ANDRAŠKO, J. (ed.). *Právne a technické aspekty kybernetickej bezpečnosti automatizovaných vozidiel.* Bratislava: Wolters Kluwer SR, 2022, pp. 13–59.

GANKEVYCH, K., LEVCHUK, V., KOROLYOV, S. Critical Infrastructure Facilities of Ukraine in the System of the Ministry of Defense of Ukraine. *Legal electronic journal.* 2021, no. 11, pp. 79–82. Available at: http://www.lsej.org.ua/11_2021/17.pdf

GAUDIN, G., MANTZARI, D. Google Shopping and the As-Efficient-Competitor Test: Taking Stock and Looking Ahead. *Journal of European Competition Law and Practice.* 2022, vol. 13, no. 2, pp. 125–135.

GERBRANDY, A., PHOA, P. The Power of Big Tech Corporations as Modern Bigness and a Vocabulary for Shaping Competition Law as Counter-Power. *Wealth and Power.* New York: Routledge, 2022, s. 166–185.

GHOSE, A., HUANG, K. Personalized pricing and quality customization. *Journal of Economics & Management Strategy.* 2009, vol. 18, no. 4, pp. 1095–1135.

GÖNENÇ, G., KAĞAN, A. U., YILDIZ, G. Is there a Need for a Visible Hand in Digital Markets? *European Competition and Regulatory Law Journal.* 2022, vol. 6, no. 4, pp. 306–317.

GONZÁLEZ, E. G., DE HERT, P. Understanding the legal provisions that allow processing and profiling of personal data – An analysis of the GDPR provisions and principles. *ERA Forum.* 2019, vol. 19, pp. 597–621.

GOSSE, Ch. "Not the Real World": Exploring Experiences of Online Abuse, Digital Dualism, and Ontological Labor. The Emerald International Handbook of Technology Facilitated Violence and Abuse. 2021. Available at: https://www.semanticscholar.org/paper/"Not-the-Real-World"%3A-Exploring-Experiences-of-and-Gosse/4b39d472fb8f95fbc7c48d3ec7322c1f2ae75904

GOSZTONYI, G. European Court of Human Rights: Internet Access as a Means of Receiving and Imparting Information and Ideas. *International Comparative Jurisprudence.* 2020, vol. 6, no. 2, pp. 139.

CRAIG, P. *The Lisbon Treaty. Law, Politics and Treaty Reform.* Oxford University Press, Oxford, 2010.

GRIFFITHS, M. D. Is the buying of loot boxes in video games a form of gambling or gaming? *Gaming Law Review.* 2018, vol. 22, no. 1, pp. 52–54.

HACKER, P., CORDES, J., ROCHON, J. *Regulating Gatekeeper AI and Data: Transparency, Access, and Fairness under the DMA, the GDPR, and Beyond.* Working Paper, December 9, 2022, pp. 1–41.

HACKER, P. Teaching Fairness to Artificial Intelligence: Existing and Novel Strategies Against Algorithmic Discrimination Under EU Law. *Common Market Law Review.* 2018, vol. 55, pp. 1143–1186.

HADFIELD, G. K., HOWSE, R., TREBILCOCK, M. J. Information-Based Principles for Rethinking Consumer Protection Policy. *Journal of Consumer Policy.* 1998, no. 21, pp. 131–169.

HAMULAK, O. The Variations of Judicial Enforcement of EU Charter of Fundamental Rights vis-á-vis Union Institutions and Bodies. *The Review of European Law, Economics and Politics.* 2018, pp. 98–112.

HAMUĽÁK, O., KOCHARYAN, H., KERIKMÄE, T. The Contemporary Issues of Post-Mortem Personal Data Protection in the EU after GDPR entering into Force. *Czech Yearbook of Public and Private International Law.* 2020, vol. 11, pp. 225–238.

HAN, C., REYES, I., BAR ON, A. E., REARDON, J., FEAL, Á., BAMBERGER, K. A., EGELMAN, S., VALLINA-RODRIGUEZ, N. Do You Get What You Pay For? Comparing The Privacy Behaviors of Free vs. PaidApps. Available at: https://dspace.networks.imdea.org/bitstream/handle/20.500.12761/691/Do_You_Get_What_You_Pay_For_2019_EN.pdf?sequence=1&isAllowed=y.

HEARD, A. Human rights: Chimeras in sheep's clothing. An Introduction to Human Rights Theory, 1997. Available at: https://lawprojects.wordpress.com/2012/03/01/human-rights-chimeras-in-sheeps-clothing/

CHIPIDZA, W., YAN, J. Does Flaggin Potus's Tweets Lead to Fewer or More Retweets? Preliminary Evidence from Machine Learning Models. *IDEAS.* p. 18. Available at: https://ideas.repec.org/p/osf/socarx/69hkb.html

HODÁS, M. *Implementácia autonómnej mobility – niektoré filozofické a (ústavno) právne aspekty a ich právne a metaprávne implikácie nielen pre Slovenskú republiku.* Praha: Leges, 2022, 101 p.

HÖNIG, M. Initial Coin Offering. Studie zu Kryptowährungen und der Blockchain-Technologie. Available at: https://www.frankfurtuniversity.de/fileadmin/stan dard/Hochschule/Fachbereich_3/Kontakt/Professor_inn_en/Hoenig/20180502_Bitcoin_Studie_fra_uas_Hoenig_V1.0.pdf.

HORVATH, A. Protection of consumers provided in the proposal for a regulation of markets in crypto assets. *Zaštita kolektivnih interesa potrošača.* 2021, p. 428–455. Available at: https://doi.org/10.18485/union_pf_ccr.2021.ch21

HU, H., KRISHEN, A. S. When is enough, enough? Investigating product reviews and information overload from a consumer empowerment perspective. *Journal of Business Research.* 2019, vol. 100, pp. 27–37.

CHARETTE, R. N. How Software Is Eating the Car The trend toward self-driving and electric vehicles will add hundreds of millions of lines of code to cars. Can the auto industry cope? Available at: https://spectrum.ieee.org/software-eating-car>

CHIARA P.G. The IoT and the new EU cybersecurity regulatory landscape. *International Review of Law. Computers & Technology.* 2022, vol. 36, no. 2, pp. 118–137. Available at: https://www.tandfonline.com/doi/epdf/10.1080/13600869.2022.2060468?needAccess=true&role=button

CHIRICO, F. Digital Markets Act. A Regulatory Perspective. *Journal of European Competition Law & Practice.* 2021, vol. 12, no. 7, pp. 493–499.

CHIRITA, A. Google's Anti-Competitive and Unfair Practices in Digital Leisure Markets. *The Competition law review.* 2015, vol. 11, no. 1, pp. 109–131. ISSN 1745-638X.

IBÁÑEZ COLOMO, Pablo. The Draft Digital Markets Act: A Legal and Institutional Analysis. *Journal of European Competition Law & Practice.* 2021, vol. 12, no. 7, pp. 561–575.

WRIGHT NELSON, J. Lost in Space? Gaps in the International Space Object Registration Regime. Available at: https://www.ejiltalk.org/lost-in-space-gaps-in-the-international-space-object-registration-regime/

JACKSON, N. United Nations Declares Internet Access a Basic Human Right. The Atlantic, JUNE 3, 2011. Available at: https://www.theatlantic.com/technology/archive/2011/06/united-nations-declares-internet-access-a-basic-human-right/239911/

JACOBY, J., SPELLER, D. E., KOHN, C. A. Brand choice behavior as a function of information load. *Journal of Marketing Research.* 1974, no. 11, pp. 63–69.

JAKAB, M. Google Android: Behavioural Theories of Harm in the Light of New Judgments and Regulatory Tools. *Auc Iuridica.* 2023, vol. 69, no. 2, s. 95–106. ISSN 0323-0619. DOI: 10.14712/23366478.2023.17

JASMONTAITE, L., DE HERT, P. Access to the Internet in the EU: a policy priority, a fundamental, a human right or a concern for eGovernment? SSRN Working Paper. 2020, vol. 6, no. 19. Available at: https://www.researchgate.net/publication/339860840

JENNY, F. Changing the way we think: competition, platforms and ecosystems. *Journal of Antitrust Enforcement.* 2021. vol. 9, no. 1, pp. 1–18.

JONES, A., SUFRIN, B. *EU Competition Law.* Text, Cases and Materials. Sixth Edition. Oxford: Oxford University Press, 2016.

JURGENSON, N. *Digital dualism versus augmented reality*. The Society Pages: Cyborgology, February 24, 2011. Available at: https://mxepstein.com/wp-content/uploads/2017./08/Digital-Dualism-versus-Augmented-Reality.pdf.

KALESNÁ, K., PATAKYOVÁ, M. T. Subjects of Legal Regulation – Different Approaches of Competition, Public Procurement and Corporate Law. In MILKOVIC, M., KECEK, D., HAMMES, K. (eds.). Economic and social development. Varazdin: Varazdin Development and Entrepreneurship Agency. 2019, pp. 210–219.

KAPLOW, L. Competition Policy and Price Fixing. Princeton University Press, Princeton and Oxford, 2013.

JONES, J. K. Blockchain in the Space Sector. Center for Space Policy and Strategy. March 2020, 17 p.

KARIKMÄE, T., MÜÜRSEPP, P., PIHL, H. M., HAMULAK, O., KOCHARYAN, H. Legal Person- or Agenthood of Artificial Intelligence Technologies. *Acta Baltica Historiae et Philosophiae Scientiarum*. vol. 8, 2020, pp. 73–92.

KERBER, W. Digital markets, data, and privacy: competition law, consumer law and data protection. *Journal of Intellectual Property Law & Practice.* vol. 11, no. 11, 2016, pp. 856–866.

KETTEMANN, M. C. Ensuring cybersecurity through international law. *Revista Española de Derecho Internacional.* vol. 69/2, 2017, pp. 281–289.

KING, D. L., DELFABBRO, P. H. Video game monetization (e.g., 'loot boxes'): A blueprint for practical social responsibility measures. *International Journal of Mental Health and Addiction*. 2019, vol. 17, pp. 166–179.

KING, D. L., DELFABBRO, P. H., GAINSBURY, S. M., DREIER, M., GREER, N., BILLIEUX, J. Unfair play? Video games as exploitative monetized services: An examination of game patents from a consumer protection perspective. *Computers in Human Behavior.* 2019, vol. 101, pp. 131–143.

KOCHARYAN, H., HAMUĽÁK, O., VARDANYAN, L. "The Right to be Remembered?": The Contemporary Challenges of the "StreisandEffect" in the European Judicial Reality. *International and Comparative Law Review*. 2022, vol. 22, no. 2, pp. 105–120. DOI: 10.2478/iclr-2022-0017

KOMNINOS, A. P. The Digital Markets Act and Private Enforcement: Proposals for an Optimal System of Enforcement. In CHARBIT, N., GACHOT, S. (eds.). *Eleanor M. Fox | Antitrust Ambassador to the World – Liber Amicorum*. 2021, s. 425–444.

KOMNINOS, A. The Digital Markets Act: How Does it Compare with Competition Law. Available at: https://papers.ssrn.com/sol3/papers.cfm?abstract_id=4136146

EICHENSEHR, K. The Law and Politics of Cyberattack Attribution. *UCLA Law Review*. 520 (2020). 598 p.

LABRECQUE, L. I., VOR DEM ESCHE, J., MATHWICK, CH., NOVAK, T. P., HOFACKER, CH. F. Consumer Power: Evolution in the Digital Age. *Journal of Interactive Marketing*. 2013, vol. 27, no. 4, pp. 257–269.

LAMADRID DE PABLO, A., BAYÓN FERNÁNDEZ, N. Why the Proposed DMA Might Be Illegal under Article 114 TFEU, and How to Fix It. *Journal of European Competition Law and Practice*. 2021, vol. 12, no. 7, pp. 576–589.

LAMBERT, P. *Understanding the New European Data Protection Rules*. New York: Auerbach Publications, 2017.

LAROUCHE, P., DE STREEL, A. The European Digital Markets Act: A Revolution Grounded on Traditions, *Journal of European Competition Law & Practice*. 2021, vol. 12, no. 7, pp. 542–560.

LAȚICI, T. Understanding the EU's approach to cyber diplomacy and cyber defence. European Parliamentary Research Service. 2020, 12 p. Available at: https://www.europarl.europa.eu/RegData/etudes/BRIE/2020/651937/EPRS_BRI(2020)651937_EN.pdf

LAUX, J., WACHTER, S., MITTELSTADT, B. Taming the few: Platform regulation, independent audits, and the risks of capture created by the DMA and DSA. *Computer Law & Security Review*. vol. 43, 2021, pp. 1–12.

LEE, B. K., LEE, W. N. The effect of information overload on consumer choice quality in an on-line environment. *Psychology & Marketing*. 2004, vol. 21, no. 3, pp. 159–183.

LESSIG, L. The Law of the Horse: What Cyberlaw Might Teach. *Harvard Law Review*. 1999, vol. 113, no. 2, pp. 501–546. Available at: https://cyber.harvard.edu/works/lessig/finalhls.pdf.

LIANOS, I., KORAH, V., SICILIANI, P. *Competition Law*. Analysis, Cases, & Materials. Oxford: Oxford University Press, 2019.

LIU, H. Y., MAAS, M. M., DANAHER, J., SCARCELLA, L., LEXER, M., VAN ROMPAEY, L. Artificial Intelligence and Legal Disruption: A New Model for Analysis. *Law, Innovation and Technology*. vol. 12, no. 2, 2020, pp. 205–258.

LOBSCHAT, L., MUELLER, B., EGGERS, F., BRANDIMARTE, L., DIEFENBACH, S., KROSCHKE, M., WIRTZ, J. Corporate digital responsibility. *Journal of Business Research*. 2021, vol. 122, pp. 875–888.

LOUTOCKÝ, P. Online Dispute Resolution to Resolve Consumer Disputes from the perspective of European Union Law: Is the Potential of ODR Fully Used? *Masaryk University Journal of Law and Technology*. 2016, vol. 10, no. 1, pp. 113–127.

LUCCHI, N. The Role of Internet Access in Enabling Individual's Rights and Freedoms. EUI RSCAS Working Paper 2013/47. Available at: https://cadmus.eui.eu/handle/1814/27435

LUUKAS, S., EVANS, T., CILLUFFO, F., NADEAU, A. European Union and NATO Global Cybersecurity Challenges: A Way Forward. *PRISM*. 2016, vol. 6, no. 2, pp. 126–41. Available at: http://www.jstor.org/stable/26470452

LUCKERSON, V. Americans Will Never Have the Right to be Forgotten. *Time*. Available at: http:// time.com/98554/right-to-be-forgotten/

JUN, L. V., XUAN, L. The Impact of Information Overload of E-Commerce Platform on Consumer Return Intention: Considering the Moderating Role of Perceived Environmental Effectiveness. *International Journal of Environmental Research and Public Health*. 2022, vol. 19, issue 13.

MACH, M. Streisand effect in the Content of Right to be Forgotten. *European Studies, The Review of European law, Economic and Politics*. 2022, vol. 9, issue 1.

MAK, V., TERRYN, E. Circular Economy and Consumer Protection: The Consumer as a Citizen and the Limits of Empowerment Through Consumer Law. *Journal of Consumer Policy*. 2020, vol. 43, no. 1, pp. 227–248.

MALGIERI, G., CUSTERS, B. Pricing privacy – the right to know the value of your personal data. *Computer Law & Security Review*. 2018, vol. 34, no. 2, pp. 289–303.

MÄLKSOO, L. The Controversy over Human Rights, UN Covenants, and the Dissolution of the Soviet Union. *Japanese Yearbook of International Law*. 2018, vol. 61, pp. 260–283. Available at: https://ssrn.com/abstract=3254490

MANIA, K. Online dispute resolution: The future of justice. *International Comparative Jurisprudence*. 2015, vol. 1, no. 1, pp. 76–86.

MARTIN, K. D., BORAH, A., PALMATIER, R. W. Data privacy: Effects on customer and firm performance. *Journal of Marketing*. 2017, vol. 81, no. 1, pp. 36–58.

MARTÍNEZ-RAMIL, P. Discriminatory algorithms. A proportionate means of achieving a legitimate aim? *Journal of Ethics and Legal Technologies*. vol. 4, no. 1, 2022, pp. 3–24.

MARTÍNEZ-RAMIL, P. Is the EU human rights legal framework able to cope with discriminatory AI? IDP. *Internet, Law and Politics E-Journal*. vol. 34, 2022, pp 1–15.

MAZÚR, J., PATAKYOVÁ, M. T. Regulatory Approaches to Facebook and Other Social Media Platforms: Towards Platforms Design Accountability. *Masaryk University Journal of Law and Technology*. 2019, vol. 13, no. 2, pp. 219–242.

Mc CHESNEY, R. W. *Digital Disconnect: How capitalism is turning the internet against democracy*. New York, NY: New Press, 2013.

MEESE, J., NANSEN, B., KOHN, T., ARNOLD, M., GIBBS, M. Posthumous personhood and the affordances of digital media. *Mortality*. 2015, vol. 20, no. 4, pp. 408–420.

METZGER, A. Data as Counter-Performance: What Rights and Duties do Parties Have? *Journal of Intellectual Property, Information Technology and E-Commerce Law*. 2017, vol. 8.

MIŠĆENIĆ, E. The Effectiveness of Judicial Enforcement of the EU Consumer Protection Law. In MEŠKIĆ, Z., KUNDA, I., POPOVIĆ, D., OMEROVIĆ, E. (eds.). Balkan Yearbook of European and International Law. Cham: Springer, 2019.

MONTI, G. The Digital Markets Act: Improving the Institutional Design. *Journal of European Competition Law & Practice*. 2021, vol. 12, no. 2, pp. 90–101.

MORTEN HAUGEN, H. Is Internet Access a Human Right – for Everyone, or only for Persons with Disabilities? *Kritisk juss*. 2014, vol. 40, no. 1, pp. 26–51.

MOSKAL, A. Highlight Digital Markets Act (DMA): A Consumer Protection Perspective. *European Papers*. 2022, vol. 7, no. 3, s. 1113–1119.

NEGROPONTE, N. *Being Digital.* I. New York: Vintage Books, 1996.

NEWMAN, J. M. Antitrust in Attention Markets: Defintion, Power, Harm. University of Miami. *Legal studies Research Paper.* No 3744839. Available at: https://ssrn.com/abstract=3745839

NICOLI, N., IOSIFIDIS, P. EU digital economy competition policy: From ex-post to ex-ante. The case of Alphabet, Amazon, Apple, and Meta. *Global Media and China.* 2023, vol. 0, no. 0, pp. 1–15.

NOLAN, D., DAVIES, J. Torts and Equitable Wrongs. In BURROWS, A. (ed.). *English Private Law.* Oxford: Oxford University Press. 2017, pp. 927–1030.

OSULA, A. M., KASPER, A., KAJANDER, A. EU Common Position on International Law and Cyberspace. *Masaryk University Journal of Law and Technology.* 2022, vol. 16, pp. 89–123.

PAPAKONSTANTINOU, V. Cybersecurity as Praxis and as a State: the EU Law Path Towards Acknowledgement of a New Right to Cybersecurity? *Computer Law & Security Review.* 2022, vol. 44, pp. 1–5.

PARK, D. Individualization, information asymmetry, and exploitation in the advertiser-driven digital era. *The Political Economy of Communication.* vol. 5, no. 2, pp. 22–44.

PARKER, G., PETROPOULOS, G., VAN ALSTYNE, M. Platform mergers and antitrust. *Industrial and Corporate Change.* 2021, vol. 30, no. 5, s. 1307–1336. DOI: 10.1093/icc/dtab048

PATAKYOVÁ, M. T., MAZÚR, J. Facebook – Global Issue without (Existing) Solution? In KLIEŠTIK, T. (ed.). 18th International Scientific Conference Globalization and Its Socio-Economic Consequences. Žilina: 2018, s. 2298–2306.

PATAKYOVÁ, M, T. Notion of Anticompetitive Agreement Challenged in Digital Environment. *European Studies. The Review of European Law, Economics and Politics.* 2020, vol. 7, no. 1, pp. 237–252.

PEÑA, J., GARCIA-SEGURA, L. A. The Critical Role of Education in Every Cyber Defense Strategy. *Northern Kentucky Law Review.* 2014, vol. 41, no. 3, pp. 459–469.

PETIT, N. The Proposed Digital Markets Act (DMA): A Legal and Policy Review. *Journal of European Competition Law and Practice.* 2021, vol. 12, no. 7, pp. 529–541.

PETR, M. Twice about ne bis in idem: Conflicting Approach of European Courts to the Same Principle. *Czech Yearbook of Public & Private International Law.* 2017, vol. 8, pp. 210–222.

PICHT, P. G., FREUND, B. Competition (law) in the era of algorithms. *Max Planck Institute for Innovation & Competition Research Paper.* 2018, no. 18–10. Available at: https://doi.org/10.2139/ssrn.3180550. Accessed 23. 2. 2023.

PINO, G. The Right to Personal Identity in Italian Private Law. Constitutional Interpretation and Juge-Made Rights. In Van HOECKE, M., OST, F.(eds.). *The Harmonisation of Private Law in Europe.* Oxford University Press, 2000, pp. 225–237.

PIRIS, J. C. *The Lisbon Treaty. A Legal and Political Analysis.* Cambridge University Press, Cambridge, 2010

PODSZUN, R., BONGARTZ, P., LANGENSTEIN, S. Proposals on how to improve the Digital Markets Act. *SSRN Electronic Journal.* 2021.

PODSZUN, R. From Competition Law to Platform Regulation – Regulatory Choices for the Digital Markets Act. *Economics.* 2023, vol. 17, no. 1, s. 1–13.

PODSZUN, R. Private Enforcement and Gatekeeper Regulation: Strengthening the Rights of Private Parties in the Digital Markets Act. *Journal of European Competition Law & Practice.* 2022, vol. 13, no. 4, pp. 254–267.

POLLICINO, O. The Right to Internet Access: Quid Iuris? In VON ARNAULD, A. K. VON DER DECKEN, SUSI, M. (eds.). *The Cambridge Handbook of New Human Rights: Recognition, Novelty, Rhetoric.* Cambridge: Cambridge University Press, 2020, pp. 263–275. Available at: https://papers.ssrn.com/sol3/papers.cfm?abstract_id=3397340

PONTE, L. M. Throwing Bad Money After Bad: Can Online Dispute Resolution (ODR) Really Deliver the Goods for the Unhappy Internet Shopper? *Tulane Journal of Technology and Intellectual Property.* 2001, vol. 3, pp. 55-92.

POSNER, R. A. REVIEW OF KAPLOW, 'COMPETITION POLICY AND PRICE FIXING'. *Antitrust Law Journal.* vol. 79, no. 2, 2014, pp. 761–68.

QUACH, S., THAICHON, P., MARTIN, K. D., WEAVEN, S. Digital technologies: tensions in privacy and data. *Journal of the Academy of Marketing Science.* 2022, vol. 50, no. 1, pp. 1299–1323.

RAFEL, R. M. The Directive Proposals on Online Sales and Supply of Digital Content (Part I): will the new rules attain their objective of reducing legal complexity? *IDP: Revista d'Internet, Dret i Política.* 2016, no. 23.

RASO, F., HILLIGOSS, H., KRISHNAMURTHY, V., BAVITZ, Ch., LEVIN, K. *Artificial Intelligence & Human Rights: Opportunities & Risks.* Berkman Klein Center Research Publication, 2018, pp. 1–62.

REGLITZ, M. The Human Right to Free Internet Access. *Journal of Applied Philosophy.* 2020, vol. 37, no. 2, pp. 314–331. Available at: https://onlinelibrary.wiley.com/doi/abs/10.1111/japp.12395

REINARTZ, W. Customizing prices in online markets. *Emerging Issues in Management.* 2002, vol. 1, pp. 55–65.

RICHTER, Š. Ochrana osobních údajů v kontextu poskytování digitálních dat spotřebitelům. *Právník.* 2021, no. 9.

RICHTER, Š. Směrnice EU 2019/770 o některých aspektech poskytování digitálního obsahu a digitálních služeb jako nástroj ochrany spotřebitele. *Jurisprudence.* 2020, no. 4.

ROBERTSON, V. Delineating Digital Markets under EU Competition Law: Challenging or Futile? *The Competition Law Review.* 2017, vol. 12, no. 2, pp. 131–151.

ROBERTSON, V. H.S.E. Antitrust, Big Tech, and Democracy: A Research Agenda. *Antitrust Bulletin.* 2022, vol. 67, no. 2, pp. 259–279.

RÖHRIG, W., SMEATON, W.C.R. Cyber security and cyber defence in the European Union opportunities, synergies and challenges. *Cyber security and cyber defence in the EU.* 2022, pp. 23–27. Available at: https://eda.europa.eu/docs/default-source/documents/23-27-wolfgang-r%C3%B6hrig-and-j-p-r-smeaton-article.pdf

ROCHEL, J. Connecting the Dots: Digital Integrity as a Human Right. *Human Rights Law Review.* 2021, vol. 21, no. 2, pp. 358–383. Available at: https://doi.org/10.1093/hrlr/ngaa063

RUST, R. T., HUANG, M. H. The service revolution and the transformation of marketing science. *Marketing Science.* vol. 33, no. 2, 2014, pp. 206–221.

SARKER, I. H. Machine Learning: Algorithms, Real-World Applications and Research Directions. *Computer Science.* vol. 2, no. 160, 2021, pp. 1–22.

SEEMMA, P. S., NANDHINI, S., SOWMIYA, M. Overview of Cyber Security. *International Journal of Advanced Research in Computer and Communication Engineering.* 2018, vol. 7, issue 11, pp. 125–128.

SCHELLEKENS, M. Car hacking: Navigating the regulatory landscape. *Computer Law and Security Review.* 2015, vol. 32, no. 2, pp. 307–315.

SCHOLZ, F., YALCIN, B., PRIESTLEY, M. Internet access for disabled people: Understanding socio-relational factors in Europe. *Cyberpsychology: Journal of Psychosocial Research on Cyberspace*. 2017, vol. 11, no. 1.

SCHROEDER, W. Limits to European Harmonization of Criminal Law. *Eurocrim.* vol. 2, 2020, pp. 144–148.

PETRUZZINO, S. Blockchain and Smart-Contracts: a New Challenges for International Commercial Arbitration. *Czech Yearbook of Arbitration. Arbitration and International Treaties, Customs and Standards.* 2020, vol., X. P., 161–179.

SKEPYS, B. Is There a Human Right to the Internet? *Journal of Politics and Law.* 2012, vol. 5, no. 4, pp. 15–29.

SKOPIK, F., SETTANNI, G., FIEDLER, R. (2016) A problem shared is a problem halved: A survey on the dimensions of collective cyber defense through security information sharing. *Computers & Security*. 2016, vol 60, pp. 154–176, ISSN 0167-4048. https://doi.org/10.1016/j.cose.2016.04.003

SMITH, B. Digital technology and the war in Ukraine. Available at: https://blogs.microsoft.com/on-the-issues/2022/02/28/ukraine-russia-digital-war-cyberattacks/

SOLEK, L. Need to Revise or Apply the Concept of Market Definition with a View to 'Zero-Price' and Overarching Markets. *Journal of European Competition Law & Practice*. 2021, vol. 12, no. 8, pp. 593–603.

SOLOVE, D. J. Understanding Privacy. Harvard University Press, 2008. GWU Legal Studies Research Paper No. 420, GWU Law School Public Law Research Paper No. 420. Available at: https://ssrn.com/abstract=1127888

SOLOVE, D. J. Introduction: Privacy self-management and the consent dilemma. *Harvard Law Review.* 2013, 1880. Available at: https://papers.ssrn.com/sol3/papers.cfm?abstract_id=2171018#

SOUSA FERRO, M. De Gratis Non Curat Lex: Abuse of Dominance in Online Free Services. *The Competition Law Review*. 2017, vol. 12, no. 2, pp. 153–170.

STASZCZYK, A. European Parliament Position on EU Cyber Security and Defense Policy. *Reality of Politics.* 2019, vol. 10, pp. 122–133.

STEZHKO, S. F. V. Cyber Security as an Important Factor for the encouragement of the Life Sustenance of the Domestic Energy Industry. *Information and Law.* 2021, 4 (39), pp. 113–120.

SZILÁGYI, F. The Implementation of Directives 2019/770 and 2019/771 in Hungary. *Journal of European Consumer and Market Law*. 2021, vol. 10, no. 6.

SZOSZKIEWICZ, Ł. *Internet Access as a New Human Right? State of the Art on the Threshold of 2020.* Przegląd Prawniczy Uniwersytetu im Adama Mickiewicza. 2018, vol. 8, pp. 49–62. Available at: Available at: https://pressto.amu.edu.pl/index.php/ppuam/article/view/21599

ŠIŠKOVÁ, N. Current Legal and Ethical Issues of Regulation in the Field of Robotics, NORDSCI Coference, Conference Proceedings, Book 2, vol. 2, pp. 397–403, Sophia 2019, www.nordsci.org

ŠIŠKOVÁ, N. *Lidskoprávní mechanismy na úrovni EU a otázky související*. Prague, Wolters Kluwer, 2021.

ŠIŠKOVÁ, N. New Challenges for the EU in the Field of Human Rights (Focusing on the Mechanism of the Charter). European Studies. *The Review of European Law, Economics and Politics*. 2014, no. 1, pp. 12–21.

ŠIŠKOVÁ N. (ed.). *The European Union – What is Next? A Legal Analysis and the Political Visions on the Future of the Union*. Wolters Kluwer Deutschland, GmbH Carl Heymanns Köln, 2018.

ŠMEJKAL, V. Abuse of Dominance and the DMA – Differing Objectives or Prevailing Continuity? *Auc Iuridica*. 2023, vol. 69, no. 2, pp. 33–51.

TABUSCA, S. M. The Internet Access as a Fundamental Right. *Romanian Economic Business Review*. 2010, vol. 4.

TALEB, N. N. *The Black Swan: The Impact of the Highly Improbable*. New York: Penguin Books, 2010.

TATNALL, A. The Internet of Things and Beyond: Rise of the Non-Human Actors. *International Journal of Actor-Network Theory and Technological Innovation*. 2015, vol. 7, no. 4, pp. 56–67.

THOMAS, S. Harmful Signals. Cartel Prohibition and Oligopoly Theory in the Age of Machine Learning. Available at: https://ssrn.com/abstract=3392860

TRIDIMAS, T. *The General Principles of EU Law*. Second Edition. Oxford University Press, Oxford, 2006.

TROPP, E. M., HOFFMANN, T., CHOCHIA, A. Open Data: A Stepchild in e-Estonia's Data Management Strategy? *TalTech Journal of European Studies*. 2022, vol. 12, no. 1, pp. 123–144. Available at: https://doi.org/10.2478/bjes-2022-0006

TRZASKOWSKI, J. Behavioural innovations in marketing law. In MICKLITZ, H., SIBONY, A. L., ESPOSITO, F. (eds.). In Handbook of Research Methods in Consumer Law. Edward Elgar Publishing, 2018.

TRZASKOWSKI, J. Data-driven value extraction and human well-being under EU law. In Electron Markets.

TRZASKOWSKI, J. GDPR compliant processing of big data in small business. In PEDERSEN, C. L., LINDGREEN, A., RITTER, T., RINGBERG, T. (eds.). Big Data in Small Business: Data-driven Growth in Small and Medium-sized Enterprises. Edward Elgar Publishing, 2021, pp. 27–39.

TRZASKOWSKI, J. Lawful distortion of consumers' economic behaviour – collateral damage under the Unfair Commercial Practices Directive. *European Business Law Review*. 2016, vol. 27, no. 1, pp. 25–49.

TULLY, S. A Human Right to Access the Internet? Problems and Prospects. *Human Rights Law Review*. 2014, vol. 14, no. 2, pp. 175–195. Available at: https://doi.org/10.1093/hrlr/ngu011

TURNER, J. Robot Rules. Regulating Artificial Intelligence. Cham: Springer Link, Palgrave Macmillan, 2019.

ULLRICH, H. Private Enforcement of the EU Rules on Competition – Nullity Neglected. *IIC International Review of Intellectual Property and Competition Law*. 2021, vol. 52, no. 5, s. 606–635.

VALUCH, J., GÁBRIŠ, T., HAMUĽÁK, O. Cyber Attacks, Information Attacks, and Postmodern Warfare. *Baltic Journal of Law & Politics*. 2017, vol. 10, no.1, pp.63–89.

VAN DEN BERGH, R., WEBER, F. The German Facebook Saga: Abuse of dominance or abuse of competition law? *World Competition.* 2021, vol. 44, no. 1, s. 29–52.

VAN DEN BOOM, J. What does the Digital Markets Act harmonize? – exploring interactions between the DMA and national competition laws. *European Competition Journal.* 2022, pp. 1–29. DOI: 10.1080/17441056.2022.2156728

VARDANYAN, L., STEHLÍK, V., KOCHARYAN, H. Digital Integrity: A Foundation for Digital Rights and the New Manifestation of Human Dignity. *TalTech Journal of European Studies.* 2022, vol. 12, no. 1, pp. 159–185. Available at: https://doi.org/10.2478/bjes-2022-0008

VÍTOVÁ, B. Limits of fairness and transparency in Internet of Things (IoT) contracts concluded with consumers. *Revue Européenne de droit de la consommation (R.E.D.C.).* Larcier, 2020, pp. 523–541.

VÍTOVÁ, B. Quo vadis, ochrano spotřebitele aneb personalizovaná tvorba ceny jako férová obchodní praktika? In *Pocta prof. Janu Hurdíkovi k 70. narozeninám.* Brno: Masarykova Univerzita, 2021, pp. 265–285.

VÍTOVÁ, B. Unfair Commercial Practices and Corporate Social Responsibility (CSR) In the Digital World. *European Studies – the Review of European law, Economics and Politics*. 2022, vol. 9, no. 2, pp. 197–212.

WACHTER, S. Affinity profiling and discrimination by association in online behavioral advertising. *Berkeley Technology Law Journal.* vol. 35, 2020, pp. 367–430.

WALREE, T. F., WOLTERS Pieter T. J. The Right to Compensation of a Competitor for a Violation of the GDPR. *International Data Privacy Law.* 2020, vol. 10, no. 4, pp. 346–355.

WELLS, P. E. Business Models for Sustainability. Edward Elgar Publishing. Northampton, 2013.

WENDEHORST, CH. Die neuen Regelungen im BGB zu Verträgen über digitale Produkte. NJW, 2021.

WERRO, F. (ed.). *The Right to Be Forgotten.* A Comparative Study of the Emergent Right's Evolution and Application in Europe, the Americas, and Asia. Champ: Springer, 2020.

WHISH, R., BAILEY, D. Competition Law. Ninth Edition. Oxford: Oxford University Press, 2018.

WHITMAN, J. The Two Western Cultures of Privacy, Dignity Versus Liberty. *Yale Law journal.* vol 113, no. 6.

WOLF, M. Algorithm-based pricing in online retailing as concerted practice. Covering the "predictable agent" with Article 101 (1) TFEU. Available at: https://ssrn.com/abstract=3536959. Accessed 16. 6. 2020.

WULF, A. J., SEIZOV, O. "Please understand we cannot provide further information": evaluating content and transparency of GDPR-mandated AI disclosures. *AI & Society.* 2022. Available at: https://link.springer.com/article/10.1007/s00146-022-01424-z#citeas

YERMENCHUK, O. The main approaches to the organization of the critical infrastructure protection in the countries of Europe: an experience for Ukraine. Dnipro State University of Internal Affairs, 2018.

LIST OF ABBREVIATIONS

ACER	European Union Agency for the Cooperation of Energy Regulators
AI	Artificial Intelligence
AIA	Artificial Intelligence Act
AILD	Artificial Intelligence Liability Directive
Art	Article
B2B	business to business
B2C	business to consumer
CEER	Council of European Energy Regulators
Charter	Charter of the Fundamental Rights of the European Union
CJEU	Court of Justice of the European Union
CMU	Cabinet of Ministers of Ukraine (Government of Ukraine)
CzCC	Czech Civil Code
DCD	Directive on Digital Content and Services
DMA	Digital Markets Act
DSA	Digital Services Act
ENISA	European Network and the Information Security Agency
ENTSO-E	European association for the cooperation of transmission system operators
EPRI	Electric Power Research Institute
ESRB	European Systemic Risk Board
EU DSO	Association for all sizes of Distribution System Operators in Europe
GDPR	General Data Protection Regulation
HunCC	Hungarian Code Civil
HunID	Hungarian Implementing Decree
ICN	International Competition Network
ICT	Information and Communication Technologies
MICA	Markets in Crypto-assets
NARUC	National Association of Regulatory Utility Commissioners
NCA	National Competition Authority of a Member State
NCAs	National Competition Authorities
NERC	North American Electric Reliability Corporation

NEURC	National Energy and Utilities Regulatory Commission (the Energy Regulator in Ukraine)
NIS 1	Directive (EU) 2016/1148 of the European Parliament and of the Council of 6 July 2016 concerning measures for a high common level of security
NIS 2	Directive (EU) 2022/2555 of the European Parliament and of the Council of 14 Dec. 2022 on measures for a high common level of cybersecurity across the Union, amending Regulation (EU) No 910/2014 and Directive (EU) 2018/1972, and repealing Directive (EU) 2016/1148
NRAs	National Regulatory Authorities
NSDCU	National Security and Defense Council of Ukraine
OECD	Organisation for Economic Cooperation and Development
PKI	Public-key infrastructure
PLD	Product Liability Directive
RTBF	Right to be Forgotten
SAEE	State Agency for Energy Efficiency and Energy Saving of Ukraine
SGD	Directive on Sales of Goods
SSU	Security Service of Ukraine
TEU	Treaty on European Union
TFEU	Treaty on the Functioning of the European Union
USAID	United States Agency for International Development

INDEX

www.ingramcontent.com/pod-product-compliance
Lightning Source LLC
Chambersburg PA
CBHW070251260926
51849CB00001BA/141
9789403502083